James G Rice
Stephens College
Columbia, MO 65201

THE SPIRIT AND
SUBSTANCE OF ART

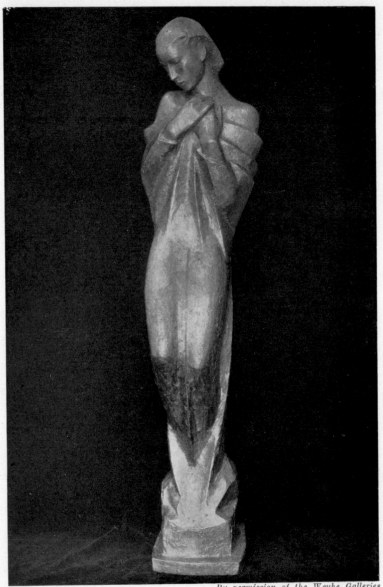

KOLBE, ADAGIO

THE SPIRIT AND SUBSTANCE OF ART

BY

LOUIS W. FLACCUS

Professor of Philosophy
University of Pennsylvania

THIRD EDITION

F. S. CROFTS & CO., Publishers
NEW YORK - - - - 1947

First Printing, October, 1926
Revised and Enlarged Edition
Second Printing, February, 1931
Third Printing, August, 1935
Fourth Printing, July, 1937
Third Edition
Fifth Printing, January, 1941
Sixth Printing, September, 1945
Seventh Printing, May, 1947

MANUFACTURED IN THE UNITED STATES OF AMERICA
BY THE VAIL-BALLOU PRESS, INC., BINGHAMTON, N. Y.

FROM THE PREFACE TO THE FIRST EDITION

This is no book for the dogmatist, who asks few questions and distrusts all problems; nor for the system-builder, who twists all things to a scheme of his making. It is an attempt to understand the substance, form, and spirit of art—to move a little closer to art as it is practised and enjoyed, and as a place for it is gained within the interests and tasks of man's life. One volume offers scant room for this. Books have been written on every one of these problems; theories have been woven and slashed through at a stroke; art has gone its own creative way at its own sweet will; time mocks at the too confident systematizer—how then escape a sense of caution born of distrust of anything final?

A text-book it might be called by one who discovers it to be informative and who attends to the headings which throw its march into convenient patterns. But it is not a mechanical toy to be wound up again and again in the classroom and sent on its short whirring way. It is meant for the use of students and for whoever is eager, keen-witted, willing to have the mettle of his mind tested—and persistently inquisitive. No student need read it who is not venturesome and adventure-loving in his thinking. No teacher ought to use it who lacks interest in thought-processes, and who is unwilling to assist in his own education—by uncovering the work that lies hidden in short chapters and occasional references, making the most of hints and drawing parallels, cutting more deeply into problems, and making the freest use of opportunities for thought. It has the welcome of open doors and open windows; if any one, thoughtfully responsive to the welcome, finds that he must walk out again, I shall not object.

The method used is the empirical one of observing and grouping facts and pushing on to general theories. This is not an easy method for aesthetics. There the facts are complex and delicate; the problems are not of a kind—some are compact and sharply limited, others spread like ink on a blotter; and general theories are apt to be incautious and personally colored.

Where firsthand experience is lacking, and there is an insensitiveness to artistic value it is useless to write. The spirit of an art must be caught from within. It is for this reason that I have given the writing of the chapter on MUSIC to PAUL KRUMMEICH, a sensitive and disciplined musician. His theories are his own. Little attempt has been made to edit them or to fit them to mine.

In what I have written I have aimed at thought tested and controlled by a personal response to works of art. The examples cited are many. Sketchy and superficial as they seem when glanced at, they were not lightly chosen. In all cases they mean something to me—an experience, an honest response, a pleasure. If I have drawn widely on art that is very old and art that is very new, and to some very questionable, it is not because I look for my pleasure shamelessly and take it where I find it, but because I do not consider it honest to reject in favor of traditional values anything that maintains itself as an experience.

It is my belief that art is a living experience—a great creative venture on the part of races and individuals; and that a study of either the creative effort or the receptive response must have about it something of a like life and enthusiasm. Scholarship need not be drab, and enthusiasm is bad only when it is ill-considered and uncritical. I have not hesitated to put into what I have written warmth and personal rhythm when I felt them to be needed. The picturesque and striking phrases I have at times used are not adventitious ornament—gold-topped nails driven at random into the wooden body of aesthetic doctrine—; they carry the enthusiasm and bring home the analysis. This way of writing on aesthetics—the only way possible to me—makes a cursory reading dangerous. The manner is not mere rhetoric; and the matter, seriously chosen and analyzed, may be had at the price of further study.

The Greek coin on the cover is meant to show how artistic feeling and decorative reshaping entered what to a less art-loving race would be merely a matter of commerce.

Grateful acknowledgment is made for permission to use copyright material to Harcourt, Brace & Company for Sandburg's "Seaslant" from *Slabs of the Sunburnt West* and his "For Christ's Sake" from *A Miscellany of American Poetry, 1920;* to Henry Holt & Co. for Sandburg's "Gargoyle" and "Prayers of Steel" from *Cornhuskers* and a few lines from *Chicago Poems;* to the *Nation* for parts of Helton's "May Jones Takes the Air" and Rorty's "Prelude," two of its Prize Poems; to Alfred A. Knopf, Inc. for material from Goldenweiser's *Early Civilization;* to the Dial Publishing Company for Waldo Frank's "Under the Dome"; and to Frederick A. Stokes Company for a portion of one of Hilda Conkling's poems.

PREFACE TO THE SECOND EDITION

A chapter on *Some Newer Developments* has been added. Of necessity it is sketchy and incomplete. No chapter, however long and detailed, can do justice to what of creative experiment and thought lies within the art of the last fifteen years. But this fragmentary account is meant to have unity. It is not to be a haphazard showing of some of the later models in the several arts, and of some of the fashionable appraisals of art, friendly or hostile. Within it is this binding thought—contemporary life has forced art into new problems and into a search for new values and forms. Thought—

reflective of that life, of its energy and subtlety or of the fear of it—stands by appraisingly while art is questingly and variously alive.

There is a new appendix of notes.

Illustrations have been added to give, here and there, something of pointedness and vividness to the text.

PREFACE TO THE THIRD EDITION

A seventh part has been added. This new material covers some hundred pages. The theory underlying the book—that art is semblance—is presented systematically. The chapter on expressionism was written too much under the influence of its earlier, bolder forms; a broader appreciative and critical study of modernism now seems called for. To the brief treatment of **tragedy** has been added an analysis of its types, of which the cosmological is stressed. There is a chapter on the dance in its relation to music and to expressionism.

Of late years a new art, that of the motion picture, has developed. It merits detailed study, for it offers intriguing problems, of time and space, of relationship to the older arts. Two special forms of painting—non-objective painting and surrealism—have interested and baffled the public. A critical estimate of both is offered.

There are new notes and additions. A few of these are methodological: is there gain or loss for aesthetics in the swing toward contextual and Marxist points of view? Others deal with arts and crafts (a much neglected phase of art), distortion, radio drama, and regionalism.

Paul Krummeich has rewritten his chapter on music in the light of his newer theories.

A few minor corrections have been made here and there in the text. Some titles have been added to the bibliography. There are a few new pictures.

L. W. F.

CONTENTS

ILLUSTRATIONS

xi

PART ONE

INTRODUCTORY

THE FIELD OF AESTHETICS

Aesthetics may roughly be defined as the theory of the beautiful. If the beautiful were a clean-cut term, and one yielding itself readily to an interest not to be distracted, a field of inquiry could easily be marked off. The beautiful is a term of several meanings; and even when taken in its widest sense it offers no more than the high spot of an interest which includes art, as it appears in the cultural history of the race, as it is created and enjoyed, as it reflects many impulses, aims, and ideals, as it gains its effects through different media, and as it seeks the disciplined expression of patterns and types. It is then not to be wondered at if writers on aesthetics differ on the question of range. While some affect the simple exclusive lines of an intensive study of beauty, others go far afield in the realms of anthropology, sociology, archaeology, and genetic and descriptive psychology, intent on gathering a varied mass of intellectual merchandise; others allow themselves to be carried far into details and problems of technique.

Historically its growth has been haphazard—a matter of uncontrolled accumulation and shifting interests and affiliations. It has taken its problems, materials, and inspirations from philosophy, psychology, and the social sciences; and has gained strength and scope alike from the penetrative insight of the reflective artist, the acumen of the critic, and the patient, circumscribed work of the scientist. Because of this, its place in the system of intellectual disciplines is ill-defined and open to controversy.

AFFILIATIONS OF AESTHETICS

AESTHETICS AND PHILOSOPHY

The philosopher is not satisfied with facts in their isolated, obtrusive presence; nor is he content to follow science in its patient and restricted uncoupling and linking. He has a passion for wholeness; what appeals to him is a well-rounded, inclusive system. The cosmos in its reaches and the mind in its tangles are his field. Again and again, from Plato to Hegel or to Croce, art has been moved within this field. Modern aesthetics has shown a desire to become independent and to keep clear of the sweeping and often vague theories of the philosopher. But further thought shows that it is impossible for the aesthetician to do without his services. Some of the problems cannot be dealt with in any other way. Thus he must come to a decision as to how art is related to life—in its origins and in its aims. No matter how keenly he is interested in the simple, tangible, concrete phenomena of art, he is sooner or later forced into far-flung conceptual thinking. If he turns to painting, he is brought up sharply against the problem of representational values and carried over into the perplexities of theories of nature, of ideal, and of reality. Again, he is confronted with cosmic forces and interests in the tragedy of Aeschylus, the poetry of Browning, the music of Wagner, and the sculpture of Rodin; and with the boldly philosophical theories of many creative artists.

Aesthetics has much to gain from a sound affiliation with philosophy; it can escape looseness in its terms and a truncated, mutilated consideration of its materials, only if it welcomes disciplined and ambitious thinking. It must, however, keep its grip on art as a concrete living thing; and use philosophy only where it ought to be used.

AESTHETICS, ANTHROPOLOGY, AND ETHNOLOGY

Anthropology is interested in man as he modifies his environment in response to impulses which, as they are expressed and satisfied, result in progressive cultural achievements. At a point in time when life must have been simple and control of it crude and meagre, art appears in skilled and interesting forms; and from that time to this, creatively reborn in a thousand variants, it has kept its freshness of appeal.

Art reflects deep-lying, persistent, ever-actively sought human values: it is one of man's ways of taking and reshaping his world. He smears his body with colored clay or uses the tattooing needle; pierces his lips and decorates himself with feathers and necklaces of teeth; delights in chipped stone and hammered brass; fills the wall spaces of his caves with pictures of the bison, the mammoth, the wild boar; and cuts the sketch of a deer in stone or reindeer horn. He builds homes for his gods and weaves his prayers into rugs or into the patterns of his dances. Fanciful as it may be to say that all tragic situations, all jokes, and all tone-structures can be traced back to a few types and motifs, it must be admitted that there are startling uniformities in early art. The drawings of Bushmen are not unlike those of the cave-dwellers of Spain and Algiers; Cretan pottery and Indian blankets are similar in their designs; folk-lore and myth-making reveal striking parallelisms. Craftsmanship in the fashioning of stone implements—in processes and forms—shows a like uniformity within a very wide geographical field. But there are differences as well in both cases. At this point the ethnologist can be of service. Studying man as he does in his racial differentiation and in groups of kinship and common customs, discovering art as not the least important factor in tribal life, and seeking to understand it everywhere in its specific cultural setting, his work must not be overlooked. It is he who holds one of the keys to the understanding of art. He can tell us what a negro idol, an Indian totem pole, a war mask, a prayer rug subtend in the way of beliefs, fears, and hopes; and what is their local script and symbolism. Art can no longer be studied *in vacuo;* it has a history and a context; and patient and cautious use must be made of every scrap of material the anthropologist and the ethnologist furnish.

AESTHETICS AND SOCIOLOGY

The sociologist studies the general forms of an articulated social life. He understands work and play in their social meanings, traces gregarious impulses in their varying expressions, catches the form and the spirit of institutions and collective enterprises, watches the social process in its spreadings and changes. His work, too, is needed by the aesthetician. For art is socially conditioned in a double sense. It appears in a close and often perplexing relation to the practical interests of social groups. The individual is to be impressed and his services are to be enlisted. Memorials in bronze or stone and mural paintings are to glorify the group in his eyes; processional pomp is to make ritual impressive; war dances are to rouse the war spirit; prayer rugs, amulets, incantations, and ceremonies of purification are used as bids for rain and a good harvest or as protection from disease; the beat of rowing or harvesting songs is to make collective work easier. All these are ways in which the group attends to its necessary business and attends to it with a flourish. Again art reflects industrial and institutional changes, and emotional, intellectual, and spiritual readjustments. Thus a truly sympathetic study of the classical, the Byzantine, the Gothic, and the baroque styles in architecture is impossible without an insight into the religious beliefs, conditions of living, emotional reactions, fashions, and customs of the times. A study of social records, readings in Rabelais or in the popular sermons of the time, and a knowledge of the medieval mind in its perplexing mixture of the naive and the sophisticated, the traditional and the rebellious, the gross and the spiritual, will assist in the understanding of the grotesque and often indecent sculptures of the medieval churches in France and Germany; without a knowledge of chivalry and of theology in their forms and spirit the French *cante fable* and the Morality and Miracle Plays must remain unintelligible.

AESTHETICS AND PSYCHOLOGY

Aesthetic experience is a psychical fact. The simplest exclamatory enjoyment of a picture, the most direct shaping of clay or putting together of sounds involve sensation, perception, imagery, ear and finger memory. However haphazard the enjoyment or wayward the creative impulse, they are legitimate material for a science whose ambition it is to reduce to order the varied mass of psycho-physical facts. Aesthetics, then, has much to gain from an alliance with psychology and can make good use of its analyses and experiments.

AESTHETICS, CRITICISM, AND ARTISTIC TECHNIQUE

Criticism is the appreciative and discriminating study of single works of art; questions of artistic technique are questions as to what specific means and methods are used to bring about artistic effects. To what extent ought aesthetics to commit itself to criticism and to the detailed and minute analysis of technical processes?

Art calls for an appreciative response; and criticism is part of the answer. At one end of its range are confessions and enthusiasms with little more than a lover's logic to back them; at the other end are painstaking analysis of works of art and reasoned valuation. Critics from Longinus to Walter Pater or Anatole France have said many things of value, and have had their share in the spreading of a more subtle and more discriminating enjoyment of art. With the play, the statue, the painting before them they have labored unceasingly to discover and fix quality and to establish canons of good taste. Aesthetics is interested, among other things, in the quality of good art, and has much to gain from criticism at its best. It needs the warm and intimate touch, and the close study of works of art. But criticism may easily degenerate into a dogmatism of impressions or into the cheap cleverness and catchiness which is all too prevalent among American critics. Even when it does not become superficial and flashy it is too neglectful of general problems and of the implications of canons of taste, and too casual and unambitious in its thought to take the place of aesthetics.

There is a question how far the aesthetician should step into the field which the technical and historical students of the several arts make their own. Each of the arts has its material and its ends, its ways of working, its resources and difficulties, and its types. Neither its forms nor its meanings can be understood apart from its own problems of technique. Thus ballad and sonnet, sculpture in wood and in marble, miniature and mural painting, sketches in ink and in charcoal, the wood-cut and the lithograph all reveal differences in pattern, creative rendering, and expressive quality. Mimetic, gymnastic, and decorative dances are different in form and spirit. Etchings can carry more in the way of symbolism and give a bolder display of the ugly than can paintings. Wood-cuts have a vigor all their own. To this must be added the traditional technique of craftsmen and schools, and the individual technique of artists. An example of the former is Greek vase-painting; of the latter, the straight brush strokes of Van Gogh or the heavy black contour line of Daumier. How far into matters of this sort ought the aesthetician to go? If he wishes to avoid mere generalities, he must follow art into much of its articulated and individualized life; but he ought not to become involved in the endless detail of endless distinctions. His main purpose is, after all, a series of generalizations revolving about the problem of beauty; and to him each work of art is the fragmentary embodiment of a narrowly circumscribed artistic purpose—one item in a column of beauty.

The policy of the open door seems to be the right one for aesthetics in its relations with philosophy, the social sciences, psychology, and criticism with their medley of facts and problems. It is like a port of entry in which, for lack of a system of imports, stores accumulate in confusion. It is best to have the brisk intellectual traffic, and to chance reducing it to some sort of order. This may be done most easily by taking beauty as the central problem and grouping as many problems as we can about our interest in beauty. But this interest must be a specialized and not a vague or general one.

THE TWOFOLD MEANING OF BEAUTY

Aesthetics concerns itself mainly with the problem of beauty.[1] Little is gained, however, if the loose popular use of the term "beautiful" remains unchallenged. Its causes lie deeper than the youthful lack of discrimination which was shown in a college girl's copy of the Odyssey with its comment "beautiful" or "pretty" on passage after passage,

[1] This seems to be recognized by the choice of such titles as *Das Schöne und die Kunst* by Vischer; *The Sense of Beauty* by Santayana; *The Psychology of Beauty* by Puffer; *The Beautiful* by Vernon Lee; *An Introduction to the Experimental Psychology of Beauty* by Valentine.

from the picture of the garden of Calypso to those of storms at sea and the grotesque, horrible blinding of Polyphemus. It is a disconcerting fact that artists and critics alike use the term in a very free and ambiguous way. When Rodin insists that beauty is not the highest law of sculpture and then contends that to the great artist everything in nature is beautiful, he is not contradicting himself—he is simply helpless before an ambiguity of language. He uses beauty first in the narrow sense of what is regular, harmonious, directly and wholly pleasing, and then in the broad sense of what is artistically effective. His *Thinker* and *Balzac* are not beautiful in the sense in which the *Hermes* of Praxiteles is beautiful. Daring marks subject and technique. In its search for the stimulating and the significant this strong, nervous, imaginative art is constantly overstepping the bounds of formal beauty. At its best it is satisfying; and it is this quality Rodin has in mind when he uses "beautiful" in the broad sense. Aesthetics would be the gainer, and much narrowing and stretching could be avoided if the use could be limited to what is formally beautiful in contrast to what is sublime or graceful or picturesque or expressive. Beauty then would be but one category among many.

A very simple system of aesthetics could be gained at a stroke if beauty in the narrow sense were the only thing artistically effective. But this is not true. Neither the social nor the personal forms and aims of art can be set within formal beauty. How little of the effectiveness of a tragedy by Shakespeare, a dramatic soliloquy by Browning, a landscape by Turner, a music drama by Wagner is to be traced to such beauty! The *Oedipus* may be well-nigh perfect in the smooth interplay of its parts and the grace and music of its language, but much of its meaning as a work of art lies in its rendering of the dark and chaotic forces of life. Bold enterprise may be seen in the forceful art of a Maillol, a Mestrovic, or a Van Gogh; in the distortions of a Matisse; in the perverse drawings of a Beardsley; and in the macabre etchings of a Rops or a Klinger. Complex and mixed as is the appeal of such art, it is nevertheless not to be neglected. No aesthetician has the right to turn away from the constant experimentation that is going on in modern art, and frown upon the search for an ever increasing range of expressiveness. If he can feel the sheer beauty of Sappho's verse

Ἦρος ἄγγελος ἱμερόφωνος ἀήδων

Spring's messenger, the sweet-voiced nightingale

and enjoy the homely lines of Whitman and the strident notes of Carl Sandburg or Vachel Lindsay, he will not attempt to limit aesthetic theory to an analysis of the qualities and conditions of formal beauty.

NATURE AND ART

Ought aesthetics to limit itself to beauty in art or ought it to include beauty in nature? Usually beauty in nature is excluded. There are some notable exceptions. Hegel attempts an analysis of animal forms; Ruskin in his *Modern Painters* gives an aesthetics of soil and cloud, of river-courses, of striated rocks—finding in all these a neglected expressiveness; Volkelt illustrates his theories of the characteristic and the sublime, and Lipps his theory of empathy, by constant references to nature.

It is difficult to see how on principle natural beauty can be excluded. There is iridescence in a soap bubble as well as in a Tiffany vase. Sunsets or light on water or the note of a bird are a challenge to art in their aesthetic appeal. The "dynamism" of the Futurists is but a poor thing in comparison with tumultuous seas, a volcanic upheaval, or the throbbing life of some wild animal snared. All the elements of strength and beauty—lines, masses, colors—are found in nature; and they are there in startling combination. The sweep of curves, the thrust of jagged or straight lines, the tilting of planes, and the banking of masses are all to be had in a single tree; and that tree may call forth discriminating and relational activities as readily as does a landscape painting. The beauty of nature may be used as the substructure of aesthetics and yields many hints as to what is pleasing and what is not. Greek sculptors sought to deduce canons from the study of human proportions; Zeising discovered in the proportions of the arm and elsewhere in nature the Golden Section Ratio and applied it widely and rather uncritically to the whole field of art. Patterns owe many of their motifs to animal forms and colors.

From a practical point of view, however, it is expedient to limit aesthetics to beauty as it is revealed in art. There the field is narrower and more definitely marked. What in nature exists in conglomerate mass, incidentally, transiently, appears in art isolated and pure, willed as such, and permanently organized. There is in nature a bewildering variety of color schemes and light and shade effects; the simplest woodland scene offers a confused medley of impressions to all the senses. Beauty in the narrow sense is incidental. The color display of birds and their song during the mating season are incidents in sex rivalry and sexual selection; perfect symmetry is rare; there are constant, artistically purposeless intrusions of the ugly and the repulsive; the complexity and irregularity of nature disturb at every step. Nor are the difficulties lessened if beauty is taken in the broad sense. However infrequent and incidental formal beauty may be in the mass of natural effects, force and significance are strongly marked. Is God then an artist in the characteristic? If he is, he is an artist on a very large scale: a scale, in fact, which taxes the

imagination, for the meaning of a tree, a flower, a form of
animal life is read in the context of a cosmic drama, wasteful, bewildering, utterly lacking the regularity of an English manor or an old fashioned garden. It matters little
whether our reading of the universe is after the manner of
Darwin or St. Augustine, the fact remains that the influence
of scientific or religious ideas is against the isolation of the
artistic in nature. If these influences are cast aside, the
conglomerate of practical associations still remains. A field
suggests tilling or pasturing; the ocean, seafaring; a grove,
holiday making; the gnarled appearance of a tree, the un-
suitableness of its timber; the sharply angled tumbling lines
of a peak invite thought on whether it can be climbed. If
all such responses are suppressed, what remains but the painful picking of bits of significant line or color from a wide
and distressingly complex display of materials? In art we
face an isolation and purification already accomplished.
We are in the presence, too, of willed beauty: of the work of
an artist whose selective skill may be responded to, and
whose purposes, while a challenge, are a challenge that can
be met. What is thus created is given permanence, and offers itself again and again to immediate and discriminating
enjoyment.

Aesthetics, then, concerns itself mainly with what is beautiful, in the sense of what is effective in art. In order to
discover the sources of such effectiveness it traces the processes by which art is produced and enjoyed. It is interested in the origins and the development of art. Stronger
still is its interest in the part played by art in life, in its
general aims, and in the highly specialized aims of the
several arts. The latter it sees cooperating or interfering;
and it follows them some distance, at least, into their technique and their types. It concerns itself with a morphol-
ogy of general aesthetic types, such as the beautiful, the
characteristic, the sublime, the tragic, the comic. In doing

this it throws the many-sidedness of both art and the aesthetic response in sharp relief. It follows the struggle between tradition and revolt; and makes a study of great diverging preferences, such as naturalism and idealism, classicism and romanticism. If it is ambitious, it invades the aesthetic consciousness of the Oriental; if it is wise, it is comparative within a narrower field—a field which, narrow as it is, holds a perplexing range of perceptions and standards of beauty. In all this work aesthetics moves within a tangle of methods and with a frequent shift of emphasis.

This is a comprehensive program, and a loose one as well. At some future time aesthetics may show a well-knit strength and trim activity within a field of whose topography and limits there can be no doubt; at present it is little more than a group of problems. But this by no mean destroys its value, for each of these problems is rich in possibilities and relations. Each challenges illuminative and correlating thought.   If the most is to be made of them, aesthetics must not be reduced to a chapter in psychology or a bit of sociology. There is little to choose between an aesthetics bound in the boards of a philosopher's system and stamped with the gilt letters of arrogance, and the loose, fluttering scraps of the anthropologist. Its true domain lies somewhere between these extremes.

THE METHODS OF AESTHETICS

A method is a means of attaining desired results; and a good method gains such results in the soundest, most forceful, least wasteful way. It is a common mistake to hold that there is only one good method for every problem. There are many effective ways of conducting a campaign or winning a battle or handling scientifically a group of facts. Whenever what is in question is a comprehensive problem which turns out to be a mass of concrete, definitely limited problems, apparently unrelated, there is need of a flexible, resourceful technique of control. Thus winning a war involves financing, provisioning, sanitation, transporting as well as a successful military use of men; and the latter in turn depends on the ground chosen, the massing and marching, the knowledge of when to join in and when to avoid battle. Every science has its field and its range of problems. Its success is in great part one of methodology. Aesthetics is hampered by heterogeneous material ranging from beauty embodied in art to the creative processes that call it into being; from social to personal values; from origins to aims; from broad aesthetic types to highly individualized technique and effects. In such a situation only the readiest shifting and combining can be of service. What often happens, however, is that the aesthetician, in response to some bias, commits himself to one method, inflexibly used, and either forces everything into its scheme or limits himself to material to which it naturally applies. Kant's *Critique of the Power of Judgment* is an illustration of the first procedure; anthropological aesthetics, of the second. The leading methods of aesthetics must be passed in review; their nature marked and their history traced; and the point indicated where they may become an autocratic menace.

THE COMMONSENSE METHOD

The commonsense method takes it for granted that the quality of good art can be seen and the essentials grasped by anyone who is alert, observing, emotionally and imaginatively responsive, and not unintelligent. It is a series of markings and casual readings in the volume of art, as that volume reveals agreements and differences in the use of colors, the organization of lines, the uses of rhythm, and in artistic ideals. Some painters use a contrasted color scheme; others a tonal scheme with one dominant color delicately shaded. Which is the more effective? Does the value of a landscape vary with the size of the picture? Many of the old masters used the circle and the serpentine; Cézanne simplifies in terms of straight and broken lines. Renoir's bodies are given a plastic rounding. Does painting gain by such a sculpturesque technique? His trees and shrubs are bursts of color and rhythm; accurately observed they are not; neither are Turner's castles. Ought surfaces in sculpture to be smooth and color in painting clear, persuasive, and pure? How much of his compactness and incisiveness does Dante owe to the closed verse-form he uses? What of the color schemes and favorite designs of this or that painter? These are samples of such questioning observation.

The method is an old one. Aristotle uses it when he says that beauty must have a certain magnitude since we do not call very small things beautiful; much of his dramatic criticism and many of his remarks on the epic are nothing but commonsense comment of a shrewd and direct type. Longinus illustrates it when he enumerates the qualities of the sublime, the frigid, the bombastic, or when he contrasts the oratory of Demosthenes and Cicero. No Homeric controversies can in any way impair the value of his contrast of the *Iliad* and the *Odyssey*. He is constantly saying things worthwhile in the spirit of an appreciative observer and analyst, and marking the here and there of beauty; but he never gets to the point of developing a general theory. The method may be seen in most instructive form in the work of certain eighteenth century Englishmen:—Hogarth, Reynolds, Lord Kaimes, and Burke. These men all kept in close touch with art; they studied the practice of painters and sculptors and poets; they observed and suggested. Burke states that smoothness, small size, and a variety of curves mark beautiful objects. Hogarth selects regularity, unity, variety; and justifies his choice of the serpentine as the line of beauty by pointing to its use in Raphael. Lord Kaimes stresses proportion and order as marks of beauty, and vastness as a mark of the sublime.

What is the value of such a method? It starts at the right point—art in its single creations—and adopts the right attitude—that of an interested observer. If sublime objects are usually vast and beautiful objects smooth and delicate or if, as Bergson maintains, the comic is not found outside the sphere of the human, why not say so and make the most of such empirical markings off and commonsense orientations? It is the only method available in some problems; and it plays a not unimportant part in even so ambitious a work as Volkelt's *System der Aesthetik*. It is often all there is to art criticisms. But there are dangers lurking in the method. It tends to stop short of a science and a philosophy of the beautiful.

Commonsense is uncritical of its data; it is superficial in its observations and fragmentary, and too easily contented in its analysis. Resting its case on common impressions, it tells us that the circle is the most beautiful figure; that squares are more pleasing than triangles and curves more pleasing than straight lines; it points to the disquieting effect of certain sounds and colors, and to the attractiveness of certain designs and color combinations.   But these facts must be tested and verified; and this cannot be done except under a system of scientific controls such as an experimental psychological method offers.   Otherwise they are little more than reasonable guesses.

Again, the commonsense method is too neglectful of philosophical implications and too slack in its thinking.   As Thomas Reid, the commonsense philosopher, suggests, it may be impossible to discover a common element in the beauties of the several arts; but such scepticism requires a most careful grounding.   Certain problems of aesthetics— the relation of art to life, the nature of the tragic or the comic, the aims and methods of idealism—are definitely philosophical; and every one of its problems, however concrete and detached they may appear to be, imperiously calls for the penetrating, supplementing, and unifying activities of the philosopher.   One problem cannot be raised without raising a host of others.   Artists have understood this:—Leonardo in his note-books; Hebbel in his diaries; Whistler and Rodin in their remarks on painting and sculpture.   The critic and the aesthetician ought to see that only in this way can they avoid a truncated aesthetics or a "commonplace book" of facts and questionable reflection! [1]

The Philosophical Method

The philosophical method ranges from enfolding, illuminating thought applied to single problems, to a world for-

[1] Lessing, a keen observer and thoroughgoing analyst, is always in search of general points of view.   In the *Hamburgische Dramaturgie* he is not content with casual criticisms, but pushes on to the profoundest problems of tragedy.   In the *Laocoon* he has built out constructively the scattered and superficial material he found in Burke, Kaimes, and others.   In both

mula, comprehensive and consistently held to, which is to serve as a key to the understanding of the facts and problems of aesthetics. It is the first in Nietzsche, Romain Rolland, and Remy de Gourmont; the second in writers like Plato, Hegel, and Croce. Both ends have their opportunities and their dangers. Nietzsche rises to art as flashily and capriciously as a trout to a fly; the waters of his reflection show swift currents and pools, swirls and eddies, clear depths and foam, and not a few tangles and rocks. He combines the virtues of boldness and reach with the vice of inconsistent, uncorrelated thinking.

A world formula as a key to aesthetics has come to be distrusted. We are too intent on keeping close to the facts of experience to accept sweeping discussions of absolute beauty, reality, ideals; and to enjoy a ghostly singlestick contest among the clouds. If after the manner of Wolff feeling is defined as confused thought, and experience is intellectualized in a high-handed manner, the burden of this original sin must rest heavily on aesthetics. Or if the latter is forced within the frame of the Kantian critical philosophy, and the dichotomy of rational self and sense self is driven into the problem of the sublime, a barren formalism and a twisting of facts result. Plato, Hegel, Schopenhauer, and Bergson all show, in one way or another, the dangers of a world philosophy autocratically used in construing the facts of aesthetic experience.

There is no discounting Plato's knowledge of art or the delicacy and quickness of his response to beauty. He is a student of the technique of music, if a somewhat unsympathetic critic of its innovations. He shows flashes of insight in his remarks on poetry, painting, and sculpture. But even the hastiest reading of the *Republic* and the *Laws*

cases we may quarrel with the result—his theories stand in need of revision—but we ought to applaud the attempt to combine what is valuable in the commonsense method with something that is quite as necessary.

reveals him discussing art as a moralist or a metaphysician. When he assumes the role of a moralist, he takes his stand on empirical ground—the observed effects of various types and forms of art. Certain kinds of music evoke amorous, others, martial moods; vocal music is to be preferred to instrumental, for it can readily be made the carrier of religious or patriotic ideas and feelings, as in community choruses; Homer and the comic poets are demoralizing; tragedy "waters" instead of starving the passions. These judgments are in turn bound up with a general theory of what human nature is and society ought to be. Back of his attacks on tragedy is the belief that to incite and indulge the passions is to slip into a primitive, pre-rational mode of living. When he writes as a metaphysician he forces on art his theory of reality and a sharp sundering of the two worlds, of eternal types, and of appearance. Not only does he limit art to this second world of everyday experience and deny it the power to render or interpret reality, but discredits it still further by holding it to be an imperfect copy of this imperfect world—a system, in fact, of surface illusions. He goes to the lengths of attempting a metaphysical classification of the arts. Plato's theory of absolute beauty has little to do with art; it takes us straight to the devotional exercises of a great idealist—and leaves us there.

Hegel vindicates the dignity of art and, in opposition to Plato, assigns it the task of revealing reality in sensuous form. He defines beauty as *Geist*, or Spirit, shining through and illumining the world of sense. He substitutes for Plato's immobile world of Ideas a developmental theory of reality and devises a method which allows an ingenious use of concrete materials. But is it not, after all, a strange treatment he gives to art? There is something at once fascinating and disconcerting in the spectacle of this intellectual giant, so fond of dramatic interplays and complications, footing the intricate path of the dialectic method and dragging along an art bound hand and foot and burdened with metaphysics. Many of his aesthetic theories are of value. His analysis of symbolic and romantic art is worthwhile; his theory of tragedy is illuminating; his discussion of the artist and of the sources and means of artistic expression repays close study. But the twist of an extreme philosophical method is undeniably present. No patient student of the history of art will accept the Hegelian method of classifying and setting in motion the several arts; no careful and sympathetic analyst of beauty, as it is so individually and variedly revealed in works of art, will weight himself at the outset with such a definition of beauty as Hegel gives. The work of men like Vischer, Carrière, and Rosenkranz reveals the disastrous results of Hegelianizing aesthetics.

Schopenhauer, with an entirely different world formula as his key, commits the like mistake of forcing on aesthetics an uncongenial and disconcerting method. Three theories of his may be cited in proof: his theory of tragedy in terms of resignation, which is untrue to the facts of experience; his fantastic criticism of still life painting as stimulating instead of suppressing the will; his analysis of classical architecture in terms of an undisguised struggle between support and burden.

Bergson, too, illustrates the dangers of the philosophical method. In his study of the comic he lays claim to walking the way of empiricism. He means to observe disinterestedly the many types of the comic, and to get what he can from such intellectual watchfulness. His selection and interpretation of facts are everywhere dominated by the contrast between the living and the inert, between life, a non-repeating series, and mechanism, a series whose very essence is repetition.

The Cultural Method

The term is meant to include the older method of Taine and the newer method of Grosse, Groos, and other social students of art. Old or new, the method sets itself the task of studying art as a thing physically and socially conditioned. It sets itself against philosophy and turns to science. Art has its roots in social life: what it is and what it bears depend on the nature of the soil, on such cultivation as is given by custom and tradition, and on the favoring trend of taste. Why then not make a scientific survey of these influences?

Taine was the first to make the attempt consistently and on a large scale. In offering a "botanizing" theory of art, he makes much of four influences: *race, climate, milieu*, and the peculiar bent, or *genius* of the artist. No work of art, be it a painting, a drama or a novel, can be understood apart from the individual genius who created it, and the race that is active in and through him; apart also from the climate, the intellectual and social cast of the age, and the prevailing taste. In response to what he considered a scientific ideal and method, Taine attempted to seize upon the cultural influences in English literature and in the great schools of painting.

It may at once be granted that race, climate, milieu, and genius are determinants of the character of art. Winckelmann, a lover of art in the concrete and a scientific student not given to generalities, was forced to consider climate and political and social conditions in his history of art. At this point or that, in the study of Greek tragedy, in the appreciation of Dutch painting or of medieval architecture, in the understanding of Chinese poetry or of the Hindu drama, a wide cultural orientation is necessary.

Unfortunately three at least of these determinants, race, climate, and genius, are too indefinite to be of much use.

The same race and climate have produced artists amazingly different; and genius appears sometimes as the exquisite flower of taste gained by the process of natural selection of which Taine speaks, sometimes capriciously, a law to itself. As for the *milieu*, or social setting, it is, at the point where Taine uses it, too complex to be of much value.   So various are the forces at work in modern society, so different is their impact on different human material, and their penetrating power, that art movements of all types and radically contrasted art works are possible in the same cultural setting.   The remedy would be to carry investigation back to simpler social situations, but Taine lacks interest in and knowledge of primitive art.   He insists that it is his purpose "to realize not an ode but a law," but his theory is only quasi-scientific.   At its heart there is a good deal of rhetoric, not so much as there is in Schiller, Herder, Croce, and Faure, but still too much.

Within the last fifty years the social sciences have forced a reinterpretation of the term culture.   Empirical in point of view and method, they have moved away from the large formulas and brilliant rhetoric of a Schiller or a Hegel and from the uncritically scientific interpretations of a Taine as well.   They show an interest in the early stages of cultural development—crude art is not cast aside—and they have the advantage of a mass of material, carefully gathered and inspected, which may be used to give content, point, and color to the reading of the culture of this or that group, this or that age.   Theirs is the further advantage of an increased knowledge of human dynamics—of impulses and interests as they interrelatedly shape and sway human life. They have gone to school with modern biology and have adopted the genetic method.

One important result of this advance as it affects aesthetics has been a marked interest shown in primitive art, as that art is related to early cultural conditions and to later and more advanced artistic forms. Grosse's *The Beginnings of Art* is a good example of this interest and of a new scientific sociological and ethnological method. Not only is light thrown on one specific problem, that of the origins of art; the book is controlled throughout by an ideal of a scientific biology of culture and reveals the use of a genetic analysis of the facts of experience. One cannot imagine Grosse taking pleasure in the botanizing excursions, vague and ambitious, of Taine or having much confidence in the cultural mesh-bags of Schiller, Croce, or Faure, through which facts are constantly slipping. He is too scientific for that—too intent on the check-up of experience. When he studies the dance he distinguishes its early mimetic and gymnastic types and sees them in relation to definite customs and beliefs and as expressive of impulses and feelings. Groos in *The Plays of Man* shows a like advance over the theories of Schiller and Spencer. It is one thing to say that man is wholly man only when he plays and to interpret art as *Spieltrieb;* it is quite another thing to trace in detail the playful activities of man and of the lower animals, show significant variants, as in the dramatic games of children, and to relate this playful activity to anticipatory instincts of use in serious living or to survivals of what was once of service to life. It is one thing to generalize with Spencer, quite another to demand and furnish verification in detail.

Art is to be read as part of a social text, which in turn is to be studied in the spirit of a painstaking scholar. The application of this method to aesthetics has resulted in large gain. Its successes are, however, most striking in the simpler and earlier forms of art. Thus may a war mask or totem pole be studied or a bit of pattern in its modifications and migrations, or a tribal dance, like the Snake Dance of the Hopi Indians. But when social influences are many, and art is advanced and personally colored, the method either slips back to its older, vague form or vainly seeks help from biological guesses, as bold as they are questionable. In such a situation the only hope lies in using the cultural method only where it can be effectively used, and in showing a willingness to be as flexible in method as aesthetics is varied in content.

THE EXPERIMENTAL METHOD

The experimental method may be roughly defined as the commonsense method made scientific by greater care in selecting and interpreting, and by the use of methods and appliances which allow a more minute, accurate, and searching study of art material and aesthetic impressions. Both methods are empirical and unembarrassed; both operate by means of introspection, observation, and analysis. Certain glaring faults in the first method are avoided in the second. Suppose I say of a certain well-known picture, "I like it"; and then look for the sources of my enjoyment in the painting. I observe balanced grouping, graceful curves, color harmonies and contrasts; and I respond to the subject and its emotional associations. To what degree do all these contribute to my enjoyment? In order to answer this question I look within and try to discover the inwardness of my response. But if I do that and only that, I am caught within a single mood—and moods change. I neither observe exhaustively nor am able to escape the capricious influences of the moment. If I seek to standardize my enjoyment by comparing my responses at different times, I have gone but a little way, for they are, after all, my responses, and, individually colored as they are, may not be shared by others. If I interview these others and seek some sort of agreement, I am exposed to the "personal fallacy" and to an uncritical acceptance of the vague enthusiasms and biased judgments I meet. I am still moving on the plane of the commonsense method and am paying the penalty. I cannot disentangle associations that carry me to the heart of a picture from such as hurry me away from it; I cannot discover the true value of a line, color, or compositional scheme.

If I am to force my way to a better method and a less subjective understanding of art, I must devise some type of experimental control. The first control that suggests itself is exhaustive analysis of the work of art itself. Observe color relations, measure distances, plot curves, trace ratios. Such a method, if judiciously used, clears away subjectivities; reveals the technique and often the aim of a picture or a piece of sculpture; and opens the way to a wider, comparative study of art. But it has its dangers. It may easily become too objective in the sense of overlooking visual illusions, personal impressions and preferences, and the part these play in the free, creative activities of art. Art, as it is created and enjoyed, is a psychical experience. A purely mathematical method may easily lead to a barren schematization as thoroughly right and as thoroughly wrong as a musical notation which awaits the interpretative stressing of a master.

The method of experimental psychology does not neglect this fact of preference. To Fechner belongs most of the credit of pioneer work in experimental aesthetics. In 1855 Zeising published *Aesthetische Forschungen*, a book whose title and table of contents seem to promise a scientific aesthetics. It turns against Hegel, contains a detailed analysis of aesthetic types, and offers studies in simple geometrical forms, in symmetry and proportion, in sound and rhythm. His aim is "to investigate beauty in the spirit of the student of the natural sciences, and to trace its causes in time and space relations, material and formal conditions; causes which produce the various effects of various aesthetic material." Pages 165-187, taken in conjunction with an earlier essay of Zeising's, *Neue Lehre von den Proportionen des Menschlichen Körpers (1854)*, gives an interesting and in many respects valuable analysis of the Golden Section Ratio. But all this promising material is too deeply embedded in philosophical terms and classifications.

It was Fechner who took the decisive step. In an early essay, *Ueber die Frage des goldnen Schnittes (1865)*, he presents "certain empirical facts" against Zeising's overemphasis on the Golden Section Ratio; in another essay, *Ueber das Assoziationsprinzip (1866)*, he makes a study of the associative factor in aesthetic experience; in *Zur experimentalen Aesthetik (1872)* he develops his method. All this, and much more of the same kind, is taken up into his *Vorschule der Aesthetik (1876)*. Modern experimental aesthetics has rejected many of Fechner's conclusions and has advanced by many steps the technique of experimentation, but the point of view and the way of going about problems remain. It is therefore worthwhile to watch Fechner at his work.

Fechner cut out of white cardboard ten rectangles of the same area, ranging from the ratio 1:1, the square, to the ratio 2:5, a long narrow rectangle. One of these figures embodied the Golden Section Ratio, 21:34. They were submitted during a course of several years to a few hundred persons of both sexes, who were asked to express their preferences independently of use and other associations. The judgments were carefully tabulated, and it was discovered that the peak of the curve was in the neighborhood of the Golden Section Ratio, the preferences sloping sharply downwards at both extremes. Fechner was too careful an investigator to stop at this point. He studied various objects in common use, books, visiting cards, portfolios, stamps and objects commonly seen, as picture frames—and discovered that the square was seldom used and that the ratios close to the Golden Section Ratio were frequent. He submitted to children in nurseries the square and the Golden Section rectangle, watched their reaching out—changed the figures from right to left to guard against right and left-handedness—and discovered no decisive preference.

What if the rectangle under consideration is a picture frame? Will not the pleasing ratio of height and breadth vary with the subject of the picture? Fechner tests this question experimentally. He puts pictures into classes: religious, mythological, genre, landscape and seascape, still life; compares examples of each class and tabulates results. Other illustrations of Fechner's method are: his study of vowel-color; his careful separation of the direct and associational factors in art; and his analysis of the direct values of sound, color, line, and of the effect of associations.

With this scientific control in terms of fact always in mind, Fechner is unwilling to reduce aesthetic experience to one principle or law. He formulates six: the principles of the aesthetic threshold, of summation, of unity in variety, of harmony and truth, of clearness, of association—and these are not given as an exhaustive list.

Since Fechner's time experimental aesthetics has developed rapidly. The technique of investigation has been improved, and the range of experimentation widened. The improvement in technique can be traced to the invention of various laboratory devices. Revolving disks with color segments allow the study of contrast and fusion; eye-movements are studied by means of photography [2] ; reaction time

---

[2] The following may serve as an illustration of how aesthetics benefits by certain technical improvements. Curves are supposed to be more pleasing than straight or irregular lines. That is an assertion on the part of commonsense which must be put to the test and, if valid, must be backed by some theory that accounts for the facts. One such theory offered was that the eye-ball, owing to the peculiar way it is set in and controlled by the muscles, works most easily in curves. But photography has shown that the eye moves not in curves but in very irregular broken lines. (cf. Valentine, *An Introduction to the Experimental Psychology of Beauty,* pp. 44–46).

is fixed; emotional effects are measured by means of contrivances which register heart-beat, breathing, dilatation and constriction of blood-vessels; the motor side of consciousness is studied at first hand. The questionnaire method has been bettered by the guarding against distorting influences of all sorts. On the basis of this improved technique accurate and ambitious experimentation has been going on. Studies have been made in rhythm, in musical intervals, in concord and dissonance; there have been numerous contributions to the aesthetics of color. What is the effect of single colors or of differences in brightness, intensity, and shade? What are the laws of effective combining? to what extent do temperature sensations (hot and cold colors) and kinaesthetic sensations (light and heavy colors) influence our response to color? Attempts have been made to study in children and adults alike reactions to lines and simple space-forms and to reduce to scientific order the time and space elements in aesthetic experience. One aesthetic theory, that of empathy, has been built on motor responses. The experimental method has been applied to the comic, and to complex rhythmic and associational problems of poetry.

No one can deny great value to the experimental method. It has put at our disposal means of testing assertions concerning the elements or essentials of beauty. But at present it is not perfected; and it probably can never wholly escape the looseness and vagueness of questionnaires or deal successfully with complex problems such as the enjoyment of a symphony or tragedy. Even the greatest care in the putting of questions and tabulating of results leaves untouched all manner of individual associations. Is not the question: Does this color please? indefinite in the sense that it may point in the direction of either the agreeable or the beautiful? and are we not dependent for an answer on the uncritical mind of the person questioned? Laboratory devices are used as correctives, but while more delicate and more ingenious machinery may be looked for, it is difficult to anticipate contrivances capable of handling effectively the more complex aesthetic experiences. The experimentalist admits that values change when they are differently combined. Fechner allows for what he calls "kombinatorische Mitbestimmung." Many of the laws of combination—of color and sounds—have been formulated. Useful experimental work of this kind may be added to. To what extent, for example, is the pleasingness of a color in draperies influenced by the texture of the cloth? Such matters are comparatively simple and may be dealt with successfully; not so the intricacies of poetry, where the experimental method, however patient and inventive, can accomplish little unaided.

The aesthetician then, if he is wise, will neither spurn nor employ exclusively any single method. He will use the philosophical, commonsense, cultural, and experimental methods, shifting choice and emphasis with the nature of his problems, and will thus develop an alert and flexible technique of observation, analysis, and thoughtful generalization.

THE ORIGINS OF ART

It is the task of the historian of art to piece together the chronicle of art; trace changes in technique and in ideals; record the interrelations of schools and their ascending and descending lines; ground the work of the artist in the character of his age and in the manner of his working; follow the ever-changing struggle between tradition and revolt. In this he receives valuable aid from many sources. With every decade of patient upturning of the soil, the archaeologist is making the story of art more complete. The excavations in Egypt, Asia Minor, Crete, and Greece; the explorations of caves and sifting of gravel-beds; the study of chiseled flint and scratched slate or ivory; the careful piecing together of bits of pottery—all this has set the formative arts in a truer light. Crude beginnings and transitions have been revealed; so have struggles with a recalcitrant material like stone and with the puzzles of facial expression, side-views, and perspective; so have technical processes. Greek coins and gems have supplied many gaps in the history of Greek sculpture and have made the study of modified copying and amalgamation of types easier; Greek vase-paintings not only show a gradual mastering of contour drawing, shading, and posing, but hint at the nature and development of painting itself.[1] Further help is necessary. The labors of the historian, the ethnologist, and the anthropologist must be called on, if this collected material is to be rightly interpreted. It matters little whether the question is one of the ancient palaces and temples of Egypt, Peru or

[1] For light on technical processes cf. Figures 2 and 4 in E. Pottier, *Douris and the Painters of Greek Vases,* N. Y., 1916.

Mexico, or of Greek athletic sculpture, or of the symbolism of Indian rugs and pottery; a correct reading is impossible without historical orientation and a knowledge of customs such as totemism and animism, and of all sorts of beliefs, ideas, and practices of magic. Two examples may serve to show how essential this social interpretation of art is. Egyptian sculpture and painting can be understood only in the light of religious beliefs and burial customs. The statuettes and paintings of the Tomb of Ti reflect curious Egyptian ideas of appanage and sustenance with reference to the dead, and offer the setting of a serious problem to the artist— that of making the retinue and workers of the mighty dead at once individual and typical of their class and work.[2] Again, in the study of decorative patterns, one might hastily conclude from the geometrical character of borders in Cretan and early Greek pottery, in Oriental and Chinese rugs, and in African and Australian masks and tattooing, that the intricate designs of modern art go back to an early delight in purely geometrical forms such as the circle, the triangle, the square, the angle, the sloping line. But there is nowhere greater need for discrimination. Zigzag lines on early Greek vases are nothing but zigzag lines, but zigzag lines in Indian rugs are symbols of the lightning. Instances of Chinese symbolism are the Knot of Destiny, the circle as the emblem of eternity, the cloud as the emblem of immortality; of Caucasian symbolism, the Latch Hook, which, like the old and well-nigh universal Swastika, is the symbol of good luck, and Solomon's Seal. To this symbolism the anthropologist and ethnologist hold the key. Again, many patterns which on the surface seem to be purely geometrical are cases of schematization of animal forms. Here are a few: the tarantula, the crab, the snake, the lizard, the kneeling camel, fishes, and birds. This schematization either marks the simplifying and modifying of animal forms for

[2] Cf. Maspero, Art in Egypt, (1912) Figures 15–29 and text, pp. 15–18.

the sake of fitting them into a decorative pattern suggestive of continuity and unity, or it is an instance of debased observation and of shorthand methods in art. Nor must the folk-lorist and folk-psychologist go unheeded, for there is in many of these designs an early delight in life and its various forms and forces: in the cresting life of the sea—the Chinese and Greek fret;—in flowers—rosettes and medallions—in sun and moon—the Sunburst and the Crescent—in running water and the growth and movements of animals.

The aesthetician, in turn, is dependent on the historian of art, and on all the others.[3] He must accept what expert opinion provides in the way of facts and adjust his theories in response to any new discovery or widening of experience. He has, of course, his own problems and his own wider use of materials. He travels the high road of theory, and he ought to do it circumspectly, with a patient understanding of what in the way of surveying and cultivating and masonry-work has been done by the special sciences. If he contents himself with a roving glance and sweeping gesture, he fails as lamentably in his way as does the archaeologist or ethnologist in his, if he lives in some one problem, as a maggot in a cheese, feeding blindly on the pulp of facts.

As a purely scientific problem, the question: How did art begin and how did it develop? is at present unanswerable, for the record begins abruptly, with a baffling lack of wider cultural facts, and proceeds spasmodically. But is it not

[3] Winckelmann's *History of Ancient Art* (1764) illustrates this problem of interdependence. It is a remarkable piece of work: solid; bristling with firsthand analyses and observations, bearing on the technical treatment of eyes, forehead, hair, costume; thorough in its use of ancient sources; suggestive in its attempt to relate art to race, climate, and social conditions; brilliant in its divination of the characteristics of the Four Styles. But all this equipment and reference to what in the light of nineteenth century discoveries seems a pitifully meagre store of Greek sculpture did not keep Winckelmann the historian from a serious misdating of the *Laocoon* and Winckelmann the aesthetician from a serious misreading of the spirit of Greek sculpture.

possible to take the problem of the origins of art in a larger sense and to trace, psychologically and sociologically, the interplay of forces to which art owes its being?

Art is very old and very human. The earliest extant art is that of the cave-dwellers, and, judging by what remains of it, it reached its highest point of excellence in Spain and Southern France. On the low dark walls of the cave of Altamira, and in many other caves, were found paintings in red, yellow, brown, and black of various animals—the reindeer, the wild boar, the bison, the mammoth. In outline, in shading, and in the rendering of animal motion these pictures show a high level of skill. There are several layers of them; the later artist covered over the work of his predecessor. This and the fact that some of the earlier paintings are clumsy and sketchy allow the partial deciphering of a long period of artistic endeavor. In beds of gravel were found stones scratched with the contours of animals, bits of reindeer horn and ivory cut into and shaped to resemble horses' heads, crouching deer, huge figures of horses sculptured in the round, and a few representations of the human figure. The age of this art has been variously set as from 30,000 to 100,000 years. The dolmens, menhirs, and circles of granite blocks found in Brittany, England, and Sweden reveal architecture in its infancy. The surfaces of many of these stone pillars are covered with intricate linear patterns. Bits of glazed pottery, polished stone axes, gold ornaments and hammered bronze implements testify to the development of the lesser arts. It matters little what is chosen,—an axe or a drinking cup, bronze armor dug up from the peat bogs of Denmark, a flint knife, the contents of an Egyptian tomb, the Swedish plaque reproduced by Reinach, with its eight point star centre, its design of concentric circles, and its rolling circle borders—everywhere art yields itself as something primitive man created, delighted in, and related to his everyday practical life. Quite as striking as its long history is its human quality.   Children scribble likenesses of trees and houses and play dramatic games with all the *verve* and finish of an artist; the camp-fire becomes the rallying point of singing and dancing; much artistry goes into the weaving of a basket or rug, the smoothing of a paddle, the fashioning of a head-piece of feathers; the story of a hunt is put on a piece of walrus tusk by the Eskimo, on a dressed skin by the Indian, on a bronze dagger, with gold and silver work, by the Cretan, on huge, modeled wall spaces by the proud Assyrian.   Everywhere art is created and enjoyed in response to common human needs.   There is no more fruitful source of errors of all sorts than the interpretation of art as something without a history and without a range wider than the creative work of a few exceptionally gifted individuals.

What are the beginnings of art?   What peculiarities of human nature make its creation so common and its enjoy-ment so spontaneous and so persistent?   Intellectual econ-omy suggests a single explanatory principle—utility, play, sex, self-expression,—but such economy means a narrow and warped theory, too high a price for any liberal-minded and observant student of art to pay.   It is impossible to run back the various types of art to one source; and it is quite likely that art sprang up in different localities and among different peoples in response to different sets of conditions. There are many sources to the stream of art; their combin-ing, the slope of the land, the nature of the soil, and the seasonal rains determine the volume of the stream and the velocity of the current as it cuts a deep and narrow bed be-tween cliffs or sluggishly takes a wandering and spreading course.   The whole river-system cannot be explained by a bit of trickling water in the mountains; the system of art, fed and feeding, changing form and velocity with changing conditions, cannot be explained in terms of a single deter-minant, physical or social or psychological.

An open mind and no favors! ought to be our motto in a review of the many determinants of early art.

Utility

It is one of the commonplaces of aesthetics to contrast the tensional response to pressing practical needs with the calm, disengaged, disinterested pursuit and enjoyment of beauty. The contrast is made plausible by taking art at its remotest point from practical life, at its culmination in a poem, a sonata, a picture. But even in the lesser arts, such as weaving, pottery, cabinet-making, silversmith work, where the product is to be serviceable there is a loving elaboration of workmanship on the part of the artist and an enjoyment of the play of form and color on the part of him who responds, which cannot be put to the score of utility.

Is it possible to take our sense of the beautiful, which in its higher forms is so forgetful of the everyday practical world and so wrapped up in an imaginative life of its own, analyze it, and show the useful as the original determinant in its forms and estimates? The attempt has been made repeatedly. Berkeley and Alison have tried to show that what is called beautiful is in some way useful; that, for instance, such architectural forms,—door-frames, wall and window spaces, arches, flat or sloping roofs,—are chosen and held pleasing as have been found most convenient and useful.

With the development of the genetic method and the comparative study of the art and culture of primitive peoples, the theory has reappeared in a strengthened and more ambitious form. Attention is drawn to the fact that the later, freer types of art go back to earlier technical processes and industrial needs—weaving, pottery, and the construction of shelters are cited as examples—that painting goes back to the sign language of pictographs; and dancing, to socially useful pantomime; that groups turn to their

UTILITY AND DESIGN

(a) A carved club, Marquesas Islands. (b) Ceremonial adze, Maori, New Zealand. (c) Wooden comb, Benin, West Africa. (d) Carved canoe prow, New Zealand.

own use the artistic gifts of their members; and that social
life, taken in the large, confesses the need of expressing and
maintaining itself through the useful activities and pleasures of art.

Facts such as these cannot be ignored. Every advance
in ethnology and folk-psychology reveals art closely related
to the aggressively self-protective life of the group. Amulets are worn to ward off evil, and masks to frighten; war
dances are to rouse the fighting spirit; rowing and harvesting songs are to make common work easy; poetry and music
speak with the voice of common exploits whose memory is
to be kept; shape in a throwing-stick and symmetry in a
paddle serve a practical purpose; rugs, bowls, totem poles
have their definite uses. But there are indications also of
a spontaneity and a surplus of pleasure which cannot be
explained either by special practical purposes or by the
larger purposes of the group. No doubt the process of
aesthetic indirection has had its share in changing work
into play and in giving man a larger field of artistic self-
expression, but it is bad psychology to trace everything
back to the perception of fitness. Symmetry is enjoyed in
objects where it never could have been useful; delicate
shading in the colors of a rug shows a discriminating taste
and workmanship far beyond anything the group expects
or can make specific use of, unless—and that is begging
the question—a social will to art as art is assumed and held
to be useful. There is another possibility also. Utility
may be taken in a comprehensive biological sense and art
explained in terms of the uses of life. It is thus that Darwin relates color and sound in birds to sex, and sex to life;
that Grant Allen traces the color-sense back to the animal's
problem of choosing food; that McDougall explains
laughter as a protective device against the pain of intense
sympathy; that art is held to be one form of the will to
health and power. The method of biological orientation

is of great value, but it lends itself to serious misuses. One of these misuses may be put as follows: Everything in nature has its use; no specific use can be discovered for A or B; therefore, A or B must be explained in terms of the general purpose of maintaining and heightening life-processes. This is like assuming that nature is a universal Fairy Godmother who is constantly bestowing gifts on us; if at any time we cannot discover a specific gift, we take refuge in the thought of some general impalpable bestowal —for is she not our universal Fairy Godmother?

IMITATION

With respect to the earliest art known to us little can be gained by a reference to utility. We know nothing of the social life of the cave-men. They were hunters with very simple weapons at their disposal. Why did these men draw and shape the likenesses of animals, and fashion decoratively their simple implements? Was it to gain control over these animals in the chase and to increase the supply of game by magic means? This answer—in terms of "imitative magic"—has been suggested by Frazer, Reinach, Spearing, and others. It treads the dangerous path of analogy. It is well known that Australians and Indians entertain such a belief in the efficacy of copies and seek to ward off a dearth of game or a drought by drawing likenesses and performing incantations. Similar motives have been assigned to the cave-men; the fact that they painted chiefly edible animals and often drew arrows on their surface is used to strengthen the argument from analogy. But the argument is largely guess-work, and may easily be carried to absurd lengths. (cf. the interpretation given by Spearing in his *Childhood of Art*, p. 96, following Reinach, of the *flayed horses' heads*). Faure suggests that these early hunters described their

kill by the vivid means of drawing and painting, but how
does such a theory fit in with either the many fragmentary
sketchings of heads or the careful detail work in shading?
In pictographs, where animal forms are used as a sort of
social currency, outline sketching is held sufficient for purposes of recognition and the forms are often debased to the
point of the utmost sketchiness.

Quite another force must be reckoned with—the impulse
to imitate and the pleasure in successful imitation.   Two of
the oldest theories of art trace it to this source.   Aristotle
speaks of man as an imitative animal; points to his practice, from childhood up, of drawing likenesses; and adds
that man delights in recognizing the original in the copy.
Our enjoyment of accurate copies of repulsive objects he
cites in support of his generalization.   Lucretius traces
music back to the imitation of natural sounds—the song of
birds, the noise of the wind among reeds.   The reed-pipe of
the peasant and the ripple and trill of song are man's attempts to master the variety of natural sounds.   Lucretius,
however, adds the restful effects of artistic exercise, and
draws a vivid picture of men coming together and enjoying
rhythmic improvisations.   Neither theory discriminates
sufficiently between creating and enjoying art.   The pleasures of recognition need not presuppose a strong mimetic
impulse; nor is imitation always conscious and pleasurably
toned.   A striking likeness is enjoyed by the artist and the
onlooker alike; and the pleasure may serve as a stimulus to
both.   But a distinction must be made between the question:
What do we enjoy in art? and the question: What impulse or
group of impulses is the cause of art?   It is the second
question which concerns us here.

The imitative impulse is strongly at work in the first
rude sketches children make of trees and houses; in the
animal dances of primitive peoples; and in the earliest pre-

historic art. The cave-men drew, painted, and carved the many animals of the chase; they caught their outline, their appearance in the round, and their movements. A sharp and alert observation marks their work. The rush of the running boar; the lumbering majesty of the mammoth; the thin, graceful foreleg of the horse; the lowered head of the bison; the stretched neck of cattle; the reindeer looking back:—all this is observed vividly and copied accurately. The detail work shows an astonishing truthfulness. The thick, long, irregular hair on the neck and back of the bison is set off from the shorter, smoother hair of the belly and flank.

The Australian paints on walls of rock or traces with charcoal on skins the likeness of the kangaroo, the crab, the shark with its companion, the pilot fish; the Bushman scratches or daubs on rocks the animals within his ken; the Eskimo works bone into the shape of sea-lions, dogs, and whales. Then there are mimetic dances, in which the dancers cover themselves with skins or feathers and imitate rhythmically, with great enjoyment and consummate skill, the characteristic movements of animals—the ostrich, the bear, the kangaroo. There are elaborate mimetic love and war dances. In the latter the thrust of spears or speeding of arrows, the rush and physical clash, the victory and the rout are enacted faithfully, to the staccato rhythms of the war cry and battle song. To these must be added other imitative poses and gestures such as the simulated movements of stalking game, of paddling a canoe, of cutting one's way through the bush.

Imitation, then, is an influence not to be neglected in any genetic theory of art; but to overplay it means a narrow and strained reading of architecture, symbolic painting, early expressionistic dancing and sculpture, and decorative art forms.

ORNAMENTATION AND DECORATION

That a decorative as well as a mimetic impulse was at work in palaeolithic art may be seen in the use of animal forms (deer, goats, heads of horses, and bulls), in throwing sticks, magic wands, and daggers. One famous dagger handle of reindeer horn shows a crouching deer, with stiff hindlegs sloping backward at an angle of forty-five degrees, hindquarters thrown up, the body sloping down to the stretched neck, the head raised to match the slope of the hindlegs and the forelegs doubled under. An admirable handle with just the right grip for the fingers! But it would not have been less admirable in a practical sense, if there had been no artistic elaboration. There is something unnatural about the pose. This must not be set down to the score of failure, for the cave-men were excellent observers and recorders of animal life. Life-likeness, however, is not their aim here: they distort in order to gain a bold decorative effect. Modern parallels are to be found in the *art nouveau*. There, in paper-cutters, weights, candlesticks, canes, the human body, flowers, and animals are all used decoratively, and in being so used are conventionalized, distorted so as to fit into a linear or curvilinear scheme. It seems plausible then to assume an early and very direct interest in decorative design and ornamental pattern. It is beside the point to refer to an accidental origin in the mechanical processes of the industrial arts. Thus it has been suggested that designs on pottery go back to thumbprints or to the imprint of a rope left on the vessels in the process of baking, and that the use of different grasses accounts for checkered color-patterns in baskets. Whatever the first occasion, the decorative impulse is traceable in the art of every primitive people.

Primitive men everywhere use their own bodies as decorative material.   Excoriation and tattooing are common; bodies are smeared with fat and colored clays till they suggest a barber's pole or a geometer's dream; teeth are blackened; ear-lobes are perforated or lengthened; lips are pulled down and noses maltreated; the head of hair is built up in all sorts of ways.   Necklaces of feathers, colored beads or pebbles, and pendants of teeth are worn.   Dressed skins, aprons, loin-cloths, masks are fringed, twisted, painted over, and striking decorative effects are gained.   It is surprising to find the flower patterns on the draperies of Gauguin's Tahiti women, which suggest the sophisticated decorative scheme of an ultra-modern painter, matched in the photographs of South Sea Islanders.

Not only the bodies but the belongings of primitive man —such as blankets, axes, spears, shields, bows and arrows, knives, paddles, arrow-smoothers—show ornamental shaping and coloring.

Such are the facts; how are they to be interpreted? Fashion and custom doubtless play their part; and back of the custom there is often a utility value.   Amulets and wands have their uses; a grotesque mask, a towering head dress, a body boldly streaked with war-paint are a challenge and a bit of bravado: they are to frighten the enemy.   The elaborate dress and the intricately carved staff of the chief or medicine man are to promote group unity and provide the touch of ceremonial impressiveness so necessary to the smooth functioning of social life.   Patterns, usually geometrical in type, are common in early art.   There are circles and rectangles, undulating and zigzag lines, lines marching in a sort of crowded obliqueness, checkerboard patterns, curves twisting and untwisting, successions of differently tinted triangles and rhomboids.   Much of this geometrical decoration serves tribal uses and is to be read in relation to tribal symbols.   Circles strung at intervals along a line mark a lapse of time—some geometrical decorations are nothing but schematized or debased rendering of animal forms. The most may be made of such explanations; there is still something unaccounted for. There is an original delight in symmetry and in orderly, intriguing variations of line. There is, also, the impulse to embellish all things, whether useful or not, by decorative edging or ridged carving, or by changing the heavy monotony of surfaces into the light, interlaced traceries of filigree work. An example of this is the Maori door lintel given by Goldenweiser (*Early Civilization*, Fig. 44).

Important as this spontaneous decoration is, it is only one influence among many in the development of art. Other determinants are: self-expression; commemoration; and the irradiations of the sex-impulse.

SELF-EXPRESSION

Many a modern artist, when asked what is back of his art and why and in what sense he is an artist, gives some such answer as this: "My art is not imitation of what in nature strikes my senses, nor is it embroidery in the sense of a sorting and recombining of colors, lines, and sounds; it is my attempt to express myself creatively by giving shape to my moods, my impulses, my dreams and imaginings. The world of objects is simply my occasion, the material in which I work, my opportunity. I am in the grip of an impulse to express and project myself—I create because I must create." The sculpture of Rodin shows this impulse at work, and the letters of Wagner testify to its overmastering force. This is, if you will, a question of the psychology of the artist, but it is something more. Expressionistic art, which deliberately breaks the stabilized world of objects to bits, and re-creates it in the turbulent image of a self as chaotic in its flashes of impulse and feeling as it is aggressive in its reaching out, goes back, for inspiration and justification, to the grotesque statuettes, of ivory and wood, of the Kongo and the African coast, and to the weird music and dancing of the negro. This sophisticated modern revolt—so Hermann Bahr and its other champions interpret it—must be carefully distinguished from an early mentality as yet unformed and a world of crude, imperfectly shaped artistic expression. But there is in early art sufficient warrant for tracing projection and expression of self, both tribal and individual.

Many primitive dances are expressionistic rather than mimetic in character. Gymnastic dances are physical expression under excitement: witness the jumping and spinning around in Russian folk-dances, the swinging of bodies and arms, and the leaping and bounding in African and Australian dances. There is a keen enjoyment of this energetic play of one's muscles, this flinging oneself about. Self-expression invades the emotional field as well. The dancers shout, fall into improvised rhythms, burst into snatches of song; the music whips up the excitement as it parallels it. A grotesque, imaginative strain is present in sculpture and painting. Acquaintance with the material of myth, folk-tale, and legend, with masks that distort rather than imitate, and with fantastic creations in the drawings of Eskimo and Australian alike, reveals the fact that primitive man, faithful observer and imitator that he can on occasion be, persists in and enjoys building at times a world of his own—a world expressive of his own energy, his own playfulness, his own moods.

In the individual artist this expressionism is partially checked by his own collective way of feeling and thinking and by traditional patterns and symbols imposed by the tribe. But within these limits there are a great number of individual variations in the working out of a general pattern and striking opportunities for an individualized iconography of supernatural helpers and hinderers. Anthropologists and ethnologists recognize this variational element. Here is a quotation from Goldenweiser, *Early Civilization*, p. 166: "We say 'expression' deliberately, for the primitive artist is not by any means as passive an imitator of traditional style or pattern as he or she is often represented to be. In those areas where careful studies of primitive art have been made, as for example, in North America, ethnologists constantly observe the great and typical variability of objects of art. Not that the tribal style is ever disregarded. The opposite is, in fact, invariably the case: the woman embroiderer of the Plains, the man carver of the Northwest Coast, the woman potter of the Southwest and embroiderer of the Iroquois and Algonquin work along well established lines of technique and design pattern. But within these fixed limits there is infinite variation, often minute, at other times radical, which cannot be explained by mere inaccuracy of reproduction due to the absence of definite measurement, but can only be accounted for by the individual technical aptitude of the artist, the peculiarity of his idiosyncrasy or the direction of his playfulness. In the Plains, for example, the minute units of the embroidery designs are combined into a great variety of more complicated patterns. New patterns of this kind are constantly originated by the women who, in this case, dream the new designs. Of course, even these dreamed designs always follow certain tribal principles of decoration and arrangement of design units. But there is room enough left for an unceasing variety of detail."

One of the simplest, and to the aesthetician most fruitful, forms of self-expression is play. In its quieter as well as in its most vigorous types it is an invasion and resetting of the external world in terms of self. When I sit down to a game of chess the two rows of men confront me with a stolid immobility. I break into this, shift them about, and use them as material for the expression of my initiative, my skill, my imaginative weaving of patterns of attack or defence. Any position which arises during the game is felt by me, not as something immobile and strange, but as tensing and relaxing purposes of mine—as life of my life. When I improvise an acrobatic dance, I break into the staid composure of my body with a chaotic abandon of physical energy, and then somehow give a new, personal pattern of skill and strength to this chaos. The process need not be self-conscious; and the playful shaping is as important as the outgoing energy.

Theorists like Schiller, Spencer, Nietzsche, and Groos have been struck by the resemblance between play and art, and by the element of self-expression in both. Nietzsche distinguishes between *Rauschkünstler* and *Traumkünstler*, between the Dionysian and the Apollonian artist. While the latter seeks to create a beautiful dream-world of his shaping, the former, the orgiastic artist, paints or chisels or bursts into ecstatic poetry from sheer pressure of his seething self—or dances to the notes of his own piping. He creates because he must express the fulness of his being. Backing his theory by references to biology and social history, Nietzsche points to the orgiastic character of much of early art, to the licence of festivals, and to the grotesque, energetic imagery which marks the lower levels of the history of art. Spencer explains art in terms of the expenditure of surplus energy; energy which has been stored because it could not be expended in the serious business of living. Groos, studying the plays of animals and of man, sees in their simulated activities an instinctive preparation for practical problems—a sort of anticipatory expression of the warrior or the hunter or the mother.

More complex in its motives than play is another form of self-expression:—that of projection and fusion. Man vivifies and humanizes nature; he attributes to inanimate objects his motor experiences and his moods—and his fellows! He constructs a world after his own image. The tree is a dryad; rocks are petrified men; the flooding of its banks is an angry gesture on the part of the river-god; the volcano is a hot-breathing giant or a fire-spewing dragon. Folk tales in which the actors are animals show little insight into animal life as such; the animals are disguised humans with a touch of the grotesque; they talk, weep, and, what is most human of all, moralize. Again there is a sort of sympathetic projection of a man's personality into his belongings, so that when he sickens the blade of his knife turns dull. There is much of this in early magic and witch-craft, and in the mythmaking artistry of early man.[4]

Self-expression then is one of the roots of art. It is well to remember, however, that a shout, whole-souled though it be, is not yet art, ecstatic language not yet poetry, and a hurling into space or time of one's emotional experiences not yet painting or music. Art is something beyond such simple spontaneity—something disciplined by its own developing technique; and often something created and formed in response to other and equally insistent impulses.

COMMEMORATION

Commemoration may or may not be a special form of self-expression. The artist feels impelled to create, and to externalize his inner life. But he also means to build something of himself into the permanent mould of immortal verse and imperishable music. Convinced as he is of the uniqueness and worth of his impressions and experiences, he records them in his art and cheats them of their evanescence. A changing sky at sunset, the sting of a salt breeze or the white chaos of a driving, blotting snowstorm—the ecstasy of love—a lost friend or leader—a cosmic protest—

---

[4] Cf. Goldenweiser's reference to the Chukchee belief in mushroom men, mice-people and earth-spirits (*Early Civilization*, pp. 202–204).

nameless fears—moods that perplex and melt away—all this
is to be immortalized. The feeling of the lastingness of
their work is strong in artists [5]; so is the human craving,
if not for immortality, at least for a greater permanence
than life ordinarily allows. The engineer who perpetuates
his vision and skill in a reclaimed desert and the man who
records his initiative and courage in the building up of a
large business have the feeling and the craving in a less
subtle form.

Undoubtedly the desire to arrest the moment for the
purpose of recording and commemorating what is felt to be
of interest is back of many a poem and sculptural design.
It varies with the artist and the period; and it must not be
confused with the release of surcharged self-feelings or the
spontaneity of play.

What then is its influence in the development of art? It
is dangerous to drag in the whole sophisticated individualism
of the modern artist. Primitive man exhibits an egoism as
naive and direct as that of a child; and this egoism is not
necessarily creative. He often seeks to perpetuate himself through the work of others. Let the sculptor catch
my likeness; let the painter fill spaces with my hunting exploits; let the tribal circle hand down my name! Art
there is in all these cases, but the commemorative stimulus
comes from without. Nor can such a desire to stand fixed
and impressive before one's self and one's fellows be made
to explain the frequency and range of commemorative art.

[5] Horace (*Bk. 3 Ode xxx*)

> A monument I've achieved more strong than brass,
> Soaring kings' pyramids to overpass;
> Which not corroding raindrip shall devour,
> Or winds that from the north sweep down in power,
> Or years unnumbered as the ages flee!
> I shall not wholly die!

and Shakespeare's Sonnet

> Not marble, nor the gilded monuments
> Of princes, shall outlive this powerful rime—

Hopi Bowl   Gold Disc from Panama

Tlingit Amulet   Eskimo Box

ARTS AND CRAFTS

There are tribal epics and tribal trophies; painted on skins or cut into stone are the records of fighting and hunting; there are shrines, burial places, public buildings, embellished landmarks of great common achievements; there are all sorts of ceremonies—pantomimic dances, processionals, ablutions—all witnesses to the egoism and vanity of groups. Social life is to cut an imposing figure, and the individual is to be impressed. The pride of the group in itself is reflected in the pride the members take in it;—nothing surprising in that, since the early consciousness is essentially a group consciousness, as befits a group life. But why is this business of fixing and glorifying the life of the group done with so emphatic an artistic flourish? A stick driven in the ground might serve as a mark and the crudest tracings might serve as a record. If activities are pleasurable, they are more readily entered upon and more tenaciously remembered. But why aesthetic pleasures? No stretching will allow us to leave out of the reckoning utility, play, sex, and other motives. Not all art is monument-making, and not even all in monument-making is self-expression or self-perpetuation on the part of individual and group.

A sort of biological registering must be taken into account in explaining the commemorative side of art. Physically and psychologically the sex impulse registers itself in physical union, biologically it registers itself in offspring. The artistic imagination and dexterity of man registers itself physically and psychologically in projection and in the shaping of inert material; biologically it scores in a permanence which links the present with the future—as offspring link the present with the future.

THE SEX-IMPULSE AND ITS IRRADIATIONS

There is a theory that art is sex. The artistic impulse is interpreted as the sex-impulse either in its adolescent undirected restlessness and excitement or in its compensatory radiating satisfactions in dress, taste, religion, art or in its rebellion against the disciplinary control of the group and the individual alike. Why then not explain the development of art in terms of an adolescent, an irradiating, a rebellious sex-consciousness?

What are the facts on which such a theory builds? The simplest and most obvious fact is the use of art in sex rivalry. Not only ornamentation and decoration, but dress itself is used as a sex stimulant, and as an attraction and a challenge. When a man courts he tries to please, and he pleases by showing his disturbed condition in a love-song, and his strength and skill in an athletic dance, by being more striking, more colorful, more imposing than any of his rivals. Women lure by showing their skill in the weaving of rugs or baskets, by singing and dancing, and by the exploitation of their physical charms. Erotic dances and songs are common; so is erotic symbolism in tattooing. Sex characteristics primary and secondary, are grossly exaggerated in very early specimens of sculpture and painting. Again art appears in close connection with religious ceremonies which are frankly sexual in imagery and technique. Phallic worship and religious prostitution may be cited as examples. A dormant or blocked sensuality finds an outlet in great social gatherings such as the Spring Festival in Greece, the Saturnalia and the Carnival in Rome, and in the repulsive abandon of such ceremonies as are described in *Batouala*— primitive negro sexuality described by a negro.

Such facts must not be overlooked in explaining the throbbing quality of the lyric, the origins of Aristophanic comedy, the meaning of many pantomimic dances, the exuberance of Rabelais, and the eroticism of Wagner, and of the "fleshly school of poetry." Directly or in overtones, sex has its part to play in artistic creation, of the most subtle as well as the most direct type. But much of art is untouched by it;—and this applies especially to the epic and the bulk of architecture and painting. Nor is all art—as some Freudians would have it—the irruption into consciousness of chaotic, inarticulate sex feelings, rebellious because thwarted, slipping by the censor and into art in the disguise,—of the Oedipus Complex and the Hamlet Complex. The fantastic explanations of art material by the Freudians are themselves a case of folk-lore and sex magic, of interest, not to the seeker of truth, but to the folk-lorist and the analyst of the Freudian Complex.

Art is something which is constantly creative and re-creative in the activities of groups and in the life and work of gifted individuals. When and in response to what forces it first appeared in the life of man is an unanswerable question. It may well have sprung up in different localities as the result of different influences. But it is by no means an unimportant matter to trace in its earlier and fresher stages the manifold causes and influences which account for this eternally interesting and significant process of creation and re-creation. Utility, sex, the impulses to adorn, to imitate, to express oneself in the sense of projecting a fluctuating life into the immobility of nature, and to commemorate in the sense of giving to oneself and one's own a striking and immobile distinction and permanence such as nature only occasionally provides—these are among the forces. To select one and only one and to sacrifice to it all the others is to practise an economy so stringent and narrow that the search for truth itself is regarded a luxury to be avoided.

NOTE. Self-expression is too often stressed to the neglect of expression. Not satisfied with copying, embellishing, or giving free play to his feelings or his bodily energy, man seeks to express some phase or object of the world he lives in. This may be the spirit of an animal or a tree, the nature of a demon, the quality of a disease, the essence of a ritual. In doing this he also expresses himself as a man and as an artist. In primitive groups there is no sharp separation between the inner and outer worlds, and their art shows a mingling and a bold, often symbolic shaping.   The study of masks will prove instructive.   There is a group of masks used in exorcising the evil spirits of various diseases and physical defects.   An attempt is made to get a form expressive of each.   Thus stuttering is expressed boldly in a mask of prominent teeth with the right half of the set out of alignment with the left.   Expressionism in this sense is to be found throughout the range of early art.

ANIMALS SHAPED AND RESHAPED

Above, left, Greek horse; *above, right,* Boar from Altamira
(Palaeolithic); *center,* Relief of the horse of a Chinese Emperor;
below, Cat and Snake by Wharton Esherick. (*The Cat and Snake
used by permission of the sculptor, the others are from the University
of Pennsylvania Museum.*)

PART TWO

THE AESTHETIC RESPONSE

THE AESTHETIC RESPONSE

The artist often insists that the great mass of people are incapable not only of appreciating good art and understanding what he is about, but of responding aesthetically at all! Their eyes and ears are untrained; and their minds run off into the world of morals, of business, of science. Has he not as an interpreter and creator isolated, given form to, and made self-sufficient impressions which ordinarily go unnoticed in the amalgam of practical experience? and are these line and color values of his to disappear once more in the common mixture of life?

The problem here is not how the artist creates, of the manner of his conceiving and shaping, and of the canons of criticism to be applied to his work. It is the more general one of discovering what is implied in the artist's response to nature and in an emerging world of art, and in the peculiar response on the part of an observer or hearer which he has a right to demand.

In dealing with this problem of aesthetic experience and its creative and appreciative aspects it is well to insist that (1) creation and appreciation cannot be sharply sundered; and (2) the aesthetic response is not a magical something called forth by art and art alone and sufficiently simple and uniform to be marked by two or three adjectives. There is an underlying likeness between the way the artist responds to nature and shapes according to his needs and the way the onlooker responds either to nature or to what the artist gives him. There is this much truth in the position of the representatives of creative criticism: every act of appreciation is in part a sympathetic re-creation of the artist's meaning, in

part an expression of the critic's own creative personality.
Again, there are personal differences within the field of genuine aesthetic experience which must not be overlooked.
There are variations in emotional and imaginative suggesti-
bility; and there are the well-known visual, tactile, and motor
types. Thus Vernon Lee's response to a Greek vase is so
peculiarly motor that few could share it; still it cannot on
that account be ruled out as non-aesthetic. Nor can art be
neatly blocked off from life and studied in isolation. The
paintings in a gallery are highly specialized products of
artistic effort and technique; they demand, but cannot always command, loyalty to an art spirit. But even they, as
works of art, are of the stuff of life and embody part of its
spirit. If, however, aesthetic experience is to be studied
in a broad and sympathetic manner, it is necessary to go
back to where art and life run together, and to where the
response, creative as well as appreciative, is less highly
specialized and less sharply marked.

The Genesis of the Aesthetic Response

Imagine a man, with little else than a gun and an axe in
his possession, set down on a desert island. The problem of
keeping alive presses; and for the first few days every
thought and every muscle is thrown into the struggle. This
Crusoe looks for a spring, digs for edible roots, hunts, fells
trees, builds himself a shelter. He observes the plant and
animal life about him; and studies closely the soil, the rocks
and the coast-line of his island. In this practical reshaping of a world, the manifold of colors, lines, spaces, and
sounds of which he originally became aware is broken up into
objects—birds, trees, plants, beach, clouds—and a study of
their natures and relations is forced upon him. An interest,
sharpened by anxiety and need, leads him to attend to like-

nesses and differences, and to the service all these objects
may render him in his struggle to maintain life; this means a
further reshaping: the birds become game; the trees, timber;
and the clouds, a possible water-supply.

With the disappearance of need in its most pressing form
it becomes possible for him to react to his environment in
two other ways: *hedonically* and *aesthetically*. Pleasure
and pain there were before this, but they were too closely
bound up with problems of well-being; now pleasure, at least,
has become detached with a savor and a value of its own: the
man enjoys his hunting or fishing, lingers over his food.
He becomes a pleasure-taster and pleasure-seeker; and ex-
tracts from his experiences something he had neglected.
Things are now valued as they affect him agreeably. Still
another response is his. He begins to see a tree, not as so
much timber or as the bearer of delicious fruit, but as a complex of lines and colors, with a life and spirit of its own expressed in the texture patterns of its trunk, in the glister
and sweep of its fronds. With senses and imagination freed
from too insistent a self-reference and from ideas of sustenance, he feels himself into this its life; and if there is something of the creative artist in him he sets himself the task of
rendering it in a charcoal drawing on stone. He responds
aesthetically; and it is the nature of this response which has
proved itself to be one of the most puzzling problems of
aesthetics.

THE NATURE OF THE AESTHETIC RESPONSE

If the problem is to be made worthwhile it must be studied
in the spirit of empirical analysis, at the risk of an initial
and possibly final looseness. The marks that distinguish
experiences commonly called aesthetic must be set down, and
their relations must be traced.

PRACTICAL DETACHMENT

Much has been made of the fact that in art the strain and the stress of practical life and its problems somehow disappear; that its point of view and activities are in this sense *detached* and *disinterested*. In this reading of experience there is the assumption that conduct is largely a matter of purposes which, in their drive and objective, bear more or less directly on the problem of self-preservation—and this, in turn, is a matter of reading things in terms of relations and relations in terms of practical control; and there is the belief that art is to be set aside as something self-sufficient and isolated. It is, however, worth pointing out that the practical and the artistic cannot be severed as can the pages of a book, and that there is danger of serious misreading if practical detachment be taken as the one and only mark of aesthetic experience.

By way of showing that it is one important mark, let us turn back to our Crusoe. For him aesthetic experience appeared at a point when there was some lessening of the strain of adjusting himself to his environment and subjecting it to a control made necessary by the desire to keep alive. He could now see beauty in the oar he was shaping; in the game that was to be his kill; and in the tree whose fruit he meant to eat. The problem of saving himself had made it necessary for him to read things in terms of the qualities of directest use: the tree in terms of fruit or lumber or shade; and to fashion things whose very meaning was one of use: oars, traps, clothing. With the coming of security and leisure it was possible for him (1) to pass from the usable qualities of a thing as they affected him to the thing itself, (2) to detach the thing from its purposive relations to other things as well as to himself, (3) to respond sympathetically to its self-expressive life.

Suppose a naturalist, interested in the habits of wild ani-

mals and hunting with a camera, sees a flash of color in the
jungle and is confronted with a tiger ready to leap.   At
that moment he can have no interest in the self-expressive
purpose of the tiger other than that of thwarting it: the
camera must give way to the gun.   But even when there is
no such crisis his interest is non-aesthetic because scientific
in a broad relational sense.   The tiger is studied within the
context of the forms, processes, and manifestations of organic life.   The reading is in terms of the actual—of life
as it has been, is, and probably will be; much of this reading
is abstract, incapable of being put into imagery.   This furnishes by way of contrast another clue to the nature of the
aesthetic response.

MOVING WITHIN A WORLD OF SEMBLANCE, OR APPEARANCE

The world of art is neither the actual world nor a copy of
it.   By the material it works in, sculpture is cut off from
the possibility of giving even the complete image of a man;
the technique of painting, in drawing and in range and combination of color, is an elaborate structure of illusion, which
is never the equivalent of the stuff or the form of experience;
and music moves within a world of its own creation.   In so
far as we enjoy art we respond to this world of appearance
and its new, superposed values;—aware, as in tragedy, of
actualities, but never, except when we are least aesthetic, applying the same measure to the two worlds.[1]   Suppose we

---

[1] Hissing the villain in a play, applying moral standards to Falstaff or
to a French farce, enjoying the extreme lifelikeness of wax figures means
stepping outside the world of semblance and of aesthetic appreciation.

All sorts of problems radiate from this idea of a world of appearance
which we playfully create and enjoy.   Here are a few set down at random: Does lifelikeness play a legitimate part in art?   To what extent
are we aware of a playful self-deception?   Is this new world more real
to us or less real than the actual world?   How is it related to a world
of dreams?   Is it possible to step out of it and back again and be the
gainer in an aesthetic sense?

now step within the experience of our Crusoe and become aesthetic appreciators of the world about us. An attitude of practical detachment has allowed us to rescue things from a relatedness to our needs and purposes, and to a system of facts; and to become responsive to a life of their own. We then—to borrow a thought and a phrase from Vernon Lee— pass from things to shapes. Color, light and shade, and sound now appear in their own right; so does form with its organization of lines and planes. A tree is no longer regarded in terms of so much lumber and fruit or of hidden items we know about but cannot see—such as the toughness and grain of its wood or its far-reaching roots—it is not an actual plant in a system of plant life. Rather is it an image carved out of space: a sensuous and formal presence compounded of colors, textures, lines and spacings, depths, and horizontal and vertical reaches; living its own life—resplendent, colorful, vigorous, closely knit—on a plane other than the actual; directly pleasing to the senses and touched with emotional and imaginative suggestiveness.

Unfortunately, words like appearance, semblance, *Schein* have embarrassing connotations; they suggest something that appears in the mirror or shadow-play of art; and they bring with them the whole problem of representational values. If we clear away this we seem to be no better off, for aesthetic experience then seems too much like a shallow enjoyment of color and design; the world of nature aesthetically responded to and the world of art, created and appreciated, seem comparable to a child's game of building triangles and polygons from tiny colored sticks and tinting the enclosed spaces. What a poor change this for the palpable, pulsing, intricate life of practical and scientific realities! Such criticism overlooks a further mark of the aesthetic response: the enriching of this world of semblance.

A WORLD OF SEMBLANCE ENRICHED

When I regard a tree aesthetically I have done something very strange. I have stripped it of its usefulness and agreeableness, and have set it apart as a shape. Three great human interests seem to have vanished in my refusal to have my experience circle about what is of use to me, what affects me agreeably, and what confronts me as an actuality. They reappear, however, in altered form and with a new and startling significance. Purpose reappears as relatedness in part of line to line, color to color, and of parts to an organic whole, in part of the visual image to conditions under which I can attribute beauty to it. Agreeableness is shorn of its reference to me and to my well-being and is infused into the shape as a quality. In this sense aesthetic experience is marked by *selflessness* and *objectified pleasure*. As for the third, the interest in something tangible, something we can knock up against and can observe behaving is satisfied in a new form. The world of artistic shapes is self-sufficient; it forces our senses and our imagination to move within the measure of its imagery. A beautiful object confronts us as truly as any other; it has laws and a life of its own; and it is palpably real.[2] When I see my face in a mirror I am in the presence of an image which interests me as a reflection, and I expect to find nothing in the image that is not in the face. But when nature is mirrored in aesthetic contemplation or is caught up and reflected in art there are two striking differences. Subjectively, the image is not held to be a duplication or likeness; we move contentedly within the appearance and hold it to be self-sufficient in its direct appeal; objectively, there is a magical quality in the mirroring which gives an additional richness to the image.

---

[2] Pirandello has in his plays exploited artistically the problem of the relation between reality and existence. In *Six Characters in Search of an Author* the life of fictional characters is held to be no less real than that of their creators or readers.

The world we live in is a practically reshaped world, in which things are modified, invented, destroyed; and in which we are constantly pressing beyond images to facts and uses. The world of art is a sensuously and imaginatively reshaped world, in which there is an initial flattening of things to shapes, and then a giving to these shapes something of our own wealth.   The acknowledgment of such a transference appears in many aesthetic theories; Lipps speaks of *lending;* Volkelt of *menschlich wertvoller Gehalt; empathy,* of which so much is made by Lipps, Groos, and Vernon Lee, is nothing but giving to inert material our motor impulses, memories, moods, and ideas.

There are, of course, other ways of enriching.   To the astronomer the moon means more than a luminous disk; the worshipper uses a cross, candles, strings of beads as symbols or as points of departure and support for religious feeling.   In both cases sense objects are caught up in a mass of orderly images and far-flung emotions, and in a sense destroyed.   In art there is no such ranging.   Sense-values are created and maintained in their own right; they are never merely points of departure.   Intellectual and imaginative values are given a sensuous form which is felt to have a reality and worthwhileness of its own; and which in turn, like a magnet, gathers to itself other values.

What is the nature of this process of enriching by means of which semblances become humanly significant and thus acquire greater artistic depth?

THE NATURE OF THE PROCESS OF ENRICHING

Nature as it is present in a landscape painting or a sculptured figure has been reshaped sensuously and imaginatively by the artist.   In one sense his work falls short of the scene or the body which furnishes the material for his art.   What he gives is something other and in a sense something infinitely more; and it is the nature of this *more* in the aesthetic response which is our present concern.

The landscape painter, unable to compete with nature in the range and grading of colors, substitutes a scale of his own, develops graded and contrasted effects, re-arranges and stresses; and thus creates an organized color image. Among the many lines which the landscape offers he selects such as serve his purpose; he places accents, relates and unifies; and in this way fashions a pattern of his own of lines and masses.

In addition, he makes these colors and lines the carriers of moods, imaginative constructs, ideas. He means his picture to be humanly significant and relies, therefore, in part, on an enriching process in which the beholder shares. One need only step up close to a picture to see how sketchy the whole thing is; how what is merely suggested must be rounded out into semblances.

The process of enriching involves a double response: *sympathetic* and *empathetic*.

However much an artist reinterprets and re-organizes from necessity and choice, he must respond sympathetically to the tree or flower or cloud he is to paint: feel the conspiracy and unity of its lines and colors, the character of its patterns, the spirit of its life. A like sympathy must we carry to the contemplation of the artist's work. The unity and originality of his design must be grasped, and the working out of his artistic purpose must be felt. This, again, leads to the artist as he expresses himself creatively. But that curious law of *not stepping out of bounds* must not be forgotten. The personal bias, the moods, and the ideas of an artist interest us aesthetically only in so far as he has infused them in his work; for it is only then that they have become detached, and part of a world of semblance, and humanly significant in the largest sense.

There is also an empathetic response. The term empathy

has been coined as the equivalent of *Einfühlung, feeling one-self into.* In a general sense it means a reading of inanimate nature in terms of human life and its attributes. It is a lending and a vivifying. We speak of lines marching or bracing themselves, of a rising mountain, of screaming reds, of a modest violet, of a weeping willow, of a forehead villain-ously low. These are not mere figures of speech. They testify to a transference whose mechanism is interesting and whose place in aesthetic experience is a not unimportant one.

Motor Empathy: Our psychophysical response to the world is strikingly and incurably motor. As we explore things our eye-balls change position and shape; our head turns to the tensed play of the muscles of the neck and back; our hands reach out. Our bodies, even at rest, are a mass of tensions and flexions; it requires only the familiar experi-ment of standing erect and of thinking of something on the ground in front to feel oneself falling. According to Ver-non Lee back of the phrase "the rising mountain," that is back of our reading of inanimate objects in motor terms, are actual muscular adjustments—as the eye seeks higher and higher levels—and the funded motor memory of like move-ments in the past. It is all this that we project in the sense of putting it in the object.

There is, however, this difficulty. Many of our muscular adjustments serve practical purposes. Thus we turn our eyes to put an object within the field of clear vision; we in-terpret a mountain in terms of the effort of climbing it; an apple means to us an agreeable biting into it, past or future; smoothness of skin, the running our hand along its surfaces. All this practical side of motor activity disappears in the aesthetic response. It is not as part of the actual world of success and failure that we see ourselves, in our tensing and stressing, in the mirror of art.

Empathy of Mood: When we speak of a weeping

Rotary

Kolbe, Dancing Girl—out-
flung, dynamic

Marc, Blue Horses—centralized rhythmic

TYPES OF MOVEMENT

willow, the angry sea, gay colors, sated browns, melancholy blues we are as truly empathetic as when we speak of skipping lines, screaming reds, the push and pull of the parts of a design; but the projection is one of feeling, of mood. We are not confessing that certain lines and colors have a depressing, others an exhilarating effect; we are endowing our world of images and shapes with the wealth of our emotional life—and we respond to it as thus embodied. These terms are not figures of speech—the whole process is too direct for that—too deeply expressive of an original animism. Inanimate nature is instinctively humanized and dramatized.

PSYCHIC EMPATHY: This is empathy in its widest meaning: a projection not only of our motor experiences and our moods but of our whole life as *lived and valued*. It is Lipps's *Lebensbetätigung* and Volkelt's *menschlich wertvoller Gehalt*. Neither the creation nor the enjoyment of art can be understood if this projection is lost sight of. Ordinarily what we call the sense of living is either a keen, vague, objectless sense of vigor, physical and mental, or a sense of effective concern with and mastery of definite purposes; and what we call a sense of human values is either a vague sanctification of life or a struggle to make good our moral, practical, and religious ideals. Aesthetic experience rids us of this double vagueness and of definite practical stress as well. The artist gives himself in his work; he offers a personal interpretation, creates new sensuous, emotional, and imaginative patterns and values. Tragedy is a good example of this interest, not vague and not practically embarrassed, in human life on its psychic side. Only the vigorous and the imaginative can enjoy this form of art. We who respond to what the artist gives read it whether we will or no in psychic terms. A few patches of color and strokes, a few sequences of sounds, a few words is all that we need to set us off on this enriching. We must see to it, however, that we are always in harmony with what of psychic value the artist has built into his picture, his poem, his symphony.

The double process, then, of creating and moving within a world of semblance, and of enriching the images and shapes of that world with our psychic wealth yields the meaning of aesthetic experience.

PART THREE

THE ARTS

THE DANCE

Back of the dance in its highly specialized artistic form are the natural rhythms, the broad utilities, and pleasures of life.   From this cosmic and cultural background emerges an art, which by the use of rhythm, pose, gesture, and setting creates a world of mobile patterns and imaginative values—a realm of its own, but reminiscent none the less of the life from which it sprang.   The old cultural dances of India and Egypt reappear in the work of a Ruth St. Denis or a Sent Ma'hesa, but with a new life and meaning put into their stiff, hieratic forms; the free rhythms and aggressive movements of the Russian folk-dance are subjected to a new discipline and bent to a new purpose in a ballet like *Ingomar* or in the art of a Nijinski or a Mordkin.   There is a wide difference between dancing—as work or pastime— and the dance, but there is an indebtedness as well; and both difference and indebtedness must be constantly borne in mind.

Rhythms and Rhythmic Organization

Natural Rhythms

One need not return to a naive nature philosophy and think of the universe as a huge breathing animal to discover rhythmic processes.   They are everywhere:—in the cycle of the seasons; in the choreography of the heavens; in the advance and recession of tides; in the lapping of water against pilings or the swaying of tree-tops in a storm; in pulse-beat and breathing; in the ebb and flow of vital forces. Then there are the rhythms of psychical reactions: the curious fluctuations of the attention, charted by the experimental psychologist, and the equally curious rhythmic expression of intense feeling—the clenching and unclenching of fists, moans, the stamping of feet, the sing-song of lamentations, the throb and drum of shouts.

Natural rhythms differ in quality, complexity, tempo, and pleasingness. The flicker's tap-tap has a quality of its own; so has the less simple whine and whirr of a saw in a planing-mill. The rhythms of a crowded city street move faster than those of a village. The jingle of sleigh-bells is more pleasing than the sliding of a trolley along its rails. Ordinarily we attend to and appreciate only a few of these rhythms; the quality of the more complex and less pleasing escapes us. We do not look for rhythms in crowds, nor for rhythmic patterns in noises. The $1:2$ and the $1:2:3$ patterns, differently accentuated, of poetry and dancing are but a narrow selection from the many rhythms of speech and bodily movement. At this point an unstable attention and a variously stressing emotional response step in and change the chop-chop of a mechanical iambic line to a finely tempered series of stresses and pauses, and the monotonous tick-tock of a clock into a swinging variety of sounds. These subjective rhythms cannot be set off sharply from the others—it is impossible to cut in two the world man takes and the thing he makes of it.

RHYTHMIC ORGANIZATION

In selecting and reshaping natural rhythms and in throwing the common stuff of experience into varied forms, man shows himself an organizer on a grand scale. The smooth play of interlocking or threading machinery; the confused mass of vehicles swung into a system of traffic regulation; the orderly variety in building and dredging enterprises; landscape gardening; aquatic spectacles and fire-works; gymnastic and military drills—such are a few samples of this work, which means the rearrangement in time and space patterns of man's body and its physical setting. It is easy to understand why such organization is undertaken. Rhythm (1) makes apprehension easier—witness memory verses and the grouping of items—(2) makes achievement easier—witness the rhythmic dipping of oars or the swing of the scythe—(3) gives a pleasurable tone to experiences—witness our delight in patterned rugs, in flower-beds, in watching troops deploying. Neither the individual nor the group need be conscious of such benefits; they may be sought after and gained in response to activities that are as spontaneous and as incidental as they are helpful. A man may dance for the love of it, improvising gestures and movements that are flung out and then bent back into a scheme of measured self-expression; a group may in a holiday mood stage a spectacle in which mass rhythms of sound and color blend in a constantly changing orderliness. No matter how stereotyped a society may be in its forms or how mechanical in its manners and pastimes, this freedom is never wholly absent. The Renaissance and the Grand Siècle had their elaborate codes of courtly behavior—the bow, the sweep of the hat, the use of the fan, the exchange of compliments; they had their hieratic processionals and their stately dances, delicately and minutely phrased. Nothing could be more elaborate and more sacrosanct than the dancing manuals of these periods. But the minuet and the quadrille, dances that are too formal for our taste, were made to yield individual variations of rhythm. Freedom is prized as well as uniformity; and no codification can put an end to it. That is why social amusements can never be standardized; and that is why a hackneyed verse-form may be made to yield new music. In the dance these impulses work themselves out harmoniously: an individual life stirs in an ordered, flowing pattern.

DANCING, THE DANCE, AND SOCIAL WORK

Dancing marks the life of even the most primitive group, and it is consciously or unconsciously practised and encouraged in order to make that life more effective. Muscular efforts are to be correlated; common feelings are to be aroused; a common will is to be fostered; social demands are to be made impressive. Work must be done, and this work—hunting, scouting, tilling, rowing, and fighting— is largely of a direct physical type, which sets a premium on strength and speed. The lack of machinery forces the constant use of capricious human material; this in turn must be made to function smoothly. Nor is the rhythmic bending of muscles to common tasks all that is needed: the absence of an advanced system of intellectual and moral values forces a direct appeal to mass impulses and mass feeling. Social consecration, again, moves along the levels, not of ideas, but of picture-thought and the childlike, sensuous appeal of processional and festival.

Gymnastic dances supply the necessary physical training and with their leaping, bounding, and whirling develop what primitive life insistently calls for—an agile strength. War dances prepare men for fighting and set them to the martial key. The sending of arrows, the brandishing of heavy war-clubs, the hurling of spears, the clinching and retreating, the taking cover must all be done smoothly and must be rightly timed if they are to be effective. Excitement is whipped up by shouting and dancing and the noise of tom-toms and war-rattles or by the crude naturalism and the equally crude symbolism of erotic dances. Religious dances with their mixture of ceremonial, incantation, and magic make social needs impressive. Dancing for rain after a drought or for the removal of a spell supposed to have been cast on the chief of the tribe impresses the individual with the seriousness of social dangers and stresses the

DEGAS, DANCERS PRACTISING AT THE BAR

world of malevolent or beneficent spirits on which ordinary life is imagined to rest. Mass dances of the more playful sort serve the purpose of spreading contentment and promoting good fellowship.

It is to be noted that the occasion for these dances (war, the gathering of fruits, an invocation, an initiation, a religious festival, a market-fair) and the staging (a hall, an open space, a tribal circle) are given by the tribe; and that these dances are for the most part group dances, characterized by a bewildering variety of shared movements and massed effects. Even when there is solo dancing, when from the crowd there leaps dancer after dancer to do his bit of gymnastic or mimetic dancing, the social motif is still present, in the spirit of rivalry and in the palpitating life of the encircling multitude of potential participants.

One thing, however, must not be forgotten. Even in advanced societies there is more loose play than is needed for smooth running; and this is more marked in primitive groups. It has been said of a certain tribe of Eskimo that with them four days out of seven are holidays. All this feasting, dancing, and buffoonery are to be explained in part in terms of high spirits, of an inveterate playfulness, and a childlike unconcern with the future; in part in terms of a life organized loosely enough to allow such things some play. To ignore this spontaneous, individual element in early dancing is to falsify the facts in the interest of a theory of utility values which cannot be upheld; to exaggerate it is to overlook the need of a process of *aesthetic indirection*, which changes this socially charged early dancing to the free, highly individualized art of the dance.

The Process Of Aesthetic Indirection

As society advances the response to life becomes more indirect and more subtle. Impulses are less headlong and less aggressive in their satisfactions. The sex-impulse, for instance, is less brutal, more playful in the matter of love and courtship, and more responsive to all manner of secondary stimuli. Feelings are less unshaded by individual differences and less instinctively social, and are organized into sentiments; motives are more complex. Practical needs as they shift and relax their pressure, at this point or that, allow the release of energy for play. Man turns aside to the contemplative and decorative uses of life; and a detached aesthetic consciousness emerges. This process of aesthetic indirection implies (1) the changing of work into play, (2) the viewing of leisure as a chance for amusement, (3) a new, subtle response to life in terms of the serious playfulness of a creative art impulse. Even at low cultural levels there is not much work that is so grinding and so eagerly pointed at results as not to allow an occasional interest in processes, an occasional enjoyment of muscle tensions, of sweeping movements, of surging or receding emotions. To the man to whom canoeing and hunting are serious business the rhythmic flash and dipping of the paddle and the gliding of the body through grass in stalking game may be a source of pleasure. Other things to be considered are the seasonal character of agricultural work; a bantering rivalry that leads to the playful trying out of muscles; changes in the nature of the needed work, allowing sportive survivals such as our camping or hunting and many of our outdoor games. Again, man becomes more acutely aware of his leisure time as something to be filled with individualized enjoyment. What he seeks is "a good time," which means getting as far away from work as possible and striking out for himself in his search for pleasure. The bulk of our dancing is of this sort; we often enjoy our art as we eat our bonbons. But this individualized enjoying oneself that has shaken itself free from work is only a first step; if art is to emerge, interest must be shifted from self

and its stimulation to an object or projected activity which
is the summing up of the artist's power and the rallying
point for the sense and the imagination of the onlooker or
listener. That means a *double indirection:* a work of art is
set over against an actual practical world and over against
a hungry and self-conscious self. Ritual dances become
art to the dancers only when delight in their formal patterns
obscures interest in what the magic of the ritual is to gain.[1]
A love experience becomes art for the lover only when it is
set over against himself, as a flashing circle of images and
feelings which are and are not himself.[2]

[1] Cf. Miss Harrison, *Art and Ritual.*

[2] This is the secret of lyric poetry. The practice and the theory of
some expressionists seem to run counter to this second detachment. They
push what they call *Ichgefühl* to the limit of egomania. Here are samples
from Gottfried Benn's *Synthese;*

> Ich aber bin der stillsten Sterne;
> Ich treibe auch mein eignes Licht
> Noch in die eigne Nacht hinaus.
>
> . . . .
>
> Ich wälze Welt. Ich röchle Raub.

But even in such poetry the projection is felt as projection and the images
count as images. Kurt Heynicke's *Mensch* is a good illustration:—

> Ich bin über den Wäldern,
> Grün und leuchtend,
> hoch über allen,
> ich, der Mensch.
> Ich bin Kreis im All,
> Blühend Bewegung,
> getragenes Tragen.
> Ich bin Sonne unter den Kreisenden,
> Ich der Mensch,
> ich fühle mich tief,
> nahe dem hohen All-Kreisenden,
> ich, sein Gedanke.
> Mein Haupt ist sternbelaubt,
> silbern mein Antlitz,
> ich leuchte,
> ich,
> wie er,
> das All;
> das All,
> wie ich!

THE DANCE AS A WORK OF ART

Each type of the dance has its own technique, and its own peculiar resources, problems, and sets of meanings. The more highly specialized the dancing is—as in the clog dance, the acrobatic dance, and the toe dance—the more difficult it is to set its special significance within a general aesthetic theory of the dance. This is a problem which confronts the aesthetician in every field of art. How much of what is peculiar to a sonnet, a roundelay, or a ballad can be carried over to a theory of poetry? How much of low relief into that of sculpture? How much of a pastel into that of painting? It amounts to a struggle between the desire for unity and a delicate responding to differences. The best thing to do in this predicament is (1) to attempt to mark the aesthetic meaning of the dance—making reservations where they are needed; (2) to characterize the different types of the dance; (3) to break up the total effect of the dance into its component elements—rhythm, pose, gesture, costume and setting—and their varying relations; (4) to recapture and restate in intellectual terms the life and spirit of a dance, and the idea—symbolical or otherwise—of which it is the living expression.

THE AESTHETIC SIGNIFICANCE OF THE DANCE

Fusion of Space and Time Impressions: Imagine an oblong box, tilted up and with the lid taken off, and let it represent the enclosed and bounded space of the stage. For the simpler effects it is lined with black or edged with silver and cloth of gold; for the more complex all the illusionist devices of stage-craft are used. Cutting across this space, from side to side, from front to rear, diagonally and vertically, the dance swings its varying pattern. With a pause in the music, the dancers come to a momentary rest, the whirl of impressions settles to a clarified picture of blotches of color and an angled criss-cross of bodies, arms, and legs. This decorative ensemble every new onset of music shatters to bits. There is no other art which combines so directly and effectively the visual and the motor appeal. It is not a matter of alternating rest and motion, for the pause with all its decorative poses is felt to be the resolution of a movement and an urge toward new rhythmic developments; and every motion in turn utilizes to the full the sensuous beauty—in mobile form—of color, of light, of bodily lines.

THE VISUALIZING AND IMAGINATIVE ORDERING OF IMPULSES AND EMOTIONS: Responding to the manifold character and tempo of the music and adding a spirit and gesture of its own, the dance moves up and down, back and forth between the slack and the tensional, the impulse to relax and the impulse to fling oneself about, to whirl and leap, yielding and fighting, calm and anger, stinting and lavishing, lust and playful courting, elation and depression, pleasure and pain, joy and sorrow. In ordinary life impulses are felt by us in their direct, outgoing pressure, emotions are more or less formless, and both feed on feelings of self or are worked up into purposes. It is we who have the impulse to jump, higher and higher, to the point of exhaustion; it is we who are angry and are carried along in a gathering flood of anger; it is we who give anger an object and shape it toward a definite scheme of revenge. In art much of this formlessness, purposiveness, and self-relation is lost; impulses and feelings are cut loose from self, set over against us, and projected into a visual and imaginative world, and in this world are reduced from chaos to order or from an organization in terms of practical stresses and purposes to an organization of line, color, sound, rhythm. In the dance, of all the arts, this change is most marked, for there impulses and feelings are presented in their transitional developments—something that sculpture and painting cannot do—take visual form—an impossibility in music—and are shown—as they are not in poetry—in the closest relation to the motor life of the body.

A CONSTANTLY RENEWED INTERCHANGE OF FREEDOM AND ORDER: The traditional ballet of the early operatic stage shows an almost complete schematization of dress, pose, and movement. The dancer is put in tights and a short gauze skirt, is schooled in the difficult technique of toe-dancing, is drilled in the *rond de jambe, pirouette, cabriole, entrechat, glissade*,[3] and taught to dance in an ensemble in which everything is reduced to rule.[4] How effectively this destroys the spontaneity and individuality of the body and its movements may be seen by watching a toe-dancer take a few walking steps. It is only a great dancer—a Genée or a Pavlowa—that can get fine artistic effects from such a system; it is only a great organizer that can gain from it decorative and pantomimic effects such as are to be found in *Les Sylphides*, in *L'Oiseau de Feu*, and in Rimsky-Korsakov's *Snégourotchka*.

In other freer forms of the dance at least a large part of the aesthetic pleasure may be traced to our being conscious that the dancers are creatively active with their bodies and to our witnessing free individual energy taking rhythmic form

[3] Many of these steps and movements occur in folk dances—the pirouette in the *Gypsy Flamenco*, the arabesque in the *Tarantella*, the rond de jambe in the *Slavonic Obertass*, the battement and pirouette in the *Scotch Reel*. Emmanuel, in *La Danse Grecque*, has traced them in the old Greek dances. He has, however, made the mistake of interpreting too much in the spirit of the ballet master of the French Classical School, and hence slighting the freedom that governs their use here as well as in folk dancing.

[4] The musical comedy stage has escaped the mechanical in dress, but still shows a deadly misunderstanding of art in its stereotyped deploying of masses of girls, its marching and counter-marching, and grouping. Its patterned dances suggest the process of painting kitchen borders through perforated paper. The "perfect stepping" of the London Palace Girls is an example of complete mechanization.

and form being turned back to energy. The tumultuous but ordered choreography of *Schéhérazade* or of Fokine's *Bacchanal* may be cited in proof. The dancing is individualized and in some measure improvised; it does not shun an occasional clash with the music and the settings; it does not lose sight of the fact that the dance is a living thing and not a drill or a set of rules. Nor need this free, living character be lost when revelry and abandon are not the subject of the dance. *Petrouchka* with its marionettes and mechanized movements was never mechanical, as Bolm and Massine danced it.

In practical affairs we ordinarily put the stress definitely one way or the other, on form or on free life. If we have clipped a hedge, we look with disfavor on new, irregular shoots; if we have built a factory, we are anxious to have it grow and hum with life—let it grow if it will beyond the original scheme. In the arts the emphasis is not so strong, but it is still there. We look in poetry for either freedom and substance or for form; it is only occasionally that we find a perfect blend. In poetry, painting, and sculpture the form that has been gained is appreciated as a permanent achievement; there is no temptation to break it up. Music and the dance show a constantly changing succession, and a balanced stress on sensuous beauty and form. In the dance the form is not permanent: it is ever dissolved and renewed. A gesture or a movement as direct as life itself strikes into and scatters the group of dancers; a note of strength or grace escapes the ensemble; and then all this free variety is led to a new pattern, as individual and as full of latent life as the old one. The life interests as much as the form; and it is the incessant passing from the one to the other that is one of the secrets of the aesthetic appeal of the dance.

THE TYPES OF THE DANCE

In discussing the various types of the dance—the gymnastic, the decorative, the mimetic, the pantomimic, the interpretative, or "classical"—it is not my purpose to go beyond the point at which dancing emerges in the field of art. Originally expressive of simple instinctive needs, (mimicry, vigorous and various physical expression, control, rhythmic order) and serving social purposes, the dance, due to a process of *aesthetic indirection*, shifts the stress from the work to the pleasure which originally furthered the work, and changes this pleasure to a peculiar kind of satisfaction. It offers itself as an artistic content of movements, colors, lines, and projected feelings and ideas; it reflects the purposes and capacities of the dancer; and it is danced to elicit an artistic response from the spectators. It is the dance in this its varied detachment that is of interest to the aesthetician.

THE GYMNASTIC DANCE: The gymnastic dance shows many varieties. It includes violent gyrations and twists of the body, balancing and pirouetting, the volte and the caper, dancing with flexed knees, stamping, whirling, and spinning in Russian peasant fashion.[5] It is independent of all but the most rudimentary music, but may parallel effectively simple changes in tempo and musical flare-ups. I remember a Russian dancer who rolled across the stage like a ball, to the accompaniment of a ripple of music and a quick unslinging of notes. The gymnastic dance is almost purely motor; what it presents is not varied rhythmic motion or beauty or grace, but strength, agility, skill. We feel the life of the dancer in the dance, and tense our own bodies in answer. But is physical abandon art, and is the doing of

[5] Lucian in *On Pantomime* (34) alludes to a gymnastic dance, the *Phrygian*—"that riotous, convivial fling which was performed by energetic yokels to the piping of a flute-girl, and which still prevails in country districts."

stunts anything beyond acrobatics? it might be asked.
It is true that the gymnastic dance frequently moves to one
or the other of these extremes. If it avoids them, it has a
genuine and characteristic aesthetic appeal. Life, abundant and at high pressure, is there, and so is a forming principle, which concerns itself with the matter of control rather
than with the ordering of space and time. How lightly he
leaps; how deftly he gets every ounce of strength from
his body! How freely and surprisingly he does it all!

THE DECORATIVE DANCE: The decorative dance puts
beauty in the place of strength, and organization of sound,
color, and line in the place of muscular control. Processional and ceremonial dances, pageants, circular dances
with shifting and interlocking patterns are of this type.
They appeal frankly to the eye and make much of the music.
Examples are: the Greek *Chain Dance*, the *Saraband*, the
Minuet, and the *Quadrille*. Among folk dances the *May-
pole Dance* and the *Farandole* are strongly decorative.[6]
Loie Fuller's Serpentine dances are purely decorative in
their use of flowing draperies thrown into constantly new
forms by undulating movements of the arms and in their
changing color reflections.

THE MIMETIC DANCE: Of this, the simplest and the
earliest are the animal dances.[7] To these must be added
imitations of jointed dolls, wooden soldiers, leaping flames,
the dress and manner of other people, and movements such

---

[6] Kinneys, *The Dance:*—"The Farandole is popular in the South of
France. Under its name a chain of boys and girls, united by handkerchiefs
that they hold, 'serpentines' and zigzags in directions indicated by the
caprice of their leader, perhaps traversing the length of the streets of the
village. From time to time the leading couple will halt and form their
arms into an arch for those following to pass under; or again stop the
procession in such a way as to wind up the line into a compact mass."

[7] Examples are:—kangaroo, frog, and bear dances: sword and spear
dances; the *Sailor's Hornpipe*, with its imitations of hoisting sail, rowing,
hauling in rope; the Dance of the Wooden Soldiers in the *Chauve Souris:*
the *Whistling Boy*, danced by ten year old Ruth Goodwin of the Helen
Moeller School.

as throwing the javelin, playing ball, tracking game, ford-
ing a stream, rowing, courting, praying. It is a mistake
to interpret such dances and our enjoyment of them simply
in terms of a delight in mimicry and appreciation of skill.
Copying if well done affords pleasure, but there is often no
literal copying in the mimicry dance. There is a rhythmic
reinterpretation, a rounding off of gestures, an exaggeration of movement, such as swaying or strutting, an extravagance of costume—all pointed at greater beauty or greater
expressiveness. There is a distortion which reflects the
dancer's impish joy in falsifying persuasively, and his free,
accentuated reading, serious or burlesque, of material ordinarily not stressed or artistically valued. In like fashion,
the blank verse of Shakespeare is a rhythmic ordering
of words and a distorted transcript of common experiences.
In the mimetic dance we are as acutely aware of differences
as we are of likenesses. We do not expect to see blood flow
in a war dance nor do we look for a literal rendering of
lunging and retreating, of sword and buckler play. There
are rhythmic repetitions, phrases of movement in answer to
musical phrases, and changes in tempo which raise the
performance beyond a copy of how men fight. In a *Jointed
Doll* dance we enjoy the puppet-like appearance of the
dancer and her skilfully mechanized movements; but the
greater part of our pleasure is gained from the consciousness
that while the dancer is more mechanical than any puppet
she is using varied characterization and grotesquerie to make
the doll more expressive of free, personal life than any doll
could possibly be.

THE PANTOMIMIC DANCE: This is a dramatic elabo-
ration of the mimic dance. In a passage in *Daphnis and
Chloe*, Longus has described two such dances: the *Vintage
Dance* and the *Dance of the Reed-Pipe*:

Philetas obeyed, and Dryas began the *Vintage-Dance*, in which
he represented the plucking of the grapes, the carrying of the

baskets, the treading of the clusters, the filling of the casks, and the drinking of the new made wine. All this Dryas imitated so closely and admirably in the pantomimic dance, that the spectator might fancy the wines, the wine-press, and the casks to be actually before him, and that Dryas was drinking in reality.

Each of the three old men had now severally distinguished himself. Dryas in his delight gave Daphnis and Chloe a kiss, who immediately sprang from their seats, and began to dance a ballet representative of Lamon's fable. Daphnis assumed the character of Pan, and Chloe that of Syrinx. While he endeavored to entice her to his embraces, she smiled in scorn at his attempts. He pursued her, and ran upon his tiptoes in imitation of the cloven feet of the god; while she, making a semblance of exhaustion, at last hid herself in the wood, making it a substitute for reedy lake. Upon losing sight of her, Daphnis seizing the large pipe of Philetas, breathed into it a mournful strain as of one who loves; then a love-sick strain as of one who pleads; lastly a recalling strain, as of one who seeks her whom he has lost.

Philetas himself was astonished, and ran and embraced the youth and kissed him: and with a prayer, that Daphnis might transmit the pipe to as worthy a successor, bestowed it upon him as a gift. The youth suspended his own pipe as an offering to Pan, kissed Chloe with as much ardour as if she had really been lost and found again, and led his flocks home by the sound of his new instrument.

Here are all the marks of the pantomimic dance. In the *Vintage Dance*, which shows clearly the relationship to the mimetic dance, there is a rhythmic imitation of a series of actions dominated by one purpose, and dramatic because of that. In the *Dance of the Reed-Pipe* there is that and much besides. The fleeing nymph and the pursuing god furnish an action full of contrasts, and dramatically and decoratively interesting. There is, too, in dance and music alike, the portrayal of emotional changes. Then there is a story taken from a legend. Embedded in the legend is a certain amount of symbolism—

compacting with wax unequal reeds in order to show how the course of their love had not run smooth—

to this must be added such symbolism as the technical limitations of pantomime demand. The pantomimic dance is as a mute drama in miniature, impoverished by the absence of the spoken word, enriched by the presence of music and the lavish and more detached use of decorative effects. In Lucian's list of myths utilized in dances those of a dramatic character predominate: the battle of the Titans, the theft of fire by Prometheus, the destruction of the Python, the birth of Pan, the rape of Helen. The Marion Morgan Dancers have built a series of dances around the story of Helen. The *Thamar* and the *Schéhérazade* of the Russian Ballet are of the very essence of the drama.

If not mechanized or flattened emotionally or strained to the point of grimace, the pantomimic dance is capable of a varied and forceful appeal. Lucian is right when he speaks of its "subtle harmonious versatility" and of its effects on the beholder—"training his eyes to lovely sights, filling his ears with noble sounds, revealing a beauty in which body and soul alike have their share." It must, however, be added that the pantomimic dance often aims at the characteristic rather than the beautiful. An example is Isadora Duncan's interpretation of Tchaikowsky's *Marche Slave*.

THE CLASSICAL, OR AESTHETIC DANCE: Within the last twenty years, at first under the leadership of Isadora Duncan, a new type of dance has become prevalent. It is variously named: classical, because it is Greek in dress and patterned in part after ancient vase-paintings; aesthetic, because it is art in a pure and direct form; interpretative, because it seeks to render the spirit of musical compositions like *The Blue Danube*, Mendelssohn's *Spring Song*, Chopin's *Funeral March*, Gluck's *Iphigenia in Aulis*, the Symphonies of Beethoven.

It has taken on many forms and has become weighted with many aesthetic and educational theories. In the Dalcroze Institute it becomes eurythmics, a sort of musical hygiene aimed at the right tuning of mind and body; in the Elizabeth Duncan School at Darmstadt it is a training in plastic harmony, supposed to be ennobling; in the Free School Community at Wickersdorf it is an attempted recovery of spontaneous social self-expression. With Mensendieck it becomes gymnastic hygiene; with Ruth St. Denis it turns into the costume dance and the exotic drama. The Morgan Dancers put the stress on pantomime, and the Chalif School, on schematized movement. It retains much of its early pure form in the work of the Duncan Dancers and in the Helen Moeller School.

The dancer is clad in a chiton and short diaphanous draperies that leave the limbs bare. Aesthetically, such a costume means, first of all, a frank use of the sensuous beauty of the body. The effect is not sensual or gross, because the bust is felt in relation to the shoulder and arm; the thigh in relation to the torso and the leg; and the whole body, trained away from the too soft and the too muscular, is felt in relation to a rhythmic beauty, of which it seems the living expression. It means, next, the recovery of freedom and naturalness of movement. It means, last of all, a costume which shares in the natural expressiveness of the body, and adds a fluttering decorative life of its own, and a color or two, with the effect of tinting.

The freedom is carried over into the movements of the dancer. In the rendering of dance music, the march becomes less rigid; the minuet softer and less schematized; the gavotte, the mazurka, and the waltz are given a freer life. The motor appeal of the uniform beat of the music is slighted in favor of the motor appeal that lies in a changing rapidity of motion, in an alternation of violent and gentle gestures, in the fluctuating lines of draperies.

THE AESTHETIC ELEMENTS OF THE DANCE

The aesthetic elements of the dance are four: *rhythm, pose, gesture, costume and setting.*

RHYTHM: Rhythm relates the dance to the motor and the formal side of music. It is a matter of accents and pauses, of a changing tempo of tensed and slackened muscles, of the transition from a slow to a fast, from a calm to a startled or frenzied movement. This physical energy, caught in all its intensity and variety, and enjoyed by every motor impulse of our being, is reduced to ever changing formal patterns. There is, fused with this motor response, an emotional response in terms of mood: rhythms are gay, sad, solemn, dreamy, restless, calm. For the rendering of such emotional values the dance must rely in part on music and in part on the cooperation of pose and gesture.

POSE: Pose relates the dance to the expressional and decorative side of sculpture. There is a momentary resolution of the musical, and the attention is shifted from the rhythm to the body as a visual object, interpreted either as an achievement in balance and negation of gravity or as a purely decorative ensemble or as a mould of feeling. Of the first, toe dancing and gymnastic dances offer many examples—such as the balancing on the toes of one foot with the other leg at a right angle or the throwing of the body backward with a violent upthrust of one knee, as shown on page 215 of Genthe's *Book of the Dance.* Of the second, illustrations are to be found in Genthe on pages 43, 61, 149, 165, 167. Of the third, the drooping, mournful poses of the Duncan Dancers in Chopin's *Funeral March,* are an example. These three phases are paralleled in sculpture by *The Flying Mercury, The Maiden Tying Her Sandal,* and *The Niobe Group.*

GESTURE: Gesture relates the dance to the decorative

and expressional side of sculpture, painting, and poetry. It differs from pose by a more definite pointing, and by an emphasis on arm and head movements. It is easy to show by rough schematizations how different positions of arms and hands give a different decorative tone to the whole body. Besides, gestures mean something, emotionally and dramatically. Arms are stretched out with upturned palms in supplication; flexed with vertical palms in a warding off movement; bent about the head in grief; flung out laterally in joyful abandon. Two dangers must be avoided. Definite as gestures are, in their purpose and pantomimic value, they are not definite enough to be turned into routine movements. The gesture of despair is spontaneous and differs from person to person. Gesture must not clash with pose; the expressiveness of the arm must have its reason in the carriage of the body.

SETTING AND COSTUME: Setting and Costume relate the dance to the decorative and expressional side of architecture and painting.

There must be chosen for the dancers a space neither too large nor too small, harmonizing with the spirit of the dance, allowing complete freedom of movement, toned so as not to distract, yielding intensifying aid. It is evident that the old style stage settings with their false realism, their rigidity, their clutter of stage properties, their artificial isolation of the figure by means of a spotlight, and their pretentious and distracting settings, are unsatisfactory. The dance has benefited greatly by new methods and ideals of stagecraft. Two paths of development may be followed. One leads to the use of draperies and changing lights, whose varying folds, colors, and luminosities give a living setting to the life of the dance. The other either seeks highly specialized settings for highly specialized dances—cubist angles for a Burmese dance, arabesques for a rococo dance, grotesque, teetering lines for a *danse macabre,* splashes of red and black for a dance of passion—or aims at monumental effects and a bold massing of color. If the danger of too static and too obtrusive a stage picture is avoided, striking effects may be gained in this second way. Examples are the elaborate pantomimic dances of the Russian Ballet, and a choreographic composition by Fokine, in which dancers weave their lateral and diagonal patterns on huge, terraced stairs.

The costume presents similar aesthetic problems. It ought to be decorative, in the sense of revealing and enhancing the beauty and grace of the body. Delicately tinted draperies do that, for they respond readily to the motion of the body and offer an infinitely moulded, fluttering life of their own. It ought to be expressive, directly or symbolically, of the nature of the dance. In elaborate dramatic dances the Bakst costumes count for much. The grotesquerie of *Till Eulenspiegel* is heightened by the use of grotesque costumes. But I have seen a girl of ten without the help of a special costume render with great expressiveness the mechanized life of Poldini's *Waltzing Doll.*

The decorative and the expressive in costume may clash. The costumes of Adolf Bolm in *Prince Igor* and of the Lady in *Papillons* are aimed at the characteristic at the expense of decorative beauty; the *Narcissus* costumes are purely decorative. The costume of the Eunuch in *Schéhérazade* shows a balance—it is grotesque in its extravagant lines, decorative in its red, yellow, and orange, and its gold zigzags and sapphire spots. The emphasis of necessity varies with the character of the dance. Exotic dances invite exotic costumes; historical dances set truth above beauty; the soul of Pierrot lives and dances in his black and white.

The costume, like the setting, ought to reflect the meaning of the dance. Pleasing or expressive as its lines and colors are, they are there only by right of their service; and they serve by adding to the visual splendor and by intensifying the emotional and dramatic life of the dance.

Unless all the elements—*rhythm, pose, gesture, costume* and *setting*—are unified and interrelated, the dance fails of its meaning as a work of art. There must, first of all, be visual organization. Gesture must be related to pose; there must be harmonies of color and line and of grouping; and a converging visual splendor. But that is only part of the task, for the meaning of the dance lies in time as well as in space, and so there must be rhythmic organization. Imagine a series of poses, revealed by flash-light stabs at the darkness. Each pose would strike us separately with a sort of visual self-sufficiency. Not so in the dance! The visual splendor changes from moment to moment, pose melts into pose, lines flutter and settle and flutter. This is not a mere scene-shifting. Every pose, every line, is felt to be mobile and transitional. The dancer carries the principle of continuity in his body; with him, therefore, rests the task of modulating the changing life of the dance and throwing it into rhythmic patterns. But there is more work to be done. Rhythms, poses, and gestures are the carriers of emotions and moods; through their aid dances may express gaiety, sadness, exultation, passion, absorption, grief, melancholy, lightheartedness. One of the problems of the dance is to achieve a single emotional color-tone or the complex unity of an emotional color-poem. There remains the need of dramatic organization. The dramatic theme, or idea, of the dance must not be confused with the subject or story. The subject may be Salome before Herod or the drowning of Narcissus or a tragic love-tangle. Around such subjects the dance, enlisting the services of music, weaves a system of dramatic values—of contrasted passions, of startling gestures and sharply accentuated movements, of tumult and repose, of visualized emotion.   In the bending of its manifold expressiveness to this unity of theme lies the most difficult task and the greatest opportunity of the dance.

NOTE 1.   In early group life, dancing, with little evidence of form, appears in a day's work and a day's play.   At first glance there seems to be as wide a gap between this and the elaborately patterned religious, ceremonial, commemorative dances found in primitive cultures as there is between ballroom dancing or the quick rhythmic movements of a boxer sparring for an opening and a dance recital designed as art.   However, there is no such wide gap.   Play and serious social work spontaneously develop form and pattern in and through which they are integrated.   In certain Indian dances of serious religious import two buffoons parody the ceremonial and add to it playful arabesque.   The ritual itself becomes stylized.   Mimetic and gymnastic dances reveal at many points an instinctive or deliberate quest for artistic form.

NOTE 2.   Floor patterns in the dances of a ballet group are overlooked because we do not see the dancers from above.   Ice skaters, like dancers, are aware of such patterning as they cut their figures into the surface of the ice.   The motion picture camera, with its angled shots from above, has drawn attention to this aspect of the dance.

ARCHITECTURE

Architecture, of all the major arts, keeps closest to practical life. Whatever else it may be, it is first of all the art of building; and as such it must submit to an alien will, which chooses the material, sets the cost, fixes a constructive program and carries it out through the genius and craftsmanship of the architect. Because of this it has been set by Kant as a dependent art over against the free arts, in which the artist is allowed to express himself unhampered by practical dictation. Two facts wreck such a theory. Any and every art may be dependent without losing its artistic value. Of this, monumental sculpture, religious dances, and commemorative poetry are examples. Again, in architecture, where the practical control is strongest, this very control serves as a challenge and an opportunity to the architect to be an artist as well as a builder, and to form a variously accented and patterned beauty with the material he has been set to work in and within the specifications of type and cost which are not his.

The close relation, however, makes it difficult for us, engrossed as we are in the technique of living, to respond to a building aesthetically instead of seeing it as part of the business or setting of social life. If we succeed in avoiding this, there is still a difficulty. The will to art in architecture is complex; it does not allow an easy survey and conquest, but demands for its appreciation a disciplined eye and the power to grasp unity of design in intricate masses of heavy, inert material.

What is the aesthetic soul of architecture, and how is

this soul expressed in the living body of architectural effects?

The Aesthetic Meaning of Architecture

A building is a block carved from cubical space. It lacks the simultaneity of impressions which is possible in a painting, and the easy roundness and compactness of a sculptured figure. The spirit of isolation to be found in these arts is lacking in architecture: the block is shaped in relation to the surrounding space and its objects. The site and the setting offer artistic as well as practical problems and opportunities. There are good reasons for the position of a medieval robber castle: it was difficult of access and dominated the road below; when studied as a work of art part of its meaning is to be found in the countryside it gripped and ruled.[1]

The more or less massive shell of this hollow block contains either smaller blocks, each separated from the other by ceilings, floors, and interior walls or a large interior broken up into related and communicating spaces. No reading of architecture is complete which neglects interiors, for it is in their fashioning and elaboration that much of the genius of the architecture is revealed. In the Pantheon, a circular temple, there is one vast interior losing itself at its periphery in the depressions of a panelled dome and sweeping past Corinthian columns into the recesses of seven niches. In Gothic cathedrals spatial continuity is combined with bewilderingly complex dividing and stressing. The nave in its reach from portal to choir is flanked by single or double aisles and galleries marked off by pillars and arches and is cut across by transepts; semi-circular chapels break up and individualize the sides; and groined or ribbed vaulting, the

---

[1] Architectural responsiveness to environment may be studied in the California hillside bungalow; and in city planning, which is coming to be looked upon more and more as a problem in art.

By Ewing Galloway

EMPIRE STATE BUILDING

roof. This modulated unity of the interiors of churches, halls, and theatres cannot be gained in office buildings and conventional houses. The modern office building is committed to the "boxes within a box" scheme; the parcelled offices and the mechanical connection of floors by the rectangular block of the elevator shaft or uniformly regular stairs make an artistic interior in the fullest sense impossible. Architects in planning houses are abandoning this scheme. They are doing away with doors, making rooms responsive to each other, and treating halls and stairways in a new manner. In the bungalow superimposed stories are eliminated because of their vertical estrangement, and the rooms are made to share in a common horizontal life. The use of an inner court, or *patio* offers a combination of seclusion—an exterior serving as an interior—and a freely circulating domestic life.

Looked at from the outside, a building is seen as a mass of marble or brick or stone and mortar whose artistic effects are tri-dimensional and manifold, and whose full meaning as a work of art can be grasped only by series of eye-movements and measurements of spaces, planes, and angles in their relations, and of diverse visual excursions and motor responses. This is true of the simple, stacked triangles of the Pyramids as well as of the domed, turreted, and arched exterior of St. Mark's or of a Gothic cathedral with contours that play in and out, filigreed surfaces, flying arches, buttresses, spires, pinnacles, and gables. We never see the exterior all at once, nor do we see it flat. When we are limited to one side of it we see that side as composed of projections and depressions. The limiting lines are felt as edges, windows and doors as openings, and window-facings as planes slanting into the frame. Cornices and pillars are not seen as horizontal and vertical lines; porticoes and doorways thrust out at us or draw us in after them. Surfaces are broken up by mouldings and the plastic help of sculptured figures.   The third dimension is actually there; it is not, as in painting, an illusion created by means of the art of perspective.   The eye is forced to adjust itself to varying depths.   There is a direct and empathetic response to weight and pressure; there are muscle strains and tensional adjustments as the eye follows the upsweep of the Campanile at Pisa or the Eiffel Tower and the low expansive spread of the Parliament Houses at London or of Hampton Court.

So far the aesthetic meaning of architecture has revealed itself as a single and varied life, responsive to its type and setting, expressed through lines, masses, and space-forms, richly and harmoniously planned and elaborated, giving itself quietly and successively to an exploring observer—a life of many accents and one spirit.

This life, however, is incompletely understood if it is not read imaginatively in terms of the creative mood of the builder as that mood becomes visual and gains a meaning far beyond the visual—a meaning which discloses itself only to the imaginative observer.   Architecture lacks something of the easy sensuous appeal of painting and sculpture; it demands for its creation and understanding imagination of a high order.   The architect uses material—stone or brick—which has very little original sensuous and imaginative value and which is not readily endowed with a significant life; he faces the task of an elaborate organization of space-forms; and he must make what he creates larger, somehow, than the practical need it is meant to serve.   Not only must the complex forms of architecture be grasped in their interrelations, as are the cuts in a text-book of solid geometry, but the artist's enriched reading of human life must be shared, and the spirit and life of his work, caught. A Gothic cathedral is at first glance a bewildering mass of intersecting planes, supports, enclosed spaces, and decorative detail—all of which must be felt as a manifold orderliness—but it is also a place of worship, in which must be sensed the mysteries of religion and must be heard the resonant voice of the medieval Church; and it also expresses the spirit of its builders, and through them that of race and period, with special ideals of art and modes of expression— a spirit to be recaptured.

If the artist is a reshaper of images and feelings and if his work is one phase of the imaginative life of mankind, an interpretative reading is needed. But there are dangers to be avoided. A cultural reading may easily degenerate, as it sometimes does in Ruskin, Taine, Cram, and Faure, into brilliant rhetoric or a social rhapsody. It is difficult to withstand this temptation to looseness in arts which like poetry, music, and painting depend in part for their effects on irradiations of feeling and marginal associations. In arts in which craftsmanship is palpably *there*, as in ornamental metal-work, basketry, rug-craft, intaglio-work, and in sculpture and architecture, there is a natural corrective to such fantastic interpretation. The classical and the rococo are interesting as moods and phases of the creative spirit of mankind, but little can be made of them unless their reading is checked up in terms of actual forms. Again, while it is necessary to see the artist in his work, little is gained by taking what he has set aside of himself and made objective and self-sufficient, and putting it back into the personal chaos that was its source. It is better to work down to the aesthetic elements of a building as they appear in combined effects.

THE ELEMENTS OF ARCHITECTURAL EFFECT

LIGHT AND SHADE, COLOR, TEXTURE

The architect has incomplete control of light and shade. The site of a building, constructional needs, the diurnal and seasonal shifting of the position of the sun make mastery impossible. Still, his are many chances of catching lights and fixing shadows.

In the interiors of churches this is a matter of (a) openings to admit light, (b) pillars, arches, and recesses, (c) cornices, projections, and grooving, (d) light and dark stone-patterning in floors and walls. In the Pantheon there is only one source of light, a huge opening in the roof; in the Church of St. Godehardi in Hildesheim the light slants in from the side with mottled effects on floor and pews; in the Liebfrauenkirche in Trier and in Notre Dame it pours, softened through tinted glass, down the nave, casting shadows on pillars and slipping past them into aisles. Where there is much structural complexity and breaking of surfaces by means of ornamental carving and fluting, light and shade effects show great variety. Light and dark stone-patterning may be seen in St. Paul Before the Walls.

In the exteriors of Gothic buildings there is a complex system of accents: angled walls, turreted and differently pitched roofs, flying buttresses, arcades and clear-stories, deeply set portals, traceried windows, and filigreed stonework allow a sharp and varied contrast between bright lights and dark, quieting shadows. In simple and massive rectangular buildings like the Palazzo Strozzi, the Palazzo Riccardi, and the Boston Public Library, almost the only accents are those of cornices and mouldings. Mouldings have another, a decorative use. They have also been called devices "whereby, with the help of the light and shade they produce, definition is given to the salient lines of a building"; and they have been shown to be most delicate and least deep and massive where brilliant sunlight and a clear atmosphere make it possible to gain "strong shadows from slight projections."

Color, in architecture, plays its part in the choice of material, in joining, in setting, and mosaics, in the tinting of surfaces, and in mural decoration. Brick, blackish basalt, the granular mixtures of granite and porphyry, green limestone, and Pentelic marble offer strikingly different color values. Elaborate and variegated inlays of wood and stone in exterior walls seem to us to interfere with the dynamic flowing and stretching of the lines of a building; it is, however, a Moorish liking. In domestic architecture greater latitude is common. Effective variety is gained by combinations of weathered shingling or painted boards with cement or stone substructures. As for the decorative use of color, it is to be found everywhere in a minor rôle: in the gilded and tinted triglyphs and metopes of the Parthenon, the stained glass and the painted timber roofs of the English Gothic, the mural paintings of basilicas and of the twelfth century cathedrals at Hildesheim and Braunschweig; and in the frescoes, colored porcelain tiles, roof framing, and gilt metal work of Indian, Chinese,[2] and Japanese architecture.[3]

Texture as an element in architectural effect is too much neglected in aesthetics. Stones may be roughened by chipping or left with a central projection; rubble may be used; laths in a house may run vertically or horizontally; bricks may be glazed or left rough, and they may be joined by grooved or ridged lines of cement. Porous limestone differs in *feel* from granite; a shingled roof has none of the smooth unbending hardness of a slate roof. Such differences are as marked as are those between a Senna and

---

[2] Banister Fletcher, p. 812.

[3] Banister Fletcher, p. 826, "Colour decoration, introduced from China in the sixth century, is very generally applied to the interior and exterior of Japanese temples. Beams, brackets, carvings, and flat spaces are picked out in gilding and bright colours, such as blue, green, purple, madder, and vermilion. Wall paintings are generally on a gold ground and represent animals, birds, and flowers. Supporting pillars are usually black, red, and gold.—All the accessories of architectural design, lacquer-work, enamels, faience, bronzes, and ivories vie with one another in minuteness of accuracy, softness of colour, and profusion of detail."

Kazak rug or between tweed and broadcloth. Least interesting in point of texture is a smooth stucco surface; it is as
featureless as a piece of plain oilcloth and must be redeemed
by weathering. Filigree work suggests lace. The term
texture need not be limited to the compactness or looseness,
the smoothness or roughness of surfaces; it may be applied to
the patterned weave and gathering of details in the interior
of a mosque or a cathedral.

VASTNESS

Vastness strikes the note of the sublime in architecture.
Peculiar effects are gained by great size and height in buildings. Standing within its space, we respond to a vast
interior in terms of a kind of muscular space-experimenta-
tion. The initial stages of stretching and reaching are
combined, in the absence of objects within easy reach, with
a quickened sense of extension. If the interior is in semi-
darkness, the sense of vastness is more intense; in like manner a lifting fog increases and makes indefinite distances at
sea. When a building is looked at from without, the sense
of great horizontal and vertical extension is gained, not
from eye-measurements and definite estimates, but from
movements of the muscles of the eye and neck, and suggested walking or climbing. This may be proved by a simple experiment. Standing at a distance and looking up
at a tower or wall, it is possible to get a clear linear image,
which on the basis of knowledge is interpreted as great size
or height. But to get such an impression directly we
must take our position close by and look along the wall
or up at the Eiffel Tower or the façade of a cathedral;
there is then a sense of on and on, and up and up with no
chance of linear limits or easy surveying and measuring of
spaces.

TOWER OF THE CHRYSLER BUILDING

MASS AND BALANCE

The material in which the architect works is heavy, and he combines blocks of stone to a structure whose weight and downward thrust are tremendous. Part of the kinetic appreciation of architecture is the response to this exploitation of his of the force of gravity. The Pyramids, simple and massive, offer little else, the effect of an equally colossal pyramid of cardboard would be quite different. Ideas of solidity and durability enter into the creation and enjoyment of the masonry of heavy walls, of heavy beams or metal work, but there is present also this rudimentary delight in the affirmation of great weight.

There is an analogous pleasure in sensing the pressure of one's body—in feeling oneself firmly set. The analogy may be carried further. There is pleasure in stretching upward, in standing on tiptoe—in a denial, as it were, of the force of gravity. In architecture the impression of lightness is given by tapering, as in spires and gables; by the use of slender columns or long, narrow openings; and by strongly accented verticals.

Pressure and upward thrust are in architecture, structurally and artistically, a contest between burden and support. This is one phase of balance. A heavy structure held up by slight pillars suggests strain and top-heaviness as well as squatness; massive pillars under a flimsy superstructure seem to exert more force than is needed. The use of spiral, or corkscrew pillars as supports seems a violation of balance: they suggest buckling and collapse under an excessive burden.

Lateral balance implies success in dealing with the inward and outward thrust of structures carried to great heights. Stability must be given; there is to be no collapse by caving in or bulging. The main lines must be straight up and down or with uniform rounding or slanting, as in a spire or a dome. A leaning tower is displeasing; it suggests toppling. There must be balance of subsidiary lines. Buttresses slant in and up to brace the walls; in the pointed arch a lateral thrust is met by a thrust from the right; in a spire there is a meeting and stacking of many diagonals; in the rounded arch, as it appears between pillars or in the vaulting of a dome, and in the arch span of a bridge there is an equilibrium of forces which is pleasing quite apart from its structural use of stability.

Balance is here used in a kinetic sense. It may also be used in the sense of bilateral symmetry. In the latter sense an unbalanced arrangement is an unsymmetrical arrangement. The two uses differ widely. In a stick of the same circumference throughout its length and with weight evenly distributed, the point of balance—in the middle—will also give symmetry of line. Bore a small hole in one end and insert some lead, and the balancing of the stick on a forefinger will result in asymmetry of line. In architecture symmetry has a place apart from any question of weight and balance.

Balance itself is not always a matter of actual weight and stability—it is not merely a structural concept. The Leaning Tower at Pisa stands, but it seems to fall; and in this *seeming* is to be found a large part of the secret of our response not only to architecture but to all art. It is a question of empathy. We throw ourselves into the leaning of the tower, follow it down, muscularly and imaginatively, and feel it falling.

PATTERNED COMBINATION

The simplest form of patterned combination is a row composed of a unit repeated over and over, with the units separated by the same unarresting interval. A row of windows in an office building is an example, so is a colonnade. Such rows have the practical purpose of serving as openings or supports, and the aesthetic purpose of breaking up walls into smaller ordered spaces. Unless windows and columns offer a pleasing architectural form or arrest the eye by some bit of decorative elaboration, this simple repetition seems uninteresting. Sunken windows, projecting stone facings, columns whether used in their full roundness in a colonnade or in relief as decorative items in a façade, complicate and enliven the effect by adding to the flat horizontal rhythm along the surface a waving rhythm of varying depths. When the façade itself is rounded or waving, variety results from optical illusions.

Somewhat more complex is the simple alternating row in which there is repetition of ornamented intervals, as in the Lian Cathedral. The ornamentation may be like or unlike; in the frieze of the Parthenon triglyphs alternate with metopes, and the latter are individualized by means of varying sculptural compositions.

Instead of the simple 1,2–1,2 alternation there may be a 1,2,3–1,2,3 series or in fact the repetition of any complex pattern. No art equals architecture in the gaining by simple means of manifold effects, striking and intricate, in the integration of forms. In rows of windows one above the other where there are plain intervals there is no integration beyond that of the *feel* of the whole wall surface. With the introduction of panelled columns of greater length than the window frames and of vertical patterning, the harsh separateness of the different stories disappears. Of this the arcades of the Doge's Palace offer an illustration. The columns in the lower row are bound together by the swinging rhythm of the arches; the upper, more slender columns end in arches whose points in turn run into the rolling rhythm of a series of pierced circles—the parts are thus made responsive, and the patterning becomes fluent and variable.

Other complicated patterns may be found in serrated roof lines and in the decorative detail along cornices.

SYMMETRY

By a symmetrical arrangement of parts is meant bilateral inverted repetition swinging on a pivot: as abcIcba. An approximation to this is the human body with its branching from an axis.   In architecture symmetry applies to (a) the working out of an architectural scheme and to (b) the decorative ordering of spaces and lines.

ARCHITECTURAL SCHEME: The temple at Edfu, the front of Rheims Cathedral, Notre Dame, St. Mark, and the Town Hall at Antwerp offer examples of almost perfect lateral correspondence.   But there are deviations from such a scheme.   In many French Romanesque churches—S. Giles, for instance—there is a central symmetrical arrangement flanked by towers of dissimilar height and structure. The Chateau de Chambord seen from the north shows a startling symmetry carried up and over into a many-turreted sky-line, but the wings are of different lengths.   Such deflections from absolute symmetry can sometimes be traced back to practical needs or to growth by accretion, as in the Palais de Fontainebleau, but a distrust of the mechanical effect of complete inverse repetition must also be counted in.

DECORATIVE ORDERING OF SPACES AND LINES: Symmetry as it applies to the ordering of parts and to decorative detail may be seen in a threefold arrangement of portals, as in Notre Dame and Rheims Cathedral, in converging mouldings, in stone tracery work in windows, in altars and stone screens, in Buddhist gateways and in the Emperor's Palace at Pekin.   In the Doorway of C. S. Pablo at Valladolid an exuberant and florid mass of carving is thrown into a rich and measured correspondence of lines.[4]

---

[4] Banister Fletcher, pp. 438, 539, 813.

PROPORTIONALITY

Proportionality refers to (a) the relation between the length, height, and depth of a building, and to (b) ratios worked out and repeated in the various parts.

(a) Make a drawing of the Parthenon with proportions radically altered, push the sides in and lengthen the vertical lines, or make of it a squat, expansive building: in either case there will be distinct loss of beauty. This simple experiment proves that there are certain relations between length, height, and depth which are more pleasing than others. One of the most widely used is an increase by half. It would, however, be a mistake to carry the rationalizing of preferences to the point it was carried to by Fechner in his experiments with rectangles. One of Fechner's least acceptable rectangles, a very long and narrow one, is used with pleasing effect in the Campanile. The truth of the matter is that the nature of a building, whether it is to serve as a tower or a lighthouse, as a bungalow or a temple, and the exigencies of the site, as in the Flatiron Building, are unconsciously taken into account in our reading of proportions.

(b) Ratios are to be found in the mutual relation of the parts of a building. The façade presents a wall to be individualized in many ways: by patterned rows, decorative detail, contrasted accents of texture, depth, and color. If the impression is not to be confused, some sort of horizontal and vertical organization must be had. The openings between columns must bear a fixed relation to the columns themselves; the height of the column, to the breadth; and the several vertical partitions, of cornice, entablature, and support, to each other. At first thought, simple ratios such as 1:1, 1:2, or 1:3 might seem best to serve the part of binding the spaces of a façade to a common life. But try the experiment of combining toy blocks of different colors to a

façade illustrative of such simple ratios, and you will find
a shallow interest in easy patterning soon followed by a
slackening appeal: the effect is as monotonous almost as
that of verses with the caesura always in the middle or that
of music with an unvarying, undisguised 1,2 or 1,2,3 beat.
At the other extreme, ratios which can be expressed only by
high numbers, such as 19:21 or 37:39 do not yield a felt
relation of lines and spaces.

Measurements made on ancient temples by Penrose,
Cockerill, and Stuart and summaries and comparisons
offered by Hittorf and Raymond prove that Greek architects consciously sought a mathematical scheme. In the
Temple of Aegina the width of the raking cornice, the
corona, the abacus, and the ovolo is the same; and the
tabulated measurements of the parts of some twenty Greek
temples, given by Raymond on p. 221 of his *Proportion of
Harmony and Color*, reveal the recurrent use of ratios of
approximately 1:1, 1:2, 1:3, and 2:3. It must, however,
be pointed out that (1) the divergence from perfect correspondence cannot be explained by dwelling on the difference between measured relations and perceived relations,
which reflect illusions. The Greek artist knew the value
of slight irregularity even in the visual image: he carried
the roundness of the middle portion of pillars a little beyond
the point at which the lines appear straight to the eye;
and (2) the simple ratios apply to capitals and entabla-
tures, where it is possible to vary visually the lines of division, and where when a breadth of space recurs it recurs
at wide intervals. Greek architectural proportions in the
large run to the less simple ratios of 4:7, 5:7, 5:8, 2:5,
3:8, 9:10. The range of pleasing proportions was held to
be a wide one, and too marked a regularity and mathematical transparency was avoided. Architect and sculptor
were interested in developing a canon of the proportions
of the human body. Vitruvius, whose work subtends lost

Greek speculations, gives what he considers normal human proportions.[5] Not only is there more than one unit of measurement used—head, forearm, and foot—but the relationships show great variety. There were many such canons, for the range in the human body of the normal and the pleasing is very wide; and the architect and the sculptor readily carried over into their arts something of this breadth.

HARMONY

Harmony in architecture is gained when all the diverse parts and items of a building—masses, lines, spaces, angles, textures, colors, and sculptural ornaments—agree and conspire to give (1) the impression of a single and successful creative will, (2) a single pleasing visual image, (3) unity of spirit and emotional tone. If the architect falters in making arbitrary changes or fails to achieve perfect control over his material and his problems or if many successive artists work in an ill-coordinated way at some huge structure, like St. Peter's in Rome, lack of harmony of the first kind results. Visual harmony is a difficult matter. It is violated when there are: disorderly mixing of rectangular and rounded pillars, a shingled roof on a brick building, a sudden unmotived bending of lines or sharpening of angles, flimsy looking supports to a frowning and heavy superstructure. Patterning and proportionality lead the eye and the attention into rhythmic paths; a sudden jolting from that path is felt to be disagreeable. It is not a question of always expecting and looking for the same. There must be variety as well as unity. Rather it is a matter of the like or the not too different. Curves and angles must be varied, but within the range of a dominant scheme, such as that of circle segments in St. Sophia, of slender, piercing

5 Vitruvius, *De Architectura*, Bk. III, chap. 1.

triangles in the Cathedral at Cologne, of blunt triangularity in the Cathedral at Orvieto enlivened by sharp thrusts into space. Visual harmony must be interpreted more liberally in architecture than in painting, for a building gives itself in sets of images and must in its organization conform in part to practical demands. Harmony of spirit and emotional tone, the third type, refers to a conglomerate response made up of visual impressions, associations, and suggested emotions. There must be nothing in the interior of a church inconsistent with devotional feeling; and gloom, contrition, and hope must find something of themselves in its darkened spaces, stone floors, high vaulting, and the blues and reds of its large windows.

ORNAMENTATION

The most extraneous forms of ornamentation are sculptures in the round, as in the flat roof triangle of the Parthenon; mural paintings, as those of Polygnotus; fountains, trellises, and shrubbery in enclosed spaces. In all such cases there is a nice adaptation on the part of independent arts, whose contribution to a general decorative scheme is easily set apart. Quite different is the situation when a pillar is sculptured as a Caryatid or an Atlas, a waterspout as a gargoyle, and when, as in the Palazzo Borghese, an elaborate fountain is built into the wall. These things have no structural value—an unadorned pillar or spout would serve as well—they are illustrations, however, of a process of *indirection* discoverable in all the arts, by means of which the useful is disguised and subordinated to a freely working decorative will. This will becomes most expressive and most closely bound up with the spirit of architecture when by virtue of the stone-cutter's art the wall itself becomes decoratively alive. In the façade of the Cathedral of Milan the wall seems to disappear in a network of windows and delicate lace-like perforations; sharpness in sky-line and spires is lost in elaborate carving. Again, the heaviness and simple strength of a wall may be made more expressive by the use of massive cornices, sparse openings, broad and plain window-facings, huge oaken doors sunk into the wall.

The range of ornamentation in architecture is a wide one: it includes fluting, panelling, tinting and gilding, stone and wood carving of capitals, pulpits, and benches, patterned bands, sculptured friezes, medallion work, inlays and edging, and work in metal. It offers many special problems: of craftsmanship and technique; of the historical development of patterns and their relation to styles; of tradition and innovation; of the invention and use of complicated geometrical designs; of imitation and adaptation of forms of plant and animal—the leaf, the lotus blossom, the rose, the nautilus, the snake,—of the use of symbolism.

Ornamentation in architecture serves to (1) give variety of interest to surfaces, (2) give animation, variety, and rhythmic swing to lines subdividing spaces and relating planes, (3) offer varying relief to masses and afford the eye points of support and interest in its plastic excursions, (4) guard against the impression of inert heaviness.

Certain aesthetic principles follow from this its function. It must not be superfluous or obtrusive, like a lot of flashy jewelry; far from being incongruous, it must fit into the general architectural scheme and its spirit; it must be smooth and persuasive, without inner discords; it must help rather than interfere with the rhythms of lines and masses; it must have a beauty of its own and a share in the life of what it adorns.

FITNESS

Vitruvius, having enumerated *venustas*, *utilitas*, and *decor* as the three architectural demands to be made, interprets *decor* in a way which combines and confuses what suits the practical purpose of a building and what seems suitable in the sense of fitting in with our associations and our feeling of what is suitable.   Picture galleries, he says, ought to have windows facing north so as to admit an even light; a building ought to be fitted to its site; temples dedicated to moon deities ought to be roofless; those dedicated to Mars ought to be of the simple, severe Doric order, while the soft, luxuriating Corinthian is suited to those in honor of Venus.

Fitness is one of the elements in the total aesthetic effect of architecture; the term itself must, however, be cleared up and its various uses separated.

Examples of three of these uses are: (1) a shoe fits, (2) a man is fit, (3) it is not fitting to laugh in a church.   In the first there is the recognition of a definite purpose accomplished, with little or no interest in the manner and means of accomplishment; in the second it is a question of a whole set of purposes together with an interest in what physical fitness means and how it expresses itself; in the third the reference is to congruity rather than to purpose.

A building serves a purpose: it is a church, a railroad station, a home.   In its construction and in the planning of details specific means are employed to solve specific practical problems.   If our pleasure in architectural fitness were merely this, that we took delight in such detailed adaptedness, and in nothing else, we should not get beyond a Babbitt-like enjoyment of a well appointed, well painted, efficiently floored, tiled, lighted, impressive, *bang-up* twentieth century home.

Fitness as an element in architectural effect is to be found in the second and third meanings of the term.   It is an adaptedness to sets of purposes and interest in processes through which a general purpose unfolds itself and arouses a sense of the suitable.   There must be added historical and emotional associations and a feeling for harmonious organization. In the Grand Central Station in New York we are interested in the way in which a general purpose takes on articulated and differentiated form in train-shed, waiting-rooms, ticket-offices. Crowding, confusion, and waste of space are avoided. There are several train levels easily reached by sloping passages; the huge arched train-shed, rendered unnecessary by an electrified service, has disappeared; the large central hall allows circulation where it is most needed, around ticket offices and gates; and the waiting-rooms are set aside and spared all confusion. Whenever a general purpose is worked into a structure in such fashion, a pleasurable sense of fitness results. All the parts cooperate efficiently; they are congruous, offering harmonies of line, mass, and color. Theirs is a common artistic as well as a common practical life. When Vitruvius calls it indecorous to combine a large and showy entrance and a shabby interior he is using fitness in the third sense. When he suggests that a temple of Venus ought to be of the Corinthian type he is basing his argument on religious and historical associations. Modern parallels are easily found. The Greek Temple is to us not only a triumph of strength and harmony of line, but an embodiment of the religious and civic life of the Greeks—a life and spirit it was admirably fitted to serve. There is then something incongruous in having this type used in a serving-station or having it house a banking enterprise, in which instances there is a lapse in function, and a lack of harmony between exterior and interior.

Such are the elements of architectural effect: light and shade, color and texture, vastness, mass and balance, patterned combinations, symmetry, proportionality, harmony, ornamentation, and fitness. Named singly, they play their part in combination; and it is well to remember that there are many pleasing ways in which they may be combined. Architecture is an art of many forms, of many moods, of many voices.

SCULPTURE

Sculpture in its historical development is closely related to architecture. In the great temples of Egypt, Assyria, and Greece; in the huge and intricate Gothic cathedrals; and in the slighter, commemorative and civic structures— tombs, shrines, triumphal arches, town halls, and fountains —it has served the double purpose of giving varied decorative effects to masses and lines and artistic form to structures, and of yielding a heightened impressiveness, social and spiritual, to objects, events, ideas. The monotony of skylines is broken by winged lions, palmettoes or figures in rows, that of cornices or wall spaces by mouldings and by sculptures in the round or in relief. Architectural forms are given lightness and life through the use of the lotus, the ivy, the rose and by chained patterns of snakes, lizards, and birds; pillars take human shape as caryatides or slaves or world-bearers; niches are filled with statues; Gothic portals are rich in sculptural reliefs. Phidias and his co-workers subordinated their art to the architectural scheme of the Parthenon. A brilliant example of their success are the pediment sculptures in the low triangle under the roof. Some of Goujon's finest work is within the setting of the Clock-Tower of the Louvre. The great French stone-cutters and metal-workers and the German wood-carvers of the Middle Ages became decoratively effective in their elaboration of altars, cornices, gates, pulpits, and tombs, like the Sebaldusgrab of Peter Vischer. To this first purpose must be added a second: that of heightened impressiveness. Much of Greek sculpture was under the sway of religious and patriotic motives: time has given to many of these figures an artificial isolation by tumbling them from their shrines and breaking away their religious emblems. The Phidian statues of Zeus and Athene, by the size and majesty of their design and the use of precious gold and ivory, gave volume and intensity of religious feeling to the temple that held them. Patriotism found plastic embodiment in the group of *Harmodius and Aristogeiton* and in the *Victory of Samothrace*. In Gothic churches figures of Mary [1] and of the Saints, groups of the Crucifixion and the Pieta, wood and stone reliefs of the Birth of Christ [2] and the Last Supper, of the Bearing of the Cross,[3] and of pathetic biblical incidents such as the sacrifice of Isaac [4] give an added solemnity and emotional spirit to Christian worship.

There are, however, signs of an early independent development of sculpture. The art of the cave-men of the Reindeer Age offers many examples of animals carved in the round or in relief; that of the African negro is rich in amulets of bone and in grotesque human figures carved from wood. Some of the religious and social meaning of this work is lost to us; but the fact remains that it appears at an early cultural stage when only the most rudimentary architecture existed; and that it expresses, quite independently of decorative architectural patterning, *a will to the plastic rendering of organic life.*

It is here that the aesthetics of sculpture must begin, for it is this preoccupation with organic life that is the first mark of sculpture as an art. A world without animal life might be material for painting or poetry but not for sculpture. Mountains, huge blocks of stone, and trees are wholly unsuited as subjects, however complete the modeled likeness. There is in sculpture nothing to parallel landscape painting, where the introduction of animals and hu-

[1] Portail de la Vierge of Notre Dame.
[2] Pisano's Baptisterium at Pisa.
[3] Adam Krafft.
[4] Ghiberti or Brunelleschi.

mans is unacceptable to modern feeling. A rock may be used as a background or, as in some of Rodin's work, as part of the composition, a tree trunk for balance or support; trees or houses may fill spaces in a relief, and flowers may be used in a decorative design. Beyond this the sculptor cannot go. It is for this reason that a small spire, naturally felt as part of a large whole, if detached and put on a pediment, impresses us architecturally rather than sculpturally, however delicately carved.

Two obstacles to an understanding of sculpture are: variety of material and variety of type. Wood, marbles of different colors and textures, ivory, bronze, and stones like granite, basalt, and porphyry are used, singly or in combination; and their choice demands special treatment. Thus a marble statue in certain poses requires as a support a pillar or tree which the use of bronze would render superfluous. Bronze reflects light as ivory does not, and a marble surface has a granular aliveness which wood lacks. Carving in wood allows finer detail and a sharper edging than is possible in stone. Sculpture in relief, high or low, has its own decorative and pictorial problems. If analysis is to escape a tangle of qualifications, it must turn to sculpture in the round and to stone or bronze as material; in like manner an aesthetics of painting must turn to oil rather than to water color, and to canvases in preference to porcelain or ivory.

THE AESTHETIC MEANING OF SCULPTURE

In sculpture the material is tri-dimensional, heavy, and unresponsive. The tri-dimensional quality is preserved— it is not as in painting annulled and then re-created as a system of illusions. The heavy, recalcitrant block is shaped in response to an artistic idea, which means (1) exploiting sensuously the material itself, (2) building a visually and

HEAD OF AKHENATEN

dynamically satisfying system of lines, planes, and masses, (3) creating a semblance of organic life, (4) giving plastic form to psychic values. These four, with the accents differently placed by different artists, mark the aesthetic meaning of sculpture.

THE SENSUOUS EXPLOITATION OF THE MATERIAL

There is nothing in sculpture to match in intensity and range the natural beauty of colors in painting. The glister of certain stones, the luminosity of marble, the smoothness of ivory, the dusky splendors of bronze, the beauty of texture and of grain of certain woods are all less insistent, and are in part, at least, the result of polishing, burnishing, and scraping. The sculptor strives to make the most of what natural beauty there is. He chooses the marble of Paros, seeks flawless wood, sees the striking possibilities of blackish, grey-flecked basalt or mottled porphyry. He refrains from doing violence to his material with a coat of color, and does not destroy its oneness of effect by arbitrary combinations.[5]

THE CREATION OF A (A) VISUALLY AND (B) DYNAMICALLY SATISFYING SYSTEM OF LINES, PLANES, AND MASSES

VISUALLY SATISFYING: Imagine either a rectangular block or several blocks, one set above the other and at right angles to the line of vision, and then carved from it the *Apoxyomenos*. See the figure at first flat, as in a linear design. The monotony of the blocks has been broken by a varied system of lines: there is a flowing rhythm in the oval of the head, the short vertical of the neck, the slant outward of the left shoulder and inward of the arm, the gentle curving of loin and hip, and the long vertical of the leg.

---

[5] Polychrome effects are not pleasing; even a slight tinting or gilding is unacceptable to modern feeling. Inlay work—ivory eyeballs, for instance—or the use of three kinds of stone, as in a statue in the Luxembourg where porphyry is used to simulate color effects in clothing, endanger the unity of impression. This is true of Klinger's *Beethoven*.

Across the body is the horizontal of the left forearm, and on the surface of the head are the short criss-cross curves of the hair. But the contours become differently beautiful and expressive as we walk around the statue. What were held to be lines are now felt as the edges of surfaces; and the surfaces in turn in their tilting and rounding enclose masses. Thus the statue from the turned head to the downward thrust of one arm and the lateral thrust of the other and the receding plane of the right leg, from the sharply edged hair to the plastic rendering of muscles, knee-cap, and toes, becomes visually effective as an organization of interrelated planes and masses. It seems like, and still unlike, the constructs of solid geometry. Schematic drawings of sculpture can be made which cause all representational values to disappear, and which make these relations stand out. It requires but the simple expedient of setting side by side a number of models of geometrical figures to discover marked differences in the pleasingness of their systems of lines and masses. A sphere is preferred to a truncated prism, a pyramid to a cone. It is the sculptor's task to make visually satisfying the cubical arrangement he creates; to give compactness and variety to his contours; offer congruities of lines and angles, ridge and scoop surfaces; and bring a plastic imagination to bear on his stacking of planes and ordering of masses. Rodin points to this problem in his theories and solves it in much of his sculpture. Great linear beauty marks the head and bent raised arm of his *Age of Bronze*, while an ugly top horizontal mars his *Shade*. He gives massiveness of contour to his figures, and tilts planes and roughens surfaces for the sake not only of catching shadows and affording the eye contrasts and individualities, but of offering a vivid impression of depth and of exploiting artistically cubical space. This to him is the secret of modeling, and he alludes to it again and again in his conversations with Gsell. The cubists at their extremest point of "absolute sculpture" go far beyond this. Eliminating as such sculpture does all but a faint trace of representational and psychic values, it seems little else than an architectural grouping of geometrical models.

DYNAMICALLY SATISFYING: Even a cursory reading of Rodin and his work shows that for him lines, planes, and masses are *alive:* they stretch themselves, thrust, gather in, break through at this point or that; theirs is a tensional play. This dynamic quality must be traced to motor and kinetic empathy. Such empathy plays a part in other arts also: in architecture in the column, the arch, and the spire; in painting in vigorous verticals, flowing curves, marching diagonals; and in that equivalence of the suggested weight and directed power of colors and lines which is called balance.

Sculpture must not limit itself to effective visual organization; it must create mobile and balanced power. It is not by accident that the sculptor turns to organic life, which reveals such power. Franz Metzner in his *Earth* presents a seated figure with legs drawn up, back curved sharply downwards, and head bent over one knee. The composition has all the compactness of the artist's own *Leidtragender*, of Rodin's *Thinker* or of Barnard's *Hewer* but. is more geometrical than they are. It has the appearance of a sphere; and this motif is repeated in the round, cropped head and the clenched fists. But this sphere is dynamically *alive:* not only do the tensed muscles suggest tremendous force; they mark sharply one moment in a self-directed bodily life which may unclench and shift its ground. An illustration of how important organic forms are to sculpture may be gained in this way. In imagining a rhomboid sharply tilted at an angle of forty-five degrees we get a disagreeable sense of toppling. But our sense of balance is not outraged when we turn to the sharp-angled *Fighter of Ravenna* and the unbalanced position of Herzog's *Ekstase*, simply because here the moment is caught as a moment, and we feel ourselves into human bodies which do not allow themselves to fall.   Again, in Elkan's *Heldenklage*, a huge figure hewn from granite, the geometrical figure, a cube, is not allowed to absorb and annul kinetic and psychic values.

THE CREATION OF A SEMBLANCE OF ORGANIC LIFE

Throughout its history sculpture has created likenesses of animals and of the human form.   It has been frankly representational of organic life as it appears in the lines and general build of a body, in the play of muscles and variegated moulding and texture of surfaces—representational in neither a very detailed nor complete sense.   The material in which the sculptor works does not allow him to give the bloom of a cheek or delicate coloring of the skin, the fine lines of hair or cloth; and it yields him only limited chances of rendering the inner life of intellect, will, and feeling, which animates the body.   Within these limits he for the most part seeks a truthful image of natural forms and of the spirit they express.   Rodin is in the right when he exacts of the sculptor an accurate knowledge of anatomy and physiology.   The structure of the body must be understood; so must its muscular adjustments to all manner of positions; and its living covering of flesh, cartilage, and skin.   An unintentional violation of the truth of nature, in ignorance or because of a lack of technical skill, is felt to be a flaw.   A departure which springs from a desire to gain an added symbolical or spiritual expressiveness is not so regarded.   Rodin has the courage of such a practice.

Organic life is thought of in terms of a unified system and a self-expressive life, and they are related to the struggle for existence and its problems.   In a plant this organization is as delicate as it is in an animal, but there is little or no impressive manifestation of power; and we find it difficult to

From the University of Pennsylvania Museum

Egyptian   Sumerian

Easter Island   Egyptian

TYPES OF SCULPTURE

read plant life in terms of what might be called a *psyche*. The term *psyche* is not used in a metaphysical sense, but as a convenient characterization of consciousness, instincts, impulses, behavior, etc. through which human life and, in a more rudimentary way, animal life expresses itself. Rodin means something like this when he demands that sculpture reach the spirit in the form. The higher the advance in the animal scale the more individualized and the more varied and more directly revealed in the form itself does this inner life become—and therefore the more suitable for sculptural rendering. A fly-trapping orchid [6] or a spider is unsuited to its purposes; not so the king of beasts of prey or a predatory woman.

THE GIVING PLASTIC SHAPE TO PSYCHIC VALUES

The task of sculpture is not ended with the creation of a pleasing system of lines and planes, and with the lifelike rendering of bodies; the problem of gaining psychic significance remains. This involves (1) a sympathetic reading in its own terms of the life whose semblance is given, (2) an imaginative and emotional reaching into the realm of the humanly significant, and (3) the embodiment in bronze or marble of certain generic human values.

(1) The *psyche* of a spirited horse or a fox terrier is partially expressed in lines, movements, and individual responses. The rendering of an animal must not be superficial, fanciful or purely generic. It must be a creation from within the instincts and moods of this life—a patient and sound reading of some individualized text from the language of plastic forms. Such a sympathetic reading is more completely possible and of greater interest when the representation is of the human *psyche*. The sculptural effectiveness of figures like the *Theseus* of the Parthenon, the

---

[6] Some such trap may be read into Rudolf Belling's *Dreiklang,* a cubist design with an effective motor suggestiveness.

Drunken Silenus, the *Niobe* and the *Laocoon,* Rodin's *Eustache de St. Pierre,* Lederer's *Fencer,* and Barnard's *Lincoln* is to be sought here as well as in a satisfying organization of spaces, skilful modeling and lifelike rendering; they affect us from within outwards.   It is what life means to this god or death and its agony, to this or that mortal; what the strain and perplexity of thinking means to this man; what a bout means to a skilful fencer, who is bending and testing his rapier—the spiritual moment—that counts heavily.

(2) There is something to be added to this sympathetic recording of the inner life of individuals.   It is not merely what contemplative ease, grief, agony, pride in skill are to these men that the sculptor aims to show: it is what these things mean to him imaginatively and emotionally, and through him to us as sharers in a common humanity.   In this sense he is a reshaper, with a larger interpretative purpose circling about and settling into the lineaments of his work. Of this Rodin offers many instances.

(3) Very striking is the self-imposed simplicity of sculpture, which turns away from intricacies bodily and mental and contents itself with draped or naked bodies, single or grouped, and a narrow range of psychic values.   In its ideal content it favors the typical, the generic.   Man-centred like all art, it exploits in its own way the relation between mind and matter, and rests at least part of its appeal on our interest in a few recurrent complications and responses. This is an incomplete list of such values:

SELF-COMPOSURE AND THE CALM POISE OF A MIND AT REST: This is best seen in Greek sculpture.   Illustrations of it are the *Theseus,* the *Hermes,* statues of *Hera, Demeter, Athene,* and many fine heads.   It is lacking in baroque sculpture, and only a few of the figures and busts of Rodin have it.

HEALTH; STRENGTH; POWER: The youthful body in its glowing health and easy strength, the broad-based muscular and mental power of maturity, the mind in its stretch from promise to ease and forceful performance; such things we find pleasure in, in answer to an instinct in the service of life. To this preference sculpture usually appeals. Examples are to be found in Greek athletic sculpture. It may also be seen in Donatello's *David*, in Michelangelo's *Slaves* and in his *David*, and in Rodin's *Adam* and the *Age of Bronze*. When there is, on the contrary, a sculptural rendering of weakness, senility, defective development or perversion, it is because of a search for other values than those of youth or strength.

It is to be noted that a statue expressive of great power need not be beautiful in a formal sense. Muscular development may be too extreme for either beauty or balanced health. The *Doryphoros* and the *Disc-Thrower* show a union of strength and beauty; in the *Athletes* of Klinger and Stuck there is some divergence; in the *Farnese Hercules* there is an utter sacrifice of beauty.

ALIVENESS; ALERTNESS; MOBILITY: It was something of an achievement for sculpture to substitute for the inertness of a figure standing at rest, in frontal position with legs closed and arms hanging close to the sides, the aliveness, lightness, and suggested mobility of the body within a great range of positions, and to put in the place of a mask-like face, expressive of a crude and stolid mental life, an individualized, mobile facial expression. In view of this development it seems strange to find sculpture often interpreted in terms exclusively of rest.

This is not a question merely of the sweep of a body caught at a moment of extreme motion, as in the *Disc-Thrower*, or the figures from the frieze of Halicarnassus; nor one of imaginatively completed rhythm, as in Meunier's *Mower* or in Kolbe's *Dancer*, who seems to turn slowly as we watch her. Rather is it a matter of putting into inert marble something of the infinite mobility, physical and psychical, of human life, and of giving our interest in that mobility a peculiarly toned satisfaction. Wherever there is in modern sculpture a trend away from such lightness back to the heaviness of Egyptian and Assyrian sculpture it is to be explained in either of three ways: as a mistaken reading of Rodin's theory of massiveness; as an attempt to allow simple space values their full force, with no distraction on the part of the psychic (Hildebrand); or as a desire to bring art back to the elemental.

EMOTIONAL RESPONSES: Extreme emotional effects are much rarer in sculpture than in music or poetry; not even the *Niobe* or the *Laocoon* match the intensity and poignancy of appeal possible in the other arts. The *will to emotional upheaval,* which is so tumultuously present in tragedy, here adopts much quieter ways—not that the sculptor fears a destruction of formal beauty, but he understands his inability to give a searching and subtle portrayal of emotions at their crest. Within this its quieter range sculpture appeals to our interest in seeing embodied and sharing common human emotional responses and moods: grief, anger, remorse, love, adoration, ecstasy, despondency, melancholy, gaiety. Thus we are made to share in the remorse of Rodin's *Eve* and in the vision of death of his *Burghers of Calais,* in the sorrow of Michelangelo's *Pieta,* in the gaiety of dancing Tanagra figurines and Greek reliefs, and in the joyful abandon of Carpeaux' *Dance.*

PERSONALITY IN ITS PURPOSES AND COSMIC RELATIONS: Here again the resources of sculpture are limited; they fall short of those of tragedy, which concerns itself with man's character and man's fate—with the network of human purposes and with man's struggle to live his personal life within the context of the laws of a universe. Sculpture can give only a simple and brief excerpt from the mass of human purposes and only a hint of man's cosmic relations. Scraping the body of oil and sweat; extracting a thorn from a foot; dealing death or fleeing from it; throwing the discus or swinging a scythe; dancing, wrestling, hunting, bathing, mothering; the Greek holding up the limp body of the wounded; the Roman abducting a Sabine woman; the Gaul committing self-murder; a youth pouring a libation; a faun playing a pipe—such are the simple actions sculpture in the round can give effectively. If it attempts more, it becomes disagreeably topical and complicated, and unintelligible as well, for it cannot render purpose in its inception and follow it through its stages to a goal. It stops short often even of the simple actions and purposes cited, and offers bodies at rest, with a frank unfolding of their surfaces and a quiet undirected mental life.

The genius of sculpture does not lie in the domain of metaphysics: cosmic problems, of unfailing interest to mankind, are not natural to it. The philosophical content of Greek sculpture does not go beyond that of the mythology which gave the material. But the very choice from its circle of myths of the serene and humanized deities of Olympus in preference to the darker, less intelligible creations of the popular imagination and the rendering in vivid form of the struggle between Centaurs and Lapiths, between Gaia and her giant sons and Athene, and of Fate, Sleep, and Death in the sepulchral reliefs shows a thoughtful bias and an interest in an emerging Cosmos and its relation to man. The mysteries of the Christian religion find expression in certain types of medieval sculpture and give them intensity and depth. Among the moderns, Bartholomé, in his *Monument aux Morts*, Meunier, Metzner, and Rodin aim to make their work suggestive of larger philosophical problems. Rodin claims to be an interpreter of what stirs and strains in the process of life. The conception of his *Hell Gate* is a cosmic text on a grand scale; single creations of his, such as the *Hand of God*, *The Wave*, as well as his work in the aggregate, reveal the use of a bold symbolism and the presence of a philosophical purpose bearing down on human shapes as they lust, struggle, reflect, rebel, submit—as they come and go.

AESTHETIC TESTS

There is the closest possible relation between the knowledge of the aesthetic meaning of sculpture, as that meaning gives itself through a study of the elements of sculptural effect, and the question of what norms are to be applied to test the excellence of a figure or a group in marble or in bronze. The decision must not be left to mere like or dislike; nor is any service done by general principles applicable to all the arts, unless they are modified in the light of an understanding of what sculpture, as an art with problems and resources of its own, means to be, and can do.

What follows is in no sense a complete list; it is merely an attempt to mark some of the essential tests in any intelligent appraisal of the artistic worth of a piece of sculpture.

AN ARTISTIC IDEA THAT IS WORTHWHILE AND MASTERED

WORTHWHILE: Artistic idea and subject, often confused, are not the same. Two paintings of the Madonna, two statues of Apollo or David, two plays dealing with the same historical personages and events are the same in subject, but may differ widely, as Schiller's *Maid of Orleans* and Shaw's *Saint Joan* do, in artistic conception and purpose. Not only are subject and idea confused, but a moral bias is yielded to, which accepts some subjects and artistic purposes as ennobling and sets itself sharply against others as degrading—commending a statue of Joan of Arc and looking askance at Rodin's amorous groups or at his *Balzac*.

The first step in the appraisal of a work of sculpture is an understanding of what the artist means to give. He ought to be taken first of all on his own terms. The later Greek ages did not see in gods and goddesses what the age of

Phidias saw; interpretation and rendering are quite different. If there is distortion of the female figure, as in Archipenko, Mowbray-Clarke, Lehmbruck, for the sake of symbolism or expressionism, the distortion must be accepted as an essential moment in the working out of an artistic idea which must be understood before it is either approved or rejected.

The second step is to discover the degree of worthwhileness in the artistic idea and in the individualized and stressed rendering given by the artist. Not all artistic texts nor all personal readings are of the same worth.

How is this matter of worthwhileness to be decided? It may at once be said that every phase and form of life and every reading of it, ranging from humble copying through sympathetic reshaping to the wildest extravaganzas of self-expression have in them elements of worthwhileness. As for the attempt to work out a definitive scale of such values, that must always for aesthetics remain a partial failure in view of irreducible personal preferences. All that can be done is to name a few tests which can be applied to the artistic idea. These are: (1) beauty, (2) character, (3) plastic quality, (4) psychic significance. Thus the *Apoxyomenos*, the *Hermes*, the *Apollo Sauroktonos*, the *Dancing Satyr*, and the *Venus de Milo* exploit different types and stages of the natural beauty of the body; Stuck's *Athlete*, stocky and unattractive in its lines, Rodin's *Thinker*, and Barnard's *Lincoln* sacrifice beauty to character; the *Laocoon*, the so-called *Seneca of Herculaneum*, the *Dying Gaul*, the *Burghers of Calais*, and the *Vieille Heaulmière* aim at a combination of plastic and psychic values—they force us to see tensional masses and ridged, pitted individualized surfaces where we ordinarily see only bulk and smooth stretches—they arouse feeling, appeal to our imagination and widen and deepen our view of life. Hildebrand, loyal to aesthetic ideas of his own, is satisfied with mere values of line and mass.

MASTERED: Whether the artistic idea has been mastered in the sense of being completely and adequately embodied in plastic form depends on (1) its suitableness and (2) the technical skill of the artist. Certain subjects and ideas fall outside the realm of sculpture; others admit of only partial success in the carrying out. How childish the Roman allegories of the Nile and its cubits and Father Tiber and his children! Here is not the life of a river nor a vivid picture of its tributaries. The sculptors chose the unsuitable. Painting an allegorical figure of Rumor, as Apelles did, or modeling a towering helmeted God of War, sword in hand, are interesting experiments which must fall short of expressing what rumor and war really mean, and of what other more resourceful arts can do with such subjects. Rodin's *La Vieille Heaulmière*, which gives only one of the contrasted pictures of youth and old age, cannot match in symbolism Villon's ballad, which gives both. Again, there may be a failure of technical skill. The sculptor may have failed to carry through a movement of the arm to the shoulder and the back; he may have left an unresponsive stiffness in the face or the draperies of an agitated or fast moving body; he may have overleapt himself in trying for the sublime; he may have been unwise in his choice of methods.

AN EFFECTIVE ORGANIZATION OF CUBICAL SPACE AND ITS VALUES OF MASS AND LINE

In early Egyptian and Greek statues the organization is a simple one; an upright body is shown in frontal position, with arms hanging along the sides and legs close together; headdress and hair, massively treated, are made to fill the right angle of collar-bone and neck. Roughly speaking, the cubical space gained by slipping a hollow oblong over the figure is filled by the stone or bronze. But such a scheme, while restful at first in its compactness and balance, tends to become monotonous. How limited the aesthetic appeal of such a pose, quite apart from the fact that it fails to do justice to the flexible life of the human body! Turn the body into a diagonal from the feet or the hips, swing out or bend arms and legs, bend it with a thrust of shoulder or knee, or raise it to the rhythmic movement of the dance, and all sorts of patterns, interesting in their variety, will offer the sculptor opportunities and problems. There will be unfilled spaces, tilted planes, balancing masses, crossing lines; there will be motor stresses to be watched and set in relation. Variety is subjected to a discipline which does not sacrifice the least of its manifold and individual accents. A bold and in the main successful conquest of complex space values is Rodin's group *The Burghers of Calais*. Failures are his *Nuit de Mai* and *La Centauresse*. An ambitious and unsuccessful composition is Rudolph Maison's *Negro and Panther*. A panther has completed its leap from above, burying teeth and claws in the shoulder of the negro, whose body, touching the ground with one foot, is borne down straight to an angle of forty degrees. The intentional lack of balance is mannered; the right arm in its stiff separateness of line seems in no sense part of a living body; there is an ugly lack of correlation between the vertical of the panther and the diagonal of the negro; the area of interest—the meeting heads and shoulders of man and beast—is too limited.

BEAUTY AND CHARACTER OF SURFACES

What the sculptor can make of surfaces is one test of the worth of his work. Unenlivened as these are by the play of color, they must be made pleasing, significant, individually alive in other ways—by a delicate sense of touch which strokes, lingers, or hints with the slightest of touches—accentuates—differentiates. Thus the onlooker is offered tactile values that keep his interest from flagging. Too smooth or highly polished a surface is monotonous in its effects.   If, by contrast, there is an immoderate scooping, pitting or ridging, the feeling for surface as surface is lost.   In the best Greek work the nude or half draped body is made to yield an interplay of rough and smooth: in the *Hermes* the contrast between the carefully modeled irregularity of the hair and the smooth forehead; in the *Faun* a ridged diagonal of cloth against the smooth elastic skin of a youthful body; in the *Doryphoros* the contrast between the trunk with plates of muscle felt to be flexible and the long unaccented surfaces of the thighs.   Incidental decorative effects there are—the shield of the *Athene Parthenos*, the sandaled foot of the *Hermes* are examples—but in the main the elaboration of surfaces, even in Greek reliefs, is in relation to the plastic and vital motives which give sculpture its meaning.

TRUTHFUL RENDERING

Granted that there are types of sculpture that limit themselves to an organization of lines and spaces,[7] and others that seek only the expression of moods, unconcerned with the paralleling of natural forms, the fact remains that sculpture in its historical development and in its great achievements has offered itself as a representational art of definite and limited purpose—rendering incompletely, and within conventions of its own, the bodies of humans and animals.   We have then a right to ask with respect to the sculptor's work, "Is this a truthful rendering?   Does it show a knowledge of the human body, its possible positions, its muscles, ligaments, joints, and their relations?   If the sculptor has chosen a violent moment—a runner straining, a wrestling bout, a horse rearing—has he felt himself into the violence of that moment, as McKenzie does in his athletic sculpture; and

---

[7] Cf. Belling's explanation of his *Dreiklang:* "Der Dreiklang ist Raum —und Formbegriff.   Das ist meine Auffassung der Plastik: das Einfangen der Luft."

has he given in his transcription a truthful picture of what that strain would mean for each and every part of such bodies?"

Two difficulties appear: (1) nature herself is constantly varying her forms and departing from what seems to be her types, and (2) the artist often intentionally departs from nature.

Torsos, arms, and legs differ in relative lengths; heads, breasts, or hands, in shape; the distance between eyes varies from face to face. It is true that certain shapes and proportions are more pleasing than others, and that nature in her happiest, artistic moods—which are by no means frequent—suggests norms which the sculptor may turn into a canon of forms. But exceptional forms, whether beautiful or ugly, or highly individualized faces, of which Roman sculpture shows many, are not felt to be unnatural. But the line of the freakish must not be reached. Unlike painting, which is highly individualized and concerns itself with the less objective and permanent manifestations of nature, such as color and light, sculpture, narrow in its possible effects, is committed to what in nature suggests stability and type. The typical itself is an imaginative construct superimposed on the multitudinous and variational in nature. For this reason as well as for others it is difficult to apply to sculpture the test of truthful rendering of natural forms.

Intentional deviations on the part of the artist are common. Rodin's *exagération des formes* is only one striking instance. Accents are shifted; there are strange, forced unions and much slurring and dragging—all this for the sake of a reading, which instead of following quietly and faithfully the natural plastic values of the body, seeks one or all of these things: (1) individuality of interpretation and treatment, (2) added decorativeness, (3) increased emotional or imaginative intensity, (4) symbolism. Of (1)

little need be said: deforming such as is to be found in Ce-
zanne's fruit pieces, Van Gogh's landscapes, and sculptured
figures as far apart as those of Rodin, Epstein, and Archipenko is due not to defective vision, but to the stamping of
nature with the impress of sharply personal artistic technique and purpose.   Illustrations of (2) are as old as the
Reindeer Age and as new as the newest of the *art nouveau:*
proportions are altered—an unusual slenderness, for example, is given the human figure; there are decorative arrangements of torso, arms, and legs, and of animal forms; a group
of figures is reshaped and reduced to a flowing rhythmic pattern.   Manship, eclectic in his sculpture, as Davies is in his
painting, shows a fondness for such rhythmic modifications.
Great emotional intensity (3) may be gained by a boldness
which breaks through the natural, and simplifies and fal-
sifies forms.   Rodin's *Burghers of Calais*, Barnard's *Lincoln*, and Metzner's *Leidtragender* are examples.   Of (4)
symbolism it may be said that it creates or reshapes for the
sake of a meaning which is not nature's by right.   It suggests rather than imitates and inclines toward the imaginative and fantastic.   In Rodin's *Hell Gate* it parallels certain creations of the *Inferno*, which in turn is a distorted and
morally weighted vision of sin and punishment; in Rodin's
Wave, with its tumbling and crested group of figures, it
uses human forms slightly modified to express what is not
theirs to express.   In the Oscar Wilde Memorial in Paris
it assumes a bold and sinister creative form.

The Aesthetics of the Relief

Relief may be low, giving bodily surfaces with but a slight
rounding, or high, with bodies springing forth and almost
detached.   It may appear within the compactness of a
cameo, a coin, a plaque, or medallion; it may march as a
frieze straight along the walls of a building; it may wind it-

GLAZED POTTERY STATUE OF A LOHAN—CHINESE

self around a vase or be the circular pattern of a column, a fountain or a pulpit.

It is much less independent than sculpture in the round; it plays a decorative part in the elaboration of architectural effects, and is allied to painting in much of its technique.

A surface is to be filled and to be made decoratively attractive. This surface exists as the actual ground of stone or metal from which the plastic pattern or composition of figures and groups is to emerge. Another parallel surface must be construed imaginatively in the foreground, touching the projecting parts and keeping the whole scheme within an organized field of depth. A mixing of high and low relief, resulting in something like a relief map, is not acceptable to the eye; nor is a diagonal slanting away from the onlooker. Again, the figures are seen from one angle —there is no walking around them—and intervals are more obtrusively present than they are in sculpture in the round.

While sculpture in relief is capable of complex effects, it is best to take it first at its simplest. Suppose the flat circle of a coin to be almost completely filled with a head. Sharpness and neatness of line are to be looked for; so is very fine decorative detail. If a draped dancer is worked out of a rectangle, there are the additional problems of effective placing in relation to surrounding and intervening spaces, of rhythm, and of balanced coordination of lines. The impression given by such a dancer in relief is quite different from that of a dancer in the round, for the kinetic element so strong in sculpture—the muscular response to self-expressive force and vitality, as in Rodin, Maillol, and Mestrovic—is here only faintly present. It is true that in many reliefs—the metopes, the frieze of Halicarnassus, the Borghese Vase—struggle and violently gestured movement play a part, and that the feeling oneself into plunging horsemen or rapt dancers means a muscular as well as a motor response. But what impresses most is the compositional scheme in the metopes, and in the others the linear rhythms and the varied pattern.[8]   It is not from accident that dancers and processionals appear so often in reliefs, for they allow a rhythmic development and visual surprises in the way of constantly re-settling lines.   The rhythm may be slow and the design stately as in the Panathenaic procession in the Parthenon frieze where lines are repeated and varied slowly, or the movement may be fast and the curves bold as in a Maenad rout.   Many of the principles of composition in painting may be carried over to sculpture in relief, but the latter, while more complex and less dynamic than sculpture in the round, allows itself a looseness of design and often a rhythm which seems to go on unendingly.   Relatively simple and sharp in its technique, it cannot rival painting in effects of perspective and atmosphere; and it is true to the genius of all sculpture in its choice of organic life, leaving to one side many of the things the painter delights in.

The appreciation of sculpture in the round demands a geometrical imagination—a clear sense of lines and planes in their relations—and, in addition, a sense of all the straining and balanced forces at work in the linear and voluminar scheme.   This scheme presents itself with a completeness and palpableness which not every one can enjoy.

About a relief there is a suggestion of incompleteness, of pictorial allusiveness and lightness which makes it immediately pleasing.   Rodin, who in his *Thinker* and in his *L'homme qui marche* has caught the pure spirit of geometrical and kinetic sculpture, has in his *Paolo and Francesca*, *The Wave*, *Thought*, and *Springtime* given plastic form to the softer, slighter, more purely decorative spirit of the relief.

8 Movement is felt as rhythm rather than as force.   Lambeaux' *Human Passions* is an example of this.

Hicks, The Residence of David Twining in 1787

Dale Nichols, Home for the Holidays

RE-SEEING NATURE

PAINTING

Painting, like architecture, is a much wronged art, but there are different reasons for the misunderstanding. A building is useful, a picture is not. In its development as an art it has come to stand in looser and looser relations to life; if then it is misread, it must be because of other distorting influences.

The truth of the matter is this: a painting seems to represent something; the common man who is very much at home in the world he lives in—a world of familiar objects, singly or grouped, such as men and women, mountains, rivers, trees, houses, boats, flowers, animals, and of human feelings and relations to be accepted or suppressed—imagines that it is this world that the painter aims to give. He insists that everything in this world is worth putting on canvas, and holds that what is given must be a faithful copy. It is thus that he judges—and misjudges—painting. If he happens to be a paunchy profiteer sitting for his portrait, and the gift of seeing himself as he is has been mercifully withheld, he will put to the score of judicious and effective copying the colorful and subtly expressive organization which the great artist can create, even with a paunchy profiteer in front of him. Velasquez, court painter though he was of unpromising models, achieves a delicacy and mellowness of touch, a masterful and penetrative simplicity of design and execution which are peculiarly his own. Elinor Wylie's psychology in *Castilian* is probably wrong

> Velasquez took a pliant knife
> And scraped his palette clean;

He said, "I lead a dog's own life
Painting a king and queen.

.   .   .   .   .   .

"I am sick of painting painted hags
And bad ambiguous dwarves.

.   .   .   .   .   .

He squeezed out color like coins of gold
And color like drops of wine.

.   .   .   .   .   .

He burnt the rags in the fireplace
And leaned from the window high;
He said, "I like that gentleman's face
Who wears his cap awry."

This is the gentleman, there he stands,
Castilian, sombre-caped,
With arrogant eyes, and narrow hands
Miraculously shaped.

but the last phrase, *miraculously shaped*, hits the mark.
The man outside the window was merely a clue; the painter
saw what no chance passerby could see, and he reshaped what
he saw to a marvelous painting. Rembrandt, likewise, in
his portraits of himself, took common and grotesquely ugly
features, set them in mottled light and shade, suffused them
with soft reds, browns, and yellows, and gave them psychic
depth and organizational strength. He saw himself with
a painter's vision.

If painting is not to be misunderstood and its aesthetic
secret not to remain hidden, an answer must be found for
the questions: what is it that the painter means to give?
how is the world he sees different from the world the common man lives in? what does he work in and how does he
gain his effects? how does he carry his vision over into the
living world of art?

The World We Live In

By *the world we live in* I mean the world as it presents itself during any day's span to an ordinary, none too reflective consciousness. It is not the philosopher's world—puzzled over, unified, made over in the image of a subtle intellect which takes neither its objects nor the validity of its processes for granted. It is a world of time and space; an experience of sounds, colors, shapes in their changes and their spatial thereness; a world of practical relations. It is a challenge to purpose, is to be valued for its uses, and is to be reacted to in terms of feeling and thinking.

Part of this world the common man sees represented on canvas—not the changes and uses, but objects as they appear in space, and as they mean something to him practically, emotionally, imaginatively. Suppose him to be looking at the picture of a pastoral scene: timbered land in the background, barns, fields with cattle grazing, a small stream with clumps of bushes. He does not see it in terms of a *Farmer's Journal*—give him credit for that—but he does see it as true to life or not, as conforming or not, in shape, color, and general appearance, to what he is familiar with and knows to be so or so in actual life. He fails to discover here what has not been forced upon him in actual experience: delicate shadings of color, atmospheric effects, the character of lines, the relationships of masses. He is interested in the subject and expects verisimilitude and the same feelings a real pastoral scene would give him. He knows that a load of hay cannot be driven in this barn, but insists on it looking like a real barn, nevertheless. Or, in a different mood, he becomes sentimental over the quiet of a rural scene. Of either of these misreadings the casual visitor to museums is often guilty; occasionally they appear in art journals and histories of painting. It is they that provoke an equally false reading of painting as mere pattern.

THE PAINTER'S WORLD

The *Painter's World* is first of all a world of and for the eye. He is interested in objects only in so far as they can be painted, and they can be painted directly only in their visual aspects. What is called a barn has many more meanings than the visual one; and as a purely visual object it has many aspects, varying with the angle of the eye, the distance, the light. It is with these visual aspects that the painter concerns himself. Thus his world is, in the first instance, an impoverished one, made the poorer by being stripped of every purpose, by the ignoring of practical relations, and by the choice of this or that appearance, to the neglect of all others. But it is also, in a special sense, a richer world than that of the common observer, since the painter sees the slightest of shadings and varying reflections, and responds to subtle relationships of line. Passing along a street in New York, I once saw within the window-frame of an apartment a strikingly beautiful girl in a flowered dress, with a parrot perched on her arm. For a moment I saw with a painter's eye—the graceful pose, the curve of the arm and cheek, lights and shadows on the draperies and silk, harmonies and contrasts of color. But only for a moment, and with no power to give artistic expression to what I saw; and then I went off into a curiosity of imaginings and meanings which took me far away from the painter's world. I was back in the world we live in, wondering about the place in it of this bit of the exotic in such a uniformity of city walls and windows.

The painter has a delicately responsive eye, and is visually selective and re-creative. But his activity goes beyond this, for he unconsciously gives form to what he sees. He has a feeling for structural unity; where there is no such unity in nature he supplies it. In so structureless and amorphous a thing as the raging sea he feels the force-lines as he feels them in so completely formed a thing as a yacht. A haphazard collection of things—fruit piled, a crowd, plants and trees growing in a wild confusion—he endows with a common rhythmic or decorative life. More than that—he gives them unity of *meaning-in-form;* catching them up in a oneness of vision, of mood, of personality.

The Painter's Work

This the *Painter's World* is to be expressed. It is to be given the form and significance of art within the medium of the artist's choice, and through the disciplined resources and aims of painting. This is the *Painter's Work.* If this work is to be understood it must be studied in terms of the medium used, the devices employed, the goal aimed at, and the type chosen.

THE MEDIUM

The medium is color, extracted from various substances, mixed with different binding agencies—oil, chalk, water—and applied with the necessary preparation and finish to surfaces of many kinds—paper, canvas, stone, wood, porcelain, silk. The pigments used, the ways of mixing colors and glazing, the surfaces chosen are of great interest to the special student; they concern the aesthetician only in so far as they can be shown to make an aesthetic difference in the painting. This is not a hard task. The impressionists have proved that greater brilliancy may be gained by putting small patches of color side by side and allowing the eye to mix them than by the ordinary chemical mixing. An attempt might be made to have water color, pastel, porcelain painting, and oil painting on canvas render the same subject with an exact duplication of design and color values. Failure would result. Colors on porcelain have a peculiar transparency and flatness; pastels have a dry quality and do not favor, as oils do, rhythmic fluidity; in water colors it is difficult to gain plastic modeling. The spirit and general impression differ in the four cases. There is a charming allusiveness about water color; pastels are flaky or crumbly; porcelain painting is naive, with a direct and rather shallow sensuousness of color; painting in oil is subtle, with a depth and richness of its own.

The primary colors—red, green, and violet-blue, or yellow—and black and white variously mixed give the painter a wide range of possible effects in color. By mixing a color with that to the right or left of it in the spectrum he changes its *hue*; by adding to a color white or black he changes its *tint* and *shade*—thus there are light greens and dark greens, bright blues and dull blues; by getting a color at its purest, fullest, and intensest he gains *saturation*.

There are certain facts about colors and their combinations which are recognized in painting. They are set down here in a very sketchy way. Colors are spoken of as warm or cold, passionate or quiet, pleasing or less pleasing. The numerous studies that have been made in color preferences have proved inconclusive; so have attempts to affix to each color a definite emotional quality or suggested image. Early stages in racial and individual development show a liking for reds and yellows—two colors which are intense and inciting as browns and blues are not. All colors, however, have acquired a symbolism and an emotional suggestiveness which vary with custom, situation, and mood. Again, a color may be pleasing in one hue or shade and not in another; or its pleasingness may change with area or texture. Often colors seem to differ kinetically or in the suggestion of weight. There is a blazing energy about certain bright reds wholly lacking in pink. Orange seems heavier than lemon-yellow, and dark colors have more weight than light ones. Certain colors seem to recede, others to move toward us.

As for combinations, the first two facts to be noted are those of simultaneous and successive contrast. If two colors are put down in adjacent spaces they modify each other. Put red next to green, and it appears brighter, and the green acquires a yellowish tinge. Orange next to green appears reddish and makes the green appear bluish. In the combination black and yellow, the black appears violet or bluish; the yellow, light and faded. If green is set beside black the green is yellowish and the black gains a reddish tinge. In so far as the painter aims at visual impressions he must have an understanding of such facts of simultaneous contrast in the joining of his color patches and in the grounding or general setting of his colors. Successive contrast refers to the appearance, as an after image, of complementary colors—as of blue and orange or red and green blue.

LIGHT AND SHADE

In the visual world which the painter observes and reshapes there are accents other than those of color. Objects are in shadow or brilliantly illuminated, vivid or vague and wavering; evenly reflected or dappled; glinting with high lights or receding with edges of darkness. Such accents may be rendered by the use of blacks, greys, and whites alone; by the use of a single color in various shades and brilliancies, as of browns in a sepia print; or by an elaborate color scheme full of contrasts, and revealing in whites and blacks great wealth and depth of color.

LINE

An object shorn of its uses and presented as visual appearance strikes the eye not merely as a varied mass of color and a varying play of light and shade, but also as a system of lines. Lines have a direct natural expressiveness. Curves and jagged lines affect us differently; so do heavy and thin lines. Slanting lines have a motor quality which horizontals lack; the latter in turn are restful and relaxing in a way in which verticals are not. Delicacy, decisiveness, and emphasis all contribute to our pleasure in a line; so does its varied life in space. This life, in both single lines and their combinations, must be free and rhythmic. Simple geometrical schemes cannot be used widely in painting as they can be in architecture. Thus a line which is a straight horizontal and then turns into a half circle whose diameter is of equal length may be used effectively in a repetitional decorative pattern of a building, but seems too mechanical in painting.

Lines in our visual experience are edges of surfaces, and these surfaces are marked off by differences of color or texture. In either case there may be a sharp break or a partially defined transition. We are not ordinarily conscious of the line as something independent. It has become more and more the practice of modern painters to delimit in terms of color—to define line and linear relations as color—and of light and shade. This means that a black and white copy of a Cézanne or Renoir amounts not merely to a sacrifice of color effects, on which they lean heavily, but to a loss of, at least, part of their linear scheme.

The edging that lines give to surfaces is not only one at right angles to the eye, it is carried back from the eye at different angles into deep space. This receding expressiveness of lines forms part of the problem of perspective; color gradations and differences of shading are the other parts.

Lines also act as clues to the visual meaning of objects; this is their representational expressiveness. A clever draughtsman like Busch can put down a few whirls, dashes, and sweeping lines and make them call forth supplementary relational effort on our part—and behold, the few linear clues become comic figures of men and women. In like manner a painter can make a few color patches or lines visually expressive of objects. We need only step in very close to a painting to discover this *expressive illusion;* what in the distance seemed a complete and definitely worked out object now turns out to be nothing but bits of color and line— hints we had perceptually completed. This is merely one phase of a technique of illusion to which painting is committed in putting the semblance of a tri-dimensional, visual world on a flat surface and seeking to render within its narrower range and slenderer resources the complexities of color, light, and line which the world about us offers. This very fact forces imitation to become in part a creative reshaping. But what is back of such reshaped likenesses? What is the painter's aim in working in a special medium and in using skilfully the technical devices of his art?

THE GOAL AIMED AT

A plausible but false answer would be this: the painter is aiming at the illusion of a perfect copy of some natural object. What nature accomplishes so easily, he seeks to match, color for color, line for line—his ambition roused and his ingenuity challenged and tested by the difficulties of his task. A portrait painter in front of his sitter and a landscape painter who has set up his easel in a field seem to be doing that. But it has been shown that the artist, even before he has put brush to canvas, has stepped out of the world we live in into a world of his own—a world more purely visual, and more subtle and varied in its values of color and line. Where we see blacks he may see purples; what to us is mere expanse, is to him variegated texture. Even if he were to copy what he sees, we should be far from admitting it to be a likeness of objects as we know and see them. The impressionists were criticized for what was held to be a lurid, unnatural coloring.   But the painter does not copy literally the object he sees.   He modifies it, partly from necessity and partly from choice.   The nature and the resources of his medium make a paralleling of line and color values impossible.   There is also a voluntary modifying of what he sees: a rearrangement of lines, an intensifying of contrasts or a soft blending, new accents of light and shade, a new massing of effects.   Back of this rearrangement are the transforming influences of a personal vision.   When distortion has a place in this vision, as in El Greco or Cézanne, it is often mistakenly read as a physical flaw in seeing or as some mental twist—as copying still, but under a fatal handicap.

If imitation is to be rejected as the painter's goal, what is it he aims at?   It is what has for want of a better name been called *pictorial form*.   The secret of the aesthetic value of a painting lies not in the verisimilitude of its colors and lines—its representational accuracy and lifelikeness—but in a certain creatively personal organization.

The painter's response to what is about him has been shown to be one of seeing objects as shapes, and of feeling himself into the subtle relationships which visually mark such shapes.   Thus he sees a chair, not as a thing in common use, but as a system of lines and planes in color.   To have this painter's vision is not yet to be a painter.   The task remains of using the materials of life—its colors and forms —as starting-points for the creation, on canvas or something else suitable and by means of brush and pigment skilfully handled, of a new and significant unity, representational and intensely personal, which may be called *pictorial form*.

What is this pictorial form and how is it gained?

At the very outset there is this difficulty: pictorial form is in its organized variety and meaning one and indivisible, and yet cannot be discussed except in terms of a seriatim

analysis of what has a part in its creation—artistic idea
and subject, design with all its special values, and representational and imaginative factors.

The matter may be put to the test in this fashion. In a
black and white copy of a painting one important part of its
aesthetic value—color—has dropped out; there remain the
compositional unity of mass and line, and the representational values. Turn the black and white copy upside down,
you have altered the perspective, destroyed the compositional scheme, and broken down the relation between the
subject of the painting and the design. Such a piecemeal
elimination of elements of aesthetic effect might incline to
the belief that what is called a picture is a subject arranged
in a linear scheme, with values of mass, aerial perspective,
and color added. Nothing could be farther from the truth.
Rather is the subject seen as personal vision, emotionally
and imaginatively touched, and as design—the colors and
lines at once play their part in relating, setting off, and individualizing planes; and the lines have motor, decorative,
and emotional expressiveness. The aesthetic meaning of the
picture lies in all these together—and in none of them separately. Such a word of caution ought to precede a seriatim
analysis.

PICTORIAL FORM

A. ARTISTIC IDEA AND SUBJECT: In choice of subject
the painter has much greater freedom than the sculptor.
Inanimate nature is moved within the field of his choice;
so are complex groupings; so are incidents varied in detail
and appeal. All this is beyond the interest and the powers
of sculpture in the round; and even sculpture in relief, pictorial in inspiration and technique, falls short of painting.

It is usual to divide painting, according to its choice of
subject, into the following classes: (1) landscape, (2) still

life, (3) genre, (4) historical, (5) portrait, (6) figure. Of these the first gives a fragment of the appearance and life of nature; the second offers, with a frank interest in their *thereness*, a few objects grouped in a simple way—a dish of fruit, swords and armor, a side of beef, game birds and fish, a section of a room. In the others the interest is shifted to the human side of life. Genre painting offers groupings, incidents, actions not as they occur or have occurred, but as they reveal again and again some humanly significant trait or phase or interest in the recurrent and variational drama of human life. The Interiors of de Hooch, *Boys Eating Melons* by Murillo, *The Night Watch* by Rembrandt, *Kermess* by Tenier, *Peasants Dancing* by Breughel the Elder, court life depicted by Watteau and Fragonard, Manet's *Races at Longchamps* and *Music in the Tuilleries*, Renoir's *Piano Lesson* and *A Cup of Chocolate*, and Cézanne's *Card Players* are examples. In historical painting, secular and religious, there is a definite orientation within the stream of life. This thing has occurred at such and such a time and in such and such a place. The Adoration of the Magi, the Marriage at Cana, Christ in the Temple, the Last Supper, the Crucifixion and the Transfiguration were used again and again by the Italian painters; Rubens, Delacroix, Gericault, and Gerard glorified in more or less monumental style court and battle scenes.

Subjects differ in moral, imaginative, emotional, and pictorial value. Millet's *Angelus* has a moral quality which Jordaens' drinking scenes and Manet's *Bon Bock* lack; there is more for the imagination in the mountains or the sea than there is in an eighteenth century garden; a moorland is depressing; a drug fiend arouses disgust; a dance is exhilarating; the pictorial value of a banquet is great because of the opportunity for variegated grouping, effective massing, striking accents in color, splendid detail work.

Painting is in part a representational art, with the visual

aspects of nature for its material. An attempt to do away with subject must remain a questionable step. The impressionist motto "any subject will do" and the reduction of painting to pattern or music by moderns like Russell or Kandinsky mean a distrust of alien interference with the work of the painter. It is easy to lean too heavily on the sentimental, religious, and historical values of an incident, to the neglect of all else. This is a common misreading of pictures. It can best be avoided by passing from the commission given the painter to the subject, from the subject to the *artistic idea* he seeks to express, and from the artistic idea to its realization through paint. An artist is given the task of painting the walls of a church or doing a portrait. In the former case he may be allowed to make his choice from a range of suitable biblical incidents or he may be set a very definite task—Italian church painters were often limited in that way—in the latter case he must paint this or that man. But when we pass beyond the commission we find that the subject interests the painter as subject in so far as it is bound up with some general human value—splendor, grandeur, pathos, tragedy, delicate charm. In this sense the subject even of an historical painting is timeless. The Pieta is an eternal tragedy. The transition from subject to artistic idea is through the individual interpretation the painter gives his subject. Even if the whole matter of his technique is set aside, a personal vision remains. Leonardo's *Mona Lisa*, Titian's *Man with the Glove*, Van Dyck's *Charles the First*, Velasquez' Infantas, Rembrandt's self-portraits, Whistler's *Carlyle* all show quietly posed bodies and heads, and character expressed in pose, line, and color. It matters little who the originals were or whether they were faithfully represented. All these pictures are personal, sharply individualized visions. The fanatic, twisted spirituality of some of El Greco's figures contrasts with the sweet and shallow complacency of most of Raphael's Madonnas, and the

naiveté of the early Germans.   The nude figure as material
for painting reveals a personal influence.   The muscular
massiveness of Michelangelo's nudes is quite as far removed
from the animalism, heavy and soft, of those of Rubens
as it is from the immature forms chosen by a Boucher or a
Fragonard, the decorative modifications of v. Marées or
Davies, the full blooded naturalism of Zorn, and the angular
figures of Hodler.   It is not a question of models.   It is
true that Rubens in a letter refers to the large, flabby women
he was forced to use as models.   But there are deeper influences.   In none of these men is there an actual copying
of the model; in each case the human body as it is painted reflects an artistic idea, and back of that idea there is a personally colored vision, influenced in part by the cultural setting.[1]   The difference between subject and artistic idea may
be driven home by two illustrations, one from sculpture and
one from painting.   Mussolini is the subject of a bust by
Wildt, but there is hardly a suggestion of likeness there.   To
the artist Mussolini was a symbol of strength, and in true
expressionistic fashion he has built that idea into his medium;
he has stretched the lines, broadened the masses and tensed
the features with that in view.   In El Greco's *Laocoon* the
subject is a tragic incident, but it is artistically fashioned
along decorative lines.

In a painting in which pictorial form has been achieved
subject and artistic idea have a legitimate place, but the
subject is not allowed a separate and distracting life, and
the artistic idea is reflected in an organized variety of line,
mass, color, and light.

B.   DESIGN: A picture viewed merely as a framed section of canvas must have unity in the sense of an integration
of parts.   This unity is called design; and the manner of
gaining it, composition.

[1] Hausenstein has shown in an instructive way the personal and cultural
mutations in the use of the nude figure.

(1) *Pattern:* The first step toward an understanding of design is to look for a system of relationships which can be enclosed in a simple geometrical figure such as a circle, a triangle, an oblong. These general patterns keep eye and interest from sliding into space. To them may be added the cross, horizontal or tilted, and the diagonal, straight or curved, as main organizing lines in a picture. Examples are: of the circle, Andrea Solario's *Madonna and Child* in the Louvre; of the triangle, Raphael's *Madonna del Prato;* of the oblong, Gainsborough's *A Morning Walk;* of a triangle set on a rectangle, the *Sistine Madonna;* of the half-cross, Hobbema's roads with tall trees; of the diagonal, Rubens's *Descent from the Cross* and many of the slanting designs of Degas.

There is danger in making such general patterns excessively geometrical. A sympathetic study of pictures reveals a great variety of combinations, ranging from an arc above a rectangle, as in del Sarto's *The Last Supper,* to a circle filled with diversely slanting lines, as in Rubens's *The Rape of the Daughters of Leucippus.*

Design is a matter not only of holding the parts of a picture within a general pattern, but of divided spaces and patterned relationships within that scheme. In a figure study there is first of all the question as to how, with reference to the vertical and horizontal limits of the frame, the body is to be posed—straight up and down, in the middle, as in Gainsborough's *Blue Boy,* slightly tilted as in Cézanne's *Peasant,* near the right as in Whistler's portrait of his mother. There are two other problems: how is the figure to be drawn and the space it contains to be filled and articulated? and how is the space surrounding it to be treated? Is that surrounding space to be given as flat surface, contrasted, homogeneous, and either neutral as black or grey, or with the independent, directly pleasing effect of an expanse of gold or silver? Or is it to appear as deep space, in which the figure is placed or out of which it seems to step? Is it to remain unaccented, as mere unvaried background and is it to be unfilled—without objects of varying depth and cubic individuality? Is this surrounding space, whether flat or deep, decoratively or cubically accented or not, to be independent of the figure and its design? These questions, here as well as in group painting, can be given only this answer: the background is an integral part of the pictorial form and the design; the treatment ought to depend on the form intended and the artistic idea the painter seeks to express. In Renoir there is often a delicately varied decorative elaboration which abolishes the background as such and moves all space within one scheme of color, line, and light. Matisse purposely gives the impression of flat decorative patterning, and shows little interest in deep space. Cézanne does not aim at such effects; either the background is left almost neutral, as in some of his portraits, with the full solidity and weight of his painting thrown into the face or the figure, or it is filled, not decoratively as in Renoir but with part of the plastic meaning of the picture. In the *Bathers* by Cézanne, which Cheney in his *Primer of Modern Art* has for different purposes set by the side of Courbet's *Bathers*, there is no background, properly speaking. Trees and foliage are not a flat pattern, but in light and shade and line they are at one with the nude figures; and this oneness is essential to the meaning of the picture. In Courbet's painting we are conscious of two figures in the foreground and of a photographically rendered receding forest as a setting. The interest is sharply focussed; the design is faulty in its looseness. In Cézanne's *Bathers* there is no setting—man and nature are one. Formally this unification is gained by soft indecisive lines and shadows in the nudes to parallel the broad indecisive masses of foliage. Van Gogh, again, counts on his flaming and linearly agitated backgrounds to convey part of the meaning of his pictures. It follows from all this that extreme caution is necessary in appraisals of paintings. If moderns like Matisse, Soutine, Pechstein, Marc, and Walt Kuhn seem to deal arbitrarily with deep space and awkwardly with perspective, they must not be condemned hastily; their purpose must be looked for and tested in terms of an original and satisfying design.

When we pass from backgrounds to the total space occupied by the objects rendered we discover various orderly sub-divisions and patterns. One of the commonest is a triple arrangement—a central mass flanked on either side. In Titian's *Assumption* there is the unusual integration of three levels.[2] In Leonardo's *Last Supper* the *three-motif* is indicated in the three windows and is carried over into the grouping by threes of what would otherwise have been an uninteresting extension. In *The Virgin and St. Anne* by Quentin Matsys there are three arches and at the lower part of each arch two figures whose heads cut into the space of light to about the same height. Often architectural effects are used in such patterning of space.

Space-patterning may be followed into other details of a picture. Recurrent lines or patches, ratios of division similar to those in architecture, rhythmic units of light and color, lines continuous, linked or abruptly broken—all this may be taken as part of the design. It is better, however, to take pattern as a general compositional arrangement, and to discuss separately certain organizational features as part of the design and as ultimately factors in the pictorial form.

(2) *Relationships of Line and of Mass:* A study of paintings reveals a relational use of lines little short of infinite variety. Long or short, horizontal, diagonal or vertical, broad or thin, straight or curved, single or massed lines help to carry and express the painter's meaning. Their value lies far beyond the mere building up of an object and the marking of its contours. In their own right,

2 Cf. the analysis in Barnes, *The Art in Painting.*

and in their tranquil or sweeping interrelationships they serve to give motor, decorative, emotional, and dynamic value and individuality to a picture.   They may be organized into sequences—a curve or a short broken line may appear with an intriguing orderliness in the different parts of a painting.

Sequence may also be found in masses.   What has been called measure harmony is either simple repetition of a space in its bulk or the carrying of a ratio through masses of different sizes.

(3)   *Relationships of Color:* It is well to recall certain things about color.   The fact that we speak of *sky blue, sea green, flesh color* shows that we think of color in relation to the natural appearance of objects to the eye.   Some colors we find more pleasing than others.   We distinguish and respond differently to the various shades and hues of a color.   Adjectives like *gay, bright, heavy, warm, cool* are applied to colors.   We know that colors when set side by side modify each other.   We speak of contrasts and harmonies; and find certain combinations pleasing, others jarring.

All this is of importance in the study of painting in so far as an attempt is made to read the colors of a picture in their organizational unity—in their relation to the pictorial form.   In modern painting especially color rather than line is what defines and gives unity to a picture.   Little is gained by taking the marvelous light blue of Renoir's *A Cup of Chocolate* or the patches of deeper blue in his landscapes, the subdued and mellow browns and yellows of Rembrandt, the reddish yellow and bright green of Kisling, and the dark and dull greens of Rousseau *le douanier* or the reddish flesh color of Renoir's last period and to respond to them in isolation.   Nor will simple matching of them with adjoining colors mean much.   Painters choose colors neither arbitrarily nor in the spirit of the interior decorator.   Rembrandt, Renoir, Soutine, Kisling, Kandinsky, Pascin have

Above,
CÉZANNE,
LAND-
SCAPE;

below,
MONET,
POPLARS

their own individual color ranges.   This is not because they could not paint others or combine in a different way—what it means is that these colors thus combined seemed to them the best means to what they wished to express.   A black and white copy of Renoir is blotchy and thoroughly unsatisfying; the larger part of the meaning has escaped.   To show how intimately color expresses what a painting really is, the simple experiment of transposing may be used.   Copy Soutine's pictures but put blues and whites in the place of the reds and deep yellows, and most of the wild vigor has disappeared.   Put a color closer to flesh values on Kisling's nudes or transpose Picasso's emaciated *Man in Blue* to any other color or even to a different shade of blue, and the painter would at once disavow the new picture, not as necessarily less pleasing but as utterly alien to his meaning. Every color then is to be studied in relation not only to its neighbors, as harmonizing or contrasting, but to the pictorial form and its details.   There may be a design of many contrasts, phrases, accents, and sequences of color or there may be a delicately graded tonal scheme of one or two colors. It is to be regarded, too, in its plastic and structural use; in the way it may be made to catch and hold light; in its relation to balance and to rhythm; and as it affects and is affected by texture.

(4) *Light and Shade; Light and Dark:* Nature offers objects in color set at varying distances and angles from the eye.   The colors themselves are of lighter and darker shades; and the surfaces absorb and reflect light in different degrees.   Seldom is the illumination uniform over a surface of even small size—there are high lights and shadows. Outdoors it is relative also to the time of the day and the season.   With diminished light, color disappears, and what remains is a mass of greys and blacks.

The painter in his work has at his disposal white and black with their scale of greyish mixtures; or he may render the effects of light and shadow by mixing either white or black or grey with any of the colors, or color with color—striking, for example, the high note of orange in a reddish brown scheme.   His means are much simpler than those of nature, and his range of effects, narrower.   He may in a landscape seek to retain the ratios of nature, keeping, at least, the accent and measure in the contrasted surfaces of a tree that is partly in light and partly in shade when he cannot duplicate the full intensity of either, and giving their proper values to objects differently set and related in deep space.   Or he may disregard these ratios altogether and strike out boldly for an original design, quite remote from what nature offers in graded and contrasted effects.

The neutral scale—white, grey, and black—is not used much by modern painters.   Such neutrality has been taken away even from backgrounds of portraits.   It was the impressionists who saw color in shadows; it was Renoir and Cézanne who in different ways used patches of dark and light color to give solidity, variety, and rhythmic integrity to their compositions.

There are many technical uses of light in a picture.   In an interior light may be shown as striking objects from one point, a candle or a lamp, and the aim may be to give the reflections on the walls, the objects with their edges and spots of light and the deepening shadows about.   Or there may be an even, diffused light, revealing only the natural accents of the various things in the room.   There may be a culminating point of light, not necessarily in the centre of the picture, with a tonal scheme of gradually darkened color.   Delicacy of light may be aimed at, as in Corot, or the contrast between high light and depth of shadow, as in Rembrandt.   It is hardly the task of aesthetics to go into the detail of these many uses; it is the duty of an appreciative critic of any painter to study carefully the peculiar light and shade effects in his work—to see whether he sets a light patch next to a dark one or puts a transitional value between; to what extent he is responsive to the density of the atmosphere and its effect on surfaces; in what ways he uses light structurally, plastically, and rhythmically. But it is the task of the aesthetician to discover whether the lights and shadows in a picture have a patterned relation to the design, and whether they, like everything else, contribute to the pictorial form. Whether or not the colors are true to nature is unimportant; what really matters is the aim of the artist and the form he has selected and created.

(5) *Texture:* When woven stuffs are compared in point of texture, they are spoken of as rough or smooth, compact or loose, hard or soft, glossy or dull, thin or heavy in effect. All this may with only a slight stretching of words be applied to painting, for, at least, a part of the aesthetic meaning of a picture is to be found in texture.

Roughness may be gained mechanically by the thick, irregular use of spots or ridges of paint; smoothness, by an even thickness spread over the picture. The pointillists, Van Gogh, and painters like Prendergast or Soutine use the former method; Raphael is a good example of the second. Only a simple use of large color areas makes possible the latter; any aim at complex effects, any painting of one bit of color over another, interferes with evenness of surface. But smoothness or roughness is not a matter merely of what you get by running your hand over a picture. Color may be evenly applied, and yet the impression may be of roughness. In such cases the impression is given partly by abruptness and shortness in the brushwork, partly by bold contrasts in color and sharp temporary halts in the linear patterns. In this sense much of the work of Matisse, decoratively flat from the point of view of perspective, is rough in texture. Flowing brushwork and fluency of color and line, on the contrary, suggest smoothness.

Compactness and looseness may be caught in the contrast

between the earlier and later Manet or Renoir. It is easy
to see in a picture, less easy to explain. A Chardin still life
is neat, persuasively complete in color and drawing, firm
and compact in texture. A still life by Cézanne shows
greater freedom in the handling of paint, strong contrasts,
and a less obvious togetherness. Flesh as Rubens and Renoir came to paint it was not the tightly drawn uniform surface it was in some of the early Italian and German painting,
nor yet a tinted, non-porous thing like porcelain; rather was
it suffused with light, individualized through lights and
shades, and made arresting, intriguing, and living by varied
coloring. The difference between a Van Eyck or a Holbein
and a Rembrandt—an Utrillo and a Monet or Seurat—a
David or a Marie Laurencin is between a knot tightly or
loosely drawn. In the second of each pair of artists the
form is there, but it is not pulled tight; if there is detail, it
does not function neatly and sharply—there is a loose,
swinging technique.

Hardness or softness may be gained in many ways.
Sharp lines, clear-cut detail, large areas of certain uniform
colors or of unrelieved blacks or greys make a picture hard.
Delicately drawn, finely varied, wavering, rhythmically related lines, tonal arrangements of color, and shimmering
luminosities give the impression of softness. Holbein, Courbet, Leibl, Rousseau le douanier, Picasso, and Kisling are
hard; Corot, Monet, Whistler, and Renoir are soft.

Allowance must be made in any reference to glossiness
and dulness for the finish of the surface, and also whether
time has either softened or destroyed in part an original
brilliancy of coloring. Pigments, oils and other binding
materials, and varnish differ greatly in their effect on the
maturing or weathering of a picture. But after allowance has been made for this mechanical influence, there is
an intentional shininess or dulness of surface to be reckoned
with.

A picture may seem thin, flat or thick, heavy, with body to it. The mural painting of Puvis de Chavannes is thin and flat, so is the *Man in Blue* by Picasso. Certain shades —light blue or yellow—favor flatness; so do large, uniform masses of color. Wherever color is broken up, or light, or line; wherever there is bold, emphatic brushwork and structural use of perspective, there a picture has substance and depth.

(6) *Balance:* Balanced arrangement in a picture is a matter of equivalence of parts. The equivalence may be horizontal, diagonal, or vertical; it may be kinetic—weight and pull—or one of interest arrested, held, satisfied. Lateral balance is the simplest; there the idea of a stick and a fulcrum can be easily applied. The obvious arrangement would be to have the fulcrum in the middle, with equal weight on either side. Simple as it is, it is avoided by painters. If they give a figure study, they move the figure slightly to the right or left; and they get an intriguing variety by using vertical and diagonal equivalence as well. Suppose a picture is cut horizontally in strips an inch wide. For every strip the fulcrum would be differently placed. This would hold also of vertical and horizontal strips. Paste four or five of these strips together, and the question of balance becomes a complicated one.

Filled space has more weight than unfilled space; and certain colors are weightier than others. A painter gives a lateral view of a man seated. To put the axis of the upper part of his body in the middle of the picture would result in poor balance: the lines of the chair and the horizontals of his thighs and the greater mass of color would weigh down the right or left. This must be allowed for by shifting the figure to one side. Again, unless there is some compensating touch of color in the upper half of the picture, there would be too little weight there for a satisfactory balance.

Lines have kinetic value, and this value enters into the problem of balance. A picture with many parallel lines all strongly slanted must, if it is to satisfy as design, offer something to counterbalance their leaning and thrust. But painting shows less strongly kinetic balance than architecture or sculpture. Colors and lines, as they fill space and subdivide it, appeal to *interest;* their meaning is not one merely of movement and force and a balanced kinetic scheme. This interest is one of stress and arrested attention. What holds us may be either some striking detail of color or line, some accent in the artist's work, or something psychic. Thus a very small patch of bright color may balance a large expanse of color less bright. The small oval of a face balances because of its psychic appeal the larger but less arresting and significant area of a cloak or dress. In poor painting there is often a lack of correlation between these two sources and types of interest—one or the other may easily be so handled as to yield nothing of value. A good painter skilfully combines them. In one of Pascin's pictures there is to the left the figure of a small boy—an object of direct psychic appeal, charmingly drawn, slight, delicate and soft in color; on the right there is decorative compensation in a palette-like splash of many colors.

(7) *Rhythm:* Rhythm in painting is variational orderliness felt as movement. It involves (1) *recurring accents and stresses of line, mass, color, and light and shade;* (2) *suggestion of movement;* (3) *fluency of design.*

Painting has been called a space art and as such has been held to be limited to the rendering of objects coexisting in space at one moment of time. Such a theory, if held to too closely, may lead to serious errors. It overlooks the time element in the appreciation of a painting, and it fails to see that the painter can by various devices render on his canvas two or more successive moments.

We do not rest satisfied with the first general impression a picture gives as a whole. Our eyes travel from one part to another, they explore and relate. Our interest shifts and stresses. There is a time element in this organizational response through which we make a picture our own. The painter may boldly step beyond the limit set him, as Watteau does when he gives successive moments in the procession of life, or he may choose a pictorial form and pattern design which enlist strongly our relating and supplementing activities, perceptual, motor, and imaginative, with the result that space turns to movement. This is the use of rhythm in painting. Rhythm naturally suggests music or poetry —arts which give it directly and depend on it strongly for many of their effects. But it may be made use of by the architect in the variational orderliness of his marching patterns, by the sculptor in the interrelationships and projections and fallings away of his lines and masses, and by the painter.

(1) One of the sources of rhythmic quality in paintings is a recurrent stress of line or color, comparable to the repeated ins and outs of a pattern. The accent may be one of size or of brightness or of shape or of interested appeal. There is a strong triple rhythm in Leonardo's *The Last Supper*. In Caravaggio's *The Entombment* there is a group of five men and women, two of whom support the limp body of Christ. The general pattern is an arc beginning at the upper left of the picture and pulling the interest down irresistibly to the head of Christ. The six ovals show an orderly difference of slant and of the following patterned arrangement: single, double, double, single.

(2) A second source of rhythm is strongly suggested movement, quick or slow, slight or forceful, striking or subdued. Here rhythm may easily come in conflict with balance. There is an unbalanced rhythmic movement to the right in Guido Reni's *Aurora*. The pull upward in Hod-

ler's group *Concord* is very strong; Hobbema's tree-lined roads, quite as uncompromising in their use of verticals, give a quieter and slighter movement. Rhythm may be gained by a gradual lessening of shades or by the hardly noticeable movement from white to black or from light to dark color through all the values of greys and tints, or shades of the color.

(3) A third source of rhythm is fluency of design, gained by an *interflow* and *interglow* of parts. An object or any part of the sensuous image of that object is robbed of its static individuality and independence, and is distorted, if necessary, in order to give the impression of a fluctuant scheme of color and mass. Distortion of this sort is most violent in painters like Marc, Kokoschka, and Soutine, whose pictures illustrate rhythm of the second and third types. Other, less extreme examples are El Greco's *Laocoon*, Cézanne's *Bathers* and many of Renoir's paintings. Rhythmic fluency as it modifies natural forms in Renoir's *Bathers* has been well analyzed by Barnes in *The Art in Painting*. One of the largest of the Renoir canvases in the Barnes Foundation Collection, *La Promenade*, is a brilliant example of how light and shade may be made to carry rhythms throughout a picture, and soften and etherealize the hard and unattractive fashion in dress of the nineties.

c. PERSONAL VISION AND ECSTASY: Painting, we have seen, is not merely a matter of subject and technical detail. It is personal throughout. Back of the subject is the artistic idea, which is a personal vision, and which, in its embodiment in the pictorial form, affects the execution at all points, through all the detail of the design.

What we are concerned with here is the recognition of this personal element as it appears vitally in the pictorial form.

Vision and *ecstasy* are terms applicable most directly to poetry. It is in the appreciation of poetry that they are best explained. Here they may be sketchily marked as a sharp and individual way of seeing, interpreting, and rendering through paint; and a heightened emotional and imaginative responsiveness, personal, intense, and resonant, which finds expression in the work of the artist and appeals through its embodiment to the imagination and the feelings of the onlooker.

Unfortunately there is a less liberal attitude towards the personal in painting than there is in poetry. It is considered the less subjective art. Individual variations in technique are accepted and studied, but highly individual interpretations in the large and renderings are either ignored or distrusted. A large measure of this distrust may be traced back to the idea that painting ought to copy accurately natural appearances or to improve on them in socially acceptable standardized ways. But why should the painter not be himself—project his personally colored vision and be carried on its crest to ecstatic rendering? If he can make himself worthwhile in giving body to his vision and can give and evoke a vibrational quality of feeling—what else can be asked of him? Good poetry need not be of one pattern or of one voice or of one mind. Good painting ought not to be forced into one formula. Let the painter be honest and as aggressively personal as he need be, let his work be regarded sympathetically and critically. If he has little to express, he will soon find his level as a faddist; if he has created new imaginative and emotional designs and values, he ought to be welcomed in the realm of an art which has room for many eyes, many minds, and many methods.

POETRY

All definitions of poetry suffer from one or the other of two vices: either they are very simple—like Wordsworth's "emotion recollected in tranquillity"—and then they fall short of an art which is various in its types and structures, various also in its appeal and its music, and subtle in its shaping; or they seek to give in compact form the complex meaning of poetry, and then they seem stiff and indecisive, for there is still the problem of how much stress is to be put on each of the several qualities.

Of these two vices I shall avoid the first. At the risk of a pedantic and congested use of words I offer this formula:—*Poetry, in an enraptured, visional spirit and within a metrically ordered, articulated, and rounded scheme, conveys images, moods, and ideas by means of language that is rhythmical and musical, decoratively patterned, vivid, vibrant, and revelational.* All that can be claimed for it is that it is a starting place; it carries in convenient form what to me are the essentials of poetry. What is meant by them and how they are related must be left to further analysis.

The Medium

The medium of poetry is language. Whatever else he may be, a poet is first of all a worker in words. But so is the prose writer; so is he who makes use of living, meaningful speech. Words singly or in combination are symbols of meanings. They represent man's world as he itemizes its appearances; as he reflects on it and responds to it emotionally. Much of this world he shares with his fellows as an experience or as a matter of give and take; he is in need, therefore, of the standardized currency of common speech. Through language he becomes articulate and communicative. Of this commonly used language it may be said that it is a makeshift standardizing; it is largely arbitrary in its symbolism; and it is pointed at the practical. It is makeshift in the sense that a word may blanket experiences which must, as from man to man, be different and may serve as a superficial marker for many dissimilar objects and images. Thus *love* means many things to many persons; and *river* might be visualized in any one of many ways. The symbolism is arbitrary, for words are not intrinsically related to what they stand for. To this there are exceptions. Words like *hum, buzz, murmuring, swish, bubble* are a vocal evocation of sounds; *river, flumen, fleuve* give directly the slow flowing of the river in a way in which *potamos* or the short, sharp *Fluss* does not. *Gebirge* has about it an architectural appropriateness which *mountains* with its falling rhythm lacks.[1] There are emotional evocations in words like *melancholy, merriment, thrilled, monotone.* Some words are harsh and hard; others soft and insinuating; some are sharp and quick, others, slow and expansive. Again, language becomes more practical-minded as it becomes efficient in labelling and recording. The mark left by picture-thought has grown dim. Gone are the warmth and color from common speech; with the exception of its imaginative slang and forceful profanity, it is drab, abstractly discursive—a cold saving logic or a wasteful inartistic use of words.

The consciously creative, artistic impulse seizes upon language as it seizes upon marble, color, and sound, and reshapes it to artistic prose. Vividness is sought in the words; balance, in sentence-structure; variety, in rhythmic sequences; a personal and imaginative touch, in the phrasing.

---

[1] Whoever is tempted to take such analogies too seriously ought to read Aldous Huxley's burlesque remarks on the Etruscan language.

We are no longer to look through language as we might through a window pane; we are to become arrestingly conscious of a beauty and worthwhileness in the medium itself.

Poetry is a further step in such reshaping. It weaves a rhythmic magic of words. But there is more to it than this. In poetry the world is sensuously embodied in a slighter degree than in painting. Beyond the tone-color and music of words is something else to be reached and to be made vivid and unforgetable. To get more than a faint euphony from the word *daffodil* we must pass from the arbitrary symbol to a memory image of the flower—we must imaginatively recapture an experience. This is what the poet is constantly doing. Imparting to his medium new values of music and word magic, he uses it in this sense also: of projecting through it feelings caught in their fleetingness, and personally colored ideas and visual images. Not only does each poet have a form and music of his own; he also has a world of his own which he builds into his verse, using words as symbols. To see rippling waves under the image of laughter; to speak of *the still-closing waters;* or of music *climbing the long grey stairways of the sky* or of night as *star-shouldered* means more than the coining of unforgetable phrases or, as the literal-minded would have it, an imaginative mauling of language. These phrases, of the Greek, the Elizabethan, the Imagist, the ultra-modern, one and all are bold intermittent flashes of an inner vision of a world individually built, enriched for the eye, and emotionally deepened.

There is a great contrast between what these words— *cloud, West Wind, skylark, autumn, sea*—mean to any imaginative individual and what they are to a Shelley, a Wordsworth, a Verlaine, a Swinburne—in imagery, rhythm, and mood. What a picture spray there is in Shelley's *To a Skylark;* how the melancholy of autumn is voiced in the very music of Verlaine's *Chanson d'Automne;* and how the

tumultuous and encroaching life of the sea is caught in
Swinburne's lines

Inland still at her own wild will swells, rolls, and revels the
surging sea.

Even to what in nature is fixed in form and assertive in
color—birds, trees, flowers, stars—the poet responds in an
intensely personal and inspirational way. Of this striking
examples are Wheelock's *The Fish-Hawk*, Aldington's *The
Poplar*, Sara Teasdale's *The Tree* and *Stars*, Oppenheim's
Lilac Magic.

Here lies the aesthetic meaning of poetry: in this vivid
projection of what might be called a soul's intimate vision
and supreme venture in words evocative and revelational.
The revelation differs in the three great types of poetry.
The lyric—its very name suggestive of song—reveals in
emotionally vibrant language a mood, a caprice, a vision.
The epic, with a personal touch and in a welcoming, other-
minded spirit, unfolds a world of characters and events.
The drama lives sympathetically within the will and heart
of men and women, gives their inner life, and offers a personal reading of its clashes, feelings, and meanings. But
whatever the type, we are lovers of poetry only in so far as
we can share in the vision as well as become attuned to the
music and sensitive to the magic of words.

The Elements of Aesthetic Effect

THE STRUCTURAL SCHEME

Looked upon merely as printed, a poem is a succession,
short or long, continuous or interrupted, of lines sent off
in the more conventional forms with capitals and stepping
part way across the page with some regularity of length or
patterned alteration. The sequence is all but continuous in
the epic; it is cut into dialogue in the drama; there is a

grouping by stanzas in the lyric. In the less conventional forms the capitals are dropped; vertically there is still a blocking of print, suggestive or not of the stanza, and horizontally there seems to be a ranging of print arbitrary in its wide swinging stride or short halted step.

As soon as the poem is read a new articulated structure is revealed. The lines appear metrical with controlled sequences of long and short or accented and unaccented syllables; there are pauses and rhythmic onsets, cadences, phrase-units and patterns, and often rhymes.

Still another structural unity is the inner one of content —of the meanings sensuously embodied in a poem. It is then a question of how image follows image, of how moods and ideas are unfolded and transformed—of how the inner life finds a sharply varied, well modulated form.

Of these three types of structural organization the first is of little importance. Examples of the second are the Greek choric ode with its measured correspondences, the sonnet, intricate in its rhyme-form, the triolet, and the rondeau. There are many possible schemes which allow the craftsman to create delicate or involved patterns of form. Natural affinities and tradition connect certain verse-forms with certain types of content. There are "heroic" and "elegiac" measures; the ode and the sonnet demand solemn, lofty ideas and images; the triolet is a slight thing that trips lightly to lilting music. It is dangerous to disregard such associations. Edna St. Vincent Millay in her Fifth Sonnet fills a solemn verse-form with commonplace imagery and language, thus giving to an idea instinct with tragedy a satiric turn, which is uncongenial to the spirit of the sonnet. Translators are often infelicitous in their choices. Sappho has been mistranslated again and again. Put into a religiously tinged idiom, set to the weighty rolling organ music of triple rhymes and other hymnal patterning, the charm, the lightness, the sharply edged pictures, and the direct passionateness that mark her poetry are sacrificed.

Structural organization is present not only in its verbal and rhythmic scheme but in its spiritual content. It is then a matter of how the artistic idea is made articulate in a sequence of images expressive of a mood present in every part of a poem, as in Verlaine's *Sagesse* or in Swinburne's *A Forsaken Garden* or a mood sequence, as in a chain of sonnets or in Tennyson's *In Memoriam*. Goethe's *Ueber allen Gipfeln* fuses eight simple lines to a harmony of image and mood. Other poems perfect in this inner organization are *Autumn* and *Ode on a Grecian Urn* by Keats; *Fragmentary Blue* by Frost; *Pear Tree* by H. D.; *Sea Slant* by Sandburg. But Sandburg fails in the poem *Bones*

> Sling me under the sea.
> Pack me down in the salt and wet.
> No farmer's plow shall touch my bones.
> No Hamlet hold my jaws and speak
> How jokes are gone and empty is my mouth.
> Long green-eyed scavengers shall pick my eyes,
> Purple fish play hide-and-seek,
> And I shall be song of thunder, crash of sea,
> Down on the floors of salt and wet.
> Sling me . . . under the sea.

A fine poem is marred by two disturbing notes: the allusion to Hamlet, with its stark literariness, and the literary imagery near the end. Sandburg has called the past a bucket of ashes; but here he has taken from those ashes a few bits of shiny glass and has packed them incongruously in the strong salt wet spirit of his poem.

METRE, RHYTHM, MUSIC

The metrical unit is a foot: a succession in ancient poetry of long and short, in modern poetry of accented and unaccented syllables. Of feet the most commonly used are the iambus ⌣ –, the trochee – ⌣, the dactyl – ⌣ ⌣, and the anapest ⌣ ⌣ –. A metrical line is formed either by the simple repetition of one of these measures, as in blank verse, or by such repetition with a change at the end, as in the hexameter, or by a combination of measures; and if great complexity is desired by a mixing in of such unusual units as – –, – ⌣ – or ⌣ ⌣ ⌣. But verse is not a matter of the metronome; only the poorest writing or reading of it can make of it something utterly mechanical. It shows its life in the irregular sliding back and forth of the caesura, or break, in the verse; the running of one verse into the next; the varying length of line; its modulated pauses and stresses; its rhythmic breathing. Interest, which plays an important part in pictorial balance, is not to be neglected in poetry. The lingering feel of a word or the tasting of its meaning may add time or stress and redeem what seems a mechanical fault or slip in the verse. The fact that our metrical unit is one of stress, and not of quantity, makes it difficult to reduce either the rhythm or the music to a succession of beats. For affecting the metrical scheme at every point are natural and interested variations.

The rhythm of a poem depends partly on the metrical unit used, partly on metrical patterning, and partly on the swaying modulation, free and disciplined, which is the life of the verse.

Different units have a different motor *feel*. The iambus differs as sharply from the trochee as going upstairs differs from going down. The dactyl has about it a light running and rippling quality; the anapest is a long swinging stride. The number of times a unit is repeated in a line affects its rhythmic character. Thus the iambic tetrameter used in Greek tragedy is more stately, less flexible and decisive in movement than the pentameter. Few poets rival Aristophanes in complexity and subtlety of versification, and in the delicate sense of what is suited to movement and mood. The appearance of short broken lines within blank verse of regular length, as in Shakespeare's later diction, not only reflects the excitement of a Lear or an Othello but gives to the verse itself an occasional staccato note of passion. Variations are gained by the varying appearance of other feet in a line or strophe. A dactyl in a trochaic line is like a flurry of movement in the even tread of a marching song. The greatest variety of measures and rhythms is to be found in lyrics; it is needed there to express changing moods—slow and accelerated psychic rhythms—and the play of a roving and flashing imagination. Of such variety the first two stanzas of Shelley's *Night* are an illustration.

> Swiftly walk over the western wave,
>   Spirit of Night!
> Out of the misty eastern cave,—
> Where, all the long and lone daylight,
> Thou wovest dreams of joy and fear
> Which make thee terrible and dear.—
>   Swift be thy flight!
> Wrap thy form in a mantle grey,
>   Star-inwrought!
> Bind with thine hair the eyes of Day;
> Kiss her until she be wearied out.
> Then wander o'er city and sea and land,
> Touching all with thine opiate wand—
>   Come, long-sought.

The sharp decisiveness of

> Wrap thy form in a mantle grey

contrasts with the slow wandering rhythm of

> Then wander o'er city and sea and land

Of the four short lines the first two correspond; their rhythmic scheme is $-\cup\cup-$; that of the third is $-\cup-$;

the fourth, – – –, presents three words of equal psychic weight, and a slow amplitude of feeling.

An unintelligent reading would make of the first line of Shelley's *Ode to the West Wind*

O wild West Wind, thou breath of Autumn's being

a regular iambic line, but it ought to be read – – – – ∪ – ∪ – ∪ – ∪. The four successive longs set the impressive theme.

To what point can rhythmic complexity and irregularity be carried? Experimentalists have carried it to the extreme of *free verse;* they hold that the traditional forms of poetry fail to use all but a few of the rhythms of speech; that these few forms have become mechanized in the using; that there is need of new music. Their opponents see in *free verse* little else than prose printed in segments to catch the eye; and find it as unmusical as the "rough scratching of a pencil on slate." It may be granted that much of it is nothing but bad prose; but so is some of the older poetry nothing but the chop-chop of a cleaver mincing meat. *Free verse* at its best does not lack music, but it is not a facile music easily caught. Nor is modern verse so revolutionary as it seems. Greek prosody, after all, by admitting *resolution*, with restrictions which the grammarians noted and overstressed, allowed very free rhythmic variations. A line like ∪ – ∪ | ∪∪∪ | ∪∪ ∪ | ∪∪∪ | ∪∪∪ | –, gained by resolving a long into two shorts, must remain rhythmically strange; and unlike a trochaic line. The choric odes of the *Prometheus* of Aeschylus show complex patterning. In both the recitative of the *Prometheus* and the long opening chorus of the *Agamemnon* there is a free use of short broken lines, and a natural varying music. Of this free type is the *Prometheus* monologue of Goethe. So are the *Dionysus Dithyrambs* of Nietzsche. If music and the rhythmic spirit are allowed there, how can they be denied to Amy Lowell's *Patterns;* to Lola Ridge's *Reveille;* to the delicate and intense phrase units of Toller's *Schwalbenbuch* and *Masse Mensch;* and to lines like Sandburg's

> Stormy, husky, brawling,
> City of the Big Shoulders

or again

> One they killed.
> One lives on;
> Cross, thorns, head, against the moon.
> Nails was their answer,
> Nails,
> Nails.

The musical quality of a poem is not a matter merely of a metrical scheme, and of rhythmic accent and movement. There are peculiar tonal qualities in vowels, vowel-combinations; in consonants and in single words. Here are three words: *thrill, throb, thrum.* Their vowels slip down the scale; the final consonants have a persistency of sound and length which a final *t* could never give. The initial *th* has a vibrancy which is utterly lacking in words like *shrill* and *scum.* The *i* and the *u* are as different as the violin and the bass viol. Single words are soft or harsh, quavering or full-toned, intense or soothing. Vowel sequence, assonance, alliteration, the way words are put together—all have their share in the expressive music of verse. Here is illustrative material from Keats

> O soothest sleep!

from *To Autumn*

> Thy hair soft-lifted by the winnowing wind;
> Or on a half-reap'd furrow sound asleep,

Drowsed with the fume of poppies, while thy hook
Spares the next swath and all its twinèd flowers;

from *Last Sonnet*

Of snow upon the mountains and the moors

. . . . .
. . . . .

To feel for ever its soft fall and swell,
Awake for ever in a sweet unrest,
Still, still to hear her tender-taken breath,
And so live ever—or else swoon to death.

There is a delicately varied vowel-music in all these lines.
An example are the weight and volume of *swoon* as it appears suddenly in a sequence of *i's* and *e's*.

THE MAGIC OF WORDS

The music that is gained, not from rhythm, but from such
combining of words is only a special instance of a magic
practised by every real poet: the *magic of words*.   Even the
writer of artistically shaped prose has something of this
art.   He puts the right word in the right place; intent as he
is on the meaning of what he writes he does not neglect the
manner; he knows when to be decorative, direct and vigorous, persuasively smooth or harsh.   Far beyond him in a
feeling for word-values and word-power is the poet.   He has
the magician's gift of doing with words what no one else
can do.   He makes them sparkle, flash with a living fire,
darken with emotion or become translucent.   He turns
language into something beautiful, supremely expressive,
haunting and unforgettable.

Here are a few examples of this magic of words; set down
to be studied in their variety of devices and effects:

Sappho

> And I flutter like a child after her mother.
>
>   .   .   .   .   .
>
> I love delicacy, and for me love has the sun's splendor
>   and beauty.
>
>   .   .   .   .
>
> Over the fisherman Pelagon his father Meniscus set
>   wicker-net and basket, memorial of a luckless
>   life.

Shakespeare *Sonnets*

> And Summer's lease hath all too short a date:
>
>   .   .   .   .   .   .
>
> When to the Sessions of sweet silent thought
> I summon up remembrance of things past,
>
>   .   .   .   .   .
>
> Then can I drown an eye, unused to flow,
> For precious friends hid in death's dateless night,
> And weep afresh love's long-since-cancell'd woe,
> And moan th' expense of many a vanish'd sight:
>
>   .   .   .   .   .   .
>
> . . . proud-pied April, dress'd in all his trim
>
>   .   .   .   .   .   .
>
>   Sweet roses do not so;
> Of their sweet deaths are sweetest odours made.
>
>   .   .   .   .   .
>
> That time of year thou may'st in me behold
> When yellow leaves, or none or few, do hang
> Upon those boughs which shake against the cold—
> Bare ruin'd choirs where late the sweet birds sang.

Austin Dobson *A Garden Song*

> Here in this sequester'd close
> Bloom the hyacinth and rose,
> Here beside the modest stock
> Flaunts the flaring hollyhock.
>
>   .   .   .   .   .   .

Stephen Vincent Benét *King David*

> Her body shimmered, tender and white
> As the flesh of lilies in candlelight.

. . . . .

John Hall Wheelock *Nirvana*

> I have forgotten you, long, long ago;
> Like the sweet silver singing of thin bells
> Vanished, or music fading faint and low.
> Sleep on, I lie at heaven's high oriels,
> Who loved you so.

. . . . .

Carl Sandburg

> I came sudden, at the city's edge,
> On a blue burst of lake,
> Long lake waves breaking under the sun
> On a spray-flung curve of shore;
> And a fluttering storm of gulls,
> Masses of great gray wings
> And flying white bellies
> Veering and wheeling free in the open.

. . . . .

The magician's conjuring ways are many; and it is well to follow him into some of the ways of his magic.

FELICITY AND FINALITY OF PHRASE: These lines offer many instances of felicitous phrasing: *trim* is just the word to go with *proud-pied April; death's dateless night* and *love's long-since-cancell'd woe* show imaginative range and intensity gained through verbal condensation. *Flaunts the flaring hollyhock* is the perfect rendering of a vivid isolated impression; *memorial of a luckless life* is a brief epic of the sea; *blue burst of lake* and *spray-flung curve of shore* by their boldness and force move familiar objects within the circle of truth and distinction.

As for finality, that is the mark of all great art. We rest in it—we are not tempted to go beyond. When we do seem to go beyond, as in tragedy, with its cosmic riddles, it is the spirit of art that urges us and sustains us, and still holds us within its confines. Nothing in the magic art of the poet is simpler and more illusive than finality of phrase. Shelley gives an image of night *in a mantle grey, Star-inwrought!* Never have I seen her that way, but Shelley forces me to remain spell-bound within his image; I find sustenance and rest there. Another poet sees her differently; she is *Star-shouldered;* to Helton

> The night is nailed aloft with gold . . .

Again I welcome and become the sharer in what is offered. Finality in a scientific view of the night and the stars would mean a set of ideas: artistic finality means the satisfied acceptance of numberless images creatively projected and vividly made part of my imaginative life. What a stretch is demanded if we are to see with Shakespeare wintry trees as *bare ruin'd choirs*, but how consummately possessive the picture and the phrase become when their meaning is reached! We are held; and are thrilled and supremely content in the holding.

DECORATIVE PATTERNING: The order and arrangement of words in a verse differ widely from the order natural to prose. There are inversions like *bloom the hyacinth and rose;* alliteration like *sweet silver singing;* there is assonance; there are balanced arrangements like *sweet deaths—sweetest odours.* Much of this rearrangement is rhythmic, and some of it is for musical effect. A large part of it may be called decorative patterning. The line

> When yellow leaves, or none or few, do hang

lacks natural directness and logic but offers a pleasing pattern of words. Shelley's line

> Yellow, and black, and pale, and hectic red

has an interlocked sequence of colors, within which the *and*'s are cradled. In Swinburne's *Itylus* there is decorative variation in the line

> Sister, my sister, fleet sweet swallow

and there is in the first lines of all but two of the stanzas, in the adjectives applied to the swallow—*fair swift; fleet swift; soft light; singing; fleeting; shifting, rapid*—not merely a picture painted in successive touches but word patterning that is subtly reminiscent and ever new. Even Sandburg, who is as remote as can be from the intricate word embroidery of a Keats or a Swinburne uses decorative patterning in poems like *Sea Slant* and *Slabs of the Sunburnt West*. He strikes again and again the same phrase-note at the beginning of lines; he plays such variants as

> A bluejay blue
> and a gray mouse gray

and

> Into the night, into the blanket of night,
> Into the night rain gods, the night luck gods,
> Overland goes the overland passenger train

FIGURES AND IMAGERY: In every Rhetoric there is much space given to figures of speech:—apostrophe, asyndeton, hyperbole, metaphor, simile, and the rest. All these are part of the mechanics of poetry; and they all, in their several ways, reflect its spirit and deeper life. Apostrophe and hyperbole both reveal emotional intensification, and the former serves lyrical projection as well; asyndeton favors vigor and swiftness. Simile and metaphor deserve a place apart, for they are closest to picture thought, and to the imaginatively reshaped and revalued experiences which are the stuff and form of poetry.

The simile is a transference in the sense that the poet in picturing or describing something calls to his aid another image or set of images. The uses and types of such transference are many.

Sappho in the lines of a marriage song

Raise high the roof-beams, carpenters. Like Ares comes the bride-
    groom taller far than a tall man.

wishes to give a vivid impression of the height of the bridegroom, compares him to Ares, and then, lest the irrelevant and too fantastic mar the picture turns back to the tallness of a very tall man.

In Browning's

And her eyes are dark and humid, like the depth on depth of lustre
Hid i' the harebell

mere vividness is not aimed at; the image gained from the transference is elaborated; the value is for the moment shifted to it. This is true also of Shelley's four similes in *To a Skylark: glow-worm golden, rose embowered* add nothing to the vividness of an imaged bird; they are given a rich poetic life of their own.

Different again are the long descriptive similes used by Homer, Virgil, Dante, and Milton. There, too, the value is in the second image, but the image is chosen because it is naturally and vividly expressive of the first.

The finest type of simile is the one of which the second stanza of Meredith's *Love in the Valley* is an example. Speaking of his love he calls her

Shy as the squirrel and wayward as the swallow

and, elaborating on these two images, has them sparkle and glint with a brilliancy that adds lustre and gives defining light to both.

In the closing lines of Andrew Lang's poem *The Odyssey*

> They hear like Ocean on a western beach
> The surge and thunder of the Odyssey

there is a transition from simile to metaphor. Calling a metaphor a condensed simile has the authority of Aristotle. The example he gives—*like a lion he leaped on them—a very lion he leaped on them*—fits many cases, but is misleading, none the less. The origin of the metaphor in language, and its use and spirit in poetry are to be sought elsewhere. Many common words are faded metaphors. What they expressed originally was the imaginative seizing of something, rather than a clearly grasped and sharply visualized likeness of two things. The Homeric simile presents the incisive lines of a well worked out painting—luminous and illuminating; the similes of Keats and Shelley even at their boldest have this quality. But the metaphors of Aeschylus, Sophocles, and Shakespeare are quite different. They are direct, intense, bold; and they are not meant to be expanded into pictures. Metaphors like *flame-eyed fire; the multitudinous laughter of the sea; the sea blossoming with dead; heaven-kissing hill; Come seeling night, Scarf up the tender eye of pitiful day* are a snare to the literal-minded; they do not lend themselves to complete detailed visualization. Nor are they purely decorative embellishments of language. Rather are they the direct presence of an intense, imaginatively and personally touched spirit seeking expression at all costs. Sophocles applies the word *chloros, grass-green*, metaphorically to tears and life-blood. If the visual image is too definitely kept in mind it blocks the way to an understanding of what he wishes to express;—tenderness and youthful vigor. In the sonnet of Shakespeare quoted the court scene suggested by the legal terms—must not be visualized. H. D.'s *Oread*

> Whirl up, sea—
> Whirl your pointed pines,

> Splash your great pines
> On our rocks,
> Hurl your green over us,
> Cover us with your pools of fir

has been unintelligently criticized as far-fetched and straining in its imagery. But metaphors are not condensed pictures. In them, to use a Sophoclean metaphor, the poet *tears up words from within him.* They may be reckless and they may be mixed. They must be imaginative and personal; and they must have the breath of life. In this sense metaphors are not a technical device but the very essence of poetic speech. To them may be applied the lines of Wheelock

> On the wide waste the web of twilight, trembling
> Hangs low with stars and night

EVOCATIVE LANGUAGE: Part of the magic of words in poetry lies in the choice of phrases which are evocative or revelational—of feeling, of mood, of visions, of ideas. Here are examples to be looked into:—
Shakespeare *Hamlet*

> tears seven times salt
>
> .   .   .   .   .   .
>
> If thou didst ever hold me in thy heart
> Absent thee from felicity awhile

Keats

> The weariness, the fever, and the fret—
>
> .   .   .   .   .   .
>
> My heart aches, and a drowsy numbness pains
> My sense, as though of hemlock I had drunk,

Masters

> The days went by like shadows,
> The minutes wheeled like stars

Keats

> Rounded by thee, my song should die away
>   Content as theirs,
> Rich in the simple worship of a day.

Of these the Shakespearean phrases are evocative of feeling. The second of the lines from Hamlet's dying words has been cited by Matthew Arnold as an instance of happy phrasing, but the first

> If thou didst ever hold me in thy heart

is much more than that. Of thousands of phrasings none could give as this one does the intensity and preciousness of love; none could give as *tears seven times salt* does the bitter essence of unrestrained grief. The marvelous thing is that the poet while he vibrates responsively to feeling gains what is not in the feeling as commonly experienced—a music, a mystery, and a personal consecration. In the examples from Keats the words are held together in the vibrational unity of a mood. The verses from Masters show how a poet can take what is common—the passage and marking of time—and make of it, by means of circling imagery, something which has all the grandeur and reach of a cosmic drama. A phrase, again, like *the very flame of love* has this quality of calling forth the imagination and forcing it to share in a bold excursional ranging. When Wordsworth speaks of the winds as *upgather'd now like sleeping flowers* he has made calm imaginatively meaningful. Much of the evocative language of poetry is evocative in this sense. The last example from Keats shows phrasing evocative of thought—revelational of thought. Thought springs forth, not in the nakedness or in the marching gear of prose, but polished, rounded off in vivid, colorful dress—at once itself and more than itself in this intensely personal adornment.

It is only a step, and a natural one, from this last phase of the magic of words—evocative language—to what might be called the triple soul of poetry: feeling, mood, thought. It is they that stir in the sensuously precious body of a poem.

FEELING, MOOD, THOUGHT

The question here is not one of structure, music or phrasing. It is of the inner life and spirit of a poem as a whole; —its artistic idea. The matter is not a simple one: there are many types of poems; and many and subtle are the effects aimed at.

Short lyrics—the love song; the ecstatic nature poem— come from the heart, and mean to speak to the heart. Simple human feelings such as love, grief, joy, hatred, reverence, regret, hope, despair lose something of their obviousness and downrightness as they are projected and held within an objective artistic form. Intensely personal feelings, which are subtle and complex, changing or clustered, as in Sara Teasdale's sequence *Sea Sand* or in Wheelock's *The Black Panther*, are in like manner given value. Some experience—the sight of a girl, the loss of a friend; some object seen—dunes, a meadow, clouds, the sea—or some sensation—the call of a bird, stinging salt spray—mean an emotional response, but the feeling as it takes form gains its drive from imaginative forces and an elaboration from an artistic impulse which is consistently marked by *indirection* and *enriching*. A lover's eyes are notoriously inventive; grief and joy in real life are inarticulate and chaotic, and sharply pointed at actualities. To the poet feeling becomes a psychic color wheel, of one color or of many, revolving slowly or rapidly in a world of his own. Of this Shakespeare's dirge *Come away, come away, death*, Browning's *Home-thoughts from Abroad*, and

Keats's *Last Sonnet* are examples.   If poetry is to be made anything of, this emotional colorfulness must be seen.

What is true of feeling is true also of mood.   A mood is a mass of feelings in tonal unity.   It matters little what the mood is—melancholy, desolation, revolt, lightheartedness, adoration—it is there in the music, the rhythm, the imagery, the rounded structure and the indwelling spirit.   Mood is pervasively present in Swinburne's *A Forsaken Garden;* Baudelaire's *Spleen;* Tennyson's *St. Agnes' Eve;* Heine's *Lorelei;* Burns's *My Bonnie Mary* and drinking songs; Whitman's *Song of the Open Road.*   Doom hangs heavy over the *Oresteia;* a warlike spirit breathes in *The Seven Against Thebes;* there is a rollicking mood in Aristophanes; a pensive mood tinged with sadness in Swinburne's *Ave atque Vale;* religious fervor gives the tone to the *Paradise* of Dante. A slight study of these poems is all that is needed to reveal how rich a thing mood may become through the sensitive and creative genius of a poet.

Often the purpose of a poem is thought, artistically shaped, taking on vividness and brilliancy from the way it is expressed, and thus made arresting as well as compelling. The thought may be a simple one—a bit of meditative analysis called forth by some incident or experience.   Or it may be built on such a contrast as the thoughtful man meets in the spending of his life.   Such is Henley's *Invictus* with its last line *I am the captain of my soul;* such is Shakespeare's twentieth sonnet:

> Poor soul, the centre of my sinful earth—
> My sinful earth these rebel powers array—
> Why dost thou pine within and suffer dearth,
> Painting thy outward walls so costly gay?
> Why so large cost, having so short a lease,
> Dost thou upon thy fading mansion spend?

or Wordworth's sonnets *The World* and *Mutability*. This is criticism of life; and it may, as in Empedocles, Lucretius, and Dante expand to a world philosophy and an intellectual panorama of life and its forms and forces.

In certain poets—Dante, Browning, Whitman may be chosen as examples—this thought-content is strikingly and persistently present. But all poetry has some of it. Only a large-minded reading of it will save us from seriously misinterpreting poetry. Clearness and consistency are a logician's virtues; and a poet does not present and pursue thought in the spirit of the logician. Rather does he seek it for what it is worth to him, imaginatively and emotionally, and for what he can make of it as he casts his magic spell. That spell need not be one of beauty; and he is not committed to an idealistic, ennobling reading. He may contemplate a Golden Age or he may, as Sandburg and Vachel Lindsay do, attempt to understand as well as get the *feel of* the ugly and tremendously alive modern scene; he may with Whitman study the patterns of the living garment of God or he may unravel it till nothing remains but strands of dirty wool. He may be optimist or pessimist; idealist or cynic. To him man may be the creator or stormer of heavens—or a poor naked two-pronged thing. What he can make of any of these ideas is what counts; how he can exploit them for the imagination and make them vibrant for feeling; how he has them live in the imagery and the music of his verse.

RAPTURE AND VISION

Rapture and vision crown and complete the meaning of poetry. Words like rapture, ecstasy, inspiration all refer to something that has been felt again and again—that the poet is slightly mad in his art. *Seized, beside and outside himself, breathed into and blown through* are their meanings.   Plato in the *Ion* and the *Phaedrus* reflects on poetic madness; Shakespeare alludes to it in his phrase *the poet's eye in a fine frenzy rolling.*   Shelley voices it in the *Ode to the West Wind:*—

> Make me thy lyre even as the forest is:
>
> . . . . . .
>
> Be thou, Spirit fierce,
> My spirit!   Be thou me, impetuous one!
>
> . . . . . .
>
> Be through my lips to unawaken'd earth
> The trumpet of a prophecy!

Sandburg shows it in his *Prayers of Steel:*

> Lay me on an anvil, O God,
> Beat me and hammer me into a crowbar.
> Let me pry loose old walls.
> Let me lift and loosen old foundations.
>
> Lay me on an anvil, O God.
> Beat me and hammer me into a steel spike.
> Drive me into the girders that hold a skyscraper together.
> Take red-hot rivets and fasten me into the central girders.
> Let me be the great nail holding a skyscraper through
>   blue nights into white stars.

Here is what Plato says:

For all good poets, epic as well as lyric, compose their beautiful poems not as works of art, but because they are inspired and possessed.   And as the Corybantian revellers when they dance are not in their right mind, so the lyric poets are not in their right mind when they are composing their beautiful strains; but when falling under the power of music and meter they are inspired and possessed; like Bacchic maidens who draw milk and honey from rivers, when they are under the influence of Dionysus, but not when they are in their right mind. . . . For the poet is a light and winged and holy thing, and there is no invention in him until he has been inspired and is out of his senses, and the mind is no longer in him; when he has not attained to this state, he is powerless, and is unable to utter his oracles. . . . The poets are only the interpreters of the gods by whom they are severally possessed.

.   .   .   .

But he who, not being inspired and having no touch of madness in his soul, comes to the door and thinks that he will get into the temple by the help of art—he, I say, and his poetry are not admitted; the sane man is nowhere at all when he enters into rivalry with the madman.

Ecstasy and *frenzy* are less suitable terms than *rapture* and *inspiration;* they suggest too strongly great intensity or sublimity. *Rapture* is not altogether free from this, but is on the whole the best word to use.

It is a familiar fact, observable throughout the range of human action, that at times a level of performance is reached, not only beyond the ordinary but even beyond our known reserve power. We play or work as if inspired: something seizes us; sustains us we know not how; drives us headlong —we are possessed. In like manner the poet if he is not a mere craftsman of phrases and musical virtuoso is swept along with his theme; is carried beyond himself.

Rapture is not a quality found only in great poetry, although few poems that are great have none of it. It is a natural gift, appearing at times even in children's poems as an imaginative throb in simple motifs. Here are two examples, the first taken from *Adventure* by Hilda Conkling; the second a poem by a twelve year old boy.

> Come quickly to me, come quickly,
> I am waiting.
> I am here on the sand;
> Sail close!
> I want to go over the waves. . . .
> The sand holds me back.

Oh adventure, if you belong to me,
Don't blow away down the sky!

* * * * *

A CLIPPER THREE DAYS OUT

How I love to feel
The tug of the wheel,
And the swaying deck beneath my feet;
With the chill salt spray
On the deck at play
While the foresail yanks at the sheet!

How I love to be
With the restless sea
On a clipper three days from home;
With a crew strong and hale,
And a frolicking gale,
And our bowsprit buried in foam.

It is the life-giving quality in poems as different in theme
and volume of feeling as Sara Teasdale's *Blue Squills*—
which gives rapture at its intensest and purest—Vachel
Lindsay's *I Want to Go Wandering;* and Roy Helton's *May
Jones Takes the Air*

Proud queens, old queens, pale and dead and fair,
Who will be waiting to match her beauty there?
The night is nailed aloft with gold—the wind is on her hair.
And love is searching through her eyes; if time has love to spare
Bring love!   Show love!   Raise it like a crown!
   May Jones of Filbert Street is walking into town!

Nations are marching.   Cities yet unseen
Roar on the pavements where her feet have been:
New worlds!   Wise worlds!   Worlds all gold and green!
This is your birth night.   Rain your splendors down!
   May Jones of Filbert Street is walking into town.

A little street walker seen through a poet's eyes! Plato is right in calling him divinely mad.

Rapture may be a force that rushes imperfect poetry to great heights. An example of this is Rorty's *Prelude: When We Dead Awaken.* It begins haltingly, wavers close to the ridiculous, and then as the poet is swept along ends in a magnificent crescendo

And I shall play a dawn prelude over the white faces of the hundred
    million sleepers till they brighten and smile as the violins
    shimmer and sweep;
And the bells will ring out in the steeples, and the tall towers rock,
    and light will come blowing high horns out of the east, and
    the world will wake sweetly to the smile of a bluebird's warble
    and the gold-blue morning bugles of a thousand cock-crows;
And I shall caper and smash among the kettle drums until not one
    sleeper is left asleep, and the laughter of all the gods will
    roll out with the sunrise, and we shall live, we shall live, we
    shall live!
O that day!

Rapture may be started by a thought, an image, a mood. In Browning's *Home-thoughts from Abroad;* Swinburne's *When the hounds of spring are on winter's traces;* and Shakespeare's *When daisies pied and violets blue* there is the same thought—of spring; and there is in each case rapture personally colored. Note the seizure; the involuntary rush of imagery and rhythm; the cumulative extravagance; the whirling and flashing imagination. There may be an image, as that of the crashing forest trees in the second part of Faust; we are then hurled with the poet into the very midst of splintered and shattering wood. Something of this rapture is retained. There may be a mood, a subtly personal one, as in Verlaine's *Sagesse,* or a cosmic one, as in Swinburne's *A Nympholept* and *The Temple of Pan* or in Sandburg's *Leather Leggings;* we are again made to feel that the poet is inspired—breathed into by his theme and resonant of its tone.   The voice need not be a beautiful, clear, and full sounding one; it may be raucous, a thing of weird sounds, for the poet may be possessed by such huge gargoyle gods as Samuel Butler creates in *Erewhon*, with the wind sweeping strangely through their hollow spaces.

When rapture is lacking poetry becomes poor and commonplace.   Without the touch of the master who is himself mastered it sinks to a mechanical performance.   In lyrical poetry rapture is often strongly emotional.   In the epic it need not be that: there, as in Homer, it may be a sustained and sustaining beauty and force which lifts a world lived in to heights ordinary, normal-minded perception does not often reach.

Not only is the poet enraptured, but he has certain visual experiences and imaginings which may be called *visions*. Here again he is slightly mad.   Madmen have visions:— they see things that are not there; and their way of seeing is vivid, intense, emotionally unstable, personally distorted, and in a practical sense false.   The poet, like all self expressive artists, sees with the inner eye; across it flash objects common to the outer eye—clouds, birds, daffodils and roses, a mountain pass or waterfall, spring and winter, youth and old age, a brook, street scenes, farming, lovemaking, seafaring, war.   But all these are strangely illumined and changed.   As they become part of the poet's vision they become *charged*, in the sense of being more vividly seen, more intimately felt, more individually colored.   They are imaginatively transmuted; made vibrant for feeling; turned into something uniquely personal.   It is part of the genius of the poet that he can *"live vision into deed"*; not as the madman does with what he imagines but in the sense of giving through the imagery and structure of his verse artistic form to his visions—casting them forth and giving them a

disciplined life of their own. This is true equally of transmuted visual images of common objects, and of such elaborated purely imaginative creations as Dante's *Hell*, Coleridge's *Kubla Khan*, and Baudelaire's *Don Juan Aux En-
fers*.

Examples of poetic visions are: war as it lives in Homer
and Aeschylus; hell and heaven as they take form in Dante
and Milton; the skylark, the nightingale, the stockdove, and
the swallow as they are glorified—and distorted—by Shelley,
Keats, Wordsworth, and Swinburne; the rural scene of
Burns and Frost; machinery as Sandburg sees it in *Gargoyle;* Chicago and the vast grain fields of the West as they
work on his imagination; the tombstones of the *Spoon River
Anthology;* Vachel Lindsay's *My Lady is compared to a
Young Tree;* gardens as Amy Lowell sees them. They are
all, as visions should be, vivid, striking, and personally inspired.

To the imagination of both Homer and Aeschylus the
Trojan war was vivid and fraught with infinite possibilities
for testing the mettle of men and calling forth human passions, but a comparison of the *Iliad* and the choruses of the
Agamemnon reveals sharp differences in the spirit and substance of their visions. A nightingale is differently envis-
aged by Wordsworth and Keats; a swallow, by Swinburne
and Toller. Only a Shelley would call dead leaves driven by
the wind *pestilence-stricken multitudes*.

Visions must not be reduced to a single aesthetic type.
They may be beautiful or fantastically distorted; sublime
or idyllic; tragic or comic. Nor is their relation to the actual constant; it varies from a mere added glamour to violent
distortion. The question whether Falstaff, Caliban, and the
mad Lear are true to life, is beside the point; they are magnificent visions existing in their own right. Rossetti's picture

> It lies from heaven across the flood
>   Of ether, as a bridge.
> Beneath, the tides of day and night
>   With flame and darkness ridge
> The void, as low as where the earth
>   Spins like a frightful midge.

is astronomically absurd; but it is a splendid vision, nevertheless, by such tests as poetic fire, imaginative force, cosmic emotion, and original seeing.   These and inner tests like them are the only ones that ought to be applied to visions. Poetry is not photography; it is neither science nor logic. To see as Sandburg does in *Gargoyle* a bit of machinery as mouth and smashing fist

The fist hits the mouth over and over, again and again.
  The mouth bled melted iron, and laughed its laughter of nails
    rattling.

seems strange, violent, and defiant of logical analysis.   But in its bold and personal reinterpretation it shows the true visionary spirit of poetry—the same spirit that is to be found in quieter and less disturbing ways in the simple forms and unobtrusive visions of Wordsworth's *Daffodils* and *To the Cuckoo*.   What he says of the cuckoo

> Even yet thou art to me
> No bird, but an invisible thing,
> A voice, a mystery

may be applied to all experience as it flashes across the inner eye of the poet.

  The aesthetic meaning of poetry then is to be found in the created unity of structural scheme; metre, music, and rhythm; word values—decorative and evocative—; imagery; thought, feeling, and mood as they express an artistic idea;

and rapture and vision. These, separated in discussion, but interrelated in fact, are the *one soul-in-body* of a poem. They live in its spirit and find form in its substance.

CRITICAL TESTS

It is from the meaning of poetry as an art that all attempts to set values must start. The game of setting values, of calling this poem good and that poem bad, is fascinating and dangerous. It is often played with a narrow, unfair mind directing a heavy hand. To play it in this fashion with poetry as the stake is rash and dangerous, for here is an art which is intensely personal, imaginatively adumbrated in even its simplest forms, and with a very wide range of technical problems and resources. If there is a lack of sensitiveness on the part of the critic, if he is unimaginative, emotionally cool or matter of fact or distrustful of what is new, the poet pays the price.

A fair critic of a poem looks upon it first of all as an individual bit of creative self-expression. He seeks to capture its spirit and become a sharer in its life. That at least is a debt we owe to the living. He then applies certain general tests gained from a sympathetic study of what poetry means to be and how it gains its varied effects. Music, word-power; sensitiveness, vivid and original reshaping, feeling projected and enriched, freshness, rapture, vision—these are some of the things to be looked for in good poetry. There is no one formula for an effective mixture. The proportions differ from poet to poet, from theme to theme. Modesty, flexibility, and urbanity are three virtues the critic too often lacks. Let those who will play the hazardous game of caging within their prejudices that *light, volatile thing*, the poet; and let him who must, suffer.

MUSIC

BY PAUL KRUMMEICH

Introduction

Music, as an experience, is shared by most of us; many seek it, and few escape it. Perhaps more would crave and fewer avoid it if all knew the right approach. Admittedly the most popular of the arts, music is nevertheless but superficially understood. Aside from the purely sensuous pleasure it affords, art is a product of the mind,—for the mind.[1]

THE LAYMAN'S ADVENTURE

The reason for the popularity of music is by no means self-evident. The choice of the masses must be accounted for, and this is best begun by analyzing the layman's experience. Untutored and unspoiled, he enjoys what he hears in the most natural manner; he accepts what is offered without question or doubt. This is also the artist's way. The moments in which he has subdued his analytical self are wells of pure blessedness. This the layman cannot know. While he may darkly suspect he has struck the golden vein, he has no way of judging the value of his claim. Being what he is, he cannot analyze, and his shortcoming is his salvation. He listens as he must, which is as he should: *synthetically*. As long as he keeps faith with Nature, he will be guided, and his trust will sustain him. But it works both ways: for let him falter in this faith, and he is lost. No

---

[1] The mind is to be regarded as a functional ensemble, which includes both reproductive and creative types of imagination.

longer then will he delight in those reverberating harmonies which somehow revealed to him the depths of his being. Now he will seek enlightenment of a different kind: he craves to understand what is beyond the reach of conceptual thought. Before long he gains in knowledge and in power, so he thinks; and soon enough the immortal *Eroica* will be for him no more than a tuneful illustration of a Napoleonic campaign. Also, pure music will have been dethroned, and a free art reduced to a subject of polite conversation.

THE ARTIST'S PROBLEM

The artist, too, has his problems; but curiosity is the least of his afflictions. He knows the primordial vigor of his art, and never questions its rational nature. He holds what he has and feels secure in his wealth. He heeds instinctive warnings, and wisely refrains from defining what he could not analyze if he tried. Not so the half-trained layman, who readily talks, wholly unaware that he lacks the proper equipment. Yet if you would know what music is, ask the musician and you will be disappointed. When the artist turns philosopher (with a mere handful of exceptions) he presents a most distressing spectacle. Untrained in introspection, notoriously weak in analytics, he attempts the impossible and soon enough is caught in the vortex of his temerity. Realizing his predicament, he resorts to the familiar strategies of far-fetched analogies and tedious circumlocution until total confusion results and his audience gives up in despair.

MUSIC THE LANGUAGE OF THE EMOTIONS

We are constantly reminded that music is the language of the emotions, as though that were a definition. Nothing could be more ambiguous and misleading than this popular saying. Granted that music is art, no one today could subscribe to the Darwinian interpretation of emotions. The term language is equally ill chosen. It is usual to hold that language deals with concepts, logically ordered; but no conceptual data are to be found in music, and very little is known of its logic. So that, while the intelligent music-lover resents the Darwinian shadow, he prefers to keep language within its established functional limits. Though it may seem paradoxical, he readily believes that music expresses feelings, but never inquires into their nature, nor into the manner in which they are expressed. The first of these pseudo-definitions is as good as the second, and the second as bad as the first. Divorced from their vagueness, and rightly interpreted, they are equally true; in their dogmatic rigidity, they are meaningless, which is worse than false.

SPACE AND TIME

At the outset, art was defined as a product of the mind, for the mind. While this definition seems vague, it is all-embracing; it covers every step from creation to appreciation. As we approach the subject more closely, the need for a narrower definition is indicated: Art is the medium through which man expresses his ideas in image form. To avoid confusion, the terms *idea* and *image* must be defined. No matter what an idea may be, it cannot be less than a circumscribed state of mind, which functions within its boundaries. This statement is easily understood when one considers that the idea of justice is one thing, whereas the idea of expediency represents a different state of mind. The term *image* stands for form regardless of dimensions. It may be a three-dimensional structure, a two-dimensional surface, or a one-dimensional pattern floating along the time axis. Images are either spatial or temporal; the former have their parts simultaneously, the latter in succession. It must be understood that space stands for simultaneity, and time for succession. Music is a pure time-art, and one who would fully enjoy it is advised occasionally to undertake a journey from the world of space into the less familiar world of time.

In the contemplation of a sunset at sea one beholds a luminous disc gradually approaching an undulating surface, beneath which it slowly disappears. As a mere event, this commonplace spectacle is hardly worth mentioning: yet it has thrown countless people into rapture and ecstasy. Beautiful, they call it,—gorgeous, sublime; and one wonders what may be the cause of this extravagant language. It cannot be the sober fact of a disc and a surface,—that would be incongruous. For those who incline toward spatial imagery, movement is a negligible factor; their experience soon terminates without appreciable after-effects. There are others who are keenly susceptible to the charm of movement. For them, object-images pale imperceptibly as movement gains in strength; it assumes control as the objects drift into the background of attention. Careful introspection shows it is not so much the objects as their moving that makes one exclaim. That this is not immediately obvious is because of our initial object-consciousness, and the unfortunate habit of identifying object and movement. The deeper effect is caused not by the object but by the movement; even its aftermath seems to haunt us long after the object has disappeared.

The Elements of Music

RHYTHM

One who watches his own behavior will sooner or later discover a certain regularity of movement, especially in those organic functions over which he has little or no control. He takes for granted the even flow of pulsation and respiration, and so inhibits the most casual inquiry into those forces which govern this orderly procedure. There is much talk about rhythm in the realm of music; what is actually under discussion is not rhythm but its tonal manifestations. There are many examples of organized phrases in the textbooks, but rarely a word about rhythm itself. It should be possible to show that all rhythmical behavior may be traced to a common source.

When life is defined as a series of interconnected pulses flowing along the time axis, one must suspect some kind of governing force. If life began without rhythm, it had need of speedily adjusting itself to a mode of existence free from undue shock and friction, or perish prematurely. It seems more reasonable to assume that the force which generates life would also protect a living organism against conditions hostile to its survival. Some governing power is certainly most intimately linked with life itself. No continuity of being seems possible unless the organism functions rhythmically. Rhythm may then be defined as the governor of the flow of life.[2]

The monotonous ticking of a metronome has as little to do with rhythm as the tedious time-beating of a third-rate conductor. Such devices are bound to weaken or destroy an innate sense of rhythm. The function of rhythm is to integrate interrelated individual parts into a balanced organic whole, for the purpose of establishing the restful harmony so essential to the needs of man. Rhythm is the arch-organizer of all temporal structures. The best way to discover how a thing has been put together is to take it apart. A lucid example of rhythmical grouping is presented in Appendix II, Sketch I; a more extended one is found in Sketch III. In both cases the point of division is indicated by the

---

[2] The rhythmic force which regulates the behavior of organic life must not be identified with mechanical rhythm. The former is flexible, the latter rigid because coerced.

comma. Sketch XA presents a complete four-bar phrase, which may readily be divided into two equal parts. Sketch XB is constructed in the same way, and may be similarly broken up. It is an intensified repetition of XA. These musical aphorisms emerged spontaneously, and were recorded as they came.

A perfectly clear tripartite division will be discovered in Schumann's "Of Foreign Lands and People" (*Scenes from Childhood*). The first section of this composition, comprising eight measures, falls naturally into four groups of two measures each. Place a comma after the second measure, a semicolon after the fourth, a colon after the sixth, and a period after the eighth,—and a perfect rhythmical pattern appears. Another example, entitled "An Important Event" (from the same cycle), is worth investigating. Here are three sections of eight measures each, which may be subdivided into groups of four and two measures respectively. This will be further discussed in a subsequent section on forms, where the tripartite construction will be explained in terms of thesis-antithesis-synthesis (A-B-A).

MELODY

What is a melody? Definitions are plentiful. The most popular one reads: Melody is a succession of tones pleasing to the ear. Unfortunately this easy definition is neither wholly true nor altogether false; it is a dangerous half-truth. No self-respecting composer would be satisfied with a mere succession of tones; nor would he ever try to please anyone's ear,—not even his own. He shapes his ideas to the best of his ability, regardless of all other considerations. Significance is the keynote of all good art; the Beautiful and the Ugly are inevitable consequences of legitimate creating. It must be remembered that art draws its raw material from experience,—from life itself,—much of which is far from pleasant. When a musical idea is born, it appears in the shape of a temporal image (better known as a sound pattern), which is projected through the medium of tone. Not until then may one speak of melody; and now the definition is simple enough: a melody is the significant tonal projection of a temporal image.

HARMONY

The meaning of the term *harmony*, when employed as a label for one of the musical elements, must be regarded as distinctly different from its usual interpretation. It does not stand for that atmosphere of restful balance engendered by the contemplation of an artistic structure; it is the label given to a science which has made possible the vertical combining of many tones. Thus an array of tone-complexes (chords) may be interconnected to form an organic whole. In music we speak of horizontal and vertical listening, or reading. When listening to a hymn sung by a four-part choir, one may follow four individual melodies simultaneously, or else a progression of chords. The former is the horizontal approach, the latter the vertical.

Harmony may be either homophonic or polyphonic; a brief analogy will serve to explain the meaning of these terms. The homophonic structure may be compared to an autocracy. Like the unquestioned ruler, the melody governs all; its accompanying figures are no more than serfs. Simple chords, either compact or broken, furnish a background for the all-important melody; there is not a trace of melodic participation or competition. The reverse is true of the polyphonic system, which is based on democratic principles: not the will of the one but the wisdom of the many. True, a keen individualism may assert itself here, claiming and granting ample freedom, but a common interest assures concerted action and due coördination.

Music devoid of harmony is as old as humanity; but its evolution into a fine art depended upon the creation of a science of music. The reason for this is twofold. In the spontaneous shaping of a melodic or rhythmic pattern, the composer yields to vital forces which seem to dominate him for the time being. On the other hand, the vertical joining of many tones or melodies requires some reflection. Harking back to the folk-song, it must be observed that every single tone can belong to many modes, both major and minor. This multiple relationship is responsible for the peculiar indefiniteness which is felt in an unsupported melody. Any harmonic background is born of a craving for greater stability and direction. Harmony, even in its simple homophonic form, establishes the all-important element of positiveness, and so guides and supports the melodic flow. This type of treatment must not be underrated; it is a most useful device, and a source of aesthetic delight.

The plain chordal accompaniment employed in Schubert's "Serenade" is both adequate and significant,—an excellent example of homophony. A beautiful melody, reminiscent of folk-song, is supported by a guitar-like setting—a typical serenade. But could such a simple means suffice Brahms in the creating of his first symphony? Anyone familiar with this colossal structure must realize that a different type of harmony was required to effect a homogeneous flow of many individual melodies and conflicting rhythmic patterns. It has been said that the nature of polyphony is amply demonstrated by two or more individual interrelated melodies sounded simultaneously. This is quite true, provided the term *individual* is stressed. In a complex idea, one phase is often at war with another, causing an atmosphere of acute strife; the same holds in a complex musical idea. The tone-poems of Richard Strauss contain many warring tone-complexes; an uninformed listener is tempted to call such music chaotic. It never occurs to him that in music too inexorable logic reigns. In larger compositions, several melodies are logically developed, and respect for their individuality generates those screaming dissonances resented by the lovers of sweet sound. There is an unwritten law which decrees that every melodic strain is entitled to a logical growth and a reasonable freedom of movement. The organic development of melodies and rhythmic patterns must be given precedence over euphony. Richard Strauss had this in mind when he exclaimed, "Could I but slay euphony!"

But how can the composer function freely when a science, with its many laws, hems him in on all sides? This query is born of a misunderstanding. The science of harmony is not a system of musical mathematics which laconically decrees what is right or wrong. What may be expediently applied in a mechanical universe cannot possibly succeed in directing and controlling the behavior of genius. If a symphony were nothing more than a combination of tones arranged according to strict laws, then composing would be a matter of accuracy and patience. Much of this type of "learned" music has been created, and there are many who enjoy trying to "solve" it. Needless to say, such music is artificial and therefore not art. Compositions that have stood the test of time are sound; they are the work of genius. From the study of these masterpieces, men of insight and patience have gleaned much information which seemed to indicate that the composer was guided by some mysterious force. It required the wisdom of Kant to discover that the laws of the mind govern the labor of genius.[3] The theorist *collects* the laws; genius *makes* them. That many rules and regulations are apt to enslave the half-trained is easily understood; to the true artist they furnish the key to freedom,—freedom within the law. All that is good in art is the product of this union of the Dionysian and the Apollonian.

[3] "In genius, Nature works according to her own laws."

Tonal Raw Material

The musical idea prior to its projection should be regarded as a mental stream which runs its course within self-imposed boundaries. It is a temporal phenomenon, and requires a temporal medium for its adequate individuation. This singular vehicle must share the fluid properties of the idea, and must be capable of portraying joy and grief in all their nuances. Like the idea, it must be energy-born and energy-sustained until its mission is fulfilled. Such a medium is tone.

TONE

Periodic vibrations emanating from an elastic body disturbed in its tranquil state result in organized aerial structures. These silent vibrations constitute the physical or real tone. For the psychologist this spectacle presents no more than potential tone. To attain psychical existence, vibrations in space and time must be aurally apprehended and cortically localized. Physically received and psychologically understood, a single tone is complete and self-sufficient; musically, it is less than a fragment. No individual tone can be considered a musical tone when thus separated from the tone-complex to which it belongs. Melodies and harmonies cannot exist unless and until related tones are interwoven in horizontal series and vertical columns. Only in a logically evolved musical structure can tone enter the service of the idea.

SCALES

Primitive tools have always served the ends of primitive man. Just so, the virile pentatonic or five-tone scale has held undisputed sway wherever primitive emotions have been felt and expressed. It was found simultaneously in old Japan and in the African jungle, in the Scottish Highlands and in the tepees of the American Indian. Wholly devoid of the comfort in the half-tone intervals, it indulges in steps greater even than the whole tone, thus exhibiting its lusty strength. Because of its two semi-tones the familiar diatonic scale furnishes two periods of relaxation. No doubt they were considered necessary or they would not exist. There is also the strange six-tone scale,—a most unusual mode, and worthy of closer inspection. Composed of six whole tones, the equivalent of six long and even strides, it may begin anywhere and seems to end nowhere. Unlike other scales, it does not gravitate toward a tonal hub (tonica) and so defies our natural craving for finality and central control. Common chords superimposed on this scale generate weird and strident tone-complexes, whereas the harmonies built on the diatonic scale prove surprisingly mellow. We must not overlook the chromatic scale, shunned by Brahms and glorified by Wagner. There is more chromatism in the prelude to *Tristan and Isolde* than in the entire Brahms literature. This scale is composed exclusively of half-tones. Like the whole-tone scale, it lacks central control: it may begin or end anywhere. Unlike the six-tone scale, it glides, and does not stride. It is close-knit and tenuous, flexible and sinewy. When contrasted with the sturdy pentatonic, it seems to crawl and wind its way about like a parasitic vine, encircling something stronger than itself. Wagner seems to have discovered something sensuous in this scale, suitable to the portrayal of erotic moods.

KINAESTHESIS

Hearing is involuntary auditory sufferance; listening is active gathering, which involves volition and intelligence. Hence the phrase aural, or auditory, thinking. When music is apprehended through the ear, it is correct to speak of auditory thinking, if one intends to indicate the nature and origin of the sensory data with which the mind operates. The composer also thinks, but not aurally; he composes with his mind, not with his ears. Here the term auditory is out of place. Like so many others it is but vaguely defined; it seems to have acquired three meanings, which is two too many.

The spoken language may be regarded as a system of sound-signals the meaning of which has been agreed upon. But sounds like "house" or "tree" not only convey their conceptual meaning but also conjure up distinct three-dimensional spatial images. Since all linguistic sounds reach the mind by way of the ear, it is possible even here to speak of auditory thinking. However, when a mere sound-signal is translated into a space image, the ear functions *vicariously*. Auditory thinking is *autonomous* while listening to pure music, because the tympanic function of the ear is not rendered subservient to visual, tactile, or conceptual thinking. Finally, the kind of thinking the composer employs remains to be defined.

Kinaesthesis, correctly translated, stands for perception of movement. So understood, the meaning of this symbol grows broader, and should enjoy a corresponding extension of application. Speaking of movement, two types must be stressed: the kinematic and the dynamic. When an object in space changes its position, the movement so created is kinematic. The other type is equally important but less familiar. Not object-begotten, and therefore not kinematic, it is wholly internal and is called dynamic. It refers to the flow of psychic life, in its ceaseless undulations. There are definite changes of intensity indicative of positive movement, in the rise and fall of joy and grief, in the variations of hope and despair, of expectancy and resignation. These internal phenomena are as substantial as they are intimate; they, too, can be observed, measured, and recorded.

Obviously, observation deals with appearances; however,

what appears in space and time is the product of a creative force. Be it a gesture or a melody, these temporal patterns must be designed before they can be observed. The apprehension of music must be considered in two ways, kinematically and dynamically. When a melody is heard, the movement so perceived is induced by vibrations in space and time. Thus far, it is necessarily kinematic; but the immediate transformation of the kinematic into the dynamic presents another problem. Some analysis of the mind will greatly facilitate a thorough understanding of kinaesthesis. The function of the mind is to think, and thinking is either synthetic (joining) or analytic (separating). It is clear that joining and separating must remain abstractions unless a substance is involved.[4] Whenever thinking is discussed, it is imperative to differentiate between the thinking process and the thought substance. There are three kinds of material with which the mind may operate: temporal images, spatial images, and concepts. The thinking process is governed by the *a priori* laws, and no change of substance can affect the act of thinking. Kinaesthetic thinking, which includes the autonomous type of auditory thinking, operates with temporal images; visual and tactile thinking operate with spatial images,—and conceptual thinking, with concepts. Because observing implies creating, it may be said that the observing mind thinkingly reconstructs what the creative mind has thinkingly built.[5] The moment has come to stress the type of kinaesthetic thinking which creates. In the creative sphere, the composer functions as the designer of temporal patterns; and what he so builds he may observe and record.

[4] It must be understood that *joining* and *separating* refer not only to concepts and connectives but also to images and image-units. The process of joining or separating is what is important; it matters not so much *what* is so manipulated.

[5] Creating and observing are discussed separately for the sake of expediency; in the end they have their consummation and identification in understanding, which is identical with intelligent self-contemplation.

When a silent melody courses through the composer's mind, his self-contemplation is of the basic kind; it deals with temporal patterns exclusively. Once the nature of kinaesthetic thinking of the creative type is fully grasped, man has acquired a most powerful tool. Now the deepest accessible level of the ego can be reached, and its most recondite manifestations be measured and recorded, as they reveal themselves to kinaesthetic observation. What lies above this basic level (spatial imagery and conceptual thought) is relatively superficial; what lies below is chaos,— the "microchaos." In pure kinaesthesis, in inner observation of inner movement, lie the essence and goal of all aesthetic delight. In the temporal sphere, objects and the material interests they may generate are not yet or else no more, and all extra- and non-aesthetic acts are impossible. This basic self-contemplation is identical with Kant's "interessenloses Wohlgefallen" (disinterested joy) ; it is here that the Beautiful resides. Were it to exist on a more superficial level, then music could have none of it. Music is a pure time art; it has neither spatial images nor concepts. But if the Beautiful does function as explained above, then it operates at the base of all things apparent, and must cast its radiance upon all that rests on this base. The Beautiful—this strange flower of the mind—is never a surface creature; it blooms in the depths of temporal regions. *Its essence is of the soul in its simplicity; its form, an act of the creative mind.* It is in these depths that Nature freely yields her treasures; it is here that man must find himself. To go deeper is to plunge into chaos; to go less deep is to forfeit one's birthright—the understanding of the Self.

THE CREATIVE PROCESS

When the creative urge crowds the threshold of the composer's mind, a musical idea is born. By a strange process, oscillating between rumination and reflection, tonal strands are woven around this nucleus, until a musical embryo is nurtured into a mature work of art. Of all this the composer is blissfully ignorant. As long as he may somehow observe the flux of his agitation, he is well served. Even so, the idea unfolds itself to him in the most lucid manner. The absence of spatial imagery and concepts does not embarrass him; he could not use them, as such, if he tried. When questioned, he says that he hears his music ideally; but reflection shows that he thinks kinaesthetically. In this way he apprehends the ideational flow in all its nuances as distinctly and comprehensively as you and I contemplate our familiar day-dreams.

Since all art is imagery, the artistic idea must exist in image form to serve the artist's purpose. Even in music this is true, although the imagery here employed is of the less common temporal variety. The idea, as it first presents itself to the composer, is a nucleus or germ-cell. Being a product of inspiration, it appears spontaneously; it conditions and controls all artistic effort. It is the proverbial "gift of the gods." It comes unbidden, but with the force of a command; it is to be had for the taking, but cannot be kept without a struggle.

Program Music

The drama is universally accepted as a rational product; and everyone is willing to *think* himself into, through, and out of it, in order to assimilate its message. This unanimity of opinion and directness of purpose do not obtain in the layman's approach to music. How does the average intelligent man act when a symphony is poured into his ears? Does he remotely suspect he is apprehending a legitimate drama in tones? He seems darkly conscious of a peculiar insufficiency, until Nature responds to his struggle by luring him into a state of pseudo-contentment. With her facile magic, she conjures up in his mind all kinds of fanciful spatial imagery, to fill the void she abhors. Thus a Chopin nocturne may yield visions of colorful gardens or lovely pastoral scenes—-most welcome gifts to an eager listener who now believes he has found the "meaning" of the thing. How could he know that these creatures of the painter's fancy are but substitute-images, extra-musical by-products of his own creating? The reversal of this procedure explains the nature of program music. To avoid abstract discussion, let us take Schubert's "Erlking" as an example. In Goethe's famous poem one may discover three distinct phases: the text, a pageant of spatial imagery, and the all-important emotional undercurrent which falls into the category of temporal imagery. The text finds its pictorial illustration in the spatial imagery it evokes; but the essence of the poem must be looked for elsewhere. One who has never known love and hate, hope and despair, will never write such poetry. "The Erlking" rests on an emotional basis; and it is this basic temporal phase that found significant expression in Schubert's immortal song. The root of all imagery is kinaesthetic; this fundamental type not only represents the *prima forma* of the poem but also functions as the composer's lodestar. All the information he may gather, all the colorful spatial imagery it engenders, are of no earthly use to the composer unless reduced to the one-dimensional level of kinaesthesis. Only in this manner can the poem grow into a song. The composer's contribution is not to be regarded in the light of an organic change; on the contrary, it is the last step in the realization of the poet's dream. Whatever music is gleaned from poetry slumbers at the base of the poetic idea. The composer brings it to life, and so reinforces the essence of the poem by giving it a musical underpinning. All program music originates in this manner.

Program music is often preferred to pure music, because the program somehow elucidates the music. There are some, however, who claim that because of its hybrid character, program music must necessarily be inferior to pure music. While this attitude is understandable, it must seem rather strange to question the value of masterpieces like *The Mastersingers* and *Tristan and Isolde*. To be sure, the program governs the composer and thereby guides and restrains him. But this is also true in pure music. Minuet, rondo, fugue, and sonata represent strictly defined formal frameworks; and whatever freedom the composer craves he must exercise within fixed boundaries. Again, there are those who think that program music is a new entity, the product of a complete fusion of program and music. It is clear that this is impossible. The program furnishes the composer's inspiration; the music is his response. And while the causal nexus exists, cause and effect should never be identified. The reason for any misconception of the value of this type of music lies not in the influence of the program but in its coexistence. All program music is a coördination of program and music. No matter how close their affinity, the program remains program, and the music will always be music. Program music is neither better nor worse than pure music; it is *different* because it is a combination of two or more arts.

PURE MUSIC

The listener who fails to approach music as he should is apt to turn painter, sculptor, or poet. The substitute-images referred to are not only out of place in pure music but actually destructive. Pure music expresses types,—the graceful, the beautiful, the sublime, and their countless nuances. To interpret such music by way of a single object-image reduces the typical to the specific, and so dilutes the vigor and narrows the scope of the composition. If the ear were as well trained as the eye, temporal images would be as clear, as vivid, and as significant as the common spatial variety. Until this equalization is achieved, kinaesthetic thinking must remain dim, and kinaesthetic imagery correspondingly vague. It is this unsatisfactory vagueness which causes vicarious imagery by way of discontent. Thus, substitute-images emerge to reinforce an all too faint kinaesthesis. Under these conditions, the natural process is reversed. Instead of the spatial factor becoming subservient to the temporal, the temporal is spatially interpreted.

There is no end of evidence to show that the average music-lover is deeply moved by good music, despite his inability to account for his reaction. Kinaesthesis plays an all-important part in every experience; but it must be observed in its pure state to be thoroughly appreciated. Pure music furnishes this opportunity. External stimuli (vibrations) are not experienced as such; the transformation of auditory data into musical sounds is immediate, and no intrusion of object-images or concepts deflects man's inward gaze. One who is stirred by a symphony knows that something worthwhile has happened to him. Being unable to define his experience by way of spatial imagery or conceptual thought, he believes that he *feels;* and in this faith he has many followers. The meaning of the term *feeling* is sufficiently vague to be generally accepted; therefore the popularity of the old saying, "Music expresses feelings." It has been carefully explained that the listener thinks even as the performer and the composer. Why then does he declare that he feels when his behavior proves that he thinks? One who proclaims a composition beautiful pronounces a judgment; this act presupposes intelligent cognition and discrimination. The answer is simple enough. He has been taught to think conceptually and is wholly ignorant of the nature and scope of kinaesthetic thinking. What the layman calls feeling is identical with kinaesthesis in its temporal purity.

Owing to its spontaneous inception pure music cannot be attached to the retinue of an external power. It is born autonomous, and maintains its exalted rank. The composer's message is conditioned by his peculiar imagination; its appearance is governed by the particular medium through which it is projected. Because pure kinaesthesis furnishes no object-images or concepts, the composer cannot recognize his work in terms of object-data or language. Notwithstanding this, he has the keenest knowledge of the *essence* of his message. This is all he needs; he can convey no more. Pure music expresses the essence of the composer's past— the dynamic residue of his experience, reorganized into temporal images and crystallized in tone. The musician cannot paint pictures or carve statues; nor may he give verbal information like the poet. Music portrays those recondite soul states which *underlie* all spatial imagery and conceptual thought. This makes it the basic art. By way of summary, we are ready to answer the question, What is music? Music is the significant tonal projection of the idea in its temporal form.[6]

Some Musical Forms

It is well known that all art music rests on song and dance, the music of the people. It should not appear strange then that a host of musical art forms can be reduced to these two basic types. Fortunately, a most compelling proof can be found in the common source of song and dance. For want of a better term this parent form shall be called arabesque.[7]

---

[6] In the same way, the dance may be defined as the kinematic projection of a temporal image (or image-complex).

[7] It must be borne in mind that the term *arabesque*, as here used, is not to be identified with some compositions so labeled. It is no more than a vague tonal pattern, wholly devoid of rhythmic organization and melodic significance.

ARABESQUE

This crude pattern (Fig. A) represents no more than musical raw material; it becomes meaningful and may be intelligently apprehended when duly organized. Since we shrewdly reduce what is too large for convenient cognition,

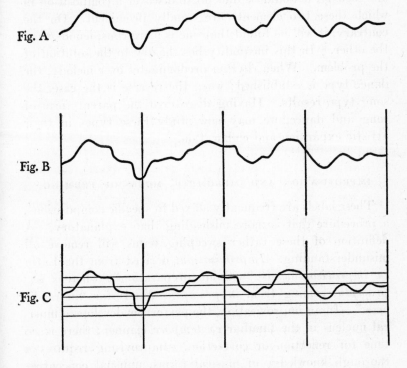

Fig. A

Fig. B

Fig. C

Fig. A is divided and subdivided into equal parts, small enough to be comfortably manipulated. That these vertical dividing lines appear at equidistant points is due to our innate sense of rhythm. Thus Fig. B shows Fig. A *quantitatively* bounded; and the rhythmic element, dormant in Fig. A, is now established. There remains the necessity of awakening its latent melodic features. This is accomplished by the horizontal or *qualitative* division, as shown in Fig. C. The varying intensity apparent in the rise and fall of the pattern may now be easily measured and accurately judged. The original quasi-chaotic arabesque (Fig. A) is now sufficiently developed and matured to give birth to song and dance. While all music shares the dual charm of rhythm and melody, it would be difficult to discover a composition in which these two elements are equally prominent. On the contrary, it will be found that one is more conspicuous than the other. In this inequality lies the key to the solution of the problem. When rhythm predominates over melody, the dance type is established; when the reverse is the case, the song type results. Having discovered the parent form of song and dance, we may now study these types in their artistic expansion and elaboration.

IMPROVISATION AND IMPROMPTU, MODES OF FORMING

These labels are frequently affixed to specific compositions, a procedure that is more misleading than explanatory. A definition of these rather sweeping terms will remove all misunderstanding. *Improvisation*, derived from the Latin *ex improviso*, means "without preparation"; whereas *impromptu*, coming from *in promptu*, stands for "in readiness." In an improvisation, the performer develops a musical nucleus in the familiar *ex tempore* manner; there is no time for reflection or correction. Improvising requires a thorough knowledge of musical forms, unusual concentration, a fertile imagination, and a flexible mind. The great masters of the past excelled in this spontaneous type of musical utterance; and history informs us that the improvised fugues of J. S. Bach were regarded as nothing short of miraculous.

Just as every healthy idea is the product of spontaneity,

so an entire short composition may be born mature and complete. One must here assume an unconscious genesis, since the composer consciously contributed little or nothing. Examples of this type are to be found in Schubert's songs and dances and most likely in some of Chopin's shorter preludes. The writer has reason to know that this is possible; it has happened to him more than once. While the gifted composer may improvise a symphony, such a complex and extensive composition could never come about in the impromptu fashion. It is reasonable to claim that the title "Impromptu" is out of place except in small and relatively simple compositions.

CHORALE PRELUDE

In its simplest form, the chorale may be defined as a sacred song, which in the chorale prelude acquires its artistic setting. It is natural to assume that a chorale prelude is a prelude to a chorale,—but this is far from true. Musical literature shows that this type of composition is a kind of polished improvisation on a chorale theme. Further investigation will show that this is exactly what the composer intended it to be. The Germans not only borrowed the Latin term *praeludium*, but also coined the corresponding verb *praeludieren*, which means to "preludize." A correct definition of the chorale prelude is rather difficult unless the investigator knows that in the German language the term *praeludieren* is synonymous with improvising. Almost every chorale prelude exhibits that free treatment of a theme so peculiar to improvisation. This is particularly evident in the well-known "Awake! the Voice Commands" of Bach, in which the theme itself is divided into several sections, preceded by a prelude, connected by interludes, and closed by a postlude. The chorale prelude has preserved for posterity many inspired sacred tunes; incidentally it shows that a god-given play instinct can perform its wonders in an incense-laden cathedral atmosphere.

SONG AND DANCE FORM (A–B–A)

When the formula "thesis-antithesis-synthesis" can be justly applied to a composition, three essentials are indicated: homogeneity, a tripartite structure, and a functional identity in spite of structural disparity. The alphabetical formula A–B–A would be of greater service if modified as follows: A^t–B–A^s. A^t stands for thesis, or statement; B for antithesis, or counterstatement; and A^s for synthesis, whose function is to unify A^t and B. It is not by accident that most songs and dances are so constructed; our task is to account for this phenomenon. The writer's "Lullaby," published in this volume, will furnish a practical example, and the missing text here supplied will simplify the analysis.

Lullaby

Hush my darling, hush my baby,
    Twilight hovers everywhere;
Sweet repose may heaven grant thee:
    Dreamland's vision, bright and fair.

Evening shades are falling faster,
    Purple hills in darkness glow;
Starry hosts attend their master:
    Guarding all who sleep below.

This two-stanza poem is obviously an A–B structure; yet in the song, the repetition of the first stanza adds a third section. This addition was found imperative, and the reason for it must be discovered. A sharp contrast between the two stanzas of the poem will be noticed; the first represents a nursery picture, while the second paints a cosmic image.

This chasm is easily bridged unconsciously by referring to the first stanza after having read the second. It is human nature to join things thus into a unity.

It has been said that in the song the music intensifies the emotional phase of the poem. In doing this it also strengthens its contrasting features. Because of this intensification, the first stanza, which now functions as synthesis, had to be repeated. In the song, the A–B poem structure is enhanced in scope and intensity; and the need for the A^t–B–A^s structure stands explained (Fig. D). In Chopin's Prelude, Opus

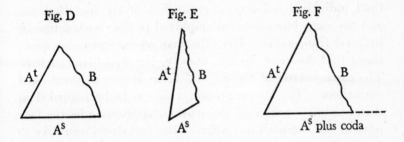

Fig. D   Fig. E   Fig. F

A^t B A^t B A^t B

A^s A^s A^s plus coda

28, No. 6, A^t contains fourteen measures, whereas A^s has only four. This is explained by the fact that the contrast between A^t and B is so slight that the shortened A^s suffices to establish a balanced unity (Fig. E). A very different A^t–B–A^s structure may be observed in Brahms's Intermezzo, Opus 117, No. 1. Here the contrast between A^t and B is so glaring that a stronger synthesis is required to achieve a complete unification. In this example, A^s presents an embellished repetition of A^t plus an extra four measures [8] (Fig. F). While basically identical, these compositions are individually different. This proves that a musical idea is not to be forced into a pre-fabricated formal strait jacket. On the contrary, the idea, conditioned by a given mood,

[8] This four-bar appendage is known as the coda; its function is to augment the unifying powers of A^s.

predicates the form in which it is to appear. Again we see that "in genius, Nature works according to her own laws."

THEME AND VARIATIONS

It was the great Kant who unwittingly defined this form when he said: "In order that a change may take place, it must take place on something; this something, however, dare not change." While this may sound like an amusing word-play, a simple analogy will show that Kant was right. A builder may erect a number of skyscrapers which show distinct individual differences, regardless of the fact that one and the same blueprint was employed in the construction of the steel frameworks. Here the changes take place on something that does not change, namely, the structural nucleus. The same is true of the musical form known as theme and variations. The theme proper, which is to be regarded as the composer's source of inspiration, appears to be the best part of the composition; whereas the variations seem like so many attempts to approach the perfection of the theme.[9] A variation may be sketchy or elaborate, graceful or ponderous; it may even change from song to dance; there can be no objection as long as the theme is somehow recognizable in the variation. For a better understanding of this form, it is imperative to consider that a theme may be skeletonized. This is accomplished by divesting its rhythmic, harmonic, and melodic features of all but the essentials necessary to the preservation of its individuality. This denuding process lays bare the structural nucleus of the theme. Not the perfect theme but the skeleton is responsible for the variations. The composer's imagination is fired by the formal immaturity of the nucleus, and then sustained by its inherent strength. In this wise the same idea may assume many dif-

[9] Beethoven, Easy Variations (ed. Steingraeber); also Sonata, Op. 26, first movement.

ferent appearances. Organic unity, a wealth of colors, and an ever-changing surface constitute the charm of this form. There are scores of excellent variations, all of which repay careful study. As might be expected, even here the gradual growth from simplicity to complexity may be observed. In the early variations, the composer had but little freedom; whereas, in the later examples, he wanders far afield. In these compositions, the relation between theme and variation is often vague; but closer inspection shows that the composer has not ignored the nucleus in the far-flung flights of his fancy.[10]

RONDO

The French rondeau, a dance-song of medieval times, is generally accepted as the prototype of the instrumental rondo. This form shows a marked development and strong central control. As in the variation, the theme functions as the composer's source of inspiration, but there the resemblance stops. A rondo theme generates a number of lesser strains known as responses. While they are organically related to the theme in structure, they are quite different. They do not represent the same idea in varied garbs (as in the variation); they express the several phases of the idea. Fig. G indicates the cyclic principle here employed. The theme (T) generates its first offspring, A; the second appearance of T is followed by the new issue, B; and this procedure continues until the fecundity of the theme is

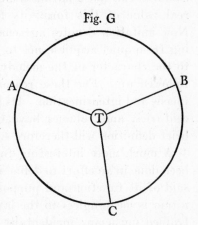

Fig. G

10 Brahms, Variations on a Theme by Haydn.

exhausted. Assuming that there are three offspring, A,B,C, the structure could be explained as follows: A is the product of T; B, the issue of T plus A; and C, the fruit of T plus A plus B. Since these responses, A,B,C, are born of the same theme (T), they are also controlled by it. This is indicated in Fig. G by the circle which joins and unifies the diverse sections of the composition. The rondo is frequently employed as the closing movement of the concerto and the symphony. It is a lively tune, jolly and often exuberant; it springs from a surplus of vitality and breathes the joy of living.

CANON AND FUGUE

Structurally speaking, the canon merely embodies imitation. The same melody is presented by two or more voices in such a way as to overlap; they seem to crowd one another like shingles on a roof. So regarded, the composing of canons seems like a harmless musical pastime; to discover the real value of this form, its function must be considered. Now imitation denotes agreement and corroboration, ranging from quiet acquiescence to vigorous approval, according to the character of the melody and the speed in which it is followed up. For these reasons the canon is used for emphasis and intensification. Its historical genesis covers many centuries, and volumes have been written about it. This brief definition will therefore suffice in this place.

A much more interesting form is the fugue. Much has been done in an effort to define its structure. Little has been said of its function and purpose. The best structural definition is meaningless to the layman, and superfluous to the trained musician; incidentally it fails to explain why such a thing as a fugue should be. The young composer is confronted with a set of strict rules which he must implicitly obey. Having successfully finished his task, he has a tonal pattern which happens to be called a fugue. The structure he now understands, but of its artistic value and usefulness he knows little or nothing. This would be a sorry state of affairs if it could not be remedied.

Since art is a transmutation of the data of experience, every art form should be definable in terms of experience. What is not somehow found in life will never be discovered in art; and the fugue is no exception. It has been repeatedly stated that all laws are culled from the masterpieces; and this raises an interesting question. What set of laws guided the composer who wrote the first fugue? The answer is not so difficult as would appear. This man had a particular message, and discovered the only possible way in which it could be significantly expressed. That this form should have been called a fugue is of no great importance; it might very well have acquired a more appropriate label. Let us propose a definition here, more likely to startle the professional man than the layman.

It cannot be denied that the symphony is a drama in tones; in the same way the fugue may be defined as a *tonal symposium*. This is not a mere structural definition, but covers function and purpose as well. It will also explain the reason for the fugue's existence. In this form, a given theme is soon joined by a number of counterpoints (companion melodies) which are closely related to it. The theme proper suffers no organic change throughout the composition, but the counterpoints are individually different. Obviously the argument so essential to the fugue cannot emanate from the theme; it is rooted in the disparity of the counterpoints. As the conflict grows in intensity (the stretto section), some of the counterpoints seem to fall by the wayside, while one or more survive because of their superior strength.[11] When terms like *theme* and *counterpoint* are translated into *statement* and *commentary*, the fugue can be discussed in terms

[11] Bach's "Well-Tempered Clavichord," fugue in C sharp minor.

of everyday experience, which the layman as well as the professional man can understand.

A group of men who have agreed to discuss a given problem may wander far afield, but they will be careful not to lose sight of the chosen topic. A parallel situation exists in the fugue. Here too is perfect agreement as to the theme which is to be exploited. Its constant repetition preserves its individuality and rank. As soon as the topic is agreed upon, each member of the symposium presents his individual commentary and maintains his standpoint until defeated. Later he may try again and offer a different point of view, or join in the opinion of his rival. This too is found in the fugue, where different counterpoints seem to strive for survival. Just as in the heat of an argument extreme care must be taken to hold to the point, so in the fugue, in the stretto section, the theme crowds in upon the counterpoints by appearing in the overlapping manner of the canon.[12] Any topic to be defined must be regarded in terms of a problem, and the argument as the road to its solution. The initial presentation of the fugal theme also presents a definite problem, as every composer knows. Many difficult approaches are employed, which culminate in the argument; and the ultimate reëntry of the theme is the solution of the problem. While this form is far too vital and important to be toyed with, it has furnished much sport to the musical mathematicians. Thousands of structurally perfect fugues have been written—and forgotten. They lacked the living substance, the *sine qua non* of all formal expression.

THE SONATA MOVEMENT

The sonata, and its orchestral equivalent the symphony, should not be confused with the sonata movement. In this compact form, the A–B–A pattern (already referred to in

[12] Bach's "Well-Tempered Clavichord," fugue in E flat minor.

song and dance) achieves its highest development. Now thesis (A^t), containing both statement and counterstatement, constitutes what is known as the *exposition*. Antithesis (B) stands for *thematic development;* and synthesis (A^s) refers to *recapitulation*. A more specific description will be furnished in the next paragraph.

SYMPHONY

The symphony represents the masterform; it may be likened to and discussed in terms of a complex drama. It is a composite structure which embraces many of the lesser forms; but its basic strength and cohesive power are due to the fact that it is anchored in the sonata movement.[13]

Let us then proceed from the familiar drama to the less familiar symphony. Fundamentally, the drama can be defined as the acting out of an idea, and its principal characters as the chief interpreters of the ideational complex. The same is true of the symphony—it is a drama in tones. It too expresses an idea, and its themes spring from the same nuclear source, and serve the same elucidative purpose. In like manner the lesser characters of the drama correspond to the counterpoints of the symphony. These unassuming creatures are more important than their modest station would imply. They represent and interpret their superiors, by whom they are begotten; they furnish the connecting tissue which welds the contrasting elements into an harmonious ensemble. It is clear that these two forms have much in common. They are identical in substance and structure, function and purpose. The obvious disparity is a matter of imagery and medial projection.

[13] For clarity's sake, it must be understood that "theme" and "counterpoint" are applicable to every section of the symphony, whereas "thematic development" refers exclusively to those parts which are constructed according to the pattern of the sonata movement.

The relationship between drama and symphony stands in the following formula:

Drama:	Exposition	Argument	Dénouement
Symphony:	Exposition	Thematic development	Recapitulation

The motives of the symphony represent the highlights of the idea, and should be treated as such. It is equally important to show that they spring from a common parent. The connecting tissue also must be considered if this relationship would be discovered. There is also the thematic development, a kind of musical argument which serves to establish the unity of the whole by revealing the affinity of the parts. The highlights are all-important, but the function of the lowlights must not be underrated. It is they that bridge the gaps, and so fuse a manifold into a synthesis. All this is quite simple, easily explained, and readily understood; yet error usually prevails over truth here because of a shallow conception and a superficial approach.

The sophisticated layman is wont to favor the themes of the symphony at the expense of the ensemble. He may be likened to the casual opera-goer who singles out the "stars" and thereby misses the play. Both are star-gazers, who stare in awe and wonder at the major constellations, but never behold the glorious firmament. They give little and get less, because discrete attention inhibits concrete apprehension. In centering their interest on the highlights, they unwittingly *de*compose a work of art. They do not suspect that art *apart* is no longer art. Now sporadic audition begets rhapsodic thought; and an organic structure soon disintegrates into a litter of fragments. A meaningful synthesis degenerates into a vague synopsis, and a symphony into a rhapsody.

The naïve music lover intuitively avoids the pitfalls of "easy sophistication." He listens as he must, which is as he should—*synthetically*. Like the composer, he joins phrase to phrase, section to section, and movement to movement. He reconstructs the original. He is the creative listener, the performer's silent partner, and the legitimate heir of genius. If he is wise enough to choose the easy road from the simple to the complex, he will soon learn that a wholesome enjoyment of music is his natural due, and not the privilege of a favored few.

OVERTURE

The overture has suffered many changes, both in structure and in function, since the early days when almost anything was used and accepted as long as it preceded a musical play. It was not until Gluck presented his *Iphigenia in Aulis* that the essential question of organic relationship and true significance was successfully answered. What he established was nurtured by Mozart; it reached perfection in Beethoven's "Leonore" Overture No. 3. This superb composition is in itself a musical drama. Although the idea of *Fidelio* furnished the inspiration here, the overture seems to surpass the opera.

There are two distinct types of this form: the concert overture and the operatic overture. Notwithstanding this difference, they are more easily confounded than distinguished. Beethoven's "Egmont," inspired by Goethe's drama, is a typical concert overture. It portrays in bold strokes the emotional highlights of the underlying program. By virtue of the intimate relation between music and drama, this same composition would function as an operatic overture if the composer had chosen to give this drama an operatic setting. There are prologues of this type in which all specific mention of the details of the opera is avoided. Conversely, there is the potpourri variety, which lays no claim to structural individuality; it is satisfied with the collective presentation of melodies taken from the play proper. Wagner, who fully understood the nature and purpose of the overture, speaks of it as an "ideal prologue." This definition is both sound and significant, if the term *ideal* is understood as the adjective form of *idea*. In "The Mastersingers" the idea of life in Renaissance Nürnberg is portrayed; and the overture presents a compact and meaningful orchestral preview of the drama. Even so this overture has found its way into the concert hall. Like Beethoven's "Leonore" it is an outstanding example of symphonic writing, and is easily accepted as a concert overture by those who do not know the opera. Brahms' "Academic Festival Overture" is built on German student songs; it has overture character and belongs to the concert type. Like "Egmont," it would have answered operatic purposes had the composer chosen to use the idea of German student life as an operatic subject as Wagner did with Renaissance Nürnberg.

RHAPSODY

The rhapsody, as its name implies, presents a tonal structure in which individual musical units are elaborately embroidered and cleverly strung together. Unlike the other forms here defined, it contains material that is not organically related. While the rhapsody gives the impression of an harmonious ensemble, it is not a synthesis; it is a manifold. For this reason it lends itself to the collective presentation of many musical gems, provided they have enough in common to form a more or less balanced ensemble.

SYMPHONIC POEM

Liszt has frequently and successfully used the symphonic poem; but he did not create it. Forms are never plucked out of thin air, nor are they manufactured overnight. They have their prototypes, from which they gradually evolve. The orthodox symphonic poem (*e. g.*, Liszt's "Les Préludes") is an orchestral composition based on a single flexible theme. This accounts for its compact unity and brevity. In this work, the theme is not exploited by analytical dissection, as in the sonata movement; it is developed by modifying its rhythmic, melodic, and dynamic features. A melodic curve may easily be changed into an angle, thus transforming a gentle strain into a vigorous one. Its appearance may be further varied by stretching or foreshortening, a process which augments or diminishes its original structure. Dynamic changes are employed to increase or decrease the intensity of the original melodic curve or angle.

It has been held that "Les Préludes" has two distinct themes. On the surface this seems true; but a close investigation proves that some people underrate the vast possibilities of dynamic modification. The original theme begins with C, descends a half-tone to B, and then rises two and a half tones to E. The mythical second theme descends and ascends in half-tone steps, which is a clear example of dynamic deflation. Its greater mobility is also explained by the half-tone progression, which encounters less resistance than a larger interval. Errors of this kind are understandable, but can be avoided if judgment is withheld until all the potentialities of a flexible theme have been carefully studied. Richard Strauss, who learned much from Liszt, has not adhered to the orthodox form of the symphonic poem. He uses two or more themes and wisely employs such titles as "tone poem" and "tone painting." These compositions follow the ever-changing character of the underlying story; they lay no claim to strict form, and may be classified as orchestral ballades. There are two well-known exceptions, "Till Eulenspiegel" and "Don Quixote." The former takes the rondo form, while the latter is fashioned as theme and variations.

It is futile to speculate on the future of musical forms; all that can be said with certainty is that the greatest composers have invariably succeeded by observing the principle of freedom within the law.

Speaking of freedom and discipline, of beauty and simplicity, one is tempted to think of the immortal Schubert. Like all the truly great, he built on bedrock—the music of the people. He leads us back to the source of all music, to the very soul of man, away from sophistication and artificiality,—in short, back to nature. Clarity of substance, simplicity of form, and an unimpeded flow of melodies and harmonies characterize this music; it is as true as joy and grief, as indestructible as life itself.

PART FOUR

AESTHETIC TYPES

AESTHETIC TYPES

Art and the pleasure it gives may be thought of in two ways. It may be interpreted in general terms: as something discoverable throughout the range of human experience—in a game, a bit of organized business, religious feeling, some social amenity—and as yielding pleasure through the art in all these things. Or we may turn to the artistic impulse as it takes definite and varied form in the several arts; study it as it expresses itself in the medium and through the aims and methods of each of these arts; and read our responding pleasure always within the qualifying context of whatever art calls it forth.

Of these two ways, the first is unreservedly bad. It is true that what is called art in the narrow sense has emerged from larger practical life-interests and from vague artistic shapings of the whole stuff of experience; and that, once independent, it again finds its way into larger and vaguer life-contexts. But no aesthetics worthy of the name can stop with generalities. If it is not to become loose-lipped it must turn to fine art, seek to understand its processes, capture its substance and its spirit, taste of its creative wealth and order, and get close to its ideals and pleasures. This is the reason for the second way—an analytic study of the system of the arts.

Another problem, however, remains: that of aesthetic types. Often when we pass from painting to painting, from poem to poem we become aware of differences of purpose and effect within a general artistic effectiveness. Such differences may also be found as we pass from one art to another.

Virgil, the sculptors of the *Laocoon*, and the painter El Greco have made creative use of the same material. The effect in the three cases is startlingly different. Peculiarities in the aim and the resources of poetry, sculpture, and painting have something to do with this—there is this much truth, at least, in Lessing's essay—but they do not explain why tragedy and pathos are so arrestingly present in the poem and the group and are all but absent in El Greco's painting. If Michelangelo had painted the picture they would have been there. The reason must lie in personal preferences and aptitudes. El Greco meant to be decorative.

Cutting across the arts and expressive of a personal bent and definite aim, are certain broad aesthetic types. Sublimity marks the genius of Aeschylus; Sappho, Catullus, and Keats are voices of grace and beauty; Whitman's poetry naturally falls within the characteristic; Tennyson is idyllic; and Byron is picturesque. There is sensuous beauty in Titian, tragedy in Michelangelo, grace in Praxiteles, pathos in Scopas, rough strength in Van Gogh, idyllic charm in Watteau, decorative appeal in Botticelli and in Gauguin. Music may be any one of these things. In single works of art, the creative impulse is seen pointed in its choice and shaping at one or the other of these types. Their meaning lies there. If it is to be grasped a careful understanding must be gained of the substance and spirit of the *beautiful*, the *characteristic*, the *sublime*, the *comic*, the *tragic*, and of *minor* types.

Again, if we pass from the work of art to the response to art, we must seek to understand appreciation in its specialized forms. Beauty of structure and beauty of language or organized sound may be discovered in the *Oedipus Rex*, in *Hamlet*, and in Chopin's *Funeral March*; but with reference to all three the exclamation: "how beautiful" would be pitifully inadequate. This is not what they mean to be; they are quintessentially tragic, and as such they grip and hold us. They all give pleasure, it is true, but unless the specific nature of this pleasurable response is looked for and its roots in human nature are searched for, our comprehension of art and of the enjoyment it yields to him who knows its secrets will always be uncritical and shallow.

These are but two sides of one problem—the markings in art and the forces in its diversified satisfactions. It is the problem of the following chapters.

THE BEAUTIFUL

The beautiful may be used widely and loosely to mark the aesthetically effective. In its narrower sense, however—the immediately, smoothly, and wholly pleasing—it is one of the aesthetic types, with a will and appeal of its own. Attempt after attempt has been made to get close to its quality and to understand its relations to other types. But the difficulties are many. It appears differently in the several arts and shows a perplexing variety even in a single art. People may agree as to how the term is to be used and yet retain their sharply individual preferences in their choice of objects to be called beautiful. There is also the danger of slipping into the wider aesthetic use. More insidious still is the temptation to take the term over into the realm of metaphysics, away from art, into a mystical and spreading light. Plato is guilty of this; so are Hegel and Schopenhauer in so far as they force beauty within the general formula of their systems. It must be enchanting to sit on the metaphysical branch of the tree of life and to utter the clear-throated, commanding notes of a world-song of beauty, but I prefer a humbler position on the ground, and the less pretentious task of keeping the beautiful close to art—and of seeking a modulated understanding of what it means there and in our common aesthetic responses. Even such a task is none too easy.

The beautiful appears in art as: *sensuous beauty, beauty of form*, and *beauty of meaning-in-form*.

SENSUOUS BEAUTY

The beautiful is somewhat loosely applied to simple sensuous material as yet unformed: to a patch of color or a

APOLLO FROM THE TEMPLE AT OLYMPIA

single note. In such cases little more can be done than to point to an immediate, fully satisfying pleasingness. Notes very high or low in the scale are not so pleasing as are notes within these extremes. The peculiar clang-tint given to notes of the same pitch by different musical instruments also affects the pleasingness. A piano note is more immediately and purely pleasing than a cornet note; the blare of a trumpet does not favor beauty as the clear smooth sounds of a violin or flute do; organ music inclines to sublimity by the sheer volume and swell of its sound, it is rarely beautiful. Blue is often more pleasing than brown, and robin-egg blue more pleasing than ultramarine. Certain greens are displeasing. Delicate tints are more easily worked into a beautiful whole than intense, obtrusive shades. A luminous, smooth expanse of color is closer to beauty than a muddy, harshly varied one. Line, substance, and texture show similar differences. A broad, straight or jagged line is harsher, heavier, less alive than a slender and delicate curve; plaster is dead, as marble and wood are not; velvet has a quiet and facile persuasiveness lacking in calico or linen.

Experimental studies have been made of preferences of color and line. They have revealed wide individual differences and hidden associational influences. They have shown that in what seems to be purely sensuous beauty a formative element enters: thus part of the secret of something subtly or brilliantly alive—a face, a woodland scene, an Oriental rug—is seen to rest in the opportunities given by such animated surfaces for the enjoyment of ever new relational surprises and varying patterns.

BEAUTY OF FORM

Art takes sensuous material, for its beauty or expressive strength, and gives it an organic unity in variety which is called form. In doing this it creates a new aesthetic value or develops an implied one. In such of its works as are aimed at the beautiful as an aesthetic type the materials are wholly pleasing in their own right or they at least do not thwart a reshaping in which the workmanship is perfect and the created form satisfies completely and easily. Keats's *Ode on a Grecian Urn* is an example of the beautiful in art. There are no harsh-sounding words, no obtrusive images; there is a "linked sweetness" in the sequence of the lines; the rhythm is smooth and flowing. Within the structural scheme and blended wealth of the poem there is nothing intense or crudely aggressive which might *jump out* and disrupt the unity of tone and mood.

There is no one formula for formal beauty. There are many materials and patterns equally and differently pleasing; perfect workmanship may be shown in many ways. Keats's *To Sleep;* Swinburne's *A Match* and his second *Rondel;* many of the lyrics of Goethe; the Temple of the Nike Apteros; the Chateau de Pierrefonds; Rheims Cathedral; Correggio's *The Virgin and Child with St. Jerome;* Fragonard's *Le Chiffre d'Amour;* Manet's *The Grand Canal* and his technically very different *Fifer*—one and all are definitely aimed at beauty of form. In all of them is beauty differently compounded and held within individual organizational schemes.

What are the marks of the beautiful as it creates special values in the shaping of what is sensuously pleasing? To attempt completeness here would be folly; the most that can be done is to pass in review some of the qualities and devices most often revealed and used in such shaping.

REGULARITY

An irregular face is not beautiful; there is very little room for jagged, purposelessly varied lines in a form aimed at beauty. A regular recurrence of pleasing musical phrases or rhythmic units, of ratios of line, of colors is sought. As soon, however, as regularity gives the impression of being mechanical or too directly desired it becomes monotonous and displeasing. If it is to serve its purpose it must suggest a spontaneous as well as an effective correlation of parts; it must admit of some measure of individuality and variety.

SYMMETRY, BALANCE

Symmetry and balance are special forms of regularity. Symmetry when used in art yields a disciplined beauty of organization through time and space correspondences and inverted bilateral repetition. Balance seeks an equilibrium which is either frankly kinetic or decorative and compositional or one of psychic weight. The façade of Rheims Cathedral is symmetrical and kinetically balanced. Many pictures, beautiful in design, show a balanced arrangement of masses of color. Psychic weight is a matter of balance of interest. In a beautiful face interest in the eyes does not dominate—as it does in the face of Raphael's *Sistine Madonna*—there are balancing attractions in the forehead or in a delicately rounded cheek or chin.

PLEASING VARIETY

Art becomes ineffective—fails of beauty in the broad sense—when there is a confusing mass of unrelated detail or intricacy great enough to baffle and annoy. The beautiful in the narrow sense, as an aesthetic type, moves far within this danger point. Intricate, involved patterns and great wealth of detail it avoids. Within a comparatively simple scheme it aims at a persuasive, engaging variety. The beautiful has not the starkness and downrightness of the characteristic; it has not the emotional subtlety of the tragic and the inciting quality of the sublime; and it lacks the ornateness of the decorative. Sappho is never complex or obtrusive, and she is never monotonous. Words, images, rhythmical forms, meanings—they all share in a simply modulated life.

DELICACY

Many of the other types show a heavy, emphatic touch. The comic and the characteristic, for instance, are constantly underscoring. Not so the beautiful! It is delicate, light, persuasive rather than mastering. Rheims Cathedral shows delicacy worked into the least responsive or aesthetic materials; Watteau and Fragonard are delicate and light in their use of line, light and shade, patterning, and color. Renoir often turns massive forms into beautiful designs by a feathery use of color and a pervasive and finely touched play of light and shade. Van Gogh is too gaunt; Hodler, too much concerned with energy; and Cézanne, too directly structural to achieve beauty in this sense—nor is it their aim.

ANIMATION

The whole beauty of a diamond is in its *life*—in its animated, colorful reflections. Only a small part of the appeal of an impressionistic landscape is to be found in its brilliancy of color; most of it is gained from making the surfaces of nature visually alive in their changing reflections. A stolid face is never completely beautiful; it has the fatal defect of deadness. There must be life and sparkle in a painting or a poem. The individual life breathed into artistic forms differs from artist to artist, from picture to picture. Manet's *Grand Canal* and *The Longchamp Races* both have animation, but they *live* in different ways. In Fragonard's *Le Chiffre d'Amour* beauty is reached through the living play of light; Renoir gains animation in his landscapes in this way, but also by rhythms of color.

DISTINCTION

Distinction is not a quality peculiar to the beautiful; the tragic and the sublime have it, while it is lacking in the comic and the charming. The want of it in a face means a drop from the beautiful to the pretty. Distinction is a matter of quality; the pretty is pleasing and lightly valued; the beautiful is satisfying as well as pleasing, and holds us with a deeper and richer appeal. It is the finer thing. In art distinction is not easily discovered in very small things—in miniatures, for example—hence they are not so naturally called beautiful. Aristotle probably goes too far when he says that a very small object cannot be beautiful. With the principle of unity in variety in mind, he saw insufficient chance of relational interpretation and shaping. But these may be possible in a single verse or in the painting of so slight a thing as a leaf or petal.

Distinction in art is not to be confused with the grand manner. It may be the mark of a simple treatment of humble things, but only if there is a large and fine rendering. The petty and the coarse kill it. Naturalistic art seldom achieves it, for in occupying itself with details, sordid and petty, and in choosing a photographic method, it passes by the chance of a largely and deeply pleasing and arresting art—an art as fine as it is rare, and of an individual and unusual perfection of form.

INTERFLOW AND INTERGLOW OF PARTS

Perfection is something we do not expect in real life. We see it as an ideal, a hopeless step or two in advance of our performance or as something infinitely remote and unattainable. In art it can be attained; the rare moments when it appears in sensuous form in a poem or song are highly and reverently prized. In aesthetic types like the pretty, the charming, the picturesque the idea of perfection has no place. What is the part it plays in the beautiful?

The beautiful is complete and all of a piece. The unity that it has is a living unity: a common life *flows* back and forth from part to part and *glows* with a warmth and glamour in every enhanced and enhancing part. Plotinus and certain medieval writers were aware of this: the smoothness and *suavitas* they pointed to in the beautiful were nothing but the result of this *interflow;* and their *nitidas* is more than brightness or brilliance, it is a shared luminosity—an *interglow* that is the living light of the form and its parts. Interflow may be seen in the *Ilissus* and the *Hermes*, in many Gothic churches, in Rodin's *Springtime*, in Corot's landscapes and Swinburne's verse; interglow, in Shakespeare's *Sonnets*, in de Hooch's Interiors, in Keats and Shelley, in the landscapes of Sisley or Renoir.

The Beauty of Meaning-in-Form

All art expresses meanings through created forms. The term *meaning-in-form* is clumsy, but it serves to mark the intimate relation that exists in all good art between content and the form it is given. The *Eve* of Rodin is not merely a nude woman, it is a guilt-stricken one; this idea is worked into material and sculptural form, and through them finds a voice. Drooping melancholy becomes articulate in the imagery and rhythm of Keats's ode; youthful vigor and poise, in the *Apoxyomenos;* sheltering mother-love, in the pose of the *Niobe;* tense struggle, in the *Laocoon;* and utter abandon, in the *Drunken Silenus.*

Of meanings there is this to be said: they differ in aesthetic value in two ways; not all of them can be given form in art that is worthwhile, and not all of them favor the same aesthetic type. There are ideas and things so essentially trite or inexpressive as to foil the efforts of the most gifted artist.

No imaginative attempt can redeem them. Others that are aesthetically worthwhile may more naturally take form in the comic, the tragic, or the sublime—in types other than the beautiful.

A form must be studied in relation to the meaning it defines and expresses; and *meaning-in-form* must be referred to the artist's purpose. A tragedy or an elegy may have great beauty of language and structure, but these beauties are incidental; what is willed is the vibrational setting forth of spiritual clashes, of feeling, of moods. It is this, the spirit breathing in the form, that must not be missed—and this spirit need not fall within the single type of the beautiful.

Here are three poetic pictures from the *Agamemnon*. Each is art at its highest: flawless in workmanship, imaginative and compelling. Not one of them is aimed at beauty.

The first refers to the sacrifice of Iphigenia:

And as she let fall to the ground the saffron dye, she smote each of her sacrificers with a piteous glance from the eye; and she lay beautiful as in a picture, wishing to speak, for oft in her father's hospitable walls she had sung, and a pure virgin with her chaste voice she had lovingly honored her dear father's thrice-blessed joyous life.

The second is a vision of war:

And Ares the broker who deals in human bodies, and holds the scales in the contest of the spear, is sending home from Troy to the friends the sad dust burnt in the fire, wept with tears, loading the urns with well-packed ashes in the place of men.

The third gives a picture of the army camped before Troy:

—for our beds were before the very walls of the enemy, and the meadow-dews distilled from heaven and from the earth, a constant destruction to our garments, making our hair like that of beasts.

And should I tell of the bird-slaying winter, what an unbearable one the snow of Ida brought us, or the heat, when the sea in its windless midday bed fell waveless to sleep;—but why lament all this; the labor is past.

Whatever beauty these passages have is merely incidental; their main aesthetic purpose lies elsewhere.   The first means to be pathetic; the second, tragic; the third combines the elegiac and the decorative.   In all three instances we are carried beyond imagery and formal structure to meanings which no form can adequately contain.   Feelings are stirred; imagination is roused and sent off into cosmic problems.   Phrases like *chrysamoibos Ares* and *bird-slaying winter* are marvelous, they conjure unforgettable pictures; but whoever sees only the picture misses their greatest quality, that of emotional intensity and imaginative force.   A phrase like *star-inwrought* is within the beautiful; there we can rest within the image—nothing carries us beyond.   Not so with the others; they force us into the pathetic and the tragic with their shaking and spreading suggestiveness.

It may be said then that beauty of meaning-in-form is sought and gained when materials immediately and wholly pleasing are given perfect form; and when the meanings embodied in these sensuously satisfying forms are such as allow a resting within the charmed circle, which is not broken at any point by too intense an emotion or too propellent an imagination.

Here lies the clue to what the beautiful ultimately means in its contrast to the other aesthetic types.

THE CHARACTERISTIC

Beauty in the narrower sense—pleasing colors, clear sounds, curves, and their smooth, satisfying relations—exhausts neither the meaning nor the purpose of art. There is a distinct aesthetic type, the characteristic, which either makes for a larger, more expressive beauty or contests with the beautiful the title of supremacy in art—a struggle marked by the introduction of repulsive materials, by shattered harmonies of line or sound, by troubled and disconcerting meanings.

It has become the fashion to trace in art and aesthetic theory alike a gradual turning away from the beautiful to the characteristic. This claim seems to be borne out by the fact that (1) the term beautiful has undergone an expansion which carries it into realms—the symbolic, the sublime, the ugly—held at one time to be beyond the frontiers of the aesthetic; (2) a not to be neglected group of radical artists, the expressionists, set themselves a task quite other than the rendering of beauty; (3) even conservative artists have been forced into a bolder and harsher use of materials and methods.

The Nature of the Characteristic

What is meant by the characteristic? The term is often used interchangeably with two others: the significant and the expressive. It is mostly a matter of shading: the characteristic refers more directly to destructive opposition to beauty, truth to type, and sharp individualizing of impressions; the significant, to the association complexes we call meanings; the expressive, to certain suggestive, provoking, and stimulating qualities of colors and lines and their combinations.

The characteristic implies (1) a peculiar technique, (2) the choice of certain materials ordinarily thrown aside as unsuitable, (3) peculiar relational activities.

The technique is one of rough brush strokes, bold daubs of color, short, straight lines, sharp angles, harsh sounds, asymmetrical arrangements in architecture, discords in music. The result is an art of striking, emphatic, tensional impressions: an art which instead of insinuating itself into our graces does enjoyable violence to our senses. Walt Whitman in poetry, Van Gogh in painting, and Rodin in portrait sculpture are artists of this sort. The effect may be a stinging strength not destructive of beauty—such it is in Browning's best work—or it may be an extreme distorting of impressions—Van Gogh's breaking telegraph poles, Cézanne's lop-sided houses, Matisse's dancers, the crazy geometry of cubist heads, the expressionistic technique of a Hasenclever or a Waldo Frank, which by a sudden switching on and off of lights, a merging of the self and the universe, and the ascription of a jerky mobility to everything produces smarting eyes, confusion of soul, and a cosmic *malaise*.

When Cézanne makes oranges angular or when Hodler takes the slight curves out of a young girl's body and makes its outlines stiff and harsh, it is all a matter of technique. The material selected was pleasing and beautiful in the narrower sense; for purposes of his own the artist has reshaped it in the direction of the strong, the harsh, the incisive, the challenging. But there are materials which invite, or in fact demand such a technique. There is not much room for pleasing curves in the face of a Lincoln or in a Christ on the Cross. When Rodin chooses an old, shrivelled body, as he does in *La Vieille Heaulmière*, his selection means a

CARVED WOODEN STOOL, URUA REGION

peril and a definite and peculiar opportunity. The theme
is disillusionment; the material, revolting; the technique,
brutal. It is a bold stroke—in the soft, pleasing art of
Springtime Rodin plays for lesser stakes. An extreme instance of stark ugliness of material is Walt Whitman's *I
Sing of the Body Electric*, with its repellent anatomical details. It is useless to judge such work in terms of beauty.
It means something else to the artist, it ought to mean something else to us. With all such material the redemption is
partly technical—a masterful virility—and partly imaginative—a broadened and intensified reading of life.

There is, again, the relation of a rendering, or image, to
(1) the thing represented or our construct of it, (2) the
type, (3) a system of images and meanings, (4) human life
and its values. The terms expressive and characteristic
apply most directly to the first two; the term significant,
to the last two. (1) On seeing a full length portrait of a
friend, we exclaim: "How expressive the face! How
characteristic the pose!" The original is evidently in our
mind. (2) We look at the portrait of an Old Man by
Lucas Cranach or at Rembrandt's etching of his Mother
and interpret them as studies in the characteristic. Why?
We know neither of the originals, but we have often seen
people like them. They suggest types of aging. The very
script and sign of that aging, as it marks the lower part of
the face, has been revealed by the painters—the mechanical
pressing together of the lips by Cranach and the slackening of lines and trembling infirmity of mouth and chin—
old age caught off its guard—by Rembrandt. In animal
sculpture we demand, in addition to life-likeness, truth to
type; we look for the litheness of the panther or the grotesque lines and lumbering movements of the hippopotamus.
(3) Suppose I say of a line in a poem or a scene in a play,
"How expressive! How significant!" I am clearly marking the large part played by scene or line in those wholes of

images and meanings which I call poem or play, but I may also allude (4) to that larger whole of relations and meanings which I call life.   Hamlet's and Faust's soliloquies are clues to character and moments in a dramatic action, but they are more than that: they stir thoughts and rouse feelings as deep as life itself, and reveal man as a passionate seeker, a puzzler, a wrestler with the cosmic odds against him. In this sense, significant art makes the doors of experience swing on their hinges and open out on the mystery of things.

THE ENJOYMENT OF THE CHARACTERISTIC

Why do we enjoy the characteristic—an aesthetic type which contrasts so sharply with the beautiful?   The problem may be best approached from the side of formal beauty. Beauty implies soothing, restful effects, a resting in the image, and a weakened sense of actuality.   Of these the first needs no comment other than the appeal to common experience.   As regards the second, sheer beauty of sound or color or form holds us and yields a haunting and satisfying pleasure.   Even the slightest sketch of a Leonardo, a Boucher or a Fragonard has a beauty and a charm of line that does not allow us to consider it incomplete or invite to its completion; a water-color of delicate beauty does not admit the thought that a painting in oil could give a deeper and richer semblance of the object.   In view of the "mixed" character of ordinary experiences and the rare emergence of the utterly beautiful from the varied and straining forces of nature, it is small wonder that the formal beauty of art appears to us a charmed circle into which what is dangerous and oppressive cannot step.

All this is reversed in the field of the characteristic.   There is no question of soothing effects.   The characteristic, in its extreme forms, strikes into us like a chill and grips us like a fever. Short of that, it stimulates, excites, unsettles. It does violence to our feeling for harmony, outrages our sense of decorum, and is a challenge flung at our peace of mind. Nor is there a resting in the image. Back of the drawings of Blake and the sculpture of Rodin; of the drab picture of Ibsen's *Ghosts* or Tolstoy's *Power of Darkness*, of the physiology of Whitman's *Songs of Adam* are cosmic visions and cosmic ideas: of stress, of heredity, of natural law, of the breeding of men. Back of the distortions of expressionistic art—from Matisse to Kandinsky or Epstein —is the surging of a chaotic subconsciousness. There is no charmed circle: the actual world breaks in everywhere— strong, rough, ugly, sinister, as the case may be.

The secret of our appreciation of the characteristic lies in a twofold tensional adjustment: clashing elements must be fitted together within a work of art; and that work of art must be harmonized with our "will to beauty." Instead of curves that melt into each other there are short, brusque lines, with an angry tilt to them; there are warring sounds and strained metres; there are aggressive colors that smash into an orderly color scheme. The task of unifying such material tests our mettle, and the victory is never quite complete. Even less complete and hence more tensional is the second attempted adjustment. The "will to beauty" reflects, in part at least, the attempt to rebuild the world closer to our heart's desire. Disquieting, jarring things are cast aside; the ground is cleared. The artist in the characteristic undoes all this; he reawakens our sense of actuality and litters our steps with cosmic débris. In real life the slouching walk, the pasty complexion, and the twitching lips of a drug fiend form a picture which clashes with too complacent a view of things. Make of him material for art, and there is forced within the circle of aesthetic enjoyment something bitter and recalcitrant. The "will to art" lifts the material to the aesthetic level; the "will to beauty" cannot completely adjust itself to material that is straining away from it: the result is an enjoyable tension.

Enjoyable? in what sense and for what reasons? First in the list of the pleasures of the characteristic is *the pleasure of mastering.* This is not so much a matter of achievement as it is of a heightened sense of power. To be able to look at a drug fiend in terms of art is in itself a source of such pleasure; so is the organization of colors and masses that threaten to break loose. There is *the pleasure of tensing ourselves.* Much has been said of the pleasures of relaxation, but any athlete knows the intense enjoyment of tensed muscles and any intellectual worker that of a braced mind and an alert attention. Our attitude toward the characteristic is tensional and furnishes pleasures of this sort. There follow *the pleasures of intensified and broadened experience.* A play like O'Neill's *The Hairy Ape*, made up as it is of the pungent and bitter stuff of life, yields a pleasure that borders on pain—a sense of being keenly alive and of reaching into the tortured recesses of consciousness. Or take this passage from Walt Whitman's *Song of Myself:—*

The blab of the pave, tires of carts, sluff of boot-soles, talk of the
    promenaders,
The heavy omnibus, the driver with his interrogating thumb, the
    clank of the shod horses on the granite floor,
The snow-sleighs, clinking, shouted jokes, pelts of snow-balls,
The hurrahs for popular favorites, the fury of rous'd mobs,
The flap of the curtain'd litter, a sick man inside borne to the
    hospital,
The meeting of enemies, the sudden oath, the blows and fall,
The excited crowd, the policeman with his star quickly working
    his passage to the centre of the crowd,
The impassive stones that receive and return so many echoes,
What groans of over-fed or half-starv'd who fall sunstruck or in
    fits,

What exclamations of women taken suddenly who hurry home and
  give birth to babes,
What living and buried speech is always vibrating here, what howls
  restrained by decorum,
Arrests of criminals, slights, adulterous offers made, acceptances,
  rejections with convex lips,
I mind them or the show or resonance of them—I come and I
  depart.

A welter of images! the turmoil of life! noisome ingredients!
Here are an eye and an ear that catch the very spirit of
city life with a quivering intensity; here is an imagination
that ranges over fair and foul alike. In this intense and
broadened reading of life we sympathetically share. The
fourth pleasure is that of *biting into things*. The analogy
is a humble one from the realm of eating. We enjoy sinking our teeth into something hard and crisp; the soft and
all too yielding is not to our taste. In the characteristic
there are a strength and coarseness of fibre and a gritty admixture that we enjoy.

THE USES OF THE CHARACTERISTIC

In early art the characteristic stands out sharply, but
there is a strange thing about its use. Whether the art be
Mexican, Assyrian or East Indian, the linear patterns, the
hammered work, gem settings, textiles, glazed trinkets and
amulets reveal a "will to beauty." The two striking exceptions are music and dancing. Flower forms such as the
lotus or the rose and animal forms such as the crane, the
lizard, and the beetle, pleasing in themselves, are decoratively
shaped toward greater beauty. In their schematization the
characteristic fades out. In the *Wild Boar* of Altamira
there is apparent a delight in the life-like rendering of
sharply characterized shape and movement, but there is also
a manifest pleasure in the beauty of sweeping and tapering

lines and delicate shading. The same is true of the *Golden Cups of Vaphio* and the Mycenaean dagger, depicting a lion-hunt. When, however, early art turns to the portrayal of men and gods it is under the sign of the characteristic, usually in its more grotesque forms. Examples are: the hideously fat *Venus* found in Austria, the African drawings of men and women, the Cretan *Vase of Reapers*, the Mexican God Quetzalcoatl, the Hindu god Siva, and the *Nike of Delos*. It is not sufficient to say that these misshapen humans embody a primitive ideal of personal beauty, for there is conscious exaggeration, often along the line of the sexual. In such instances the aesthetic ideal of woman has not yet become differentiated from the sex ideal. When the exaggeration is not sexual, as in the clay vessels of Peru and old Swedish rock carvings, (large eyes and mouth, ridiculously short bodies, feet that look like rakes, huge hands), part of the explanation is to be found in certain religious beliefs, part in a naive technique dealing with difficult human material, part in a delight in human grotesquerie. Again, the visual representation of gods and goddesses reflects a crude world with the ugly and the terrifying always close at hand, and a crude symbolism. The gods of myth-making man came by their beauty even later than they came by their goodness.

In modern art there is much deliberate use of the characteristic. Conservatives insist that it means disordered vision, emotional perversions, inability to render form, pose, egotism, *réclame*. There may be such a taint in individual cases, but there is much to be said in favor of even an extreme use of the characteristic. It is in response to healthy impulses that art freshens itself by experiment and turns to a tonic of bitter taste. The experimentation may produce nightmare shapes, but these often mark the transition to new themes and undreamed of values. Think of Whitman's vision of the diverse American scene, Carl Sandburg's

Poems of Steel, Pennell's etchings of shipyards, Meunier's sculptured miners and factory workers, revolutionary expressionistic stage settings! The difficulties of material and technique alike act as a tonic and strengthener of art. The man who contends that the sole concern of art is with the narrow rose-strewn path of beauty is like the old lady who wished geraniums planted along the rim of the Grand Canyon to have it less desolate. Art is, after all, a reflection of life. If it is not to die of a languid aestheticism, it must occasionally turn to the harsh, the acrid, the poignant, the ugly. It then acquires a gaunt strength and a hard-fistedness; to give it that strength is the mission of the characteristic.

It may seem strange to find that the characteristic plays a small part in purely naturalistic art. Naturalism in its extremest forms, it is true, makes use of repulsive material and employs a technique marked by vigor, harshness, and starkness. But it lacks what is always present when there is a bold and extensive use of the characteristic:—the motif of idealization. This motif can be traced in primitive sculpture and in modern expressionistic art. Very little of the oldest, and even less of the newest art is naturalistic in inspiration and manner of rendering.

This idealization shows itself through distortion—a deliberate moving away from natural appearance. The distortion is idealistic in purpose in one or all of three ways.

First, objects are reshaped for the sake of creating forms which are more purely and insistently expressive. This is done by simplifying; by exaggerated stress on this or that quality; by the use of force-lines; and by tensional energy in the arrangement of compositional values. Grigorieff's [1] portraits deviate from the natural, and they have about them a great expressiveness and forcefulness. Expressive simpli-

[1] The works of art referred to may be seen in Cheney's *Primer of Modern Art.*

fication at the cost of lifelikeness marks Derain's *Italian Woman*, Pechstein's *Woman with the Cat*, Van Dongen's *Portrait*, Walt Kuhn's *Caucus*, Barlach's figures of old men done in wood—and creates new values in art. Force-lines are seen in extreme dominance in Pechstein's *Boat;* Barlach's *Panel;* and in Hodler, Marc, and Soutine. Tensional organization is revealed in the art of Cézanne, Maillol, Whitman, Vachel Lindsay, and Grigorieff.

The second use of the characteristic in modern art is in extending the range of materials utilized and of organized and significant forms without the heavy price paid by extreme naturalism of a loss in imaginative force. Sandburg is not a naturalistic poet. Even when he moves closest to crudely expressive, common speech and crass actuality he is saved from prosiness by the creative virility and sweep of his imagination. The expressionistic drama in no sense aims at normal beauty. It does not shrink from the ugly:—Toller in *Hinkemann* takes the acrid stuff of life; and makes a searching tragedy from materials to which the common response would be ribald laughter. Modern painting seeks new effective patterns far beyond the facile pleasingness of the beautiful.

The third use is bound up with what has been called a spiritual rebirth of art. If "mixed" materials are to be moved within the task of art they must be redeemed imaginatively by original and stimulating workmanship, and by new visions. Among these visions the one that counts, as none other does, is that of the spirituality of nature—not in the old sense of a refuge and a solace, but as something which stretches sympathetic effort to the point of pain—something that lives gropingly in us and possessively in the life that lays hands on us. Painters have confessed to this mysticism; poets have voiced it; and it lives strongly in the work of Toller, Werfel, and Kaiser. Gothic conceptions of Christ were uncompromisingly spiritual. Something of a return to

MASKS

Above, left, Iroquois "False Face" Mask; *above, right,* Man's Secret Society Mask, Ivory Coast; *below, left,* Stone Mask, Aztec; *below, right,* Woman's Secret Society Mask, Gaboon, West Africa. (*From the University of Pennsylvania Museum.*)

their intensity is to be seen in Nolde's *Prophet*, Lehmbruck's *Mother and Child* and Mestrovic's *Mother*.

The characteristic demands a toughmindedness and a far-flung sympathy which not every one has or can summon. But to exclude it from art because one has not a taste for it is to cut down the range and dwarf the growth and meaning of art to a narrow and delicate beauty, or an amiable pleasingness.

THE SUBLIME

Nature rather than art furnishes the easiest approach to the problem of the sublime. Not only is the sublime a rarer artistic phenomenon than either the beautiful or the characteristic, but it is overwhelmingly present in nature—in the human drama and its cosmic setting. The very term hints that the response—the feeling of sublimity—is the important thing; but so commonly is this feeling provoked by certain objects and experiences that a preliminary list may be drawn up, with little danger of cavil or disagreement. Sublime are: the starry heavens, the endless stretching of the years, the expanse of the desert or the ocean, an earthquake or a tidal wave, wind driven clouds, beetling cliffs, the Grand Canyon, a lofty tower, a volcano, a storm at sea, a plunging cavalry charge with flashing sabres and thunder of hoofs, a blast furnace, a sunrise, some great human achievement or sacrifice, an exceptionally noble purpose, a blast from the hell of human desires. This varied assemblage may be made to yield certain recurrent types; and they in turn may be used to open the way to the sublime in art, and to the many delicate psychological problems which are bound up with the appreciation of sublimity.

THE TYPES OF THE SUBLIME

THE SUBLIME OF SPACE

Space has been recognized by Longinus, Vischer, Volkelt, and others as one of the chief sources of the sublime. Our glance travels along the horizontal plane of desert or ocean, along the vertical plane of tower or chasm. In neither case

248

must it be arrested by details, such as ships or islands dotting the surface of the sea.[1] The impression must be sweeping. In that impression the imagination plays the major part: it conjures up the thought of receding horizons, distances not to be traversed, heights unscalable, and depths not to be plumbed. In the sublime of cubical space—the astronomer's worlds upon worlds—distances and dimensions are such as afford the chance of an excursional imagining with no blocking or distraction.

THE SUBLIME OF TIME

From the vantage ground of the present moment, the past and the future offer themselves as intellectual and imaginative constructs. The human significance of space lies in the motor conquest of distance and in the ordering of simultaneous impressions; that of time, in *filling* and *change*. Memory, as it stretches over a length of years, construes the past in terms of what has happened; imagination reads the future in terms of what is likely to happen. Suppose I take a small section from my life—to-day flanked by a remembered yesterday and an anticipated to-morrow; there is nothing of sublimity there. Nor does the sublime of time appear if I take the wider time-span of my birth and death. If, however, I take a larger cycle, that of the earth—a fiery ball with a cooling surface swinging through space and time to a frozen death—or the still larger one of the making and unmaking of worlds, there is something that defies *human filling*, and the *changes* involved are beyond the grasp of man. Herein lies two-thirds of the sublime of time. Temporal extension emptied of such content is not sublime,

[1] Cf. F. T. Vischer, *Ueber das Erhabene und Komische, S. 54:*—"If the different stories of a tower are painted in different colors, or if an extensive plain presents itself as a variegated picture of cultivated lands the impression of the sublime is lacking, for every new color, every new jutting part means a new object for the eye."

even when carried to infinity. The last third is the suggestion of great power.[2]

THE SUBLIME OF SIZE

Great size and magnitude favor the feeling of sublimity. One of the simplest types of the sublime is the *colossal.* The Grand Canyon, a grove of giant redwoods, huge boulders, a massive mountain, the Amazon with its broad sheet of water are examples. All such objects affect us impressively by their sheer bulk in space. But they bulk largely in a different sense also: they have *grandeur* and they have *majesty,*—which means there has been an infusion of ideas of beauty and distinction. Things done on a large scale are sublime:—the massing of men and batteries on the Flanders front; the swarming migrations of early times. In both cases radical reduction of size and number means the disappearance of the sublime.

A huge city affords a sublime spectacle when caught spatially in images of tall buildings and far-flung streets; rhythmically in the pulse beat of its traffic; imaginatively in terms of range of living, concentration of power, variety and reach of purposes. Put in the place of this city a bee-hive or an ant-hill. There is the same intricate social organization, the same manifold achievement, and sharing of great tasks. Why then are bee-hive and ant-hill not sublime objects? The diminutive scale has something to do with it. But there is also the thought of their insignificance when measured in terms of human power and permanence. From their point of view the ants are performing herculean feats, from ours they are moving straws. A stick in the hand of a child may in a moment obliterate their work. The rela-

---

[2] These things are strikingly present in a passage near the end of Nietzsche's *Will to Power.* There is here the mark of momentous and baffling changes, of vast rhythms, of tremendous and exhilarating power.

tional apprehension of power then must be reckoned with even in the sublime of size.

THE SUBLIME OF POWER

The manifestion of great destructive force in nature is felt to be sublime. A cyclone, a volcanic eruption, a tidal wave, an earthquake all exhibit a power utterly beyond the control of man. Not only is there no possibility of effective interference, but there is a taxing of our senses, a reverberating rush and roar, an uprooting of ideas, which make the experience border on pain. Something like this Kant had in mind when he explained the dynamic sublime in terms of a sense of physical helplessness followed by the invigorating recoil of a feeling that we as moral beings rise above the nature that threatened to smash or engulf us; and the mathematical sublime,—the starry heavens yield his example— in terms of a feeling of sensory and intellectual bewilderment followed by a sense of mathematical mastery. In both instances he misses something. In his example of the stars he insists that they be felt simply as numberless luminous points and not as a swarm of worlds. But what of a pile of sand with its millions of grains, which patience and a long life would enable me to count. There is no sublimity here; but there is in the vast stretching of the sands of the sea. Distance and magnitude and the strain they put upon the imagination make the difference. Again, in his analysis of the dynamic sublime Kant fails to take into account the direct imaginative response to volume and rush of power and the technical mastery of nature implied in a vast irrigation project, a blast furnace or an aeroplane flight. It is not only uncontrollable power that is sublime; sublimity attaches also to great power controlled by the ingenuity of science.

This much may be said for Kant's analysis: moral power

is one of the sources of the sublime. Christ's attitude on the Cross; the strength of a Socrates or Luther; the contemplated sacrifice of the Burghers of Calais; Parkman's struggle against ill health; the soldier's dicing with death; Scott's grim losing polar fight as recorded in his diary—these are illustrations.

MINOR TYPES OF THE SUBLIME

THE WILD; THE CHAOTIC: These must be grouped together and moved close to the sublime of power. The wild suggests uncontrolled power, and the chaotic, disruption—smashing up. A mountain torrent is an example of the first; a crevasse-scarred glacier or a boulder-strewn mountain-side of the second. Why then are these to be given a separate place? It is because there is another imaginative appeal. The tumbling wildness of the *cirques* and crags of Glacier Park, as seen from a trail, is sublime apart from the thought of early upheavals and moving masses of ice. It is true, however, that a *cosmic reference*, in terms of immensity of time and space, of significance or of power, tends to intensify the feeling of sublimity.

THE MYSTERIOUS; THE WEIRD: The sea and the forest; Northern lights; birth and death; certain spiritualist phenomena yield a sense of mystery; weird effects are produced by wandering lights in a fog, by the darknesses and luminosities of a moorland; by a queer stillness broken into by the soughing of the wind, the call of an owl, the baying of a hound. In all such cases there is a sense of the strange, the unexplained, the portentous. The imagination is irresistibly carried beyond the sense-impression and plunged either into cosmic problems—as in the mystery of death—or into a mass of objectless and spreading fears.

THE GLOOMY; THE DREARY; THE BLEAK: An example of the first is a pine forest at night; of the second, a stretch of waste land; of the third, the Straits of Magellan. Darkness has long been recognized as a possible source of the sublime. Longinus comments on it, and Homer and Dante use it effectively. Gloom is often oppressive; we sense danger and cannot set ourselves to meet it. But there are two compensatory factors in the situation: the fear is objectless and diffused, and there is the exhilaration of a ranging imagination. In the dreary and the bleak, fear is absent, but there is a sense of remoteness and strangeness, and a one-tone scheme of imagining; which must, however, be on a large scale.

THE FANTASTICALLY MISSHAPEN: Not everything that is misshapen is sublime. A hare-lip, a goitre, a club-foot do not give that impression. Sympathy with the sufferer can hardly be offered as a reason, for if this sympathy is removed the effect is comic rather than sublime. Is it then because our imagination is not stirred; because we cannot get away from this or that precise distortion? A battered hulk of a ship or the storm-twisted cedars of Monterey are sublime; there we are carried to the force of sea and wind. What then of the battered face of a boxer or the bent back of a peasant? The idea of distorting power is present there also, but I suspect it is the very definiteness of that power—a smashing fist or a burden of wood—which does not allow a feeling of sublimity to arise.

THESE TYPES OF THE SUBLIME MAY BE MATCHED IN ART

THE SUBLIME OF SPACE

Byron, *Cain*, Act 2

>   Oh, thou beautiful
> And unimaginable ether! and
> Ye multiplying masses of increased
> And still increasing lights! what are ye? what

Is this blue wilderness of interminable
Air, where ye roll along, as I have seen
The leaves along the limpid streams of Eden?
Is your course measured for ye? Or do ye
Sweep on in your unbounded revelry
Through an aerial universe of endless
Expansion—at which my soul aches to think—
Intoxicated with eternity?

Byron, *Heaven and Earth*, Sc. 3
Milton, *Paradise Lost*
Book of Job
Swinburne, *On the Verge*
Cathedral spires and interiors
Byron, *Cain*, Act 3

                                The dead,
The immortal, the unbounded, the omnipotent,
The overpowering mysteries of space—
The innumerable worlds that were and are—
A whirlwind of such overwhelming things,
Suns, moons, earths, upon their loud-voiced spheres
Singing in thunder round me, as have made me
Unfit for mortal converse:

THE SUBLIME OF TIME

Swinburne, *The Triumph of Time*
Byron, *Cain*, Act 3, Sc. 1

The mind then hath capacity of time,
And measures it by that which it beholds,
Pleasing or painful; little or almighty.
I had beheld the immemorial works
Of endless beings; skirr'd extinguish'd worlds;
And, gazing on eternity, methought
I had borrow'd more by a few drops of ages
From its immensity: but now I feel
My littleness again. Well said the spirit
That I was nothing!

THE SUBLIME OF SIZE

Byron *Cain*, Act 2, Sc. 2

> How silent and how vast are these dim worlds!
> For they seem more than one, and yet more peopled
> Than the huge brilliant luminous orbs which swung
> So thickly in the upper air, that I
> Had deem'd them rather the bright populace
> Of some all unimaginable Heaven,
> Than things to be inhabited themselves,
> But that on drawing near them I beheld
> Their swelling into palpable immensity
> Of matter, which seem'd made for life to dwell on,
> Rather than life itself.

The Pyramids; the Colossus of Rhodes; a many-voiced choric
    composition
The fall of Ares in the *Iliad* (Bk. XXI)

THE SUBLIME OF POWER

A shattering crescendo in music
King Lear
Michelangelo's *Last Judgment*
The closing verses of the *Prometheus Bound*
Homer, *Iliad* (XIV), simile of the storm
Iliad (XXXI), the deep-eddying river overwhelming
Achilles "and rushed in tumult on Achilles, raging from
on high, thundering with foam and blood and bodies of
dead men."

MINOR TYPES OF THE SUBLIME
The wild, the chaotic

The battle scenes in the *Iliad*
The jealousy of Othello
The tempest in *King Lear*

The mysterious, the weird

The statue in *Don Juan*
The giant figures in Butler's *Erewhon*
Macabre music
Sound and light in Dante's *Inferno*
Blake's drawings

The gloomy, the dreary, the bleak

Dante *Inferno*, Canto IV

True it is, that I found myself on the verge of the valley of the woeful abyss that gathers in thunder of infinite wailings. Dark, profound it was, and cloudy, so that though I fixed my sight on the bottom I did not discern anything there.

Dante *Inferno*, Canto XXVIII

And one who had both hands lopped off, lifting the stumps through the murky air so that the blood made his face foul, cried out . . .

The fantastically misshapen

The drawings of Rops and Klinger; the character of Caliban.

THE SUBLIME AS AN AESTHETIC TYPE

The sublime in art is the result partly of the choice of certain natural materials: ocean, desert, mountain, darkness, pomp, power; partly of the use of a certain technique. The materials are either actually built into the work of art or are suggested in terms of imagery, visual devices, and motor experiences. Thus huge size marks the Temple of Ammon at Karnak and the Zeus of Phidias; gloomy coloring many of the paintings of Rembrandt; bulging muscles the sculptured figures of Michelangelo and Rodin; great volume and vibrational intensity the music of Wagner. If this were all, the range of the sublime in art would be a narrow one, and arts like poetry and painting would be seriously handicapped: only a small part of what is sublime in nature can be carried over bodily into architecture, sculpture, and music; mountain and desert exist in poetry only in the form of word-symbols and their imaginative values, and in painting, only as color-symbols and their imaginative stretching. Even the architect and the sculptor must rely on something besides the actual height of a spire, or spread of masses of stone, or the bulk of a Zeus in marble. There must be splendor and grandeur of treatment; and a tensional appeal to the imaginative and motor activities of the onlooker. By the skilful use of light and darkness, the multiplying of court spaces and columns, a temple grows beyond its actual size,[3] sweeping lines force us to carry spires into clouds; the Zeus of Phidias grows under our eyes until we see in him the vast arbiter of human destinies, the boundless sky, and the shattering thunderbolt.

With the beautiful the sublime has hardly anything in common. It lacks the clear-cut, reposeful, self-sufficient nature of the response to beautiful objects. With the characteristic it shares the quality of not resting in the image and the admixture of stress and pain, but it has an exhilarating effect all its own. With the tragic it shares emotional intensity and imaginative suggestiveness; like the comic it uses exaggeration; not, however, to belittle but to aggrandize.

THE MARKS OF THE SUBLIME

Suppose an artist has successfully aimed at the sublime. That means he has chosen materials and employed methods which effectively provoke a certain response:—the sense,

---

[3] Banister Fletcher, *A History of Architecture,* p. 29.
"The effect produced by this forest of columns is most awe-inspiring; the eye is led from the smaller columns of the side avenues, which gradually vanish into semi-darkness and give an idea of unlimited extent, to the larger columns of the central avenues lighted by the clear-story, which is formed in the difference of height between the central and side avenues—"

or feeling of sublimity.   We may study either the quality of the art that is thus effective or the effect art of such quality has.   Both courses amount to the same thing: for it is impossible to walk on the surfaces of art without thought of the sustaining realm of formative feeling and design; and equally impossible to move within the realm of aroused feeling without thought of the forms and images provocative of such feeling.

The problem of the sublime has always been treated as a predominantly psychological one.   Longinus, a neatly observant critic of literary technique, dwells on *ecstasy*, Burke on *fear*, Kant on *depression* and *recoil*, as marks of the sense of sublimity.   All these answers explain too simply a psychic response which is subtle and complex.   This response shows the following marks:—

A SPREADING IMAGINATIVE SUGGESTIVENESS

In a sense all art is imaginatively suggestive.   This is as true of Keats who rarely leaves the confines of the beautiful as it is of Rabelais who never enters them.   Keats in *The Eve of St. Agnes* has made a catalogue of dainties significant by allusions to the East,

from silken Samarkand to cedar'd Lebanon.

Here is a case of decorative suggestiveness.   This world of mystery and romance is a world of images and suggestions to lend glamour and color;—a festooning as decorative and unemotional as are Japanese lanterns at a garden-fête.   The floating images are not like a bluish mountain range in the distance appealing to the wanderer and the climber; they are strung on the fine wires of phrases that have distinction, smoothness, compactness, finality.   It is not Samarkand that rouses us; it is the phrase *silken Samarkand* that satisfies us decoratively, and in turn sends us back to the original decorative touches of *blanched linen, jellies soother than the*

creamy curd, lucent syrops. There is then a centrifugal
force in the imaginative suggestiveness of the beautiful, and
the decorative, in the sense of a resting in the image. The
circling imagery of the lyric is another example of it.

Contrast with this the sublime, which disappears as soon
as the art becomes decorative. In a seascape there are
several feet of canvas covered with grey, green, white, and
black. There is beauty in the organization of lines; additional beauty in the rendering of the life of the sea as it
breaks against the cliffs. But the effect is sublime only if
our imagination steps into and out of the canvas, carries with
it the stimulus of certain impressions—bleakness, strangeness, power, formlessness—and gathers image after image
in an onset which knows no limit—and no stepping back
within bounds. Arts like painting and sculpture are too
circumscribed, too decorative, and too insistently formative
to achieve sublime effects often; no painter of the sea could
give the equivalent of Swinburne's stretching imagery,[4] no
landscape painter could rival Goethe's picture of the crashing trees in *Faust.* Music, on the other hand, has much of
the spreading suggestiveness the sublime requires.

A SENSE OF TWOFOLD STRAIN

THE CONTENT STRAINING AWAY FROM THE DECORATIVE
USE OF FORM:—Longinus has pointed out that ruggedness
of style goes well with sublime effects; and that the smooth

---

[4] Swinburne, *On the South Coast*
Up from shoreward, impelled far forward, by marsh and meadow, by lawn
   and lea,
Inland still at her own wild will swells, rolls, and revels the surging sea.

. . . .

A Nympholept
   . . . as the
   shifted sands
Speak forth and show but the strength of the sea's wild will
That sifts and grinds them as grain in the storm-wind's mill.
In thee is the doom that falls and the doom that stands:
The tempests utter thy word, and the stars fulfil.

and purely decorative are to be avoided. This suggests a conflict between the sublime and the beautiful, and such a conflict there undoubtedly is. By this is not meant that, for instance, a sublime passage in poetry cannot have beauty of rhythm and language. But there must be something in the form to arrest us and something to send us on, and the urging must be the stronger. This accounts for part of the strain, and for the dynamic character of the sublime. In Swinburne's *By the North Sea* the persuasive lilt and decorative patterning of the verse are too strong to allow a full sublimity of effect; in his *Tristram of Lyonesse* a rhymed form is used so unobtrusively and skilfully that image after image strikes the imagination with full vibrational and tensional force.

THE CONTENT STRAINING BEYOND THE FINITE: There is a strained forming of the formless and the not-to-be-formed; a pushing beyond the finite. As Swinburne puts it, our quest is of

> The goal that is not, and ever again the goal.

The imagery is of endless time, space vast or boundless, huge size, infinite possibilities in the way of the heroic or the hellish:—a universe remote from the common measure of human strength and human sorrow. Such a world strains without satisfying our demand for intellectual mastery and for practical and emotional adequacy.

A SENSE OF EXHILARATION

If the sublime is bound up with fear and ideas of self-preservation; [5] if it turns on our helplessness as sense beings; [6] if it implies a hostile relation to the will; [7] if it means a jolting and straining, why is it not a depressing experience? Its very name suggests exaltation and elation. Kant

[5] Burke.
[6] Kant.
[7] Schopenhauer.

explains this exhilaration as a rebound: as sense beings we tremble at our insecurity in a world which can destroy us easily; but by shifting our ground to our rational selves we come to see that this world is of our own intellectual making and is our great moral opportunity. His analysis errs in (1) assuming an initial depression and a subsequent exhilarating recovery, (2) splitting sense and reason, and (3) binding the exhilaration up too closely with moral ideas.

The sublime, like the tragic, is an imaginative adventure; and, like the tragic, it is often an intensely emotional experience. We are roused, startled, swept off our feet. Intensity of feeling may, however, be lacking; there is none of it in the sublime indecencies of Aristophanes. There is exhilaration in the venturing: a sense of expanded life and of stretching to meet its startling possibilities. There is, too, a sense of freedom. Much has been made of the agreeableness of a well ordered, neatly packed universe. But what of the joys of intellectual disorder or, at least, of an unknown which acts as a challenge and gives us the feeling of new enterprises?—enterprises that may or may not become conquests. With this venturing comes a sense of tense activity on our part. It is like mountain-climbing, which feels sharply worthwhile in the doing, and which when done yields glimpses of the unknown, a wilderness of peaks, or nothing but dense fog. Life has seemed more direct and richer for the moment. As Swinburne puts it in *The Seaboard*:—

And a joy to the heart is a goal that it may not reach.
No sense that forever the limits of sense engird
No hearing or sight that is vassal to form or speech
Learns ever the secret that shadow and silence teach,
Hears ever the notes that ere ever they swell subside,
Sees ever the light that lights not the loud world's tide,
Clasps ever the cause of the lifelong scheme's control
Wherethrough we pursue, till the waters of life be dried,
The goal that is not, and ever again the goal.

THE TRAGIC

The term tragic goes back in its origins to the earliest stage in the development of the Greek drama; it is said to refer to the goatskin clothing worn by the actors. Werfel's *Goatsong* is a reminiscence of that early meaning. From this its first crude aesthetic use it has found its way into a dozen languages and has been stretched to cover life as well as art. It has come to mark loosely the quality of certain incidents and situations, and a peculiar psychic response they call forth. The material is not sharply set aside, and the psychic response is not clearly understood; the problem therefore arises of getting rid of the marginal raggedness of common speech and of discovering a fairly representative meaning.

THE TRAGIC IN LIFE

THE TRAGIC MATERIAL

Among things commonly called tragic are: the collapse of a great social project; a fatal accident to a child; the crumbling of a man's ideals; the suicide of a man of promise; the grinding wear of life; the effect of drug-taking. If these and similar occurrences are attended to it will be seen that death is the common mark of many. Death is held to be tragic because it destroys the chance of happiness and breaks in upon human purposes in brutal fashion, whether it appears abruptly or goes about its work with a grim slowness. But there are other tragedies in life besides this extreme physical collapse. Disillusionment, attrition or ruin, routed aims, agony of mind, disease or poverty, and loss of honor make the continuance of life rather than its termination a tragedy. In all these cases happiness is thwarted, and human interests are denied their measure of satisfaction.

Of all tragic material it may be said that the collapse must be of something of value; and that value must either be present in the midst of the ruin or be supplied by an imagination looking back. There must be a glint of splendor in a mind darkened by madness; eminence in the purposes swept aside; strength or grandeur in the man that goes under or in the forces that overwhelm him; freshness and fervor in the longing for happiness which is to be blocked. The tragedy grows with the intensity of the contrast.

THE PSYCHIC RESPONSE

What is our response to such tragic material? If we exclaim: How sad! we are merely recording an emotional depression on our part. If we say: How horrible! or How terrible! we are confessing in words to a sense of shock and a defensive shrinking and warding off. But if we say: How tragic! we are responding in a different and much less simple way. For one thing, the stress is less sharply on ourselves and our feelings and impulses. Not that we are not profoundly moved! but there is something detached and objective about our experience. The key to the first and second responses are sympathetic and self-feelings and protective impulses; this the third response shows a going beyond a suffering individual and a disturbed self; it reveals a universalizing and intellectualizing of an incident, and an admixture of enjoyment.

Is it possible to break up this complex tragic response? The elements variously mixed in different individuals and different cases are the following: (1) a shock; (2) the sense of a collapse, more or less complete, of something humanly prized; (3) an intensified sense of the value of whatever has been lost; (4) a questioning often ending in revolt; (5) a sense of imaginative compensation; (6) a dash of pleasure. Words like *moved, shaken, stirred, shattered, erschütternd* signalize the profound mental and physical disturbance which is part of the experience of the tragic. Again, we are aware of the collapse of something of value—and it is to be noted that this something may range from a simple happiness-value to complex moral, religious or intellectual values. It need not be something prized by the suffering individual himself. The loss throws into sharp relief the value of the thing lost, and rouses a spirit of questioning wonder, and, often, of revolt. How can such things be? Why are such things? Some physical or moral evil acts as a challenge flung at my ideal of a just God—a challenge I cannot meet—and so I question and rebel.[1] Some stupid accident mars beyond redemption the logical reading of life. I ask myself: Is this merely a corrupt text or is it no text at all? and halt perplexed and resentful. Something ugly eats into life like a blight and spoils it for me. Here is part of the cosmic element in the sense of the tragic: this attempted reference of an incident to a world text, which is lacking in our sense of the sad or the horrible. There is, next, *imaginative compensation.* The questioning has not been stilled; the starkness of the incident has been overcome, the range of the problematic widened, and a sweep and tension given to the imagination which prove invigorating and pleasurable.

THE TRAGIC IN ART

In art the tragic appears at many points. It outsteps the limits of tragedy and may be found in a poem, a novel,

---

[1] Cf. the instance of counter-conversion in James's *The Varieties of Religious Experience.*

a musical composition, a painting or a piece of sculpture. The materials are those of life. The *Niobe* group and the *Laocoon* give the onslaught of death; *Macbeth*, *Othello*, and *Père Goriot* a moral collapse; Turgeniev's *Spring Freshets* and *Smoke*, Thackeray's *Newcomes*, Hergesheimer's *Cytherea*, and Lawrence's *Women in Love*, the tragedy of personal relations; *Don Quixote*, *The Misanthrope*, and *The Wild Duck*, the tragic implications of ideals. Villon's *Les Regrets de la Belle Heaulmière*, Verlaine's *Chanson d'Automne*, *Sérénade*, and *Sagesse*, Baudelaire's *Spleen*, and Turgeniev's *Nest of Nobles* all strike the note of disillusionment; *Rosmersholm* and Dreiser's *An American Tragedy* are tragedies of soul-division and weakness; the *Book of Job*, *King Lear*, *Ghosts*, *The Brothers Karamazov*, and *The Hand of the Potter* carry madness and revolt to the very judgment-seat of God.

The tragic in art differs from the tragic in life in a peculiar selection and stressing of materials and a peculiarly colored response. The secret of the tragic as an aesthetic type lies in an understanding of these differences; and the first clue to the secret is given by the awareness of an imagined world. To the narrowest circle of the actual world —the circle that affects me and mine—I respond in terms of attempted adjustment, of practical protest, of defence reactions. Even the remoter circlings of that actual world —a plague or famine in India, the *Titanic* disaster, a revolution in Russia, fallen kings, a volcanic eruption in Japan affect me in a practical sense; help must be rendered, sympathy must be bestowed, a repetition of such disasters must, if possible, be averted. But what of the past, which cannot be changed and which is in a very real sense an imagined thing? What of such supremely tragic events as the crucifixion, the death of Socrates, the massacre of the Night of St. Bartholomew? Here also there is a sense of actual persons and of actual suffering and loss. But when we step within the domain of art we enter a world of whose illusory, imaginatively created nature we are subconsciously aware. This world unfolds and reveals the feelings and spiritual conflicts of imaginary persons and situations with developing implications of struggle and suffering.   There is no actual smothering or cutting into flesh in the fifth act of *Othello;* we are forced into the consciousness of Othello and Desdemona and into a mass of simulated feelings, motives, designs, and complications.   We do not seek to change things nor set ourselves on guard against them; we are taken outside ourselves into a personal life imaginatively shaped by the poet or as in Swinburne's *Faustine* [2] into the realm of interpretative comment and of a simulated response on the part of the poet.

This clue of an imagined world offers what seems to be a difficulty.   In one sense the imagined madness of Lear and the ruined soul of Faustine mean less to me than they

---

[2] Wine and rank poison, milk and blood
Being mixed therein
Since first the devil threw dice with God
For you, Faustine.

Your naked new-born soul, their stake,
Stood blind between;
God said "let him that wins her take
And keep Faustine."

But this time Satan throve, no doubt;
Long since, I ween,
God's part in you was battered out;
Long since, Faustine.

The die rang sideways as it fell,
Rang cracked and thin,
Like a man's laughter heard in hell
Far down, Faustine.

A shadow of laughter like a sigh,
Dead sorrow's kin;
So rang, thrown down, the devil's die
That won Faustine.

would if Lear were a close friend and Faustine were my wife. But in another way they mean much more. I am less directly and unbearably affected, but I realize more sharply and profoundly the universal meaning of such experiences. As a result, the shock becomes a deep, reverberating emotional disturbance; and there is an intensified and widened sense of both value and loss. There is this further change. As the emphasis is shifted from the effect on me to the inner life of others and the human quality of their problems or to the cosmic response of the artist who has created them, the questioning and the revolt which mark the response to the tragic in actual life is given a different meaning. The questions of Job and the revolt of Prometheus or Satan are set within imaginary lives and characters and are taken as their problem, not ours. If the challenging is done by the poet rather than by his characters the same thing holds true; there is a detached, hovering sense of cosmic flaws and riddles. All theories of the tragic which make a point of self-reference in whatever sense—How like Macbeth I am potentially! How precarious is my happiness! How important it is for me to avoid excessive passion! How slender my title to reason! are fundamentally mistaken; the pull is all the other way.

Two differences remain. In the tragic materials and the tragic response of art there are a stronger admixture of pleasure and a larger measure of imaginative redemption than are to be had in those of life. That the psychic response to the tragic in art is enjoyable can hardly be denied. But the source of such pleasure is not to be looked for in lustful cruelty, in the sense of a contrasting security, or in opportunities for moral satisfaction. Real life offers better chances of lashing and gloating, of tasting comfort sweetened by another's pain, of tracing patterns of justice and reading moral lessons with an agreeable gesture of rebuke. The world of art is an imaginatively created world, and yields the pleasures of a tensed, electrified, and ranging imagination. It is also an imaginatively re-valued world, with a new aesthetic value, selective of the old, superadded. This new value, as it appears in the tragic, is the *imaginative redemption of evil*. If this is lost sight of neither the tragic nor tragedy as an art form can be understood.

The evil to be redeemed may be physical or moral or intellectual or aesthetic. The methods of redeeming are many. One of the simplest is beauty of form added. Set to the measure of verse, organized, clothed in resplendent language and color, repulsive things like leprosy, adultery, incest, and jealousy are reclaimed by a superimposed formal beauty. But this is only part of the secret of such plays as the *Oedipus Rex*, the *Hippolytus*, *The Madness of Hercules*, and *The Cenci*. There is, in addition, a cleansing by fire —the fires of a hot selective imagination clearing away dross, eating its way to the hard metal of human passions and making them glow with a white heat. These two ways of redeeming are combined in Hamlet's interview with his mother, in the death sorrow scene of *Liliom*, and in Swinburne's *Dolores*. The dross and the disorder need, however, not be cleared away. Lear in his madness and Othello in his turmoil and agony of mind spew forth much that is disgusting. In such cases a third method is used, that of "absolute poetry": which means a language of large and universal accents, and a reaching beyond the stature of the tragic hero to the poet—and then beyond the poet. It is Shakespeare who stalks in the tempestuous and unhinged mind of Lear and lives in the questioning Hamlet—not the Shakespeare who made good investments and was fond of lawsuits, but Shakespeare the universal artist. Instead of being lifted out of the consciousness of the individual we may be set down at its centre and be made to share imaginatively an inner life. This is a fourth method, which Shakespeare often combines with the third. It is strikingly used by Browning. The sordid murder and the trivial characters of *The Yellow Book* are redeemed in *The Ring and the Book* by means of an elaboration of the thoughts, passions, and feelings of the persons concerned, into whose selves we are sunk. O'Neill in *The Hairy Ape* and Toller in *Hinkemann* redeem very difficult material in the same way.

This principle of *imaginative redemption*, or compensation, present even in the tragic responses of life, receives a sharper accent and wider use in those of art; and is worth carrying over into a study of tragedy as a key with which to unlock its secrets. While it is to be found elsewhere as well,[3] it appears most impressively in the tragic.

TRAGEDY

TRAGEDY AS A FORM OF ART

The external marks of tragedy present no difficulties.

[3] Imaginative redemption may be traced in Aristophanes, Rabelais, Swift, Cabell; in the hell-touched etchings of Beardsley and Rops. Other instances are *The Book of Revelation,* Dante's *Inferno,* and Jeffers' *Roan Stallion.*

Ultra-modern poetry deliberately cuts itself off from beauty of material and from the simple first method of imaginative redemption. It sets itself a very difficult task—a task at which it fails when it slings on the page incongruous facts and raw words and achieves neither intensity nor discrimination. But it is a task worth the enterprise, for it promises a new intake and reshaping of materials often cast aside as worthless. There is little of this poetry without blemish, but much of it shows the redeeming magic of an original, fusing imagination. There is a fine sweep to Sandburg's *Prairie:*

Have you seen a red sunset drip over one of my corn-fields, the shore of night stars, the wave lines of dawn up a wheat valley?
Have you heard my threshing crews yelling in the chaff of a strawpile and the running wheat of the wagon-boards, my cornhuskers, my harvest hands hauling crops, singing dreams of women, worlds, horizons?

There is a new response to machinery in his *Gargoyle:*

I saw a mouth jeering. A smile of melted iron ran over it. Its laugh was full of nails rattling. It was a child's dream of a mouth.
A fist hit the mouth: knuckles of gun-metal driven by an electric wrist and shoulder. It was a child's dream of an arm.
The fist hit the mouth over and over, again and again. The mouth bled melted iron, and laughed its laughter of nails rattling.

Tragedies may be in verse or prose; they may conform to the old scheme of five acts—exposition, mounting complication, climax, unraveling, and catastrophe—or they may disregard this traditional scaffolding and break into a loose succession of scenes. They offer by means of stage-setting, costume, dialogue, and monologue a criss-cross of feelings and purposes and a developing action ending in a tragic collapse meant to be final. Any such preliminary definition reveals tragedy as a complex form of art, with a difficult technique, a varied appeal, and a nature and purpose not easily discovered.

Four terms may be used in tracing the nature of tragedy: *motivation, conflict, suffering, tragic collapse.*

MOTIVATION: The incidents and situations in a tragedy reflect the purposes, the planful ordering, and the scheming of the dramatis personae, and they in turn reflect interests and motives. There is a double reference: the purpose is shown issuing in action and leading to complications, and it is also traced back to an interplay of impulses and impelling ideals. Thus the wreckage in the last scenes of *The Wild Duck* is not mere chance débris; it interests us in relation to the meddling of Gregers and the planning of Hjalmar and Hedvig, and all this in turn in relation to the muddleheaded idealism of Gregers, the selfishness of Hjalmar, and the adolescent mind of Hedvig. Words as well as actions are motivated; they are meant to express an inner preferential and purposive life. Since tragedy works from within outwards, setting us down within the confines of its characters and asking us to share their consciousness, it has a deep and far-reaching appeal. It looks for the logic of events in character, and for the secret of character in a logic of contending and contrasted motives. It means to be more logical than life itself, in as much as incidents that are accidental in a teleological sense are ruled out or at least subordinated, and personal experiences are unified and made more typically expressive. This very unification leads to a sharp contrasting of individuals, and a setting at odds of their interests, purposes, and acts.

CONFLICT: This tensional economy is reflected in the conflicts which play so important a part in tragedy and have so large a share in its dramatic value. Whether or not conflict is essential to tragedy is a much debated question. In 1894 Brunetière in *La Loi du Theatre* formulated what he called the law of the drama: "Drama is a representation of the will of man in conflict with the mysterious powers or natural forces which limit and belittle us; it is one of us thrown living upon the stage, there to struggle against fatality, against social law, against one of his fellow-mortals, against himself, if need be, against the interests, the prejudices, the folly, the malevolence of those who surround him." In tragedy he holds this to be of necessity a losing fight; in serious drama the hero avails himself of his one chance of success; in comedy the forces are apparently equal. In contrast to the drama which shows man willing and setting himself definite aims which clash with other aims, the novel "is to give us a picture of the influence which is exercised upon us by all that is outside of ourselves."

William Archer and Henry Arthur Jones, men well versed in the craftsmanship of the drama, have made adverse comments on this theory. Archer contends that such a conflict does not mark all drama—that there is no struggling will in the *Agamemnon*, the *Oedipus Rex*, *Othello*, and *Ghosts*. He uses the similes of the spider and the fly and of the worm on the hook; and speaks of Oedipus as simply writhing "under one revelation after another of bygone error and unwitting crime." He finds himself forced to substitute *crisis* for *conflict*, and offers this definition: "A play is a more or less rapidly-developing crisis in destiny or circumstances, and

a dramatic scene is a crisis within a crisis, clearly furthering the ultimate event." He interprets a crisis in terms of
rapid and startling changes, admits that not all crises are
dramatic, and selects *emotional excitement* and *the vivid
manifestation of character* as essential marks of dramatic
crises. Henry Arthur Jones's criticism is pointed at both
Brunetière and Archer. He agrees with Archer that the acceptance of Brunetière's law means disapproval of *Agamemnon* and *Oedipus Rex.* He insists, however, that a dramatic
crisis provokes "a sense of conflict, active or implied; and
often a conflict of the human will." To him drama is a conflict as well as a series of critical situations; it is the portrayal of a person "consciously or unconsciously 'up against'
some antagonistic person, circumstance, or fortune." But
what we are interested in is not the struggle—for there
may be none—it is the physical or psychic reaction of the
person; his response to the obstacle. This theory modifies
and combines those of Brunetière and Archer.

I am quite as willing to concede certain weaknesses in
Brunetière's law of the drama as I am ready to dispute the
justice of his critics' interpretation of it, and of the appropriateness of some of the material they use in support of
their criticisms. It may be granted that Agamemnon and
Oedipus are "up against" what Jones calls "a tough proposition," or rather a hopeless one. A family curse dooms both.
But to regard Oedipus as merely passive, writhing under
successive revelations or to put our interest simply in his
psychic response to these revelations, is to misread a great
tragedy utterly. Oedipus is active throughout. It is a
losing fight: the dice are loaded; the will of the gods comes
to pass. For the way of that will coming to pass—the
cumulative shaping of the crisis—we must look to the vigorous, aggressive will of Oedipus. It is he who forces the seer
to make his first revelation; [4] it is he who summons Creon

---

[4] Teiresias:—for thou didst spur me into speech against my will.

and accuses him of plotting; [5] it is he who sends for the servant, persists in his fatal search, and wrenches the truth from the herdsman. This will of his is active even after his self-blinding. Here is a struggling will to know the truth, with obstacles—the plea of Iocasta, the message of the death of Polybus, the fears of Oedipus himself—put in the way and overcome. Here is will as Brunetière understands it—will setting aims, reflecting decisions, moulding actions.

Apollo was he that brought these my woes to pass, these my sore, sore woes: but the hand that struck the eyes was none save mine, wretched that I am! Why was I to see, when sight could show me nothing sweet?

The *Oedipus* cannot be used to discredit Brunetière's theory.

The *Agamemnon* presents a more difficult case. There is no struggle on the part of Agamemnon to escape the fatal trap, for he knows of none; his death is too swift for any mental reaction. There is no conflict in the mind of Clytaemnestra. There are struggle and psychic response on the part of Cassandra, who seeks in vain to reveal coherently what she can neither clearly express nor avert, and on the part of the old citizens, who sense an impending doom, struggle to escape from a meshwork of fears and doubts, hurl curses at the murderess, and lay feeble hands on sword hilts. The play ends with an unresolved conflict. The dramatic and tragic meaning of the Agamemnon goes far beyond the figure of the king; it is a matter of interlocked destinies and the intertwining of divine and human purposes. It seems strange that Aeschylus, who everywhere sings the relentlessness of Fate, should be able to give, here as well as in the *Prometheus* and *The Seven Against Thebes*, splendid renderings of human will. The stress is on human initiative and human motives. Cassandra has drawn upon

[5] Oedipus: When the stealthy plotter is moving on me in quick sort, I, too, must be quick with my counterplot. If I await him in repose, his ends will have been gained, and mine missed.

herself the curse because she sought to warn the Trojans; Clytemnaestra takes full responsibility for her deed [6] and justifies it on the ground of Iphigenia's sacrifice and Cassandra's seduction; Aegisthus calls himself a rightful slayer and cites his ill treatment as a motive. Agamemnon's triumphant entry is the very apotheosis of satisfied will. When he sets his purpose against Clytemnaestra's design to have him offend the gods by treading on purple there is a brief clash of wills and a fatal yielding.

Brunetière is right in seeing in tragedy a glorification of the will asserting itself in a losing fight, but he is wrong in putting too individual and too isolated an emphasis on will and conflict. Interest in psychology and the social sciences is leading us away from the clearcut, heroic, battling tragic hero or the scheming villain to a tragedy of subconscious forces, embattled ideas, and the onset and recoil of groups. We give a wider fling to the term will, and a more subtle reading to motives and psychic responses. Brunetière fails to see that, essential as is a struggling will, the conflict must be related to such other things as motivation, psychic response, suffering, and the tragic collapse. It is this interrelationship that is vital. Oedipus, "the worm writhing on the hook," the mad Ajax, and Othello are all "up against it"; they are all struggling without success. Ineffectual struggles in themselves do not hold us—why then the interest in these tragic figures? For one thing, we imagine a worm to be aware of what it is he is "up against," and we ourselves know exactly what that is. Not so in tragedy! The situation is shown evolving; there is much ignorance and confusion. This removes from our sense of the inevitable something of the hard and fast, and introduces suspense and motor responses. Again, there is the psychic element

---

[6] Clytemnaestra:—You are trying me as if I were a foolish woman; but I with fearless heart say to you who know,—and it is all one to me whether you wish to approve or to blame me: "This is Agamemnon, my husband, now dead, the work of this right hand, a righteous worker!"

—purposes in their tensing and slackening, explosions of feeling, agony mental and physical.

SUFFERING: Quite as essential to tragedy as conflict is suffering. It may be physical,—a festering wound in the *Philoctetes;* insanity, torn eyeballs, and violent death in *King Lear;* cold and hunger in Gorky's *Night Lodging;* a staggering mixture of fear and fatigue in *The Emperor Jones;* delirium in *Hannele;* disease in *Ghosts* and *The Straw.* It may be mental—the keen ache of a halting will in *Hamlet;* the dull pain of an outrage in the *Philoctetes* and the *Prometheus;* the stab of disillusionment in *Timon of Athens, Troilus and Cressida,* and *Rain;* the pangs of lost honor in Calderon's *The Judge of Zalamea,* Hebbel's *The Ring of Gyges,* and Sudermann's *Ehre;* the tortures of loneliness, divided sympathies, and soiled ideals. Instead of being presented directly, the suffering may be shown in its results or in retrospect; both are favorite methods with Ibsen. Nor need it be limited to the hero. In modern drama there is much dispersed suffering, and more or less human wreckage about.

Why then is tragedy not a chamber of horrors or a distressing exhibition of the raw wounds of life? The answer may be found in another question. Why do we not say, "Poor Hamlet!" or "Poor Desdemona!" as we might in real life? It is because we are in tragedy led beyond the suffering, in two directions. (1) Suffering is related to reversals of fortune, and they in turn are grounded in purposes and conflicts of will. (2) The suffering of the individual is shown within the context of (a) redeeming interests such as intellectual range and depth of feeling, and admirable qualities—staunchness, patience, largeheartedness; (b) a dramatic situation whose meaning is larger than the disaster of a single person; and (3) life as a mixture of the passive and active, of the drab and the splendid, of the human and the cosmic. Thus suffering Desdemona reveals depth of

feeling and intensity of pleading; interests us in relation
to the treachery of Iago and the flawed mind of Othello; is
part and parcel of a situation which appeals to the intellect
and the imagination as well as to emotion—a situation whose
catastrophe means more than the shattering of this or that
individual caught in its coils.

A COLLAPSE MEANT TO BE FINAL: The simplest form
of final collapse is death, and in most tragedies death
takes its toll.   Short of that, there may be something equally
final—the hopeless insanity of Oswald in *Ghosts;* the utter
ruin of Peer Gynt's dreams.   In comedy, as distinguished
from tragedy, the collapse is not final and the person or thing
involved is not felt to be of great moment or value.   There it
is a matter of trivial issues, shallow plots, set-backs, and
temporarily discomfited characters.   Falstaff in *The Merry
Wives of Windsor*, Malvolio in *Twelfth Night*, Tartuffe and
Harpagon are all brought face to face with the ruin of their
schemes and hopes.   But we do not get the sense of a permanent loss or gain.   Falstaff will make another easy-going
attempt on the well-entrenched virtue of some burgher's
wife and will again be tricked; Malvolio will air his vanity
and Tartuffe his cant in other circumstances; and Harpagon actually returns to his moneybox.   Not so in tragedy!
It shows the cracking of a noble heart, the downfall of a
mighty passion or of a great cause, the smashing beyond
repair of a sensitive nature.   Something has been lost, once
and for all, and the very loss drives home the value and the
sense of the flaw that is in all things human.

Here is further evidence of how all the essentials of tragedy
are interconnected.   The *collapse* must be more than an
unmotivated fit of apoplexy; it must be the snapping of a
tensional situation marked by *conflict*—of men or principles—; it must reveal passion, purpose, *suffering*, all blending in a mental crisis; it must carry us beyond thwarted and

suffering individuals to cosmic ideas and feelings, and beyond the irreparable loss to a *new imaginative value.*

It is possible to make a series, which may serve the use of tests of excellence of tragedies. They may be stood up in a row like soldiers, passed in review, and then inspected separately.

a. *There must be unified action.*

b. *This action must march.*

c. *This march must be marked by (1) complications, (2) conflicts, (3) crises, mental and physical; and must terminate in a catastrophe.*

d. *The action, in its development, crises, and catastrophe (1) must be given in terms of (a) a direct, vivid, and consistent portrayal of character, (b) an intense and significant picture of life, (c) human suffering; and (2) must be imaginatively redeemed by one or all of these things: beauty or vigor of language, intensity of passion, sweep, reach or depth of images and ideas, and a thrust into cosmic problems.*

a. THERE MUST BE UNIFIED ACTION: This is merely a special case of the general aesthetic form of organization. By action is meant neither something violent and startling only nor something that just happens. It may be very quiet and unobtrusive, a thing of the mind rather than a matter of riot, battle, and sudden death; and it expresses purpose. *Hamlet* is more than a chronicle of the sayings and doings of the Prince of Denmark; it is the setting of a definite problem of revenge and attempted solution by means of a series of purposes and acts. Here is organizational unity in the consciousness and will of a single, outstanding personality. There are other types of unifying: the unity of intersecting lives—Io in the *Prometheus*, Dr. Rank in *A Doll's House*—the unity of parallel themes—the Gloster scenes in *King Lear*—the unity of groups—Hauptmann's *The Weavers*, Galsworthy's *The Mob;* the unity of ideas— Goethe's *Faust*, Werfel's *Goatsong*, Galsworthy's *Loyalties*. All this goes far beyond Aristotle's conception of simple and complex plots; but it is true in spirit to his underlying idea that events and incidents in a tragedy must hang together.

b. THIS ACTION MUST MARCH: Tragedy, like other forms of the drama, presents life in motion. It must not be merely static. Tempo and momentum may vary; the advance may be swift and sure, or leisurely, and there may be halting and pauses. There must, however, be no continuous marking of time. The action must not disappear in lyricism, minute characterization, rhetoric, and a smother of words.

c. THIS MARCH MUST BE MARKED BY COMPLICATIONS, CONFLICTS, CRISES, MENTAL AND PHYSICAL; AND MUST TERMINATE IN A CATASTROPHE: When the will of an individual or group issues in action complications arise, obstacles are met with, and critical conflicts emerge. If the action is stripped of such complexities it fails to hold our interest. The element of suspense is then lacking; and we are denied the chance of following a varied contest; of working out the logic of situations; of tensing and stretching our imagination as we balance on the steep and dangerous places of experience. In addition then to *unity* and *drive*, there must be a *rich and tensional action*. This may be gained in various ways; no one and only formula must be forced upon tragedy.

As for the catastrophe, it is the burning glass which gathers to a point all the forces and interests of tragedy and starts a smoky flare of disaster. The catastrophe must be necessary, gripping, tremendous in its upheaval and reverberating in its effect.

d. THIS ACTION, IN ITS DEVELOPMENT, CRISES, AND CA-

TASTROPHE, (1) Must Be Given in Terms of (a) A Direct, Vivid, and Consistent Portrayal of Character, (b) An Intense and Significant Picture of Life, (c) Human Suffering; and (2) Must Be Imaginatively Redeemed by One or All of These Things: Beauty or Vigor of Language, Intensity of Passion, Reach and Depth of Images and Ideas, and a Thrust into Cosmic Problems. Tragedy shows character largely from within. It puts on the stage persons acting out their purposes, and it reveals the consciousness in which these purposes take shape—the feelings, the moods, the deliberations, the sense of self on the part of the individual. The more directly and profoundly it does this the greater its significance as tragedy will be. The *Medea, Hamlet,* and *Peer Gynt* may be used in illustration: all three exhibit a *self-revealing* central character. The impression given is vivid and deep. The mind of Medea, torn between love of child and hatred of husband, stands revealed in its tangle of motives and moods, and flashes in vivid as well as in subtle colors. In some of Maeterlinck's earlier dramas there is a sort of washed out character-drawing; the inner life is given, but too much in mood and too little in purpose. Again, character-drawing must be *consistent*. When Aristotle made this demand he met a simple situation in a simple way. Characters in Greek tragedy are not complex and are not as a rule shown as changing. When there is change, he contends, it ought to be well grounded. The modern problem is much less simple. Much of our interest is in character as developing; the puzzle of the subconscious enters such plays as Werfel's *Spiegelmensch* and O'Neill's *The Great God Brown;* and there is a growing distrust of over-rationalized character. We still insist, however, on an interrelation of motives, moods, and actions, and on the absence of sudden breaks or inconsistencies in character-drawing. In comedy there may be such breaks. In plays like *Cymbeline, A Winter's Tale,*

Much Ado About Nothing, Measure for Measure the leopard
changes his spots in a single washing. Such facile, unmotivated changes are admissible in comedy, where character
is not to be taken very seriously, but not in tragedy, where
it is of the greatest importance.

Tragedy must give an intense and significant picture of
life. In contrast to the novel, which in its hundreds of pages
gives a branching and spreading life of many characters and
incidents—trunk, fibre, mottled bark, veined or galled leaf
—tragedy selects a few characters of special significance
and moments that are critical and packs this truncated life
of the imagination with an intensity and wealth of appeal not
to be found elsewhere, neither in art nor in actual living.
This it does in part by selection—in part by a sort of synco-
pated stressing, and in part by an imaginative quickening
of inert material.

Tragedy gains emotional depth by accentuating suffering. In real life suffering is too often purely physical, inarticulate, and related solely to this or that individual.
Tragedy makes it reflect agony of mind; gives it voice in
the imprecations of a Lear or a Timon, in the self-torture
of Othello, and in the wailings of *The Trojan Women;* and
lifts it beyond the individual to make it a throbbing sorrow
to be found in all things human.

Here is that *thrust into cosmic problems* which is one of
the methods of *imaginative redemption.* Of the need of
imaginatively redeeming, in some fashion or other, the mixed
and often repulsive materials of tragedy there can be no
doubt. The meaning of the term may be gained by pointing to examples outside the field of tragedy. Indecency is
redeemed by Rabelais, vulgarity by a bit of picturesque
slang, profanity by a phrase like *Sacré nom d'un nom.* No
change has been effected in moral values: the things remain
reprehensible. But the attention is shifted from the thing to
the artist—to Rabelais hovering like a god above dirty wa-

ters, to the coiner of an unusual turn of speech, to the blas-
phemer who shows originality and imagination even in his
blasphemy—and then to the thing, which is given an altered
aesthetic value. In Ford's *Tis Pity She's a Whore* and
Dreiser's *The Hand of the Potter* the materials are such as
to arouse an immediate moral revulsion, but they are redeemed, in the one case by form and a curious blend of restraint and passion, and in the other by building the problem
out in the universe. Dreiser's title is striking and haunting
and shares in the redemption, Ford's is commonplace and
does not. These two plays have been chosen, one of them an
idealizing, and the other a naturalistic portrait, for the purpose of insisting that (1) there are many methods of imaginative redemption, (2) it is not necessary to avoid crass situations, repulsive characters or foul speech, and (3) imaginative must not be confused with moral redemption. The
first point needs no comment. As for the second, the choice
of the sordid and the narrow imposes a task not easily met.
Natural advantages, such as stateliness and breadth of
scene, beauty of character, and pomp of language, there
are none; their place must be taken by a probing, ranging,
and fusing imagination. Ibsen in *Ghosts* and Tolstoy in
The Power of Darkness are successful; O'Neill in *Anna
Christie* and Wedekind in *The Awakening of Spring* and
The Box of Pandora fall short of complete success.

The third point demands a further clearing. Tragedy
is often viewed from a moral angle; quite plausibly so since
it has at times reflected great religious and moral beliefs
and caught the spirit of the Morality Play, and since it works
so largely in the stuff of common moral experience. Put
into play the human trait of strong partisanship in moral
matters and the widely held belief that "the right side ought
to win," and the stage is set for the theory of moral redemption. This theory of tragedy makes two closely related demands: that for a vice there ought to be a compensatory

virtue; and that vice ought to be punished and the cosmic balance reestablished. One of its special technical forms is that of "poetic justice"; every character caught in the maelstrom of suffering must have some moral flaw, otherwise our sense of justice would be outraged. Commentators like Gervinus have discovered blameworthiness in Cordelia, Desdemona, and the Fool in *King Lear*, and have looked for virtues or at least plausible excuses in the villainies of Iago and Richard III. Often the theory appears as the general demand that a world satisfying to our moral sense be presented—a world in which weakness and overreaching crime lead to commensurate self-collapse, justice is done, and the right is vindicated. We are thus to be given a chance for moral edification, often denied us in real life.

I admit that tragedies like *Macbeth* and *Hedda Gabler* and tragic novels like *Anna Karénina, Madame Bovary,* and *An American Tragedy* render the logic of sin relentlessly and with no moral didacticism. But I maintain that it is the purpose of the tragic poet, not to trace simple moral patterns and to justify the way of God to man, but to rouse us to the infinite imaginative possibilities of life. This is as true of the devout Aeschylus as it is of the sceptical Euripides. A queer justice is dispensed in the *Hippolytus* and a queer fate stalks through Synge, Strindberg, Dunsany, and Wedekind. Evil unpaid for, moral chaos, the nightmare shapes of the subconscious, cruelty and waste at the heart of the process of living—all these things have a great imaginative value, which must not be ruled out through any complacent formula. Virtues and great moral moments, it is true, have a splendor and an appeal which must be utilized; but only in the most conventional drama are they used for the purpose of either pointing moral lessons or creating faith in the righteousness of the universe. Elsewhere they count for what they are worth to the imagination. The reach and stretch of *Hamlet, Faust, Peer Gynt,* and *Goatsong* go far beyond any moral truth or moral ideal. To set *moral* in the place of *imaginative* redemption is to run the risk of seriously misunderstanding the spirit of tragedy.[7]

THE AESTHETIC SIGNIFICANCE OF TRAGEDY

An original fact must be rescued from a tangle of metaphysics and psychology and a meshwork of traditions. It is this: tragedy selects material such as reversals of fortune, disasters, suffering, vice, disintegration, which in real life would be painful, and succeeds in making of it a source of pleasure. Two questions await an answer: why are such materials chosen? and how are they made enjoyable?

THE SECRET OF THE CHOICE: It seems strange that we should in art, which is a world of our imaginative remaking, deliberately choose what is distressing, harrowing, and overwhelming. Why is there such a form of art as tragedy? What is the meaning of its lowering gloom, of

---

[7] The following may serve as an illustration of how easy it is to fall into this confusion and how difficult it is to interpret any tragedy correctly. Because of *The Box of Pandora* Wedekind was charged with an offense against public morality. The lower court found for acquittal, but this verdict was reversed by the two higher courts and the play ordered destroyed or modified. All three took Lulu for the central figure, and they concurred in the opinion that the spectacle of Lulu—the embodiment of sensuality—sinking from the height of life to the depths of a common prostitute and a horrible death was morally edifying. According to the lower court it was Wedekind's purpose to show "the demoniac power of a woman's beauty and insatiable lust from its highest height to its lowest depth, and in this crass form to warn against vice and to arouse human sympathy." The higher courts reversed the decision only because this moral redemption could not cancel the filth of the second act. Now, this is looking for a Hogarthian simplicity and moral impressiveness where they are not to be found. Wedekind, in the preface to his revised play, states that the central figure is not Lulu but the Gräfin Geschwitz, and that it was his purpose to raise to the dignity of a tragic theme a pathological perversion usually derided or ridiculed. This is evidently a problem of imaginative redemption; and Wedekind uses moral ideas—loyalty, agonized self-struggle, self-immolation—with that in view. His aim is not judgment and retribution; it is to get full psychic value and tragic tension from an abnormal type rich in the possibilities of conflict and suffering—a type neglected in tragedy because of moral disapproval.

its insistent stressing of evil of all kinds? Many answers
have been given to this question. Here are a few:

Aristotle: The secret, according to Aristotle, is to be
found in a *katharsis*, a purgation on the principle of curing
like with like. Man is preyed upon by nameless dread and
objectless pity; by indulging such passions and giving them
point he temporarily rids himself of certain pathological
elements they contain, and achieves a calm like that of the
votaries of Dionysus after their ecstatic rites. In the absence of a fuller text, Aristotle's exact meaning·must remain a matter of dispute. Is the purgation to apply to all
passions or to pity and fear merely? Are pity and fear
purging agencies? What are the pathological elements to
be got rid of? It is at least clear that the passionateness
and emotionalism of tragedy censured by Plato as a social
menace are held by Aristotle to be a curative device. The
cure yields pleasure—"the pleasure peculiar to tragedy."
Here is a rudimentary biological theory which may well be
construed within the wider context of the modern mind and
its complex responses to life. The Aristotelian terms, pity
and fear, have been thus construed by Hegel and his followers.

Hegel: Tragedy, for Hegel, is the envisaging in artistic form of the complex and tensional nature of a world-
process of developing and organized reason. All the discords of life,—suffering, defeat, moral distress, the rivalry
of ideals, the butcheries of history,—this bold thinker works
into a rolling and swelling anthem of reason. What tragedy
does is to give a vivid and searching portrayal of the tortured complications and a deepened sense of the unity and
divinity of the world. It is an emotionally stressed exercise in cosmic reading. The text is full of disturbing ideas;
the construction is difficult; there is enough to try any man's
intellectual and moral mettle. The effect of a successful
reading is a universalized pity and fear—a sense of human

kinship in suffering, and a sense of the majesty and the might of a triumphant world reason.

Schopenhauer: To Schopenhauer this triumphant system of reason seems to be nonsense. The world must be read in terms of will—a will expressing itself in murderous struggle, disillusionment, suffering, and enslaving man by means of his own aggressive desires. Why then should man add to the gloom and bitterness of life by putting within the frame of the drama a massed array of irrationalities? Why should he set himself the task of enjoying the mixture? The answer to these questions lies in Schopenhauer's theory of a partial escape from life through art. Tragedy shows a crossing of wills and a clash of interests; it shows the hero overwhelmed and purified—cleansed of willing—and it deadens the will in us also. It is man's way of driving out into the open the thing he has to fight, and of gaining calm and resignation from struggle at its keenest.

Nietzsche: Nietzsche, like Schopenhauer, explains the world in terms of will, but the setting is no longer gloomy, and will is not the villain in the play. The world is not to be denied and escaped from, it is to be affirmed even in its most questionable aspects. Tragedy is one of man's boldest affirmations. To explore the depths and agonies of life and to gain from them an ecstatic pleasure is to exhibit a supreme courage and a will to mastery which nothing can balk.

Bergson: Tragedy, to Bergson, is of the nature of a volcanic eruption. It is the hurling of a molten mass of passions and primitive impulses through the thin crust of orderliness and restraint which has formed on the social surfaces of life. It is a staging, within the non-destructive realm of art, of a chaos, a whirl of feelings, and a revolt real life no longer permits.

THE SOURCE OF THE ENJOYMENT: Some people are incapable of enjoying tragedy; they either sheer off to something lighter and more agreeable or they accept it with an heroic gesture which underscores the strain they feel.   Even those who do enjoy it respond differently, but these varying reactions show a common element—a blend of exhilaration and calm.   The exhilaration is not a mere emotional effervescence but a heightened tone of consciousness, and the calm is not the calm of resignation or fatigue.   This experience marks the aesthetic satisfaction yielded by tragedy.   It has been mine on the first reading of so gloomy a play as *Ghosts* and on the completion of a five hour performance of the *Oresteia*.   It is one thing to record it, quite another thing to trace its sources.

What are the origins of this satisfaction?   What are the pleasures of tragedy?   The first (1) is pleasure in the dramatic.   This has its humble analogue in common speech: we like to have "something doing."   In the drama there is "something doing," from physical encounters, murder and suicide to subtle but none the less absorbing sparring for advantages.   In tragedy the stakes are higher than they are in comedy, and the game is more seriously a game of purposes; there is therefore more eager pleasure in the watching. Next (2) is a pleasure in psychic revelation.   There is an insatiable curiosity on the part of man directed at the inner life of his fellows.   This ranges from indecent prying to a desire to understand their actions and to savor of their feelings.   In tragedy this curiosity may be satisfied with a completeness denied in real life, for its texture is psychic and its characters are self-revelational.   There is (3) pleasure in workmanship—the handling of a situation, the shading and rounding off of character, the deft use of phrase. Two of the most characteristic pleasures remain.   If people are incapable of enjoying tragedy it is either because they lack imagination or because they cannot universalize their sympathetic feelings and cannot detach them from the ordinary motor responses of practical life.   All art is life

imaginatively grasped and transformed. In the rendering
of tragic materials this transforming is difficult, and the
pleasure on that account greater and more poignant. Tragedy, then, yields (4) a pleasing sense of intensified life.
Packed within narrow compass are characters in their significant moments of utterance and action, events in their
significant complications; and rising above the beat and
jangle of incident and character, with a huge wing-spread
of meaning, are cosmic overtones. To all this we respond
—innervating, stretching, sensing the sweep and the pressure. This may serve, too, as a biological theory of the
origins of tragedy. One further pleasure must be added,
that (5) of universalized and detached sympathetic feelings.
Tragedy is a distillation of macerated happiness and the bitter stuff of failure and disillusionment; and this distillation,
hot and biting as it is, is pleasing to a strong palate. To
feel the pain of another as our own is agonizing; why then
is there this pleasure in a form of art which seems to put a
great strain on our sympathetic feelings? The obvious answer is that it is imaginary woes we are asked to respond to,
but this answer hardly satisfies. When we come to look at
the suffering in a tragedy we find it not localized in an individual, no matter how heavy the burden of the tragic hero
may be, but dispersed, affecting the other characters and
interpreted as the sorrows of man. It is like a wavering
light running across the clouded surfaces of many mirrors,
and losing itself in the darkness beyond. In the tragic second act of Géraldy's *Aimer*, a serious play with a happy ending, intense suffering is shown dispersed over three persons—
wife, husband, lover—. Sharply interested as we are in the
predicament of each and readily as we respond to the agony
of each, our interest and our sympathy, nevertheless, strike
at and vibrate in answer to something beyond—the tangle of
misunderstandings and the sorrow that edge life in black.
Such suffused sympathy is found everywhere in tragedy.

To this must be added the matter of divided and detached sympathy. We are asked to respond sympathetically to the feelings and purposes of individuals whose interests are set in sharp opposition, or to pass to and fro between two hostile camps within one mind. This is true even of the old fashioned tragedy of villainy—*Richard III, Othello, The White Devil*—in which malice distils its poison of intrigue, for there is a sympathy that mocks at moral values. Imagine in real life such a situation as is presented in *Aimer*, and imagine yourself seriously attempting to straighten things out. The task would be painful—like trying to catch the conflicting motor and feeling values of three pieces of music played simultaneously. Why then the pleasure in the play? It is because there is no taking sides in the sense of pushing on toward a practical solution. The sympathy is detached. The pain in real life reflects a militancy, emotional and moral, which in tragedy is hushed. Here is one of the most puzzling and significant facts about tragedy. The weight of a world awry sinks deep into our consciousness and stirs it to its depths, but there is no militant desire to set this world aright, no apportioning of praise or blame, no sympathetic rushing to relieve. We are offered an opportunity which real life rarely grants us—of tasting to the full, with a discriminating and luxuriating taste, the imaginative quality of moral conflicts, of suffering, of purposes, and of our own sympathetic feelings.

Imaginative redemption, then, holds the secret of tragedy. It discloses its meaning as a type of art, and accounts for much in the quality of the pleasure it offers.

THE COMIC

The comic differs from the other aesthetic types in not appearing naturally and freely in all the arts. Architecture in its essential, structural effects has none of it; sculpture occasionally aims at it; music and the dance use it forcefully but not widely; it has no place in painting. It is only in literature and in certain types of the graphic arts —caricatures and cartoons—that it shows its full strength and variety: a variety greater than that of any other type.

If something is to be made of this problem, whose challenge has never been successfully met and much of whose mystery will remain at the end of this study, we must (1) examine the comic as an experience, tracing the fact and the causes of being amused by nature and by art; (2) pass in review the important theories of the comic; (3) discover what things are amusing and what devices are used to provoke laughter; (4) look into allied types—humor, satire, and wit—and (5) offer a brief analysis of comedy as a mass of comic effects with a structure and meaning of its own.

THE COMIC AS AN EXPERIENCE

The comic, like the tragic response, straddles life and art. Nature freely furnishes material: grotesque shapes, queer faces, twisted plays of character, startling mix-ups. On such incongruities and mishaps of life we feed with all the relish yielded by one of the oldest indulgences of man. They in turn are reflected in the mirror of art, concave or convex, and become doubly pleasing in the ingeniously distorted mirroring.

Of the comic as an experience it may be said that it is a common one. Few people fail to see "the funny side" of something. Again, it is intermittent. Being amused is in part a matter of mood, and moods come and go; even buffoons have their serious moments. As an æsthetic response it is marked by *detachment* and *distance*. It is variously compounded of good spirits; thought, and sympathetic and antipathetic feelings. It ranges from broad laughter to Meredith's "slim, feasting smile"; from laughter tinged with malice to laughter indulgent and companionable; from a response that is naive or straightforward to one that is sophisticated or subtle.

When an experience is as spontaneous and unmindful of itself as this, there seems something strained in the question: Why do we laugh? The question itself means many things to many minds. To some it is an excursion into physiology, child psychology or biology. Laughter involves facial distortion and a shaking diaphragm; appears within the first year of life; may be provoked by tickling; and undoubtedly has a biological meaning. Studies like those of Darwin, Preyer, Hall, Shinn, Robinson and general biological theories such as those of Spencer, Havelock Ellis, Sully, Robinson, and Watson have their own value. The aesthetician, however, must not allow himself to be taken away by them from the experience of being amused— of responding to the comic—and to be marched into a tangle of genetic guesses and mechanistic devices. Of what use is it to him to connect smiling with sucking;[1] to trace the area and curve of ticklishness;[2] to explain ticklishness as a protective contrivance against attack in warfare, against parasites or as a sex survival,[3] or in terms of

[1] Freud, Allin, Greig.
[2] Hall and Allin, Robinson.
[3] Robinson.

erotic excitement? [4]   It is a far cry from the smile of a baby asleep or in distress, the laughter caused by digging a finger into his ribs, and adult hysterical laughter—which is like the snapping of a cord—to even the simple enjoyment and expression of the comic or the direct enjoyment of a game of bo-peep or the antics of a mechanical toy.   It is only at this point that laughter becomes aesthetically significant.   There is no reason for not carrying a pack stuffed with psychology and biology as valuable items of equipment, but we must be headed the right way—toward a fuller understanding of an experience which ranges from the grossest to the most subtle phases of life; an experience which spans life and the domain of art.

What then, in this broad sense, is the meaning of laughter?   It is to the credit of the many theories offered that they have kept within the realm of aesthetically significant laughter; it is to their discredit that they incline to a onesided reading.

A review of some of these theories may be combined with an appreciative recognition of the truth they contain, a rebuke for their narrowness, and further analysis of the facts.

THEORIES OF THE COMIC

LAUGHTER AS SELF-GLORIFICATION

In its simplest form this theory appears in Hobbes.   He speaks of laughter in terms of "sudden glory"; and this casual remark of his fits in well with his general reading of human nature.   Whatever a man does he does for gain or glory; since he is as vain as he is selfish he resents any sign of undervaluing, and enjoys when he can a sense of superiority over his fellows.

From this Groos has developed a theory of the comic in

---

4 Havelock Ellis.

terms of a sense of superiority in the presence of something absurd; or of some part of ourselves felt to be inferior. Our laughter is at another's expense and is set down by us to our credit; or it is at the expense of the fool in us who was nearly taken in, and then it is self-praise on the part of our cleverer or more alert self. It is to the credit of Groos that he also recognizes a natural playfulness and gregariousness in human life and thus avoids something of the narrowness of Hobbes.

What truth is there in this theory of laughter? No doubt laughing is often a bit of self-congratulatory business. My neighbor has had a practical joke played on him. What a fool to walk into the trap! no such trap would snare me! My sense of security is voiced in my laughter and that in turn gives fresh strength to my assurance. I see a man of fifty falling in love and am amused at the Indian Summer madness of his courting. If he believed himself safe and then was swept off his feet, I laugh all the harder. Never should I make such a spectacle of myself! my head is too clear, my heart too cool, for that. But suppose I, too, become a victim. May I not laugh at myself as I am hurried off into irrationalities; and is not a sense of superiority involved in this laughter? I rise with the I that calls me a fool and look down on the I that is the fool. Thus does vanity snatch victory from defeat.

There need be no malice in such laughter; the attitude may be too complacent for that. When we do develop *Schadenfreude*—a malicious enjoyment of another's discomfiture,—as in certain types of practical joking and in wit, our response can no longer be explained in terms of vanity, unless it be wounded vanity; rather does it reflect a cruelty that delights in inflicting pain, and an aggressive desire to debase. It is interesting to watch Freud, who leans heavily toward such ideas, especially in his analysis of *tendency-wit*, struggling with the "sense of superiority." He assigns to it a place in the genesis of laughter and in a theory of the comic when he insists that comparison is implied in the comic; and he tries hard to keep self-glorification out of such comparisons. He is unsuccessful, for the term slips by the censor of his reasoned thought.

The theory that self-glorification, rooted in a sense of superiority, explains the comic falls short of being anything but a useful key to certain types. There are in it dangerous weaknesses. The vain man is not a good laugher. Uncritical of himself and constantly trapped by his conceit, he is the butt of jokes and the prey of comic writers.[5] Vanity is too much concerned with itself, whereas the comic response looks abroad for something foolish or absurd. Again, there seems to be a sort of *regressus ad infinitum:* for every vain self laughed at we must assume a vainer self that does the laughing. Worst of all, the gregarious, kindly, sympathetic nature of much of our laughter is neglected.

SYMPATHETIC LAUGHTER

Comedians are familiar with the trick of laughing heartily for the purpose of having laughter start up, suddenly and explosively, in the audience. This is the simplest form of sympathetic laughter: a laughing with, as unreflective and as good an example of unconscious imitation as are the movements made while watching a fencer or bowler. Such group merriment is common. There need be nothing to laugh at; we are merely caught up in the swirl.

Less simple than this echoing laughter is responding

---

[5] Malvolio in *Twelfth Night* and Sir Willoughby in *The Egoist* are examples. Professional and group vanities—"we military men"; "we artists," etc., and upstart vanities are favorite material for the comedy of character.

laughter, another and a higher type. Our being amused at human follies cannot be interpreted altogether as self-glorification or as a rebuke directed at anything unreasonable or anti-social. There is a bit of the fool or the knave in all of us, and a sneaking fondness for this fool wherever found. We enjoy sympathetically the gross feeder in Falstaff, the muddled idealist in Don Quixote, Sancho Panza the realist built close to the ground, Micawber the carefree, and Tanner the pursued. We all have a tilt or two with windmills or build castles in the air. The romantic gilding that changes a country wench to a Dulcinea is the ready practice of every lover.

It may be said of such advanced sympathetic laughter that it (1) lacks the resonance of *touch and go* laughter; (2) is marked by indulgent understanding; (3) involves feelings of wide range, superficial, easily detached and shifted; (4) presupposes an alert and versatile imagination because an unoriginal person of strong, grooved emotions, who is one thing and cannot imagine himself anything else, is not a laugher of this type; (5) cannot be explained in terms of an "instinct of self-debasement."

LAUGHTER AS A SOCIAL REBUKE

This theory retains the gregariousness of laughter, tends to exclude the emotional, and gives a new socialized and intellectualized reading of the comic. Whatever endangers our common social life provokes a gesture of protest; if society is sure of itself and the danger is not too great, the gesture is one of playful ridicule; with a deepening apprehension, the laughter becomes sharply pointed; when the danger is great, it is embittered, yields to truculent satire or to aggressive practical measures.

Of the two representatives of this theory, Meredith and

Bergson, Meredith offers the simpler variant. He holds our
social life to be an achievement made possible by individual
self-discipline and the development of a cooperative spirit.
Some impulses must be blocked and others are in need of
refinement; the individual's whole life must be raised to the
level of rational control; and there must be a "harnessing"
and pulling together at a common task. Two dangers are
to be guarded against: a slipping back to a lower level of
primitive impulses and undisciplined feelings, and an individual fractiousness which means the breaking of the social
harness, and a bolt. There is an early "rawness" in Falstaff's guzzling, gluttony, and uncontrolled sex life, which
is rebuked by the *comic spirit*—that critical warning voice
of commonsense. The obstinate man, the man of conceit,
the sentimentalist, the moon-calf all show a lack of sobriety,
of mental balance, and of regard for the checking value of
facts, which make them a menace to themselves and to an
enlightened society as well. Nor can the swindler, the boor,
the hypocrite, the fop, the pedant, the rake, the greedy law-
yer, the shallow society woman be said to be playing the
social game as Meredith would have it played—in a spirit
of sustained kindliness and give and take; they are disrupt-
ing influences to be guarded against by laughter.

Bergson, like Meredith, interprets laughter as a gesture
in defence of social unity; a discrediting by means of ridicule of anything that might swing the individual out of line
with his fellows. But when he comes to state what society
needs and what it must save itself from he substitutes alertness and resourcefulness for Meredith's consideration and
sane-mindedness, and mechanization for backsliding. His
theory takes its clue from the contrast between life, an individual, flexible, non-repeating process, and matter, which is
inert, non-flexible, reversible in its combining.

Society, a living thing, is exposed to all manner of mechanizing influences. Our institutions harden, our speech tends to become parrot talk, and our conduct turns to mere mimicry; we run along the wire of our class or in the groove of a mechanized intellect and will of our own. Society cannot afford such mechanization; it needs flexible forms and alert, adaptable individuals. The awkward man shows absentmindedness in stumbling and stiffness in falling; it is mental sluggishness that snares the victim of the practical joker. The man who flounders about and muddles things lacks sharpness and resourcefulness; the individual who sets himself apart in dress, in manner, in speech—the queer man in short—is blocking, consciously, or unconsciously, the game of social give and take. Small wonder then that they are all laughed at, and in being laughed at are rebuked in the simplest and least expensive way open to society.

Group laughter of this disciplinary type is common and often does good service in keeping down eccentricities and in furthering a life of social accord. But there is a great deal of laughter which is neither thoughtful nor corrective. It cannot be thrown aside as being farcical. Far from being well mannered, much of it is none too squeamish—a sympathetic sharing of experiences running counter to what is most highly prized in a cultured society. It might be suggested that the comic of this type has the social value of allowing an imaginative outlet for such gross and primitive appetites as cannot be destroyed but are forced back, and of thus guarding against too brittle a refinement, moral and intellectual. This would point to the theory that laughter is a relief from inhibitions; and that theory has its own difficulties.

There are two objections to Bergson's position. The mechanical is not necessarily the anti-social. Efficiency in group life is in great part a matter of economy, and economy is gained among other things by extensive mechanization.

Settled habits, established beliefs and traditions, fixed policies are needed as stabilizing forces. Again, laughter often fails to discriminate between non-conformity that is bad and non-conformity that is good; and thus itself becomes a mechanical, reactionary thing. Caricature, when it is not merely playful, uses ridicule as a rebuke. It is a defensive measure by means of which the group maintains itself at a certain level. Whoever falls below that level is greeted with laughter. But so are often those who seek to rise above it. None of the great reform movements have been welcomed by the caricaturist; he has again and again ridiculed men and women who for the sake of a larger life have broken down barriers of class or sex. Here lies a weakness in Bergson's theory; he fails to see that society is composed of many groups of clannish interests, and that each group, jealous of its narrow circle, employs laughter defensively, and at the cost, often, of greater social values. A bourgeois group laughs at one of its members who steps out of the circle; yet there is nothing either mechanical or anti-social in his ambition; rather is the laughter mechanical and opposed to a progressive social life.

Meredith and Bergson alike fail to give full value to sympathetic laughter; and they overlook altogether the laughter of relief.

LAUGHTER AS A RELIEF

Laughter on its physical side is often a form of relief. Emotional tension is relieved by hysterical laughter. In smiling or laughing we relax, let ourselves go, work off and rid ourselves of "black humours" and taut nerves.

The comic may be explained in terms of relief from three classes of restraints:—conventional, sexual, and logical.

CONVENTIONAL SOCIAL RESTRAINTS: For the sake of

smooth living together society has developed a routine of manners and morals. We must eat and dress in certain ways; carry our religion to church and home again; give our economic and moral beliefs the approved cut. We must be good carpenters or professional men; good heads of families; good citizens. We are set within an orderly scheme. All this means being restrained, conventionalized, institutionalized. If the individual is nothing and can be nothing other than this routine, well and good! he will be an estimable, non-laughing member of his community. But if he has a little originality, imagination, and initiative he may balk at the restraint and become a rebel. Rebellion of the practical type, however, means courage and sustained effort, and is bound to prove costly. There is another and a cheaper way: relief through laughter. When I catch myself becoming a creature of habit or discover society standardizing dress, diet, religion, patriotism, I seek a momentary release through amused laughter from a routine which is gradually shaping my life whether I will it or no. There may be aggressive wit in my thrust—with a naked or a buttoned point—or satire, bitter or genial, or a freeing smile.

SEXUAL RESTRAINTS: A special set of restraints are those concerning physical needs and facts of sex. A developing society achieves and asks: (1) refinement in speech and in methods of living—the grosser bodily facts are either hidden from view or carried over into the context of aesthetic, moral, and scientific meanings; (2) a more considerate as well as a more delicate manner of living—others must not be insulted by gross actions and allusions; (3) personal ideals of purity and "cleanness"; (4) a self-discipline on the part of the individual which causes him to assign to his sex life a minor rôle. With the removal of these four restraints four types of comic emerge:—(1') coarse practical

jokes; reference to bodily functions and sexual organs;
(2') intentional indelicacies and brutalities; shocking stories; (3') smutty stories; obscenities; (4') a welter of sex
allusions; a reveling in an exaggerated sex life.

It seems plausible to argue that in all these cases laughter is a matter of relief. We become gross for the sake
of a return to primitive nature; we tell shocking stories in
an attack on the eternal refinement of others; or to slip out
of our own refinement; we enjoy smut as a camper enjoys
dirt; we indulge imaginatively in a stress on sex, which we
no longer allow ourselves in real life.

LOGICAL RESTRAINTS: What is called fooling or foolery
is a disregard of reasonable sequences among words and
ideas, and of sensible conduct. At times we rebel against
what has been slowly and painfully acquired through experience—this logical restraint in ourselves and our neighbors. Why be so "damnably reasonable"? we say. There
is a desire to gamble, to throw things in confusion; to indulge in disorderly thinking, to return to an early irration-
ality still manifest in dreams, to take a slap at the all too
composed face of reason. Certain forms of the comic—nonsense rhymes, absurd combinations of words or ideas, as in
Alice in Wonderland—may be interpreted as a momentary
enjoyable release from logic.

The theory that laughter is a relief from restraints conventional, sexual, and logical has points in its favor. But
it interprets the comic in too narrow and negative a fashion.
Gross jokes and sex references are enjoyed for their own
sake by peasant and city dweller alike when there is none of
the restraint the violation of which is the purpose of many
sophisticated obscenities. Rabelaisian humor, as it flour-
ishes in our smoking rooms, is in large part a release from
decency, but neither Rabelais himself nor our enjoyment of
his type of the comic can wholly be accounted for in terms
of revolt. Again, logical restraints are hardly strong

enough to be troublesome. Clear speech and straight thinking are about the last thing the individual expects of himself or society expects of him. The discipline of life allows a liberal margin of disorderly thinking. The positive factor which this theory neglects is that of *playful caprice*.

THE LAUGHTER OF PLAYFUL CAPRICE

Rodin somewhere speaks of a "vagabondage of fancy." The phrase may serve to mark a frequent motif in the creation and enjoyment of the comic. A tramp need not be a rebel; he may be merely a rover. Systematic topsyturvyism such as is to be found in *Alice in Wonderland*, Butler's *Erewhon*, Barrie's *The Admirable Crichton* and *A Kiss for Cinderella* is a mixture of relief from accepted values and a free roving. The caricaturist plays capriciously with lines, and the comic dancer tilts and tumbles the lines of his body. Mr. Dooley has his sport with language and current events; Lewis Carrol knocks ideas about. In all these instances it is the irresponsible laugher who enjoys the irresponsible game. Illustrations may be had from such different sources as Thackeray and Rabelais. Thackeray delighted in whimsical invention of names and crazy spelling; there are many clownish touches in his letters and marginal drawings. When during his stay in Boston he shouted and danced on hearing that all the tickets for his first lecture were sold, and insisted on sticking his long legs out of the carriage window he was simply cutting capers. The contrast to his usual gentlemanliness and to Boston decorum adds to the amusement, but the heart of the matter is a boyishness which appeals to the boy that is in most men. Rabelais is a mine of laughter of this sort. He strings words together, piles up variants, throws words on the page by the shovelful, tosses ideas about, takes a question like Married or

Single? and plays with it till nothing is left but nonsense, caprice, and high spirits.

FREUD'S THEORY

No single descriptive term serves here: Freud offers a medley of explanations which includes *relief*, *play*, *malice*, *sympathy*, and *economy*. His book *Wit and the Unconscious* presents a highly specialized theory of wit followed by a more or less tentative and muddled treatment of the comic. He connects both with the unconscious. It is here that his theory is most original and suggestive, and most questionable. He gains vantage ground for far-reaching observations and shrewd comments, but he pays a heavy price—for the streams of psycho-analysis run muddy in a double sense: they are neither clear nor clean.

Our waking adult life, according to Freud, is an achievement made possible by a discipline of impulses which suppresses, for the sake of an orderly use of words and ideas and a decorous way of living, the early loose play and experimentation of childhood (pp. 190–191) and the libidinous aggressive longings which lurk in our subconsciousness. Dream-work is a plunge into infantile memories and an evasion of the censors, reason and morality. Similarly, wit-work is a way of recovering a child's "free disposal of his mental stream" and of escaping or breaking through restraints. In the jest and in *harmless wit* the pleasure gained is chiefly that of nonsense-play.[6] In *tendency-wit*—obscene, hostile, cynical, blasphemous, as the case may be—relief is sought from restraints put on sex impulses and on

[6] "It is quite obvious that it is easier and more convenient to turn away from a definite trend of thought than to stick to it; it is easier to mix up different things than to distinguish them; and it is particularly easier to travel over modes of reasoning unsanctioned by logic; finally in connecting words or thoughts it is especially easy to overlook the fact that such connections should result in sense." (Freud, *Wit and the Unconscious*.)

aggression, and their masked satisfaction is made possible. Here is one of Freud's illustrations. Two rich, unscrupulous business men have had their portraits painted. They hold an elaborate reception. An expert, asked to pass judgment on the pictures, looks at them and then at the vacant space between and asks: "And where is the Saviour?" This clever, indirect insult is cited as an example of hostile wit. (cf. also pp. 148–153).

When he turns to the question of the pleasure-sources of wit Freud encounters difficulties. *Tendency-wit* is held to involve removal—or relief-pleasure; and even *harmless wit* is explained at times as a pleasurable recovery of old liberties. But wit is held also to involve the pleasure of "gratifying tendencies"—the regaining of an early delight in irresponsible play, sexuality, and pugnacity. The situation turns out to be even more complex. It is not enough to talk nonsense to rid oneself of the censorship of orderly thinking and to recover an infantile source of enjoyment; the nonsense must be wittily disguised. Here is a third cause of pleasure: in the technique—the clever manipulation of words and ideas. Freud is not consistent or clear in working out the relations of the pleasure of *relief*, of *play*, of *technique*. He seeks refuge in vague phrases such as: "wit-pleasure shows a kernel of the original play-pleasure and a shell of removal-pleasure." To make matters worse, he puts a vacillating stress on the pleasure of a flattering comparison—the superiority motif. Again, influenced by Lipps, he uses the terms *expenditure of psychic energy* and *economy* widely and uncritically. "It has seemed to us that the pleasure of wit originates from an economy of expenditure in inhibition, of the comic from an economy of expenditure in thought, and of humor from an economy of expenditure in feeling. All three activities of our psychic apparatus derive pleasure from economy. They all strive to bring back from the psychic activity a pleasure which has really been

lost in the development of that activity. For the euphoria
which we are thus striving to obtain is nothing but the state
of a bygone time in which we were wont to defray our
psychic work with slight expenditure. It is the state of our
childhood in which we did not know the comic, were incapable of wit and did not need humor to make us happy."(p.
384) It is true that our enjoyment of the comic owes
something to playful ease in the use of words; that in certain
types of wit we spare ourselves the pain of self-reproach or
the *ricochet* of an insult; that in humor we save ourselves
the pain of sympathy.[7] There is a pleasurable lessening of
psychic work according to Freud; a special instance of
which is what he calls the *condensation-technique of wit*.
But with the collapse of an inhibition there is also made
available, made superfluous, *economized*, a corresponding
amount of energy; and the consciousness of this free energy
is held to be pleasurable. Freud needs both sources for his
theory and makes the term psychic economy cover both;
which is like not distinguishing a man who is conscious of
saving from a man who suddenly finds himself rich. The
confusion is worse in Freud's theory of the comic. When we
watch the exaggerated gesture of a clown or a child writing
with his tongue as well as with his hands we are said to laugh
at the "excessive expenditure of energy" which we in like
circumstances should save. (p. 304) The contrast between infantile and adult self, stressed again and again, is
of little use.

ANOTHER BIOLOGICAL THEORY

A bit of analysis may serve at the start. I walk upstairs
and make a last, unnecessary step at the head of the stairs;

[7] McDougall has developed independently a theory of the comic in terms
of an economy in the painfulness of sympathetic experiences. The play
of our sympathetic impulses would be too painful, were it not for the
safety device of laughter.

I laugh, and it is not at the mechanically continued stepping but at the sudden collapse of an uncalled for motor adjustment.   I stoop to pick up a coin and discover it to be a piece of tin.   Or a strong man appears on the stage.   He tenses himself, picks up a weight and purposely lets it drop; the thump and clatter are to impress me with its weight.   He selects a larger one and lifts it slowly with every sign of great physical stress.   This effort of his I share with incipient adjustments of my muscles.   He gets it to the height of his chin; then all of a sudden his arm shoots out straight, and the enormous weight hangs suspended on a finger. Cardboard painted black!—I laugh—I have been tricked into sharing in and admiring a great show of strength which turns out to be a fraud.   In all three cases there is: (1) an interested response; (2) a needless, uncalled for motor adjustment; (3) the sense of a jolt.   Ordinarily human expectations are bound up with desires and with the practical demands of situations.   The tentative unsure movements of a child in reaching for or lifting things show that an economically adjusted kinetic response to situations is a gradual achievement made possible by the discipline of experience. Such growing efficiency is paralleled by more definitely pointed purposes and expectations.   A deviation from what is expected allows a sense of jolt to appear.   The more deeply and definitely our interest is engaged the more sharply will this thwarting be felt.

In adult life there is a circle of things that matter a great deal—things to which we are committed by our effort and expectations; and beyond this circle there is a vague world which we feel no need of construing practically or adjusting ourselves to.   To me there is a difference between drawing a check or finishing this book and a flight to the North Pole or ascent of Mount Everest.   The latter do not call out effort or commit my expectations—and so I do not resent or feel a jolt at an incalculable element.   If I were to regard this circular band as an unalterably fixed boundary line I should be making a serious mistake, for circumstances might make the proposed polar flight very much of a concern of mine. Life shifts its lines, and the circle expands or contracts. Alertness and resourcefulness are necessary. Bergson is right in discovering in corrective laughter an instinctive distrust of inefficiency in the ever changing adjustments of individual and social life.

There are, however, playful and sympathetic laughter to be reckoned with; and they make possible a biological theory of laughter which differs markedly from Bergson's. There is in all of us in so far as we are serious-minded an inclination to take all things seriously—to have the circular band stretch around the goodly girth of life. If we were to act out this *will to efficiency* completely we should limit ourselves to something like the taking of synthetic food pills, the reading of instructive books, and a practical assimilation and use of facts; we should practise the utmost economy of word and deed. In such a world there would be no play and no mirth; we should not even find the correcting of others enjoyable. Fortunately such an ideal is unattainable. There is in all living a *safety margin of inefficiency*, and beyond that there is a *will to waste*. To impose and to carry out as a crusader a single religious, moral or scientific program or in a spirit of economy to pare all things down to the quick is to overstep this margin of safety. To be able to smile at our convictions and, while moralists, to imagine sympathetically and playfully worlds of other codes and looser pattern is to save ourselves from the bigotry of assuming that life can be handled efficiently and in our one way only. Laughter is one of nature's safety devices. Its point of view is the all too human, none too perfect, all too unexpected. This extravagance, disconcerting to the directly-minded, ultimately makes for sanity. To suggest that is to give a larger reading to the will to efficiency; life if not to be mastered can at

least be managed by keeping a laugh in reserve. But there
is more to laughter than this broader usefulness, for it expresses a *will to waste*. Waste, sheer, unredeemable by
reason or moral feeling, is inherent in the process of living.
Much of it is ugly; some of it is highly enjoyable.

There is in our amusements something of the exuberant,
carefree spirit of play; they involve a slackening of tension
or working off of surplus energy which in the long run may
prove beneficial. It is not, however, as careful investors
that we amuse ourselves; nor does life in allowing us our
fun seem to be aiming at a wholesome balance of work and
play. Discipline and measure are lacking. We do not
care how much we spend or how far we are carried; for the
moment seriousness of purpose is suspended in us, and the
world may go as it pleases. There is much of this spend-
thrift spirit in laughter. When I take that last unnecessary step or a broader jump than was needed it is not a
sense of power spent and misspent that makes the experience
amusing; it is the sheer waste of effort which is enjoyed
sympathetically. I have fallen in step with nature in one of
her drunken moods of random sportive stepping. There is
no wastrel like the sense of the comic. In its development it
is often connected with bibulous waste of time; its technique
is not, like that of the beautiful, one of economy—even the
condensation Freud finds in wit is a needless exaction of quick
and ingenious thinking. It gives without stint of itself and
does not care what company it keeps. Not even itself does
it take seriously. Has it not always been, in its relations to
reform movements as well as in its playful expressions, a
jump beyond the efficient and the decorous, and an enjoyment of its own heedlessness? Admit with Bergson that it
may be corrective, but insist that it is incorrigible; that it
is lavish and wasteful like life itself; that it is the voice of
our perverse pleasure in playing the part of irresponsibles in
a game too wayward for any set of rules of efficiency and too

capricious in spirit not to trick our expectations again and again.

Such a theory must not be taken too seriously if the safety margin of possible error is not to be overstepped. Unsound theories of the comic are greeted with laughter, but even sound theories are in danger. With characteristic abandon the comic spirit of mankind keeps a laugh in reserve for all formulas of, at least, its mental life, for it sees little of its will to waste in their orderly and parsimonious logic.

The Technique of the Comic

So far our concern has been with the origins, motives, and biological meanings of the comic. Motives have been found for the creation and enjoyment of the comic in self-glorification; in an instinctive defence against the anti-social; in a flooding sympathy; in play; in guarding against too intense and painful a functioning of sympathetic impulses; in relief from inhibitions; in the safe indulgence of masked hostility or cruelty; in a contrast between adult and child life or between energy innervated and energy needed; in freedom and a sense of lordship over something that does not matter and still does matter; in a sympathetic response to the wayward and wasteful moods of life.

For aesthetics there are further problems. The comic artist uses certain materials; he gains his effects by means of certain devices. Materials and technique must be studied.

There is an endless variety of comic material in art and in life. Lines, forms, movements, characters, situations, mental states, ideas, variously compounded are utilized in a story, a farce, a comedy, a cartoon, a scherzo, a grotesquerie in drawing or dancing.

With reference to this material it may be said that (1) nothing in life is inherently funny; (2) some things provoke laughter more easily than others; (3) there is nothing that cannot be made laughable.   (1') Not even everything "mechanical encrusted on the living"—Bergson's formula —is comic.   (2') There are faces, situations, characters that make us laugh more readily than others.   (3') The comic is no respecter of noble forms or precious feelings; it excludes nothing, not even blasphemy or moral filth.   It uses devices by means of which everything in life, however lofty, repulsive, socially prized—religion, murder, marriage —is made available for laughter.

No study of the comic can afford to neglect this problem of technique.   Every artist, from Aristophanes down to Aldous Huxley or Charlie Chaplin has his own favorite comic effects and bagful of tricks.   But in this endless variety there are recurrent types of method and effect which repay analysis.

MECHANIZATION

Bergson's lead must be followed in accepting mechanization as one of the commonest devices used.   It in turn depends for its effects largely on repetition and on stressing the rigid.   The caricaturist, for example, catches a twist in the lines of the face, a set expression, a cast of character, a mannerism of gesture or dress and fixes and bears down on them to the utter disregard of everything else.   Dickens effectively mechanizes through repetition: witness the cork-like buoyancy of Micawber; the Fat Boy dropping off to sleep; the rapid stereotyped talk of Jingle; the tears of Mr. Trotter, to be turned on and off like water-works.   The comic writer often makes his characters act and speak like puppets.   He pulls the strings, and a fat person rolls on the stage or a grand air and grand clothes strut in, a stiff person creaks ominously as he tries to unbend, excited individuals whirl about like tops.   Motives, too, are mechanized to such a degree that they suggest clockwork.

Among the best examples of mechanization in the service of the comic are the *Mr. Pinhead* sketches of Cami (*L'Homme à la tête d'épingle*). In the *Drunkard's Child* there are stock phrases and characters of a melodrama: the poor seamstress, the drunken brute, the frail child. Murder is made funny, and the comic reaches its height in the child's exultant cry to his mother: "*Sois heureuse, papa est carbonisé.*" In the *Calabrian Brigand Turned Dumb* a brigand suddenly loses his power of speech. His daughter buys a phonograph and tells him all he need do is to sit in his accustomed place near the forest and have it repeat, "Your money or your life!" After a wait of seven hours in the rain, an old man appears; the phonograph is set going; but the old man steps up with a benevolent look on his face, gives the brigand a coin and says, "Don't trouble yourself, my good man, I am deaf." The brigand disconsolately goes home, saying to himself, "He could not hear my challenge, so, of course, I could not rob him." In *Little Green Riding Hood* there is the same use of mechanization. The wolf, being a well regulated, fairy tale property wolf, cannot eat the little girl because she does not give him his cue, "Grandmother, what big teeth you have!" Again and again she goes through the rigmarole of questions, but always stops short at that point. The wolf tries prompting her, but finally gives up in disgust, with the reflection, "Ah, where are the children of yesterday, so naïve and so easy to devour?"

In all these sketches an absurdly mechanized world is presented, a world unlike that of our ordinary ideas, our fluctuating feelings, and our adjusted responses. Were it not for the contrast the mechanized world would not appear funny. Bergson recognizes this in his phrase *the mechanical encrusted on the living*. But what he fails to see is the presence of sympathetic laughter. The mechanized wolf is funny, but so is Little Green Riding Hood assuming the disguise of the mechanical and impishly outwitting the wolf. In like fashion we enjoy sympathetically the one thing in Falstaff which is not mechanized: his nimble wit with its unpredictable sallies.

Why are physical exaggerations—huge bulk, a long nose, large ears—funny? Bergson somewhat fantastically explains them in terms of matter losing touch with mind and absentmindedly marching on. A man is to us a being of many moods, of many free answers to life; but how can we think of this man as a romantic or heroic figure?—his paunch is in the way or his nose is a mechanical obstacle in the path of sentiment or passion. They are jokes at his expense. If we are irreverent and think of them as a joke played upon him by God, we may laugh sympathetically with the cosmic joker. The caricaturist who draws a nose to absurd lengths depends in part on exaggeration as a direct source of laughter, but he also counts on an empathetic enjoyment of his playful caprice. In *Cyrano* there is a double response of this kind: we laugh with Rostand at Cyrano, and we laugh with Cyrano at his long nose. The dramatist and his hero make so much of this nose, play variants on it, pelt it with similes, that we laugh not at the absentmindedness of matter but at the capering and the whimsical self-depreciation. Cyrano is a romantic and heroic figure in spite of his nose; and he is a comic one not simply because of his nose, but because he invites us to join in the laugh on himself.[8]   Socrates showed a similar spirit when he undertook to prove his face with its assembled home-

---

[8] A case in point is the following (*Henry IV, Act I, sc.* 2):

FALSTAFF:—Men of all sorts take a pride to gird at me! the brain of the foolish-compounded clay, man, is not able to invent anything that tends to laughter, more than I invent or is invented on me. I am not only witty in myself, but the cause that wit is in other men, (turning to his diminutive page) I do here walk before thee like a sow that hath overwhelmed all her litter but one.

liness—bulging eyes, upturned nose, large mouth—was beautiful.

SURPRISING TURNS

Startling surprises, unexpected jolts, explosive effects have come to be recognized as part of the technique of the comic. Examples may be found in

(a) GRAPHIC FORMS: The comic draughtsman makes his lines do surprising things. They march along sedately, but suddenly stumble or start off afield. They are twisted about and combined to a distorted image—an image as striking and unlooked for as are reflections in faulty glass or a concave mirror.

(b) VERBAL FORMS: Occasional misspelling, queer prefixes and endings, monstrous compounds like *alcoholidays*, *famillionaire*, sentences built awry, unexpected verse endings are examples. Aristophanes is very ingenious in his use of comic devices of this type.

(c) SITUATIONS: In slapstick comedy and farce, mix-ups and surprises are frequent. People turn up and things happen at the most unexpected moments: our expectations are led a merry dance in a world which does not lend itself to prediction. The characters, it is true, are mechanized and give the impression of being puppets, but they move about in a playfully irrational world. A man enters a room and hangs hat and coat on a hook in the wall, only to see them glide up to the ceiling; he draws a chair to the dinner table, and the chair moves back and sends him sprawling; he tries another and another until he gets one that does not move back—notice that we laugh as heartily at the chair that unexpectedly proves serviceable as we do at the others—he seats himself, and the table trots off with his

dinner.   He is in a world unfamiliar, not to be depended on.
Here is not a case of absentmindedness rebuked by laughter;
no one can be expected to guard against a world of this sort.
The man who boils his watch and looks at the egg in his
hand is absentminded; not so, however, the man who dips
his pen in the mud a practical joker has put in his inkwell—
the example is Bergson's.   We laugh at both, but for different reasons.   To be constantly on guard against practical jokes and to dread all manner of probable mishaps is
merely to be *jumpy;* and it is hardly to the advantage of
society to encourage jumpiness.   It is the surprising turn
to a de-rationalized world of jolts and bewilderment which
is counted on to produce laughter.

INVERSION

Inversion, turning things about or upside down is a
favorite comic device.   *Verkehrte Welt!*   It may be in the
service of merriment or satire; it may be systematic *topsyturvyism,* as in Butler's *Erewhon* and *Erewhon Revisited*
or in Barrie's *Admirable Crichton* or it may be casual and
incidental.   When it is systematic it substitutes for the common world either an elaborately patterned absurdity or a
counterpart which turns out to be less absurd than it seemed.
A trick photograph which shows an acrobat holding up an
elephant with one hand is an example of the first.   To the
second class belongs Butler's suggestion that instead of pity-
ing the sick and punishing the criminal we ought to pity
the criminal and punish the sick; an inversion which is more
plausible than it looks.

An example of inversion of phrase is the exclamation of
the corpse in the *Frogs,* "Strike me alive if I do!"; of in-

version of ideas, the landlord begging his tenant to submit to a reduction in rent; of inversion of situation, the Induction to *The Taming of the Shrew*, with Sly the Tinker turned into a lord.

CONTRAST AND CONTRADICTION

Contrast is used to strengthen or create comic effects. A tall man is set off by a short one, and the diminutive page adds several inches to Falstaff's girth. Systematized contrast marks *Gulliver's Travels*. Lilliput is the world seen through the other end of a telescope; in it everything is drawn to scale, but the scale contrasts sharply with what we are familiar with.

It is but a step from contrast to contradiction. Snug the Joiner impersonating a lion and letting his nails grow long to serve as claws is funny; but when he leaves half his head uncovered, speaks reassuringly to the ladies and calls forth the remark, "A very gentle beast and of a good conscience," he becomes comic because he is lion and not-lion at the same time. Impersonations of animals on the stage depend largely for their effects on such a rapid interchange or incongruous simultaneity of man and beast. In characters and words, as well as in situations, contradiction is used. Imagine a miser who suffers from distressing lapses of generosity which he in vain seeks to control, and you have a character at comic odds with himself. Puns depend on the double meaning of words. While there is nothing laughable in a word having two meanings, there is much chance for laughter if they are embodied in a sentence with a squinting reference to either. But this spinning back and forth between contrasted or opposed meanings explains puns only in part; there is in addition much blackening or cheapening.

CHEAPENING

A caricatured face is a degraded face: by a slight shifting of lines and a touch of exaggeration it has been made uglier, weaker, more base than it was. Comic drawings which make heads look like pumpkins or pears, lean men like pencils, and stout men like sacks of flour are examples of such cheapening. In parodies enough of the original form and substance is kept to get a sort of swinging memory of values, to be smashed into and insidiously turned worthless again and again. In the *Heptalogia* Swinburne parodies his trick of alliteration; and pokes fun at Whitman's pantheism and kinship universal by having the carpenter and the woodlouse fraternize.

Poe's *The Raven* is recalled and debased in these verses from *The Vultures:*

"Smith!" I shriek'd—the accent humbler dropping as another tumbler
I beheld him mix, "be off! you drive me mad—it's striking four.
Leave the house and something in it; if you go on with the gin it
Won't hold out another minute. Leave the house and shut the door—
Take your beak from out my gin, and take your body through the door!"
    Quoth the vulture, "Never more!"

And the vulture never flitting—still is sitting, still is sitting,
Gulping down my stout by gallons, and my oysters by the score;
And the beast, with no more breeding than a heathen savage feeding,
The new carpet's tints unheeding, throws his shells upon the floor.
And his smoke from out my curtains, and his stains from out my floor,
    Shall be sifted never more!

In burlesques of the Middle Ages, such as those of Thackeray and Mark Twain, there is a swift passing to and fro

between the ultra-modern and the medieval.   Contrasts and
contradictions are skilfully used.   Sir Galahad is summoned
by telephone; knights in clanking armor are mounted on
bicycles.   But there is also a playful discrediting of the
whole theatrical knighthood business.   When Leech in the
Comic History of England draws a Queen Elizabeth smirk-
ing in all the discomforts of a medieval costume or a beefy
Henry the Eighth strutting with his hat on a slant and a
lady other than fair on his arm, he is having his fun with
royalty.   A sense of contradiction alone does not explain
why I laugh when on hearing a noise in the cupboard I
open the door, expecting to find the cat, and discover my
aunt or father-in-law.   The example and this explanation
are Herkenrath's.   It is better to follow the suggestion of
Lipps that the comic results from a sudden lowering of human dignity—debasing, in short.   The more dignified my
aunt is, the more seriously she takes that dignity and the
more playfully and triflingly I regard it, the funnier will
the situation seem.

EXAGGERATION, INFLATION, DEFLATION

The caricaturist exaggerates the irregularities of a face;
the writer of farce puts within the frame of an evening's entertainment a set of freakish characters, and pictures life
as wilder, more incalculable than it is; the artist in the
comic of words twists them and pulls them about.   There is a
frank note of excess, of extravaganza, in Aristophanes'
Birds, the verbal fire-works of Rabelais, the characters in
Anatole France's *At the Sign of the Reine Pédauque*, the
novels of Dickens and the drawings of Busch, Van Vechten's
The Blind Bow Boy, and Aldous Huxley's *Antic Hay*.

Inflation is a special type of exaggeration aimed at cheapening.   Bombast, mouthing, and ranting are used to gain

the effect of the mock heroic. When Fielding describes in Homeric language a brawl among women he gives to it a dignity and an importance out of keeping with its ugliness and pettiness, and thus makes it appear low, but he has his fling at Homer as well:—a clear case of double cheapening. This puts us within sight of deflation, which is in essence bubble-pricking. In an old fable a frog tries to blow himself up to the size of an ox and bursts. A common human temptation to become puffed up, overblown, inflated with pride or pretence gives the comic writer his chance— he assists in the blowing up, then deftly inserts a pin, and *presto!* the voluminous pomp, with a bang, turns to nothing.

THE LET DOWN OF EXPECTATION

In the examples given, a sudden collapse, a deflation, was used for purposes of discrediting—of a critical reduction of the extravagant to the common or the reasonable.

There is, however, another technical use of a sudden collapse to nothingness. It may be called the let down of expectation. We expect the big, and the little is given us; we anticipate the important and are confronted with the trifling; we look for orderly forms, sensible sequences and characters, and there are palmed off on us discarded images, mix ups, and freakish men and women. We are all set for the thing we do not get, and the thing we do get is a trifle. This is the Kantian formula of an unexpected turn to nothing. The device is common. A man takes a tremendous running start and then jumps a foot; a huge man becomes articulate in mincing speech or piping treble; a vice becomes a bagatelle, an upheaval turns out to be a tempest in a teapot. Our expectations are tensed and then slackened. These things are funny apart from any hint of corrective criticism. Nor need they be, although they often are, a sort of cheapening of themselves. Playful variants are common in music [9] and dancing.

This analysis of the comic is an incomplete one. *Mechanization, surprising turns, inversion, contrast* and *contradiction, cheapening, exaggeration, inflation, deflation,* and the *let down of expectation* are merely the chief means of gaining comic effects; not only may these be variously compounded and combined, but there are others.

ALLIED TYPES: HUMOR, SATIRE, WIT

The comic is as broad as life; within this, its realm, it is as gross or as subtle, as simple or as complex, as the mind which reflects and enjoys it; its guises are many and variously proportioned; and its appeal is to many motives. Thus the jest, the droll story, the scherzo carry an appeal to merriment; *fooling* and the *patter* of a vaudeville team combine the playful with the illogical and with the pull and release of expectation; farce and practical jokes pivot on exaggeration and casual malice; burlesque means cheapening.

There are three mixed, major types: *humor, satire, wit,* which move partly within and partly without the circle of the comic.

[9] Penkert in a paper *Die Musikalische Formung von Witz und Humor* (*Kongress für Aesthetik und Allgemeine Kunstwissenschaft*) accepts Lipps' theory of the comic and seeks to discover in song and in tone-structures instances of the sudden collapse of an expectation keyed up to something important. His first example is that of a melody sustained by quiet, massive rhythms reaching great heights only to slide down suddenly to the depths of a single low note emphatically struck. His second example is that of a melody seeking a goal, tentatively, nervously, and striking a wholly unexpected, incongruous note. (Chopin's *Mazurka in F-dur*). Penkert admits that such transitions may be used for purposes other than the comic, and suggests that in order to be funny they must impress us with a certain playfulness. Sportiveness, caprice, surprising turns, contradictions, cheapening are all used by him in his analysis of comic musical forms.

HUMOR

It is in character drawing that humor achieves its greatest triumphs.   Four outstanding humorous portraits are Falstaff, Trunnion, Pickwick, and Micawber.   They reveal the following marks of humor:

A NOTE OF EXTRAVAGANCE; OF ODDITY ON A LARGE SCALE: Each of these characters moves within an eccentric orbit of bodily appearance, manner, and speech: witness Falstaff's girth and talk redolent of grease; Trunnion's one eye, sea swagger, and salted speech; Pickwick's dumpiness; Micawber's way of making punch and talking finance. These oddities are struck with a gesture so sweeping and a touch so emphatic as to remove these men to the realm of the uncommon and the fantastic.   Such an extravagance is an inseparable part of humor.   Trunnion is a good example. Old sea-dog that he is, he lives in his house as though it were a man-of-war, has his servants stand watch, affects the roughness and punctilio of an old time commodore, and cannot, even on his death-bed, speak otherwise than in the jargon and imagery of sea-faring.[10]

A FREENESS AND BOLDNESS OF CONCEPTION RESULTING IN FORMLESSNESS AND A PECULIAR IMAGINATIVE QUALITY: The humorist lords it over his creatures; goes about his work in a wholehearted unabashed way; and gets full imaginative value from the gullibility and childlike benevolence of Pickwick, and the animalism, nimble wit, and glorious cowardice of Falstaff.   His characters in turn assert themselves freely

[10] He addresses weeping Peregrine thus: "Swab the spray from off your bowsprit, my good lad, and coil up your spirits. You must not let the toplifts of your heart give way, because you see me ready to go down at these years; many a better man has foundered before he has made half my way; tho I trust, by the mercy of God, I shall be sure in port in a very few glasses, and fast moored in a most blessed riding—"
Wemmick's Castle in *Great Expectations* and the elder Weller's letter telling of the death of his wife offer parallels.

and masterfully in the imaginary world within which he has set them: there is something of the sublime in the way they carry themselves, in their self-assurance and utter spontaneity. They are not puppet-like in their actions. It is here that the mechanization theory of Bergson breaks down. To mechanize character is to flatten it imaginatively and to lose part of its appeal; this is a sacrifice the humorist refuses to make; he holds it his business to bend a deepening and spreading imagination to the reading of character as a bit of life. The life offered is not the calm reasonable one which is the *beau ideal* of Molière's comedies; it is somewhat formless and is deepened in its appeal by an admixture of bold imagery and ideas, and poignant feelings. Humorists, with few exceptions, incline toward formlessness.[11] Rabelais, Sterne, Jean Paul, Dickens are all disorderly imaginers; so is Anatole France for all his clear-cut style. They are all bold fashioners; nothing for them is too grotesque or extravagant. Falstaff, dying, sees a flea on Bardolph's nose and calls it "a black soul burning in hell-fire"— an example of imagination boldly striking out. There is also, here as well as in the second part of *Don Quixote* and the Fleet scenes of *Pickwick Papers* an emotional vibrancy and depth, in which there is part of the secret of humor.

A VIBRANT EMOTIONAL QUALITY, WHICH RESULTS FROM THE PRESENCE OF SYMPATHETIC LAUGHTER AND TRAGIC AND PATHETIC IMPLICATIONS: Again and again attention has been drawn to the emotionalized laughter of humor, its benign quality, its merriment mixed with tears, its ready and all comprehending pity. "To understand all is to forgive all" is a saying which illustrates this side of humor. But the matter is less simple than it appears to be. Sympa-

---

11 Exceptions are Fielding, whose novels are kept orderly and cool by an opposition to Richardson and a desire to write close to everyday life; and Addison and Washington Irving, who have a decorous and quiet humor, with a slightly flat taste to it.

thetic laughter, as it is part of humor, implies not merely a larger and more tolerant reading of frailties and vices and an unwillingness to attach a moral stigma to them, but an imaginative experiencing with and sharing in, marked by *verve* and abandon. When Morgann, the critic, labored hard to absolve Falstaff from the charge of cowardice, he merely gave proof that he could not live within Falstaff's hide, as Shakespeare did for a time and meant us to do. This, by itself, again, cannot be made to explain the vibrant quality of humor, and the rich and deep effects it gains. The humorist, who has been one with his characters, disengages himself, shifts his ground, re-establishes distance but keeps the sense of kinship and kindliness, and reveals pathetic and tragic implications of which the characters and we, ordinarily are ignorant. Gargantua's sorrowing for his wife, mixed with good burgundy and a father's pride, and Trunnion's death [12] illustrate this emotional deepening—what Meredith calls *the lights of tragedy* in laughter.

Humor looks upon life with a welcoming spirit, relishes the human all too human in vice and folly, and allows them to edge in on our sympathies. Satire holds them at arm's length and shakes or at least rebukes them, unless it is in one of its rarer playful moods. Costigan and Florac are

[12] His last moments, were, however, not so near as they imagined. He began to doze, and enjoyed small intervals of ease, till next day in the afternoon, during which remissions he was heard to pour forth many pious ejaculations, expressing his hope, that, for all the heavy cargo of his sins, he should be able to surmount the puttock-shrouds of despair, and get aloft to the crosstrees of God's good favour. At last his voice sunk so low as not to be distinguished; and, having lain about an hour, almost without any perceptible signs of life, he gave up the ghost with a groan, which announced his decease. (And then his servant Pipes exclaims): "Well fare thy soul! old Hawser Trunnion, man and boy I have known thee these five-and-thirty years, and sure a truer heart never broke biscuit. Many a hard gale hast thou weathered; but now thy spells are all over, and thy hull fairly laid up. A better commander I'd never desire to serve; and who knows I may help to set up thy standing rigging in another world?"—Surely a mariners' chorus and an echo of Trunnion himself!

humorous characters; the Old Campaigner is a satiric portrait.

A RE-ESTABLISHING OF HUMAN WORTH, WITH A PROVISO ATTACHED: There is more to humor than the sympathetic sharing of any and every experience however paltry, of boon companionship with any and every character however disreputable; there is more to it than *imaginative redemption* effected through the technique of genius.

Of the four characters mentioned, two, Trunnion and Pickwick, are wholly unconscious of the eccentric orbit in which they swing; while Falstaff enjoys and laughs at his. Certain followers of Hegel, building their argument on his interpretation of Falstaff, insist that a person cannot be comic to us unless he is so to himself; and they interpret the comic, and with it the humorous, in terms of the free human spirit indulging, relishing, and working off its endless caprice and its multitudinous littleness. Their restriction cannot be upheld:—the scene in which Trunnion flounders about, proposes, and swears in his blustering embarrassment is as truly humorous as is the recruiting scene in which Falstaff considers for service a choice collection of comic originals, knowing himself to be the colossal humbug of a soldier he is. But something may be made of their general theory. The humorist, like the tragic poet, is an explorer; but he is urged on by insatiable curiosity rather than by high courage. In his excursions into the paltry and the grotesque he seems to demolish or discredit everything that is felt to be worthwhile, and to reduce life to something as shapeless and useless as an old battered hat. Then, when we least expect it, he throws the light of something worthwhile on this twisted material and re-establishes worth by an appeal to feeling or to moral and intellectual values. Tears tremble in the laughter of Thackeray's *A Shabby Genteel Story* and a broad humanity quivers in the obscenity of Rabelais and the irreverence of Anatole France; there are bright moral flakes, of kindness in Pickwick and of loyalty to his master in Sam Weller; Falstaff's wit is as appealing as it is unlooked for in so heavy a body. There is, however, this peculiarity about humor: it does not allow us to enjoy a final unruffled possession of such values; it turns us from Falstaff the wit to the feeder and sot, from Major Pendennis's worldly wisdom to his lord and dinner hunting, from Pickwick's golden heart to his hopeless figure. It plays to and fro between the sublime and the all too little. There is an intentional *wobbling* in humor: one foot steps out boldly while the other falters or drags—there is an alteration of climbing, lurching, slipping, and recovering. It is for this reason that humor cannot be appreciated fully by the single-minded climber, the possessive organizer of values, and the downright plodder; for them its playful unsteadiness holds no charm.

SATIRE

Satire is seldom found pure: it is usually blended with fun, as in Dickens and Mark Twain, or with wit, as in Anatole France, or with humor, as in Shakespeare. This blending conceals some of its peculiarities. Take away from the portrait of Squeers the fun and the gusto, from *La Pucelle* and *The Revolt of the Angels* the skirmishing of obscene and sacrilegious wit, from the Nurse in *Romeo and Juliet* the sympathetic response of humor: and what remains but the three judgments; what a social menace is an ignorant, bullying schoolmaster! what a sorry thing is superstition! what a capacity there is in woman for talk and fickleness!— and by implication three values: a humane education, clarity of life, and restraint and loyalty? Satire is a taking of sides in a war of values; it is a defence reaction of a peculiarly aggressive type. However fantastic the dress, as in

Gulliver's Travels and in *Erewhon Revisited,* underneath there is a direct interest in actualities—grievances, foibles, vices, malignant growths. The mood and the reaction vary: satire may be playful or caustic or bitter or bland or insolently cool. To use a single marking adjective here is quite as absurd as the attempt to reduce all lyrics to a single mood.

The three chief satiric responses are the personal, the moral, and the philosophical.[13] Personal satire is born of a grievance and shows the animus of wounded vanity, of sensibility rubbed raw, of a sense of personal harm. Martial, Swift, Heine furnish many examples. A poor dinner or a greedy guest is enough to make Martial write a stinging epigram; neglect dipped Swift's pen in gall; the chafed soul of Butler sent his own father to the hell of satiric portraiture. Satire of this type tends to be malicious, bitter, splenetic; but it may be lightened and softened by clever wit and an enjoyment of one's grievances, as in this epigram of Martial's:

You were constantly a guest at my villa at Tivoli.—Now you buy it.—I have deceived you; I have merely sold you what was already your own.

Moral satire shows the animus of an outraged sense of decency and morality. Entrenching behind commonly accepted values, such as fairness, kindness, honesty, clean living, it makes war upon vice—the dissoluteness of imperial Rome (Juvenal); corrupt political practices (Swift, Daumier, Gogol); hypocrisy (Molière, Fielding, Thackeray); affectation and vanity (Meredith); cruelties and absurdities in war, education, religion (Rabelais, Goya, Dickens, Mark Twain); the chicaneries and corruptions of law (Rabelais in the Gripe-men-all and the Furred Cats episodes).

13 Flaccus, *Samuel Butler* (University of Pennsylvania Public Lectures, 1918–19).

Philosophical satire is more subtle and general. It is a challenge flung at life itself. It is as critical of accepted values as it is of possible abuses. Thus its questioning may be pushed to the cynical extreme of the latter part of *Gulliver's Travels* or of *Troilus and Cressida;* it may be interwoven, as in Voltaire, Anatole France, Samuel Butler, and Bernard Shaw with the ideal of a saner, more truthful, and more brotherly life than is commonly led.

In all three types of satire there is an intentional cheapening in the interest of something seriously valued. It is this sense of something held to be important and championed—the paying off an insult, the defence of social values, the critical inspection of life—that marks off satire from the playful caprice of fun, the indulgent and provisionally constructive laughter of humor, and the light and inconsequential cleverness of wit.

WIT

Wit is purely intellectual in origin and technique. It is unlike the practical joke in that its playfulness is subtle and its malice intellectualized and pointed with cleverness; it lacks the sensitiveness and emotionalism of humor; and it is not like the downright bludgeoning of satire. Wit is rapier play, cool, brilliant, enjoyed for its own sake. Sparkle, ingenuity, aptness, a quick and often startling allusiveness, dramatic quality, and a sort of word-sorcery and word-jugglery by means of which sense and nonsense are changed to their opposites are to be found in wit.

There is about wit something of the deft theatricalism of a *régisseur* who seeks dramatic effects above all else. Many witticisms are, as Bergson suggests, telescoped comic situations. Martial's epigram,

Why, when about to recite, do you wrap your neck in wool?
That wool would be more proper for our ears,

can readily be expanded to a comic scene—a crowd of listeners with wool stuffed in the ears, unconscious of the ranting that is going on. There are, in addition, a quick thrust, a dramatic sketching in a few strokes, and a clever manipulation of words and ideas. Of the latter another epigram of Martial's furnishes a better illustration:

You admire, Vacerra, only the poets of old, and praise only those who are dead. Pardon me, I beseech you, Vacerra, if I think death too high a price to pay for your praise.

Witty word-construction uses many of the devices of the comic: reciprocal interference of series in *alcoholidays*, inversion in *ginthetic sin*, condensation in *famillionaire*, contradiction, and many of the others. When Heine refers to the condescending treatment a poor relative receives at the hands of a baron of the bourse as *famillionaire*, he makes brilliantly apt sense pop out of what seems a mere conglomeration of letters.

Cheapening by means of the employment of a kind of sham logic may be illustrated by the following bit of conversation:

A. "The law of compensation holds throughout nature. When she makes us weak in one thing she compensates us by making us strong in another."

B. "So I have noticed. When a man is born with one leg shorter than the other nature compensates him by making the other longer."

B., of course, is talking nonsense. If he does so unwittingly he becomes for us a comic character and draws upon himself our laughter. If he is keen-witted enough to see through the pompous and doubtful pronouncement of A. and pricks the bubble with nonsense persuasively dressed up as sense his remark becomes witty. Any serious interest on his part or ours in bubble-pricking would carry us over into the realm of satire. If we visualized an individual lurching along, sinking on his shorter left leg, raising himself on the longer leg, if we shared the attempt to get compensation from this tilting and yet saw its absurdity we should be in the field of humor; but if we enjoyed merely the ludicrous spectacle we should be indulging in fun as simple as that of Charlie Chaplin's walk.

COMEDY

Comedy is flanked on one side by farce, on the other by serious drama. Farce is an unblushing invitation to laughter. With an extravagant gesture it sets characters and events in a whirling, jolting motion. People are constantly running into each other or flying off at a tangent; wild things are happening. The only difference between a well- and an ill-constructed farce is this—things are kept going and food is incessantly provided for laughter. Comedy, by way of contrast, does not appeal directly to our diaphragm. To its making go fun, wit, humor, satire as well as what appeals to the serious in our thought, moods, and feelings. The mixture varies: comedies may be light and witty; they may be spun of satire and irony; they may be fantastic, sentimental, whimsical, romantic; again they may be common-sense, bright and somewhat sober-minded. Each of these types requires special aesthetic norms. It is absurd to make the same structural demands of a Barrie comedy that are made of a comedy by Terence, or to look for the same things in comedies so different as *Twelfth Night*, *The Misanthrope*, and *Fannie's First Play*. Still the general aesthetic meaning of comedy may be sketched.

The characters in comedy are of the common, the even too common stuff of life; if they are whimsical or fantastic they are given a common human touch. The situations are the common stuff of life, often, it is true, arranged in curious patterns. Characters and situations may at times be flung far out toward the farcical, but they are called back within a system of motives and an orderly structure. The interest is complex as well as sustained; it depends quite as much on the stimulation of feeling and thoughtful criticism as it does on the clever interweaving of ludicrous incidents. Comedy takes thought of the lighter side of life. Meredith goes too far when he makes of it a philosophy of ironic comment and of criticism meant to be corrective. While the comic writer is something more than a merrymaker, he is something less than a philosopher. His is a light touch suited to comparatively light matters—conflicts easily solved or comfortably patched up for future snarls, wounds easily healed, trivial incidents, surface emotions. If this, however, were all, comedy could be likened to a magic hoop of gaudy colors rolling and bounding down the street, always inconsequential, hurting or blocking no one in its on and off course and ending in a spin-wheel of laughter. There is always in comedy the implication or the promise of something more serious. Vice and virtue, marriage and divorce, betrayals and disillusions, misunderstandings, adultery, death—these are matters into which tragedy drives imagination and feeling up to the hilt. Farce turns them into trifles. Comedy, unless it is unusually flippant or serious, takes its position near the line of demarcation, on the side of the *little*, and from time to time glances at or steps over into the realm of the *much*. This *doubleness of reference* it owes to humor.

A man has lost his wife and looks about for another. What tragic meanings here: the blight of death, sorrow, callousness, the collapse of human values! Observe now the working up of this situation into a comic scene in Rabelais, II, 4:—

With these words he did cry like a cow; but on a sudden fell to laughing like a calf, when Pantagruel came into his mind. "Ha! my little son," said he,—"O how jolly thou art, and how much I am bound to my gracious God, that hath been pleased to bestow on me a son so fair, so spriteful, so lively, so smiling, so pleasant and so gentle. Ho, ho, ho, ho, how glad I am! let us drink, ho, and put away melancholy: bring the best; rinse the glasses; lay the cloth; drive out these dogs; blow this fire; light candles; shut that door there; cut this bread in sippets for brewis; send away these poor folks; give them what they ask; hold my gown; I will strip myself into my doublet, en cuerpo, to make the gossips merry, and keep them company."

As he spoke thus, he heard the litanies and the momentos of the priests that carried his wife to be buried; which dashed all his merriment again, and he was suddenly ravished another way, saying, "Lord God, must I again contrist myself? This grieves me; I am no longer young; I grow old; the weather is dangerous; I am sick; I faint away. By the faith of a gentleman, it were better to cry less, and drink more."

"My wife is dead, well, by G—(da jurandi) I shall not raise her again by my crying; she is well; she is in paradise, at least, if she be no higher; she prayeth to God for us; she is happy; she is above the sense of our miseries, nor can our calamities reach her. What though she be dead, must not we also die? The same debt, which she hath paid, hangs over our heads; nature will require it of us, and we must all of us, some day, taste of the same sauce; let her pass then, and the Lord preserve the survivors, for I must now cast about how to get another wife. But I will tell you what to do," said he to the midwives, "Where be they, good folks, (I cannot see you) go to my wife's interment, and I will the while rock my son; for I find myself strangely altered, and in danger of falling sick; but drink one good draught first, you will be the better for it, believe me, upon my honor." They, at his request, went to her burial and funeral obsequies; in the meanwhile poor Gargantua, staying at home and willing to have somewhat in remembrance of her engraven upon her tomb, made this epitaph, in the manner as followeth—

Note the interplay of the ludicrous and the solemn, of the trivial and the deeply moving; observe the sallies into the imaginative and the emotional in Gargantua's love for his son; in the dignity and depth of some of his religious utterances; in the allusion to our common mortality; in the imagery of midwife, priest, and burial.[14]

The phrase "poor Gargantua" is the key to another secret of comedy; the use of sympathetic laughter. There is an echoing sympathy—we are forced to share the exuberance of Gargantua's hilarity and grief,—and there is an interpretative and responsive sympathy. But this response is not allowed to develop fully; Gargantua cries, but he cries "like a cow"; our feelings are dashed as quickly as they are aroused; there is a turn to deeper meanings and then a sheering off. It is the incomplete and somewhat uncritical nature of this sympathy which allows comedy to treat vice as a source of entertainment and to set human folly within the text of a kindly, superficially thoughtful, clever, and stimulating, but fragmentary reading of life.

[14] There is a parallel in the playlet inserted into Chapter xvi of Aldous Huxley's *Antic Hay*. There is ghastly humor in the situation—woman dead in childbirth—and in the switching back and forth between the tubercular cow, Short-i'-the-horn and such phrases as:—"Her milk is cold in her breasts"— "All the woman in her chilled and curdled within her breasts."

MINOR TYPES

There are aesthetic types which have neither the range nor the importance of the beautiful, the characteristic, the sublime, the comic, and the tragic. Theirs is a minor part in what nature and art have to offer in material and form, and in aesthetic appeal. Still, it is a part worth something, for all its lightness and slenderness of emotional and imaginative resources. These minor types: the graceful, the charming, the pretty, the picturesque, the idyllic, and the pathetic repay analyzing.

THE GRACEFUL

Nature offers many examples of the graceful: the swallow, the fawn, the tiger; the pepper tree and the mimosa; the poppy and the columbine. We speak of the graceful lines of a yacht, of the graceful movements and figures in a dance. In art slender columns, arabesques delicately rolling and flowing in their curves, the lyrics of Sappho, the Fauns of Praxiteles, the paintings of Raphael, the landscapes of Corot are marked by grace.

Grace has been defined as beauty in motion. This may be taken as a starting-point. The graceful shares with the beautiful certain qualities: a direct and pure sensuous pleasingness, with no distracting or disturbing admixture; complete harmony of color and lines; an easy self-completeness. But there is something else: movement either present or suggested. In this sense we go beyond the form that confronts us, and through it to a spirit and a life which takes ever new forms, one and all of which reveal that spirit in its ease, delicacy, and smoothness of transformation. Thus we see the yacht as sailing swiftly and with a quick responsiveness to what the wind requires, the tiger changing the lines of his body with full control of its bulk and strength, the mimosa swaying to the breeze, the dancer creating new patterns, the lyric moving about in a play of images and cadences. Wherever we are confronted with a form in which we sense inertness or lack of easy, quick, and adaptable movement, we withhold the adjective graceful.

The graceful, then, is in part a motor concept. But not all movement lends itself to its purposes. There may be tremendous motor suggestiveness in the description of a storm, as in the cataclysmic passage at the end of *Prometheus Bound*, and the effect may be meant to be sublime. The tense restlessness of Michelangelo and Rodin, the broken lines and sharp irregular motor rhythms of Van Gogh or Kokoschka, and the rough energy of much of Browning's verse are equally remote from the graceful.

If grace is to be had, the movement must be light and delicate, and must show neither abruptness nor lack of control. We are asked to share in and enjoy movement in its lighter, smoother, livingly restful forms and traditions; our motor impulses must not be too deeply stirred nor too widely engaged. Nor must the movement be felt as something cumulative or destructive. To us it must mean the promise of new and pleasing forms. There is about the motor quality of the graceful something of the superficial and the soothing; it skims along the placid surfaces of life, innocent of storms and upheavals.

The appeal it makes to the senses and the imagination reveals a like lightness of touch and of heart. It is sensuously satisfying in the changes it hints at or carries out, but falls short, even here, of the profounder needs and satisfactions of aesthetic experience. To call a work of art graceful is a gesture of social amenity—a gracious rather than a whole-

souled recognition of worth. Nor does the graceful stir
deeply the imagination which it enlists; it is persuasive patterning rather than a bold artistic venture. It lacks the
complexity and reach of the characteristic, the imaginative
stretch of the sublime, the intensity and emotional vibrancy
of the tragic.

The Charming

Slighter and more inconsequential still is the charming.
Of all aesthetic types it is the vaguest and has least to do
with art. It has come to mean an indefinable attractiveness
which while felt to be subtle is not held to be deep.

The term is most commonly used with reference to women;
when they are said to be charming it is either in a compensatory way—in default of beauty or dignity—or because they
have about them an indescribable attractiveness which holds
even while it baffles. In any case, in nature and in art
charm bears little relation to beauty. It lacks the rounded
and articulated completeness of the beautiful, as it is without
its depth. It has little of the motor life of the graceful, and
none of its anticipated series of pleasing forms. So strong
is its emphasis on the *us* in the attractiveness that it
threatens to break through the circle of aesthetic experience.
Even when it is applied to art there is this subjective personal note. In a picture or a poem we call charming it is
what *attracts us* that counts.

To speak of something as charming, then, is to confess to
the personally colored attractiveness—vague, complex,
subtle, superficial, elusive—of something slight, pleasingly
animated, and not necessarily beautiful.

The Pretty

The pretty has less of the subjectively personal than the
charming. It may, like the latter, be used sloppily of all

sort of aesthetic responses.   But it has a legitimate use as
one of the minor types.   As such it has none of the elusive-
ness and vagueness of the charming.   When we call a thing
pretty we not only claim an impression that is perfectly
definite, but we are ready with chapter and verse to justify
it.   This is true of a pretty face, true also of a pretty china
cup.   The beautiful arrests and satisfies deeply; the sublime and the tragic move us; there is intriguing curiosity in
the picturesque; promise in the charming; rough shouldering
in the characteristic.   Prettiness is a compliment gladly and
lightly given, and forgotten as soon as given.   Dainty and
little objects call forth the compliment.

The place of the pretty in art is very limited.   In gem-
cutting, silver-smith work, embroidery, and painting on china
or silk it is often met with.   Poetry in its relaxed and trifling
moments may aim at it.   But art stretched to the full stature
of its ambition will have none of the pretty.

THE PICTURESQUE

The word picturesque and its German equivalent *maler-
isch* were much used during the second half of the eighteenth century and the first quarter of the nineteenth.   It
was applied to landscape, and its use meant that a particular
scene was fit to be put on canvas—had the qualities of a
picture.   But the qualities of much of the landscape painting of that time are not at all those of modern painting.
We do not look for rounded pictorial arrangements in nature to be given as a painting, but are willing to paint landscape as fragment; we accept as material her quiet and
common as well as her striking and unusual appearances.
We take her on her own terms—as uninterested in history
and the emotions of man.   What we shun is what marks this
older painting and helps explain the use of the term
picturesque.

Suppose we take, much in the spirit of this type of picture, four subjects: a mountain suggestive of an old fortress in form and in its sheer walls, ridges, and crenellations; a robber castle on a wooded hill; ruins ancient and gloomy, with a black-robed figure meditating on the vanity of human achievement; and a coronation ceremony. The first is a striking natural appearance calling to mind architecture; the second is an impressive conjunction of the historical past, still complete in its form, and of a landscape ever new and ever the same; the third shows the past in ruins, with nature at work on the walls or pushing through the débris, and with man emotionally stirred by this tumbled greatness; the fourth gives an unusual and historically significant event in its exotic trappings and startling displays of color and mass. All four impress us as picturesque; they reveal this minor type as applied to (1) outstanding, uncommon appearances of nature, hinting at human or superhuman workmanship, (2) the conjoined life of the present and the past, (3) an emotional response, historically stirred and regretful, to the ruins of the past, (4) impressive human manifestations which are felt decoratively and historically.

The Idyllic

The idyllic is either a reading of the past in terms of peace and plenty or a selection from the present of materials that satisfy the human longing for, at least, the semblance of contented, peaceful living. In either case there is an idealized interpretation. The Golden Age of a remote past is projected wish-work, but of a quiet relaxed type satisfied with an imaginative return to what is not poignantly regretted in its disappearance. Or there may be a reposeful, sated enjoyment of some sheltered bit of present-day life as it lends itself to such imaginative reshaping as our longing for the peacefully self-complete demands. Lucretius gives idyllic sketches of the Golden Age; Theocritus and Virgil, of the shepherd and farmer; Tennyson of the age of chivalry; and Goethe, in *Hermann und Dorothea,* of the common life of the village.

The manner must correspond to the spirit of the materials chosen: a rounding off, the use of a subdued palette, smoothly flowing verse, polished surfaces in marble, no tense imagery or abrupt intensity of feeling, no vigorous, aggressive technique.

Tennyson's *Idyls of the King* are an example of the idyllic. They portray an age which had its measure of brutality and of sharp dramatic conflicts as well as refinement, mysticism, and quiet and subtle luxuries of sentiment. This age Tennyson reshapes in the way which can satisfy neither the historian nor the dramatically minded. It is quieted down, smoothed over, set to a gentle key even in its jousting and faring, given the spirit of religious peace and good manners, caught up in verse that is smooth and sweetish. To the quiet moments of this life—its idyllic phases— Tennyson has given successful expression.

The idyllic has its place in art. The mood of imaginatively exploiting and enjoying our dreams of a Golden Age —it may be an age of innocence and chivalry or a Lazy Man's Age and a *Schlaraffenland*—with no deep regrets or sharp longings is a recurrent and significant mood in aesthetic experience. So are the poet's vision of a life that is as contented as it is replete and secure, and the soft, insinuating voice he gives to his vision; so is the painter's bucolic response to nature as he catches the very heart of a drowsy afternoon.

THE PATHETIC

The pathetic is often mixed in with the tragic or set in tragedy as an added minor appeal. Cassandra in the *Aga-*

memnon is a pathetic as well as a tragic figure; so are Niobe in the Greek legend and King Lear. Ophelia is pathetic rather than tragic. Euripides' *Trojan Women* and Sophocles' *Philoctetes* show a mingling of the two types. It would be easier to understand the pathetic were it more frequently found unmixed, with its resemblances and contrasts to the tragic strongly accented.

One thing the pathetic and tragic share is the emphasis on suffering. The Greek use of *pathos* as tragic incident bears this out, for such incidents as the burning and sacking of Troy, the slaughter of the children of Niobe, the self-blinding of Oedipus, the madness of Hercules were chosen, in part at least, for their possible revelations of human suffering.

Suffering may appeal to us, as it does in tragedy, as the common lot of mankind, as something diffused and unescapable. Or it may hit us as the pain or agony of this or that individual to which we sympathetically respond—we are then within the pathetic. Again suffering may or may not be related to a wider, imaginatively and dramatically interesting psychic life—in this respect also the pathetic is narrower than the tragic. A further difference is this: in the tragic the struggle that results in suffering and the revolt holds our attention and provokes a kinetic response; in the pathetic this note of strength and resistance is absent. Weakness, in fact, often plays a part in the pathetic. The death of a child is more naturally regarded as pathetic than as tragic. The vagaries of language reveal this stress on weakness in a phrase like "a pathetic attempt." A last difference remains: the pathetic lacks the cosmic overtones which mark the tragic and give it resonance and volume. The pathetic, whether it be gentle or piercing, has about it a quality of thinness which limits its uses in art. The death of a child? what can be made of it? something that stabs or clutches us, with nothing more to be said—or something as monstrously sentimentalized and falsified as the death of little Dombey—or a tragic happening, with the thinness and slightness surviving the admixture.

There is a grave danger in the indiscriminate use of the pathetic in painting and sculpture—the direct appeal through subject-matter to sympathetic feelings. This is an easier thing to do than to create a design that is worthwhile through modeling, color, and line; and it is a tempting and more dangerous road to travel in the appreciation of art.

The graceful, the charming, the pretty, the picturesque, the idyllic, and the pathetic are a selection from the minor aesthetic types. They represent responses and moods, special and limited, which have their part to play in the varied appreciation of art. They mark also special signs and values in the body of art.

PART FIVE

PHASES AND MOVEMENTS

NATURALISM AND IDEALISM

The terms naturalism and idealism have become part of the stock in trade of aesthetic discussion; they are made to do service in the partitioning of art and in the acceptance or rejection of its creative efforts. Unfortunately they take the color of every prejudice and the murkiness of every bit of confused reasoning. Art is to copy nature, unerringly and uncompromisingly!—but what nature?—Art is not to be a literal transcript; it must idealize!—but how, to what extent, and by what manner of means?

NATURALISM

Naturalistic art there has always been. There are many examples of it in Egyptian and Greek art; and the *Old Market Woman* in the Metropolitan Museum may be set down beside the *Vieille Heaulmière* as a boldly naturalistic piece of sculpture. But as a movement in art naturalism is most definitely associated with the last twenty-five years of the last century, and with certain forces then set in motion and persisting here and there even now.

This movement may best be studied in the novel and the drama. Painting and sculpture were also affected by it, but architecture and music show little of its influence.

The naturalistic drama of the earlier Sudermann and Hauptmann, of Max Halbe, of the Strindberg of *Fräulein Julie*, of Wedekind, and Eugene O'Neill moves away from certain conventions of dramatic technique: the use of glorified, rhythmical speech, fully articulate thought, idealized and rounded off character. The speech is to be the common speech, with its dialects, its crudities, its mixture of diffusiveness and explosiveness; it is to be haltingly and imperfectly expressive, as it is in real life, of thoughts and feelings, confused and fragmentary; men and women are to be of common clay, incomplete and ragged in outline. It seeks the less compact, more confused forms of actual life; picks at the loose ends of situations and motives; and is not afraid to present character in relation to its own chaotic self-consciousness and to larger, imperfectly understood life-processes.

But there is more to the naturalistic drama than a change in the way of shaping and writing plays. Such changes reflect the desire to move drama closer to life—to make it more natural in form and substance. In line with this is the choice of a wider range of material. A portrayal of things just as they are—yes, but of all things as they are. Nothing is to be excluded. Sex in its more brutal aspects and in its aberrations; syphilis, alcoholism, tuberculosis; the sordid, the petty, and the dull; ugly blotches in our economic life; the soiled and the degraded—all this is to be moved within the circle of an honest art which sees things as they are and is not disgusted at their nakedness and foulness.

Such extension of material is seen at its extremest and baldest in the naturalistic novel, of which the chief representative is Zola. There is not a single nauseous smell of Paris or infected sore of its social life; no single bit of peasant sottishness and brutishness; no single repulsive item of the intimate life of the body that does not find its way into the pages of Zola. All this filth is presented, not because to him *naturalia non sunt turpia*, but because he was a lover of truth, even in its unworthiest human documentation—and a moralist with loathings and ideals.

Here are the twin inspirations of much naturalistic writing. This is true of Dreiser as well as of Zola.

Of these two motives the moral one is lacking in naturalistic painting and sculpture. An uncompromising love of truth they show; and an unwillingness to move within the limits of a stereotyped idealizing technique and of such material only as is orderly, pleasing, and inspiring. Nudes as Courbet paints them are much closer to nature than those of Titian or Botticelli. Zorn and some of the moderns have carried naturalism far beyond Courbet. Their nude women are neither decorative creations nor ideal forms; they are flesh and blood with a great deal of their animalism put on the canvas; and with the shorter, less beautiful lines in the transition from loin to hip, as they exist in nature, replacing the long sweeping curve of more decorative or idealistic painting. This may also be seen in Rodin's *Age of Bronze,* which is startlingly like a cast from an actual body.

The motto of naturalistic painting, as of the naturalistic drama and novel, is: Keep close to nature! By nature is meant the world of appearance as it strikes our senses. Record what your senses give you! If you paint an interior, offer a faithful rendering of even the most trivial detail; if you present an interior on the stage, do it with a Belasco-like thoroughness; if you paint landscape, study the difference between morning and afternoon lights and shadows—the effect of light on color—color edges and color patches. Paint what you see, and be sure to see all that can be painted! Put your art at the disposal of appearances, however ignoble, chaotic, fragmentary they may be! Remain passive; do not obtrude your ideals and preferences; and curb the desire to round off and make complete what nature leaves rough and sectional. Leibl paints with extreme care part of a bodice; the naturalistic drama gives a mere loose fragment of life. Simple as this motto sounds it contains many difficulties.

NATURE IS ITSELF A TERM OF MANY MEANINGS

By it may be meant (1) a whole system of interrelated facts and laws; (2) a whole mass of loosely given, often disorderly appearances, obtruding itself on our senses and presenting itself at this point or that to shifting perceptions and to the brief focussings of attention and thought; (3) values which are independent of individual moods and preferences, and must be taken on their own terms.

Of these three meanings the first is the philosophical and scientific one. One form of it appears in aesthetic theory as the demand that things be given, not as they appear, but as they are. This is realism, which must not be confused with naturalism, although the terms realistic and naturalistic are often used interchangeably.

If nature is interpreted in this first sense art can do very little with it. No art form, unless it be the novel or the drama, can give more than a bit of the Cosmos; and even they are pitifully inadequate and meagre in their giving. In plays like Ibsen's *Ghosts*, Hauptmann's *The Weavers* and *Before Sunrise*, O'Neill's *The Straw*, Brieux' *Damaged Goods*, and Galsworthy's *Justice* there is a scientific approach to problems of hereditary weaknesses, disease, and economic maladjustment, but not one of these plays is even a single page from the great book of science—nor does it mean to be. For no art—and least of all naturalistic art—must sacrifice, for the sake of an abstract synthesis it cannot carry through, its interest in the sensuous in its isolation and sensuousness.

The second meaning has its difficulties also. If we give up the attempt to get behind appearances and to rationalize and unify nature in any final sense; and if we set ourselves the task of offering appearances—a stray incident, a bit of color or form, a mere wash and drift in the life of feeling and thought—we do not know where to begin and where to stop. Nature in its physical and psychical manifestations has its forms as well as its laws. A tree or a mountain is a unit of appearance; so is a purpose, expressing itself in terms of behavior. Ought these forms to be broken up? Ought we as naturalistic artists to be willing to turn a camera this way and that and to have our art cut into such forms at random? Portrait painting gives a mere fragment, but this fragment has original dominance and is given new unity; the same success could not be had with the painting of a section of the trunk or leaf of a tree or with a foot or a forearm. Yet all these appearances are in a sense natural. Again, if forms are respected, the difficulty remains that there are many equally natural appearances of such forms. Shall we give a near view with many details or a distant one in which detail fades out of the picture? Shall we take our stand to the right or left? It is equally difficult to know where to stop in the carrying of nature over into art. The point may be made by comparing three such dissimilar things as a snowflake, a drop of water, and the mind of Mr. Bloom as presented by Joyce. A snowflake seems to be a mere bit of white fluff; under the microscope it reveals itself as an intricate, orderly design—an artistic microcosm. The drop of water, homogeneous in appearance, shows itself under similar conditions to be the fluid binding agency of all sorts of micro-organisms. Mr. Bloom's mind, subtending simple, commonplace behavior within the space of a day, is broken up in the giving into a chaotic, disjointed thing of snatches. Naturalistic art moves away from the snowflake—away from microcosm and macrocosm—in the direction of Mr. Bloom's mind. But when it has reached that mind and offers its jumbled ideas and emotions in what is often a strained, ungrammatical mass of words and phrases, it becomes violently unnatural—and expressionistic.   How far then can it go?

Suppose, again, nature be taken in the third sense as a system of independent values to be given impartially.   There are what might be called system-values in nature: in the structural and functional adaptations of a tree or an eye, in cyclical insanity, in seasonal changes.   But such system-values (1) are dependent on larger contexts of values; (2) cannot be separated in any clean-cut way from our preferences in the choice and circumscription of materials; and (3) are only incompletely expressed in individual objects as they appear.   Naturalistic art then in driving home their expressiveness by bringing in the larger context, or clearing away inessentials in the appearance is forced to become idealistic.

NO ABSOLUTELY FAITHFUL IMITATION OF THE NATURAL APPEARANCE OF OBJECTS IS POSSIBLE

In the artistic transcription of nature certain differences are forced.   Facts lose something of their palpability, obtrusiveness, and completeness when they are put into a novel, a drama or a poem.   Natural color-values cannot be duplicated: not in range—the painter cannot reach nature's intensity; nor in delicacy and fineness of transitions; nor in broadness and massiveness of effect—what is a bit of blue on canvas to the wide sweep of blueness in the sky?   A sculptor, however naturalistic he may be in the pose and modeled surfaces of his bodies, works in a medium which differs in color and texture; and he avoids the closer resemblance which the use of colored wax might give.   No art can offer the interplay of color, space, and movement given by light filtering through the leaves and branches of a tree in a swaying breeze.   No completely naturalistic technique is possible.

SELECTION AND FORM ARE ESSENTIAL TO ART; AND EVEN RADICALLY NATURALISTIC ART MUST BE SELECTIVE AND FORM-GIVING

Free verse is an attempt to substitute for the more or less artificial verse-forms of traditional poetry the looser, natural forms of rhythmic speech. But not all common speech is rhythmic even in this widest sense; and free verse with its meandering retracing or stretched lassitude of speech is itself a method of selecting and stressing. This is true also of dramatic speech, when for the sake of greater truth to nature it becomes staccato and semi-articulate, and of the jumbled prose of *Ulysses*, which holds our interest and then wearies it as a distinct and artistic manner, and not as a bit of nature. In painting, some object, fragmentary and trivial, is recreated in terms of a design of color and line; and is thus given a new unity. However formless the naturalistic novel seems to be, it is to be understood and appreciated in terms of the desire to be direct and brutally frank in the handling and the telling; and this desire takes form in a technique of selection and emphasis.

NOT ALL THINGS IN NATURE ARE OF EQUAL VALUE TO ART

Certain natural materials are artistically more promising than others. This is true sensuously, expressively, and imaginatively. Not every face is of interest to the portrait painter, nor every subject, to the dramatist; they select what yields them their greatest chance. This must not be understood to mean that there is a definitely marked off fund on which the artist and no other may draw, and that everything else is absolutely unsuitable and unavailable for artistic enterprise. It is against this mistaken theory that the naturalist takes stand in arguing that everything, even the commonplace, the repulsive, the immoral, is good material for art.   But if in seeking to remove this ban he fails to see differences in what might be called investment-value he is in danger of becoming slovenly and uncritical in the selective ventures he must, after all, as an artist make.

THE MOTTO: COPY NATURE! NOT ONLY PUTS UPON ART
AN IMPOSSIBLE TASK BUT ASSUMES FALSELY THAT
IMITATION IS THE SOLE FUNCTION OF ART

No art can be utterly true to nature, no matter how nature is read; and no careful study of art in its origins and creative expressions allows the acceptance of a onesided mimetic theory of its aims.

Naturalistic art in its attempted duplication and faithful copying tends to become superficial; a danger which expressionism escapes, although it is quite as bold in its use of the ugly.   Part of the secret of that escape lies in a creative originality which refuses to accept the mimetic formula of art.

Naturalism then must be rejected as an ideal in art.   As a movement in art it has its shortcomings and dangers; of these enough has been said.   But it has its uses as well.   It is valuable as a reaction against too stereotyped an idealism and too narrow a formula of beauty.   By drawing attention to neglected materials, insisting on truthful rendering, and moving art closer to life, it for a time rights the balance, only to fall into an extremist error of its own.   It sweeps away false ornaments; and when it succeeds in avoiding formlessness or monotony of accent, develops strength and simplicity of technique.

IDEALISM

Some understanding of the swing from idealism to naturalism in modern art may be gained by comparing Thorvald-

sen's sculpture with Rodin's *Age of Bronze;* Hawthorne's
Scarlet Letter with Dreiser's *Sister Carrie;* Shelley with
Whitman; Goethe's *Tasso* with Sudermann's *Ehre;* the
Antigone with a play like *Desire Under the Elms;* David's
Death of Marat with much of the work of Daumier and
Toulouse Lautrec. Such contrasting pairs show differences
not only in the choice of materials but in the manner and
aim of working. To discover what these differences are is
to get close to the secret of idealism. To feel them in their
sharp contrasts is easier than to uncover completely the secrets of a term which is touched and darkened by not a few
of the problems of metaphysics.

In a passage in the *Poetics* Aristotle, referring to three
painters, states that the first paints men better than they
are, the second just as they are, the third worse than they
are. In other passages he contrasts poetic and everyday
diction; compares the nobler nature of tragedy with the
baser one of comedy; criticizes Euripides for his naturalistic character portraits—a naturalism which turns gods
and great heroes like Menelaus and Odysseus into spiteful,
petty individuals. The famous definition of tragedy and
the detailed discussion of the tragic hero alike reveal an
idealistic interpretation of art.

Greek tragedy itself must be understood as one of the
great idealistic forms of art. In choice of materials, in
language, in technique and mode of presentation—the huge
open air theatre, the cothurnus, the masks, the choric chants
and dances—the purpose of distance is served. Here was
something the spectator could not immediately feel himself
into in the sense of extending imaginatively the run of
common experiences; here was life on a grander scale, en-
nobled as well as more moving—an exceptional perfection.
Something of this same distance is discoverable in the proportions of the Parthenon, in the colossal size and superhuman majesty of the sculptured *Zeus* of Phidias, and—

to judge by later testimony—in the wall paintings of Polygnotus.

Idealism is neither a faithful, photographic rendering of
nature nor a violent intentional distortion of its appearances.   Put side by side a photographic study of the nude;
a black and white reproduction of a painter's idealistic
vision of that body; and an expressionist's distorted sketch.
The idealistic painter assumes that nature often falls short
of beauty, and is not completely self-expressive in her individual creations.   And so he smooths curves, follows out
tentative lines and rhythms, omits or modifies details that
seem to mar and disturb.   He attempts even more than
this:—he looks for the typical in the particular; he seeks to
do for nature what nature only rarely does for herself; he
offers the climactic success of a form-giving will, too often
balked of its goal.   Here, he says, is the body in its perfection and meaning.   Individual examples must be modified
if nature is to be given at her best.   If we except an outmoding of technique and convention—much of the verse
of Shakespeare and the prose of Hawthorne sound strange
to modern ears—there is none of that sense of a violation
of nature given by expressionistic art.   There is reverence
back of the idealist's changes.   Nature at her best!—We
have swung back to Aristotle's term "better."   What does
this term mean?   Morally better?   Not necessarily.   It is
true that much idealistic art moves along a high moral level;
and that in its questionable forms it exploits virtue as shamelessly as naturalistic art exploits vice.   What it does mean
is: grander, nearer perfection, more impressive in its appearances, more massive or purer in its self-expressive form
than is to be found in the average.   All this applies to vice
as well as to virtue—to the baleful light emanating from a
Super-Satan as well as to an aureole.   Clytemnaestra and
Antigone are both idealistic figures; so are Caliban and
Ariel.

Idealistic art then seeks to give nature at her self-expressive best. Not at her fullest! for that would mean detail; materiality; and a cluttered plenitude which gives itself too freely, and with too obvious and confused a good-will for the fastidious taste of the idealist. Much of the detail that goes to the fulness of a perceived object is felt to be adventitious and distracting. If the art is bad there is a vagueness about it: a shimmering cloudiness and indistinctness of description; if the art is good it is marked by the large gathering in of a few expressive qualities—the swift grace of a ship, the thunder and turmoil of war, the commanding presence of a hero, the promise of spring and the mellowness and garnered wealth of autumn. It is in this latter sense that Homer, Sappho, and Keats are idealistic poets. They are all selective in this broad detail-ignoring way; they are all intent on the typically significant. Helen is the beauty of woman in perfection; but a dozen painters could paint a dozen Helens from Homer's portrait. What is true of Helen is true of Sappho's circle of girls; of her swift simple sketching of blossom, fruit, and tree; of her pictures of passion. Keats gives the spirit of the seasons, the drowsy heart of sleep, the quality of Chapman's Homer. All three poets immerse what they select in the golden splendor of language and form—"more golden than all gold" as a phrase of Sappho's runs.

A like remoteness from the material; a like ignoring of detail; a like pushing beyond the average to the exceptional, which instead of being felt as something individual conflicting with the average is held before us as something generically significant; a like simple and lofty decorative touch mark idealistic sculpture and painting. Roman portrait sculpture shows parallel lines: sharply realistic, minutely individualized faces and idealized, deified faces and figures of emperors.

Idealistic art attempts to give the Aristotelian *eidos*, the "informing form" of things, and in the rendering of this form is simple, restrained, orderly, harmonious in manner. It combines breadth, distinction, severity, and persuasiveness; seldom is it strident, turbulent or formless.   What a curiously unnatural calm there is in the lines and the compositional scheme of David's *Marat!* what a spirit of restraint and lofty repose there is in the Greek sepulchral reliefs!   The *Niobe* group may be set over against the *Burghers of Calais;* an idealistic Christ on the Cross over against an expressionistic Christ by Grünewald; a Greek ephebos against a bather by Cézanne or an athlete by Stuck; a Greek Venus of the older style against a nude by Renoir or Matisse.

Idealism has a place in art.   Its strength lies in its search for perfection and its use of disciplined form.   Of these, the first gives it the qualities of height and distinction; the second those of quiet completeness and finality.   The sense of finality gained from the statue of *Demeter*, the description of a storm by Homer or by poems of Sappho or Keats springs from the feeling that here are the consummation and consecration of object and artistic means alike—the feeling that nothing more could have been done, and that what has been done reveals utterly both the genius of the artist and the inherent possibilities of perfection of form in the object.

But there are pitfalls in plenty.   Idealism may well impoverish art or make it mechanical and lifeless.   When materials and forms are made to move within a narrow range of a lofty and quiet beauty, and there is too insistent a preoccupation with the perfect as such and with a generalized rather than an individualized expressiveness, art is the loser, as it tends to become narrow, colorless, and even vapid and insipid; when it moves too far away from the manifold, intense, and imperfect life of nature, it is cut off from many of its possibilities and resources.   If certain verse-forms and words are chosen as being essentially poetic; or the same ideal heads are used over and over in sculpture; or language comes to mean nothing but majestic folds, and character nothing but general and imposing types, then art is in danger of becoming stereotyped and mechanized. It is no longer fresh and original; in moving away from what is living in life it has become academic.

It is as a revolt from such narrowness and mechanization that many of the modern experiments in color, rhythm, and form are to be understood. Expressionism is as truly a turning away from academic idealism as it is a setting aside of naturalism even in its subtler forms.

CLASSICISM AND ROMANTICISM

Classicism and romanticism are terms not to be understood except in relation to definite techniques, ideals, and movements in all the arts. They mark contrasting ascendencies in the work of single artists or schools. Thus Mozart is a classicist in music; Wagner, a romanticist; Racine in tragedy, Thorvaldsen in sculpture, David in painting, Chénier in poetry are classicists; whereas Kleist, Delacroix, Boecklin, Byron, Victor Hugo, Poe, Mérimée and Musset are romanticists. We may speak of the Romantic School in Germany in the first quarter of the nineteenth century—a group of men bound by the same choice of content, the same outlook on life, and by like inspirations and modes of artistic shaping. We may refer to the brief clear-cut appearance of classicism in French painting or of the French Romanticists in the lyric and the novel.

But our concern is not with literary and artistic history and controversy—what is sought is an understanding of classicism and romanticism as opposed interpretative and creative impulses—recurrent, selective, peculiarly marked, and one-sided.

CLASSICISM

Classicism, in the historical sense, is closely bound up with the revival of interest in Greek life and art. It responds sympathetically to what it holds to be their spirit and form. To us, with our fuller knowledge of antiquity, the reading seems incomplete and distorted. Certain true qualities of the Greek spirit were seized upon;—measure and discipline, simplicity and lucidity, formal beauty, calm and complete self-possession; but the life in them was missed. Neglect of other qualities led to a narrow view of Hellenism;

a view for which the romanticism expressed in stories like that of the Argonauts and embedded in the classical beauty of the *Odyssey* or the *Bacchae* did not exist.

This secondary and, in part, mistakenly inspired character of classicism must not be allowed to distract from an appreciative study of the general preferences and ideals which in it find a voice. If it ends in an imitation of Greek art, and can see no other, it is only because it finds there the completion and consecration of what it seeks and responds to.

These ideals are reflected in four representative demands and practices.

THE WORSHIP OF FLAWLESS BEAUTY

Art must be marked by restraint, complete mastery of material, and perfect workmanship. There must be no faltering line, no muddy color, no slovenliness in the execution. Harmony that is easily grasped, regularity, and economy are to be sought. There must be no display of disorderly, undisciplined genius. No materials are acceptable which are too complex or too recalcitrant to fit into a simple, polished, utterly adequate scheme.

This is indeed the spirit and the form of much of Greek art. The statue of *Demeter*, the sepulchral reliefs, the *Victory Tying Her Sandal*, the verse of Sappho, one and all, give with a subdued finality of treatment a calm and splendidly poised spirit. Even when there is another spirit stirring in Greek art—a spirit of mystery and adventure —there is, in the form at least, a simple, translucent beauty.

A COMPLETELY CLARIFIED ART—NO CLOUDINESS— NO RESIDUE

A semi-articulate life of feelings that cannot be rationalized or clearly expressed is shunned as a clouding admixture; the mysterious is rejected, as possible residue for the imagination and for thought; so is the exotic, as residue for a restless and confusing curiosity. The form must be lucid and sharp and self-complete. This means a distrust of four-fifths of life as material for art—and a technique which moves within a very small circle of perfection.

THE IMPERSONAL NOTE

Ancient art when held over against the intensely self-conscious spirit of much of modern art appears naive and all but selfless. It looks out upon the world with an unconcern that is freshening and a little chilling; it is interested in the objects rather than the processes of experience; there is no plunging into the subconscious or the intensely and subjectively personal. No ancient Greek could have written a *Hamlet* or a *Faust*. Classicism seeks this objective, impersonal spirit. Its cameo-like perfection, revealing, it is true, the personal skill of the artist, is the goal of an artistic will aimed at the elaboration of this one bit, inattentive to its relation to anything else and forgetful of personal complications and riddles.

THE CHOICE OF THE TYPICAL, THE GENERIC

What is individual in a complex, detailed sense can never be either fully grasped or adequately portrayed. For this reason classicism works away from it, and concerns itself with simple types and the simple and severely restrained outlining of their broad characteristics. Greek sculpture, if we except its last phase and some of its realistic portrait busts and statues, inclines toward such a generic spirit. It presents again and again, with the same compositional stability, and with slight variations of accent, the ephebos, the athlete, the warrior, the mourner; and gives broadly contrasted types of gods and goddesses. It seems to reduce the variety of figures and faces to a few stylistic models.

Such generalized form is apparent in Greek vase painting, where it is favored by a simple outline-technique. The classicist sculpture of Canova and Thorvaldsen sought to recapture the calm spirit, and the simplified lines and typical forms of this Greek portrayal of the body. In failing to catch the individual life that lies hidden in the simplicity, such sculpture tends to become mechanical and coldly schematic.

Classicism in painting and in poetry all but avoids the suggestion of movement as too individualizing in effect; and shows life arranged in a few simple folds. It seeks the universal in theme and the generic in expression.

ROMANTICISM

Romanticism offers a sharp contrast to classicism on all four points. As a phase of art it appears in many forms and variants; and they are all alike marked by:

AN UNWILLINGNESS TO REDUCE THE ARTISTIC AIM TO A SEARCH FOR FLAWLESS BEAUTY

It would be unjust to assert that Romanticism never attains perfect beauty of form. Some of the poems of Chamisso, Lenau, and Baudelaire are perfect in this sense. There are passages of exquisite balance and rhythm in the prose of Tieck and Heine. There are parts of the huge medieval epics that have great beauty in the telling. But, judged by the strictest standards of classicism, the mixture of prose and verse in a French *cante-fable* or a play like *Twelfth Night* appears a case of imperfect integration—of formlessness. Modern romanticism neither aims at nor often gains the flawless formal beauty so dear to the classicist. It shows itself lavish to the point of wastefulness, restive under discipline, often unclear, too subtle and complex. All this must not be set down to the score of faltering workmanship and of an artistic purpose imperfectly grasped. It subtends ideals and aims sharply at variance with those of classicism. Whereas the classicist seeks to mould to perfect beauty the small part of life that can be so moulded; the romanticist, not satisfied with a worship of beauty, seeks to express life as a whole, in its grotesque, mysterious, horrible, humorous, sentimental, problematical forms and meanings. The formlessness of Jean Paul, of Victor Hugo, of Dostoevski follows naturally and inevitably from their view of life and their desire to do artistic justice to its medley of forms and mixture of appeals.

AN ART NOT FREE FROM CLOUDINESS

The complete clarification of art which is the aim of classicism, the romanticist rejects as not to be gained with the materials he chooses and as inconsistent with the artistic effects he wishes to attain. To him art is not a delicate shaping and rounding off of something simple, sensuously satisfying, and self-complete in design; it is a magic mirror which gives, with a cloudiness suffused with light, fragments of the exotic, adventurous, mysterious thing called life. The source of much of the appeal of the exotic, the adventurous, and the mysterious lies in their associational suggestiveness. Over them lies the haze of distance;—a distance which gives wing to the imagination.

THE EXOTIC:—Over against the *Madame Récamier* of David—a classicist painting—may be set the *Fight with a Tiger*, by Delacroix. David has chosen a simple subject and handled it with great economy. The background is neutral, with no intriguing shadows; figure and furniture alike are arranged in long reposeful lines and planes; there is little psychic individuality in the face. Clarity and restraint throughout the composition! Delacroix' theme is exotic:—a distant land; strange animals and plants; alien races with unfamiliar clothing, headgear, and weapons; an uncompleted, unusual encounter. While David is content with the direct appeal of a few clear-cut lines perfectly related, Delacroix gains imaginative effects by the exotic nature of his subject. He would not be a painter if he did not also appeal through line and color. But even there the effect is as different as could be from that of the other picture: the central mass—horse, rider, and tiger—is broken and jumbled in its lines, striking in its play of colors; the tree to the left merges with the background; there is scarcely a straight reposeful line in the whole turbulent design. Boecklin, Blake, and Burne-Jones, very differently inspired, are all lovers of the exotic.

So is William Morris in his modernized versions of old material. Sea voyages, the Orient, fabled lands and creatures, precious stuffs and stones with magic powers, strange races, accoutrements, and customs form part of the substance of the great romantic tales of the Middle Ages, some of which have found their way into the pages of Boccacio and Chaucer.

THE ADVENTUROUS: Adventure, physical and spiritual, appeals to the romanticist. It is something whose form, extent, and outcome cannot be predicted. It means yearning, voyaging, risking; and glorying in something that cannot be mastered. It flashes with uncertain lights and darkens with formless shadows.

THE MYSTERIOUS: The romanticist is at heart a mystic, with mystery dear to his heart. Mystery is something elusive, not to be captured and put within the confines of a clear understanding and a simple, transparent art. It attracts the seeker of the infinite. The Holy Grail and the Blue Flower become its symbols. Romanticism seeks and finds it in religion—it was this that attracted some of the German Romanticists to Catholicism—; and glorifies it in loyalty, sacrifice, and love. Loyalty refuses to be measured and limited—Hagen in *The Nibelungenlied* and Faithful

John are examples of this; self-sacrifice is a mysterious illogical force—witness the tale of *Amis and Amile;* love is not a definitely circumscribed and pointed sex desire, but infinite, irradiating, self-expression and other-valuation.

In Byron's poetry the mystery of spaces and worlds is given voice to; in the romantic tales of Hoffmann and Poe there is a preference for the hidden, supernatural, hallucinatory; for visions and intuitions; for insanity. Baudelaire's poems seek not merely the exotic and the *outré* but the mystery of new sensations and experiences.

THE PERSONAL NOTE

At the very outset a distinction must be made between (1) an intense interest in personality and psychic experiences, and (2) subjectivism—an excessive self-concern and a capricious and biased reading of things in terms of oneself. The first of these applies to all romanticism; the second marks only certain of its developments.

AN INTENSE INTEREST IN PERSONALITY AND PSYCHIC EXPERIENCE: In French lays, in medieval prose tales, in cycles like the *Morte D'Arthur,* and in the great German epics there is little self-consciousness in the telling, but there is an intense interest in personal qualities and experiences. Loyalty, self-sacrifice, love, religious fervor, friendship, delicate personal relations are given not merely for what they exact and mean in terms of action, but for what they mean to individuals, and for what they reveal of the infinite personal life of man.

In modern romanticism there is this same interest, but it exploits the more problematical, the more delicately shaded, the more evanescent and emotionally unstable appearances of personality.

SUBJECTIVISM: Subjectivism is a development in romanticism which has brought it many enemies. It may be seen in Saint-Pierre's and Rousseau's sentimentalizing of primitive life; in the indecent self-exploitation of Rousseau's *Confessions;* in letters like Musset's; in Byron's romantic reading of history and of the Cosmos; and in the whole unedifying phenomenon of Weltschmerz. It has been given a philosophy by the Schlegels: to them the self with all its longings and caprices has the right, absolute and lordly, to express itself; to see things in its own color and to bend them to its uses. This means, as Hegel saw—himself a romanticist in the larger sense—the endangering of the whole orderly, disciplined cultural achievement of man in science, morality, and art. Small wonder then that the classicist also objects to such self-aggrandizement: to him it means the destruction of form; it puts uncontrolled splenetic hunger in the place of a calm interest in beauty and workmanship.

THE INDIVIDUAL

Classicism was seen to lean toward the generic qualities of simple types. Romanticism is convinced of the tremendous worth and the infinite possibilities of the individual. Rousseau, Byron, and Musset give the medley of their thought, impulses, and emotions as something unique and precious. While David universalizes even his historical portraits and incidents, Delacroix gives the impression of a single encounter or an historical happening that took place once and in a perfectly definite individual way. There are in the novels of Victor Hugo, Dickens, and Dostoevski a host of complex characters individualized not merely in their general traits but in their caprices and irrationalities, their hobbies, manner, and dress. To the classicist such detail is inessential; to the romanticist and the naturalist it is not. If modern romanticism, nevertheless, does not excel in character drawing, if it can show few keenly observed and sharply and consistently drawn characters, it is because it is too subjective in its coloring and too deeply committed to what in personality escapes analysis and does not lend itself to clear-cut expression.[1]

If classicism and romanticism are interpreted in the broad sense as contrasted preferences, they must be held to have a permanent place in art; for in it are needed:—beauty and a more inclusive expressiveness, form and reach, order and imaginative suggestiveness, clarity and mystery, the simple and the complex, and the pure and the mingled, the impersonal and the personal, the generic and the individual.

As movements or schools, however, they must mean little to an age like ours; an age which is seeking even in its classicist preferences a wider range, a larger pattern of order, a more inclusive beauty, and above all a more intense aliveness; and which is building into expressionism what is best in its romanticist preferences. The classicism of the eighteenth and the romanticism of the nineteenth century are sadly dated. Only an historically sympathetic or a child-like mind can get much aesthetic pleasure from most of their art. At their worst, classicism smells of antiquities and museums, and romanticism, of the exotic perfume shop and the mystification parlor. The critic who values nothing but the tenets, and the artist who values nothing but the technique of classicism are like stately hens carefully guarding china eggs. Nor is much to be gained by adopting the romantic pose. We have become impatient of the self-taster and the sentimentalist. We no longer sit melancholy-wise before picturesque ruins. A new and vigorous life sweeps us on to new standards and forms of art.

---

[1] In some of its lesser and more questionable work romanticism shows a leaning toward generalized portraiture. An interesting study could be made of romantic book illustration during the third quarter of the last century. There is an ever recurrent ideal picture of girlhood—ringlets, flounces, and ribbons; slight, frail figure, languishing looks; poetic soul. A romantic type devoid of individualizing art! Such types are to be understood as a universalized subjectivity; the emotional readjustments of every generation cause their outmoding—how strange the illustrations in *Great Expectations* seem to us—; whereas the classical heads in sartorial charts have in their very expressionlessness a sort of ghastly impersonal longevity.

EXPRESSIONISM

Expressionism is admittedly nothing new; there are many examples of it in Negro music and sculpture, and in the art of the Middle Ages. It appears as part of the aim and technique of painters like Van Gogh and Hodler. But never before has it been theorized about so much or been in such vigorous ascendancy in all the arts.

A single formula will not compass its meaning; nor can it be discredited by a single impatient gesture on the part of traditionalism. Like a living thing it has many forms and phases; and a right to life.

An approach to its meaning may be had by summarizing a letter which Van Gogh wrote to his brother in 1888. In it the Dutch painter confesses to using color arbitrarily for the sake of gaining greater vigor of expression. In order to make clear his meaning he assumes himself to be painting the portrait of a dear friend. He draws a likeness faithfully; and then takes some of the likeness out of it by a non-representational, exaggerated coloring:—distorting the blondness of the hair to a deep orange or a lemon yellow. To give mystery and intensity of feeling to his picture and to convey what the friend means to him, he sets the head against a background of deep blue. This confession must be supplemented by a glance at some of Van Gogh's paintings. In the group of houses to be seen in the Barnes Foundation Collection form is distorted as well as color— a distortion to be observed in the crazy buckling of the roof lines and in the atmospheric whorls in the upper part of the picture.

What does all this mean? It is evident that whoever looks for either verisimilitude or a regular persuasive beauty and harmony is wasting his time: such things are not achieved because they were not intended. What then is intended? The distortion, in color and line, is a deliberate moving away from nature; and back of this is the aim at greater vigor, greater intensity, a more violent suggestion of movement and force, and a psychic weighting of the picture with the projected feelings of the painter. Here are all the essentials of expressionism:—a movement which has produced much original and disconcerting art. It seems to outrage all order-loving instincts; and its opponents—photographic naturalists and "uplift" idealists alike—have called it all manner of names: damning it as a degenerate twist of the mind or flaw of the eye; as frivolous, insincere experimentation; as pose; and as the sign of a barbarous lack of discipline. A defender of it like Hermann Bahr sees in it the possibilities of a great rebirth in art; a eulogist like Richard Blunck, in a pamphlet, *Der Impuls des Expressionismus*, which subtends many other similar interpretations, praises it in prose often dithyrambic as a new religion of mysticism and democracy; while Marc the painter, he of the *Blue Horses* and of curvilinear cows and sheep, testifies in his comments on painting to a depth and sincerity of purpose which justify at least in part the fervor of its eulogists.

Modern expressionistic painting goes back to Van Gogh and Cézanne and their turning away from impressionism—that most volatile type of naturalism. The impressionists in their turn had done valuable service in holding that the subject of a painting does not matter, that everything is worth painting; in observing the difference a changing light makes in the appearance of objects; and in developing a subtle and brilliant technique of color and light and shade by means of which striking open air effects could be gained. Manet in some of his figure studies simplifies as much as Cézanne does, but the simplification reflects a belief that detail is not necessary to verisimilitude, and an interest in the purely visual, flat appearance of natural objects. Monet and Sisley render visual appearance in even its most fleeting aspects by means of a brilliant, shimmering play of color and light in which the structure of objects vanishes. It was against their passively visual and structureless painting that Cézanne rebelled. His work marks the first step in the direction of a new energism in painting; and it is in terms of this energism that the later development of expressionism is to be understood.

EXPRESSIONISM AS ENERGISM

What is the nature and what are the implications and expressions of this new energism? It means (1) intense dynamic self-projection on the part of the artist; (2) a reading of nature in terms of energy; and (3) the creation of new forms, often at variance with the natural appearance of objects—forms which give the active, self-expressive nature of the artist, the essential spirit of nature, and the union of the two.

INTENSE DYNAMIC SELF-PROJECTION ON THE PART OF THE ARTIST

Van Gogh, it has been shown, insists on the right to use color and form arbitrarily for the sake of greater emotional and psychic intensity. A fierce and vigorous spirit, which does not respect things as they are, flames in his pictures. The fruit pieces of Cézanne and the interiors of Chagall; the nudes of Matisse, Pechstein, and Pascin; the heads of Cézanne and Kokoschka; the landscapes of Soutine; the *Eiffel Tower* of Delaunay; the horses of Marc, and the *Tell* of Hodler are one and all distortions. No forehead ever looked like that of Tell, with its central groove and double bulging; no leg muscles ever showed themselves so outrageously unnatural. The truth is that in none of this work are accurate representational values aimed at. They are highly individualized projections to be felt in their outgoing energy. It is impossible to confuse a Hodler with a Soutine; the one is all harsh, measured, with little modulation and no confusion; the other has a wild, chaotic strength about him, with twisting rhythms and splashings of red, yellow, and brown. Men differ greatly in their ways of receiving and copying a world of objects; but they differ infinitely more in the active thrust of their personal preferences and impulses. Unless these latter differences are felt and there is some understanding of the will to self-expression as it has its lordly, masterful way with common objects and settles itself into a pictorial scheme, expressionistic painting will seem to us little more than nightmare shapes or caricatures.

A READING OF NATURE IN TERMS OF ENERGY

In painting of the conventional type nature appears as an orderly system of forms, independent and chosen for their visual effectiveness. But there is no binding of all these forms into a common life; no suggestion of a tremendously energetic and experimental nature working in all things. Nor does the structurelessness of impressionistic landscape point that way:—that is merely a visual unification. Expressionism seeks this energy above all else. In Cézanne's hillsides nature seems to be building herself up; to be settling herself in the folds and terraces of the landscape; in his *Bacchanal* a common dynamic rhythm of life dominates clouds, trees, and the struggling nude figures. Forms, to Hodler, are the carriers of a quiet but extremely vigorous life. The radical expressionists go beyond this. They see in nature a form-smashing energy which distorts and annuls; and they hold that the artist has the right to force his way through what is stereotyped and systematized in our ordinary intellectual and perceptual responses straight to this energy:—an energy he is to reveal even in its chaotic expressions and upheavals.

THE CREATION OF NEW FORMS, OFTEN AT VARIANCE WITH
THE NATURAL APPEARANCE OF OBJECTS, GIVING THE AC-
TIVE SELF-EXPRESSIVE NATURE OF THE ARTIST, THE
ESSENTIAL SPIRIT OF NATURE, AND THE UNITY
OF THE TWO

It would be a mistake to call expressionists the nihilists of form simply because they do not respect the form of things as they are commonly seen. They may smash the world to bits, but they recreate in their own image in terms of patterns of line, mass, and color which are not chaotic or slovenly. I know of no painter who is more disciplined and consistent in his technique, and a more constructive organizer than is Cézanne. Call it anarchic if you will, to paint apples and oranges angularly, and to tilt plates of fruit at impossible angles; but do not fail to see the economy of the design, the plastic use of color, the simplicity and forcefulness of line, the rhythmic integration. It is true that expressionism, being a highly individualized projection of self and highly personal reading of nature, allows the occasional appearance of painters who seem chaotic and formless. It is difficult to follow Soutine in his tumultuous and imperfect organization. The sketchiness and non-representational character of Kandinsky's musical improvisations in color are perplexing, to say the least. But even such extreme painters ought to be approached in a spirit of willingness to see with their eyes and to work with their creative will.

Much has been written about the mysticism to be found in expressionistic art. The painters themselves, in their letters and comments, have confessed to its presence. Still it is not discoverable in their work so readily and so fully as it is in expressionistic prose and poetry; the best examples of it are to be found in these other arts, where there is a more favorable medium of expression. What is this mysticism? [1] A double energism has been traced:—in the artist's self as it projects itself and in a nature which is in essence one will, working in and through a multiplicity of forms. The two are now to be thought of as merged; the I and the Other are to be one. The humanitarian, man-centred view of life disappears, and man is read in the larger world context; but nature as an objective system of relations also disappears, and the reading here, too, is in psychic terms. A curious spiritual pantheism results, which stresses at once the most intimately personal impulses and reactions and the communal spiritual oneness of all things. *The Bacchanal* of Cézanne may be used as an instance of "cosmological oneness"; the *Blue Horses* of Marc as an example of the passing beyond single natural forms to a life that is in all and binds them together. There are two paintings, one by Meidner, called *I and the City*, and another by Chagall called *I and the Village*. In each there is a big head at the centre of the picture; in each a scene is given, not

---

[1] Marc, the painter has confessed to its presence cited from Hausenstein, *Der Körper des Menschen in der Geschichte der Kunst*,

MARC:—"The artistic effect of a study in figure painting has not the slightest concern with the scientific laws of the formation of the body painted; they may, as they show themselves, be followed, but they need not be. In fact it was discovered that the purely artistic effect is stronger when such laws are either not seen or are disregarded. This opposing the natural form is not due to caprice or a craving for originality; rather is it the accompaniment of a deeper will which glows in our generation:—the desire to seek out metaphysical laws—a desire limited heretofore to philosophy.

"To-day we are seeking under the veil of appearance hidden things in nature which we regard as more important than the discoveries of the impressionists—things which they simply passed by. And we are seeking and painting this inner spiritual side of nature not from caprice and the desire to be different, but because it is this side that we see—as at one time violet shadows and the light hovering over things were suddenly seen."

objectively, but as it reaches consciousness in bits and snatches. Familiar objects like sheep, cattle, flowers, streets, and factories appear in sections; and the differences in size are used to indicate the foreground and background of consciousness. All this is as ego-centric and as fantastic as is the romanticism in the stories of Hoffmann. But the technique and the effect are totally different. In his merging of reality and unreality, Hoffmann gives a phantasmagoria of terror, humor, sentiment, and of perception and emotion built on the shifting sands of attention; these paintings, however, retain a vigor, directness, and definiteness in their self-conscious and somewhat intellectualized mysticism, as it cuts into objects and deprives them of their self-completeness, and as it shows them floating in the stream of consciousness.

More striking and convincing illustrations of 1, 2, and 3 may be had from the other arts.

ILLUSTRATIONS OF EXPRESSIONISM

NON-FICTIONAL PROSE

Nietzsche is perhaps the first great expressionistic writer of non-fictional prose. Everywhere he projects and affirms himself—his motor impulses, his preferences, his moods. His vigorous, intense, imaginative, colorful prose voices an energism that sweeps away the orderly thought-structures of academic philosophy; the traditional values of history; and the codes of conventional morality. The Universe, in turn, to him is nothing but energy, casting forms forth and taking them back unto itself in the restless flood and ebb of its life. There are many passages in *Thus Spake Zarathustra* which reveal Nietzsche as a mystic who glories in this oneness of all things, and in the merging of the I and the Other.

SCULPTURE

Modern expressionistic sculpture shows the triple influence of Rodin, of African art, and of medieval work in wood and stone.

Rodin was not untouched by the baroque and the impressionistic.   To the latter he owes his fondness for atmospheric effects in sculpture.   But he is in much of his work an expressionist.   He sacrifices beauty to energy; interprets the material everywhere in terms of the spiritual; distorts in order to get more intense spiritual effects.   His reading of man is cosmological; and his world image is one of an endless, varying play of cosmic forces.

Negro sculpture is of more questionable value as an inspiration.   The energizing mind of primitive man as it is reflected in idols, fetishes, and masks, grotesque and distorted, is too remote from ours in motives, cosmology, and technique.   But we may be encouraged to go back of tradition to a strong original shaping; and become convinced that there can be a significant art with little or no formal beauty.   We are carried, also, more directly to design.

In the work of certain medieval sculptors—Grünewald among others—stark ugliness and an extremely simple and forceful design are combined with great spiritual intensity. Modern sculptors like Kolbe, Minne, Epstein, Metzner have sought to make that combination their own.   To them the sensuous beauty of the human body and accurately representational modeling are distractions; these are to be cleared away so as to allow some strong impulse or intense psychical experience—lust, anger, grief, sorrow—to express itself fully; and to create an artistic form of the utmost simplicity and strength.   In quite another field, that of the wood cut, similar opportunities are offered for such psychic intensity and plain compositional strength.[2]

[2] Masereel's wood-cuts are a good example of this.

POETRY

Most of our younger poets have written some expressionistic verse. Much of this verse is violently ego-centric and
eccentrically orbited; some of it gives the impression, not of
outpouring energy, but of a projected fussiness and restlessness; of lack of creative power in the reshaping of a world
hastily pulled apart; and of a lack of understanding of the
medium of poetry, and of its limits and possibilities. But
poets like Vachel Lindsay and Carl Sandburg yield the sense
of great power; and have the gift of putting into loosely
patterned verse something of the tremendous energy that
works in the formlessness of modern life. The steel mills,
the grain fields, the factories and furnaces, the forests, the
sunsets are all given a soul; and human life is caught up
in their violent or swinging rhythms. A generation back,
Walt Whitman voiced a virile self and a spiritual pantheism.

NOVEL AND SHORT STORY

In the short story and the novel expressionism is less frequent in America than on the Continent. Waldo Frank and
Sherwood Anderson are our chief exponents of it. It brings
with it great changes in style, technique, and content. The
style is tense, abrupt, vivid, and often disjointed. It moves
in brief energetic rhythms. The technique is one of short
chapters, of abrupt transitions, of loose weaving of incidents,
of intensification and distortion, of psychic weighting. The
manner is sometimes "jazzy." Is not jazz the original expressionistic music? The content is not the painstaking in-
ventory of all things material which characterizes the
naturalistic novel nor the carefully selected material of
idealism; it is the life, spirit, and movement of the material
world as that world is subjectively read by a distorting,
changing, and ever interpretative and assimilative con-

sciousness. Here is the secret of the sense of instability and of jerkiness such novels often give. Nothing is allowed to remain immobile and safe in its materiality; everything is forced to take the stamp of motor impulses and mastering moods—to become active and spiritual.

Here are examples of such expressionistic prose:
Waldo Frank *Under the Dome*:—[3]

Her gray tilted eyes seem sudden to stand upon the farther wall of her husband's shop, and to look upon her.

. . . .

The street was a ribbon of velvet blackness laid beside the hurting and sharp brightness of the store. The yellow light was hard like grains of sand under the quick of her nails.

. . . .

In the door and the clang again of the bell, a boy with them.

. . . .

But the store moved, moved.

There was a black wheel with a gleaming axle—the Sun—that sent light dimming down its spokes as it spun. From the rim of the wheel where it was black, bright dust flung away as it spun. The store was a speck of bright dust. It flung straight. It moved along the velvet path of the street, touching, not merging with its night. It moved, it moved, she sat still in its moving. The store caught up with Meyer. He entered the store. He was there. He was there, scooped up from the path of the street by the store.

THE DRAMA

In the drama expressionism has shown its worth. It has made the naturalistic plays seem trivial, and it has discredited many of the artifices of the idealistic drama. Examples of it are: O'Neill's *The Emperor Jones*, *The Great God Brown* and parts of *The Hairy Ape*; the last act of *The World We Live In*, by the Brothers Kapek; Andreyeff's

[3] By permission of *The Dial* (The Dial Publishing Company). October, 1920.

CÉZANNE, STILL LIFE

VAN GOGH, WOMAN OF ARLES

Thought and *Thou Shalt Not Kill;* Kaiser's *Gas!* and *From Morn Till Midnight;* Kaufmann and Connelly's *The Beggar on Horseback;* Eulenberg's *Mückentanz;* and the plays by Toller and Werfel.

It is useless to look for a single formula, but certain innovations and peculiarities of technique will be found, in one form or another, within this range of plays:—

MONODRAMA:—Of this *The Emperor Jones* and *From Morn Till Midnight* are good examples. In the traditional drama the hero dominates the scene with his soul-tragedy; but there are other characters into whose inner life we are to feel ourselves; and there are plot and counterplot to be understood in their relations. Here, however, we are set within the will and the emotions of a single person; everything else is merely setting—clue—vision—shadowplay—projection. O'Neill gives merely a masterly study of an atavistic fear and its panicky responses; a study as kinetic and monotonous in its accent as the recurrent throb of the war drums. In the Kaiser play there is the incident of a bank clerk's theft of a large sum of money and his attempt to live himself out in the spending of it;—an incident round which might have been woven a plot, and the tragedy and pathos of the people affected by the theft. But Kaiser does nothing of the sort. He strips of psychic content everything but the hungry and power-intoxicated soul of the thief. Everything else goes and comes in a vague, episodic way. Andreyeff's *Thought* is pure monodrama.

A DRAMA OF TYPES:—The purely individual does not interest the expressionistic dramatist. The stress is on the type. There is nothing new about a pre-occupation with types; it is common in old comedy—proof of this are the type names in the comedies of the Restoration. It appears in his old Morality Plays. But it was frowned upon in tragedy. There is something new in calling a character He, as Andreyeff does, or Spiegelmensch, as Werfel does;

in Kaiser's refusal to individuate the clerk beyond the mere lusting for self-expression, and the characters that surround him beyond that of colorless types and projections; in choosing as a title *Mückentanz*, as Eulenberg does, and offering a gnat-like swarm of characters, individualized somewhat in their pettiness, but all alike seeking in their twisting, ineffectual ways an escape from the commonplaceness of their lives.

The most significant and revolutionary point about this new type-tragedy is its turning to types of power that go far beyond the lives, struggles, and happiness-values of individuals—cosmological forces and irruptions, as in *The Emperor Jones* and *Spiegelmensch;* monstrous subhuman forms, as in *Bocksgesang;* great social and industrial complications and upheavals, as in Toller's *Maschinenstürmer* and Kaiser's *Gas!* Individual character drawing all but disappears in the process.

A MERGING OF THE OBJECTIVE AND THE SUBJECTIVE: —Examples are the churchgoers scene in *The Hairy Ape;* the scene in Heaven in *Liliom;* the galley of slaves in *The Emperor Jones;* the dinner and the cyclodrome scenes in *From Morn Till Midnight;* also Rice's *The Adding Machine*, and Lawston's *Ralph Bloomer*, and Lenormand's *Failures.* Everything is shown in objective, tangible form; and yet as reflected and distorted by its life within a perceiving and reacting consciousness. There is something suggestive of dream-technique in this—a dream-technique shown at its fullest and wildest in *Beggar on Horseback.*

LOOSENESS AND INSTABILITY OF CONSTRUCTION:—Scenes are often short and not rounded off; and they are not built up to a terse economical structure.[4] They begin and end abruptly; and have a random quality about them. There are violent changes answering the flashes and shifts

[4] Eulenberg's *Mückentanz* offers illustrations of this.

of consciousness. This again calls dreams to mind, but it also suggests the technique of the cinematograph.

AN ENERGISTIC QUALITY:—The cyclodrome scene in *From Morn Till Midnight* may be used to illustrate the energism and the worship of great power which characterize the expressionistic drama. The clerk with the stolen money in his pocket attends a cyclodrome race. The scene is written as monodrama—racers and spectators have no independent interest; we are to see them as he sees them. He sees in the racers nothing but strain and speed and in the spectators nothing but excitement and a lustfully tensed hunger of "sensations." He flings money about, offers special prizes in order to whip up to the utmost the efforts of the riders and the excitement of the others; and thus gets for himself the taste of power, and a drunken straining and stretching. The royal family enter the cyclodrome; the wild mob turns from shouting to bowing; the clerk leaves in disgust. Force that can be controlled, energy that collapses into good manners, have no appeal for him; they cannot give him what he craves above all else—dynamic self-expression with neither admixture nor restraint.

The energism of this new type of drama is reflected in the choice of materials and in the use of language. Mass movements, as they are revealed in wars, strikes, crowds, and mobs, are a favorite theme; and they are handled with great vigor. Of this the scenes in *Gas!*, the war of the ants in *The World We Live In*, and the last act of *R. U. R.* are good examples.

The language of *Gas!* moves away from dialogue toward self-expression by means of short phrases, which might be called force-units of speech. There is an attempt to make speech more powerful by ungrammatical condensation, by inversion, and a distorted order of words.

MYSTICISM:—Here may be found in its most striking

form the mysticism which is at the heart of expressionism; a mysticism which breaks through the opposition between humanity and the Cosmos, between the subjective and the objective; and which sinks individualities and separate forms in a stream of consciousness and a self-expressive nature. There are many instances of it in the work of Werfel, Toller, and Kaiser.   In Eulenberg's *Mückentanz*, a play written in prose, there are a few lines of poetry that illustrate this mysticism.

Eulenberg, *Mückentanz*,

APPARITION

Boat after boat passes,
Sending on
From eternity to eternity
The living to-day, the dead to-morrow.

(he scoops in a handful of air)

I have thrown you a wave
From the ocean of humanity
—Sea-urchins and shells and foam,
And animalcula
Caught in the froth,
Gone with its going.

You who are standing on the beach,
Awaiting the sound of the unknown,
And only too gladly fanned by the uncertain,
Stoop and observe
Even as I kneel

(he sinks down)

Before humanity
The Imperfect,
The To Be Pitied,
And yet Alone Worthy of Worship.

To this might be added the lines spoken by the Voice of
Light earlier in the play:—

Voice of Light

> Saved is he who when he looks upon creation believes in man
> in spite of what men are and what men do!

Other examples of mysticism are Lenormand's *Failures*
and O'Neill's *The Great God Brown.*

Such then are some of the peculiarities and innovations
of the new expressionistic drama.

What is the value of expressionism as a movement in
modern art? Such a question must be asked in view of the
energy displayed in the creation of an expressionistic art
and the equally energetic protests by conservatives.

Like all transitional movements expressionism has its weak
points. It assumes too readily that all expression is valuable; that all distortion has aesthetic and psychic value;
and that all contents are acceptable. It tends to overlook
the quieter forms of energy; is too neglectful of formal beauty
as one of the sources of aesthetic pleasure; and often lacks
discipline and measure. But it has great value in (a) giving freshness, vigor, and range to art; (b) helping art
beyond a purely imitative, representational ideal and practice; (c) in clearing away the conventional and the stereotyped, and in recovering, as far as may be, a type of artistic innocence; and (d) in rescuing art from a superficial
naturalism and a narrow, academic idealism.

Above all, expressionism is a significant and promising
development in art because it reflects a force and spirit which
whether we like it or not must be admitted to be the force
and spirit that stir in modern life; and because that life,
unmannerly and undisciplined as it may be in some of its
expressions, holds within itself the promise of new hopes and
achievements; of new cosmic readings; and of new moral and
aesthetic values.

SOME 'ISMS

Certain words ending in *ism* have come to be used with *cliché*-like regularity and thoughtlessness. They appear in (a) the manifestos of radical schools, where they serve as watchwords or rallying points; (b) popular debates on art, where they are incantations or a club to silence an opponent; (c) serious aesthetic discussion, where they conveniently mark certain special movements and phases of art. These movements seem little more than fads and fashions of technique, but there is honest experimentation in most of them —and points of view and aims that ought not to be neglected.

FUTURISM

According to Marinetti's pronunciamento, futurism is a revolt against the worship of form as such, the choice of certain subjects—the nude and others—and a traditional over-emphasis on representation. It is a young man's art, setting itself the task of divining and grasping the world as force. Painting is to give the "sensation dynamic." Here are three bits of futurist theory quoted by Cheney in his *Primer of Modern Art.*

How often it happens that upon the cheek of the person with whom we are talking we see the horse that passes far away at the end of the street! Our bodies become parts of the seat upon which we rest and the seat becomes part of us. The omnibus merges in the house that it passes, and the houses mix with the bus and become part of it.

. . . .

The simultaneousness of states of mind in the work of art: that is the intoxicating aim of our art.

. . . .

—the dynamic sensation, that is to say, the particular rhythm of each object, its inclination, its movement, or, to put it more exactly, its interior force—every object reveals by its lines how it would resolve itself were it to follow the tendencies of its forces.

Such theories put in practice mean preoccupation with fast moving objects, like Russolo's *Auto* and *Speeding Train*, the search for motor simultaneity of impressions, and the shattering of the form of objects.

As a movement futurism has remained barren of notable achievements; it has produced nothing beyond works of a crude and chaotic energism. The one point of value in its program is its demand that painting, as well as the other arts, be revelational of the power that stirs in the great undertakings and in the mental and industrial turmoil of our age. It errs in (1) forcing the dynamic note in painting beyond the danger point; (2) interpreting power as chaotic and disruptive of disciplined form; (3) of injecting into art something of the immature, brash, and unquiet spirit of the cinema.

CUBISM

Cubism is neither a mere fad nor an adventure in religion. Allowance must be made for a fondness for *réclame* and startling innovations on the part of artists like Picasso and Picabia. What remains is a movement interesting in its history and of sufficient vitality to have left its mark on the newer, expressionistic painting and sculpture.

The landscapes of Monet, Sisley, and Renoir offer a new technique of evanescent natural effects—the everchanging play of light and color. They are not representational in an exact sense. Renoir's trees are often mere rhythms and whorls.   Monet's *London Bridge* is but the fleeting impression the bridge might under certain atmospheric conditions give to a sensitive eye.   Structural articulation does not lie within the purpose of these artists.   Formless they are not, but their form is not of the architectural type; colors come to be the soft, intimate, complex organizers of space.

Put alongside of these impressionistic paintings a landscape by Cézanne—a southern village, with vineyards climbing the hillside, terraced and irregularly partitioned by stone walls.   There is a distinct feeling for the architectural values of such a landscape.   The houses are blocked into planes and their lines are sharply ridged.   The impression is one of a reshaping, almost monastic in its severity, of the manifold of sensuous experience.   It is this geometrical rebuilding, with its emphasis on form rather than on color or lifelike rendering that gave the impetus to the cubist movement.

The landscapes of Henri Rousseau are simple and solidly built; a picture like Derain's *Cagnes* shows a further advance towards geometrical painting: there is a hint at verisimilitude, but the cluster of houses with their high white walls and dark slanting roofs is rendered in the constructive spirit of a child's set of blocks.   This hint at the common objects and aspects of nature becomes fainter in Braque's *Le Viaduc de l'Estaque* and in a landscape by Benes which shows a castle, a church, and some houses sketchily indicated by cubes and prisms, caught within two huge arching trees—trees whose trunks, branches, and leaves are broken into straight lines and geometrical figures.   It disappears completely in Braque's *Harbor* and in Gleizes' *Landscape with Trees*.   The world of things has vanished: fragmentary bits of it appear here and there in the midst of cones and prisms and color-segments.   Picasso's *Violinist*, his *Poet*, Braque's *Girl with a Mandolin*, and Picabia's

Dance are no longer representational: they call to mind the products of the lathe or the caprices of a jig-saw.

This development reveals the more or less unconscious purpose of cubist painters: to annul (1) the object with all its associations, and (2) the sensuous image with all its fleeting inessentials; and to give either their mere structural skeletons or, discarding even that, a new, geometrical synthesis of simple space-forms. But it is one of the paradoxes of cubism that the representational it means to kill reappears in an irritating way in a picture puzzle we try to solve with the verbal tag affixed by the painter as our clue. Again, while the cubist often gains strength by the use of angular lines and the simple and solid building of masses he fails in all but exceptional cases to achieve the unity which he as the passionate seeker of the *logos* of pure space-forms is supposed to seek. In Chagall's *Still Life* every object, from lamp to pitcher and plate of fruit, is set to the same key of a few crude distorted curves; Burger's *Let there be Light* shows an ascending dynamism of line and a pleasing integration of color effects; Marc in his *Tiger* and *Blue Horses* has gained new non-representational unity and vigor of composition. But cubist painting as a whole falls far short of the art of these men, who are to be classed as expressionists; it is chaotic in the sense that there is little linear integration of the geometrical forms into which it splits space.

DADAISM AND FAUVISM

Dadaism and Fauvism have this in common: they both turn away from what is intellectually and culturally prized, and they do it with a gesture of *je m'en fichism*—to borrow one of Huxley's phrases. Dadaism turns to infantilism and Fauvism to primitivism. Dadaist poetry seems a crazy mockery of intelligent speech; stammers, is clumsy with a child's tongue, combines a pleasure in the nonsensical with a rebellious flouting of sense. Dadaist painting is sketchy, inarticulate, infantile in its designs and use of color; in its craziest moments it outrages by making a picture of foreign substances pinned to or pasted on the canvas with all the perverse caprice of a child. Fauvism flouts cultural achievements—goes back to the primitive, the wild, and the shocking. It, too, is partly revolt and partly mystification.

These twentieth century products of disillusion and sensationalism need not be taken very seriously. In many of their manifestations they are what is simply and expressively called *bunk*. We are shocked, and suspect a swindle. But now and then a gifted artist can make something even of these.

IMAGISM

Imagists are poets with a peculiar theory of what poetry ought to be. They stated their position in their first annual anthology, *Some Imagist Poets*, *1915*, and in the anthology of the following year corrected certain misinterpretations. Amy Lowell, H. D., Richard Aldington, John Gould Fletcher were members of the early group. The use of free verse, with cadences and new rhythms, the return to direct, common speech, the presenting of images, the making of poetry hard and clear were some of the points stressed in their original manifesto:—

To present a picture (hence the term "Imagist"). We are not a school of painters, but we believe that poetry should render particulars exactly and not deal in vague generalities, however magnificent and sonorous. It is for this reason that we oppose the cosmic poet, who seems to us to shirk the real difficulties of his art.

.   .   .   .

To produce poetry that is hard and clear, never blurred nor indefinite.

The connotations of the term imagist pointed strongly to a *rapprochement* to painting. Certain short Chinese poems have all the distinctness, neat self-completeness, and visual sharpness of a picture—they could be set down on silk or canvas. The imagists at times moved close to this type of poetry. They are sensitive to color and pattern. But very few of their poems, sensuous and visual as they are, could be transferred to painting. Against these connotations they felt it necessary to protest:—

—"Imagism" does not mean merely the presentation of pictures. —He may wish to bring before his reader the constantly shifting and changing lights over a landscape, or the varying attitudes of mind of a person under strong emotion, and his poem must shift and change to present this clearly.

This is the "phantasmagoria" of John Gould Fletcher's *Goblins and Pagodas*, which are as close to music as they are to painting, and make as free use of auditory and motor, as they do of visual images. What the imagists are seeking is, I suspect, a *realization*. To gain it they use a very free and flexible form. Within this form they have gained sensuous and imaginative effects that are original and fine. They have expressed the desire to put into poetry the new spirit and life they saw stirring in the other arts. It is this desire that serves best for a check on too restricted an interpretation and too cramping a use of their formula.

These, then, are a few of the many 'isms to be found in the arts. They all easily degenerate into fads, but there is not one of them that lacks historical value in the multiform venturing of art; not one of them that has not justified itself, here or there, in what has come out of its experimentation.

PART SIX

GENERAL PROBLEMS

TRADITION AND REVOLT

Every phase of human conduct, from dress to politics or religion, offers the spectacle of a body of practice and opinion establishing itself and maintaining its rule until it either disintegrates under the slow pressure of gradual innovations or is overthrown violently by an act of revolt. The same play of forces and the same drama of conservatism, radicalism, and revolt are discoverable in art. To watch the creative art spirit of mankind as it clears, settles, and builds a home for itself, as it becomes distrustful of its solid comfort, and as it strikes out for new ground and new interests, is well worthwhile. It means a growing understanding of art as a changing, living thing.

TRADITION

THE GENESIS OF TRADITION

At the outset a distinction must be made between traditional content and traditional form; the two are not always found together. H. D.'s poems are modern in manner, classical in much of their inspiration and meaning. Examples of traditional content are: fighting and hunting as the usual, the accepted theme of the early heroic ballad and folk epic; the place of myth and legend in Greek tragedy and in old Italian painting; amatory intrigue in French farce. Examples of traditional form are various technical devices, or accepted ways of doing things: the Egyptian practice of combining a head in profile with a fronting body; choric songs in Greek tragedy; the use of rhyme; the three orders in Greek architecture; the use of refrain in folk songs;

stylization in the patterns of rugs; the use of certain colors in Italian painting. In many cases content and form cannot be separated; this is true of the symbolism in Oriental rugs and of the shapes, methods of weaving, and patterning in Indian baskets.

The social character of early art explains in part the traditional content and the many accepted and practised forms. The epic helped record common martial exploits and develop what was much needed—a warlike spirit; certain forms of music and dancing appeared spontaneously with common religious beliefs and ceremonies, and assisted in making them more firm and impressive; sculpture set itself the task of visualizing in permanent form gods and godesses or that of recording physical strength and skill as part of some great athletic festival. Tribal symbolism becomes articulate in rugs and pottery, and in the carving and coloring of totem poles. In more advanced stages of society, where a spirit of individualism is already established, fashions and the common conditions and interests of living of special groups easily swing the individual into grooves. Examples are: the comedy of Menander; the cavalier poetry and drama of the Restoration; the songs of the troubadours; the paintings of Boucher and Fragonard and their relation to the *beau ideal* of the French aristocracy at the waning of the eighteenth century. Much of the content and spirit of the ideal of a class and an age is observable in rococo art. The constant and excessive use of curves, the fondness for intricate ornamentation, the over elaborate and meretricious spirit—all this reflected a dominant social taste and a shallow, sophisticated, and highly decorative life.

Traditionalism in forms and technique results from unconscious imitation; from an economic response to what is in demand and finds a ready sale; and from the influence of apprenticeship and schooling. Of these the third is the one of greatest interest. A master's way of gaining effects

WANDA GÁG, ICE HOUSE

BRACKMAN,
TWO FIGURES

From the Minneapolis Art Institute

was copied by a pupil; and what the pupil could copy was some detail of technique or strikingly individual touch. Thus were taken over and traditionalized: the deep-set eye and sharp frontal bone of heads by Scopas, the athletic figures of Lysippus and the massive ones of Rodin and Maillol, the geometrical simplifications of Cézanne, the decorative sophistication of the Pre-Raphaelites or of Beardsley. In art schools traditionalism makes the teaching easier by giving canons of criticism and offering a fixed and convenient formula for the artistic development of the students.

THE USES OF TRADITION

Whether a particular tradition is sound depends on many things. Some mannerism or defect of vision on the part of the artist or some lack of mastery of his medium may become a tradition among his followers. But what we are interested in here is the functional usefulness of tradition itself. Its uses are three:

TRADITION MAKES FOR A DISCIPLINED ART AND A SUSTAINED TECHNIQUE: To the making of good art go the trained senses, the vivid imaginings, the insight and thought of many men. Something of this can and ought to become a cultural possession. Such were the sense of beauty and the feeling for form among the Periclean Greeks—Phidias could entrust to common workmen many of the details of his architectural and sculptural designs. There is a like traditional and sustained excellence in Greek vases and coins, in French church building, in English furniture and German metal-work of certain periods. The lack of such tradition in American art life means that art instead of being expressive of disciplined taste and conscientious workmanship blooms with the curious and often poisonous blossoms of pure caprice, or in a spirit of eclecticism—of which

Davies and Manship are examples—borrows from the past.

Excellence in art is in only rare cases the expression of crude, capricious individuality. It is more often the result of discriminating taste, quick response to what the past has to offer in the way of art values, and style, which is consistency and sureness of touch gained through self-discipline. Architecture, of all the arts, reveals most plainly the benefits of traditionalism. There is little experimentalism and there is a wholesome recognition of great achievements of the past—a willingness to have genius move freely within the patterns of good taste.

TRADITIONALISM ASSISTS IN THE SOCIALIZING OF ART: In so far as early art is commemorative it serves the purpose of social continuity; in so far as it attends or enhances group purposes—harvesting, war, religious festivals, the housing of the gods—it serves that of social solidarity. In more advanced cultural stages the situation is different. Art there appears often as an opportunity and a refuge for the individualist; he can express himself freely with little fear of interference on the part of the group. Quite possibly there are things worthwhile which never can be stated in terms of social value or appreciation—artistic attainments born of the intensest individualism; religious experiences too personal and intimate for any social formula. But these are exceptional cases. The artistic impulse is too deeply rooted in a social life, too widely expressive of a common humanity in range to admit of a purely individualistic interpretation. Again, there are certain art values, not absolute in the old metaphysical sense, but gained and established by social experience, which are a cultural possession not lightly to be thrown aside for the sake of individual caprice. Good manners are a similar possession on a lower plane. What is called good taste was a natural expression of the social life of the Periclean age: it shaped and upheld the work of the humblest craftsman, created a splendid tradition in tragedy, and showed itself in what the theatre-goer exacted of poet and actor alike. With us it is partly the form and spirit, partly the content of smaller groups. It is not as a rule sufficiently strong as a tradition or far reaching enough to stamp our art with what might be called a social excellence. Some socializing of art there is, but in default of an artistic tradition it is of a moral or political type, and does much harm to art. How much better to seek for something social and permanent in art itself, and to provide for individual genius a helpful discipline and an orientation in terms of what the past has yielded of a developing taste and a progressive mastery of art materials and methods!

TRADITION ASSISTS IN THE STABILIZING OF ART: In certain long established, conservative firms or banking houses and in certain noble families a traditional pride of standards and breeding [1] makes for solidarity and balance, and guards against lapses by the individual to lower standards than those of the group. There is a similar force at work in art. The erratic appearance and unstable nature of artistic genius are commonplace of observation. So is also, however, the fact that there is a stabilizing influence in cooperative effort and well established models and methods—as among Greek vase-painters and stone-cutters and medieval builders or silversmiths—in a sustaining and informing good taste; and in the recognition of craftsmanship and beauty in their relation to the past, and to the willingness to submit to its discipline and to move along the level of its achievement.

---

[1] In a modern German comedy (Sternheim, *Der Snob*) a nobleman is asked the hand of his daughter by a man who has not only gained millions by business enterprise but has in a surprisingly short time acquired the urbanity and sureness of manners that go with noble birth. The nobleman looks upon him with the deepest distrust—no weakness is apparent, but it must be there, he argues, for if it is not, what is to become of his pride of race if good breeding, which to him is the product of many generations of discipline, can be gained within a single lifetime.

REVOLT

THE GENESIS OF REVOLT

The will to non-conformity plays a small part in early social life. Economic welfare calls for collective action; unconscious imitation and social discipline favor conformity; and there are few sharply individual problems of living. With a rising tide of individualism comes the demand for free expression, the desire for the new, and a rebellious attitude toward what is old and insisted on by the group. The desire to set oneself apart from others and to express oneself freely is a natural and useful social development. So are a craving for novelty and a turning against the dictatorial and the mechanizing. If society is a living thing we must expect a sign of this, its life, in an inherent instability—a sloughing off and renewal of tissue, and either gradual or violent readjustments.

This is the genesis of revolt in art also. But there are many special problems. It matters little what nonconformist movement we are considering—Fielding's departure in the novel, the naturalistic drama in Germany and the naturalistic novel of the de Goncourts and Zola, impressionism and expressionism in painting, Wagner's music drama and Rodin's sculpture, imagism and free verse, secessionistic exhibitions, *art nouveau*—everywhere there is the same dissatisfaction with old materials and methods and mechanized aims, and an insistence on the right to see for oneself and to give form to that vision, no matter how sharp the clash with accepted standards. This is true always of the leaders of a radical movement in art. Their following is a mixed one, made up as it is of true disciples who seek to spread the new message, uncritical enthusiasts and iconoclasts, novelty-seekers, self-advertisers, and faddists who turn revolt into a cult of mannerisms and bad taste, and swing it back to mechanization.

THE USES OF REVOLT

REVOLT TENDS TO KEEP ART FROM BECOMING STEREO-OTYPED, MECHANICAL: Art over a long period shows clearly the waxing and waning of creative force, and the appearance and dissipating of fresh and original responses to the world. In ages when the great creative forces in art lie exhausted or quiescent after an outburst and a glorious bearing, a substitute is offered and accepted. The forms which the masters had hewn for themselves in inspired madness, often in conflict with the good taste of their times—for taste can kill art—become the desiccated formulas which sustain the mediocre, and satisfy an artist and a public who get their aesthetic impressions at second hand and never test them for the life that is not in them. The result is mechanization. Certain subjects become stock-in-trade; tradition, the parrot-talk of art schools; words and phrases are given a poetic gilding and are carried from one poem over into another; verse-forms and sculptural and pictorial conventions give a sameness and a mechanical quality to art which are worse than the worst alexandrine-chopping or the worst pseudo-classical drama.

At such a time revolt is like a life-giving wind. It clears away and fructifies. A new spirit arises and brings with it a critical attitude toward formulas. The desire to see for oneself is paralleled by the effort to make each work of art mean something by and for itself.

REVOLT TAPS NEW RESOURCES FOR ART: There is danger to art in the belief that everything worth doing has been done and that there are no promising departures possible either in subject-matter or technique. To counteract this a new rebellious, experimental spirit is needed—a spirit not content to borrow its subjects from the past and to learn by rote a technique that stands in no living relation to the present or the future. Meunier, Pennell, Sandburg, and others have done artistic justice to an industrial age which Ruskin saw approaching and could not understand; architecture has gone new ways; modern music has smashed through classical formulas; the drama and the novel have aimed at and gained new effects.

The experimentalist must risk wasting our time and his —the very nature of his work brings that with it; he should not, however, increase the risk by seeking novelty at all costs. The old is not to be condemned simply because it is old, and the new is not its own justification. There is in all radical art movements a wide margin of the worthless. Responsible for it are vanity, a childish fractiousness, and a lack of disciplined effort and aim. But the experimentalism is justified if it occasionally results in something new that is genuinely worthwhile, and if it gives new life and range to what is one of man's oldest and most distinctive achievements.

REVOLT ALLOWS THE EMERGENCE OF A SHARPLY PERSONAL ART: Both social and personal motifs are present in the creation and maintenance of art. Whenever art is traditional in its meanings and methods the social overbalances the personal. Revolt has the useful part of righting the balance. In its origins it reflects the individual's unwillingness to accept uncritically what is socially current and accredited. It is a personal, creative eruption. Great rebels—Wagner, Rodin, Walt Whitman, Nietzsche, Bernard Shaw, Van Gogh, Cézanne—refuse to compromise: they put into their art whatever of creative pressure, force of conviction, sincerity of purpose, and original technique their personalities can command. Theirs is not the fault if little minds ape their ways and reduce them to a rigmarole, or if rebels flaunt selves which are not worth expressing. The right to revolt is a dangerous one, but in spite of its frequent misuses it is a right that ought to be exercised in the interests of a strongly personal art.

The story, then, of art is one of tradition and revolt: of the interplay of discipline and creative freedom; of the steadying processes of elaboration and social mastery, broken into and saved from a deadly mechanization by the force of individual artists who are not afraid of new paths of aim and technique, and who save themselves from caprice by the weight, bulk, and masterfulness of their artistic genius.

THE RELATION OF ART TO LIFE

If much is to be made of this problem its terms must be understood. By life is here meant: (1) purposive activities on the part of man—instincts, habits, preferences, value-settings; (2) the general process of adjustment and modification by means of which individual and race maintain themselves; (3) the world-process—as read by man—in its changes and their laws, its ups and downs of health and decay, and its rhythmic ebb and tide.

Among the many purposive activities of man there are certain ones roughly grouped as aesthetic and held to find their full expression in art. Art is seen to range from the intensely personal creativeness shown in a lyric or a symphony to communal, cooperative or socially inspired creative work; such as building churches, embellishing cities; taking part in tribal dances and chants, or giving touches of beauty and artistic value to dress, gear, and furniture.

The problem is to discover: (1) the relations, friendly or hostile, that exist between aesthetic interests and the other great human interests; (2) how art is to be viewed biologically, in terms of general human adjustments; (3) to what extent an aesthetic reading can be given to the world-process, or Cosmos.

AESTHETIC AND NON-AESTHETIC INTERESTS

The chief non-aesthetic activities whose self-expression affects art in one way or another and whose claims are to be weighed are: practical interests, science, morality, and religion.

Certain of the relations between aesthetic and practical activities were traced in the chapters on The Origins of Art, The Dance, and The Aesthetic Response. There it was shown how through a process of indirection the interest shifts from the definitely useful thing to free, self-expressive satisfactions to be had in its making; and from the large relational readings of both practical life and science to a contemplative, isolating, and circumscribed concern with what is being or has been artistically created. The contemplative attitude is not to be understood as utterly passive—a sort of day-dreaming—. The motor quality is present in the shaping which yields artistic form, and present also in the shaper's empathetic and sympathetic response to his work. But all these motor activities move, as they do not in practical life, within the circle of a world of semblance; a circle which reveals a strong centrifugal force drawing art away from the practical world and from the consciousness of self in its ordinary relations of purpose and of pleasure. The aesthetic response was interpreted as a process of impoverishing and enriching:—a flattening of the thing to the shape, or image; and a passing from the image to an organized form, which means a form enriched by inner relationships of line, color, sound, rhythm, and pattern; and enriched also by the rendering of a self-expressive life which we feel to be our own at the very moment it stands over against us and invites us to an excursional understanding of its nature and complexities.

There is, however, another and more sharply pointed problem. What ought the relation to be between art and the other great human interests? There would be no question of adjusting rival claims if we had unlimited resources of energy, time, and money, and could express ourselves fully and without confusion in all five fields of values. Unfortunately, the resources are limited, so we are forced to consider whether their claims can be adjusted; on what terms there can be granted to each a free expressive life of its own; and how, in particular, art can be saved from a confused mixing of standards, and an intolerance which seeks to subject it to the alien control of utility, morality, and religion.

Nothing is gained by matching intolerances and insisting that art exists for art's sake, and is, therefore, not to be set within any larger scheme of values. There is something ingenuous and childlike about the belief that art can thus hold itself apart from a social life which has developed and must nourish it. In material and aim alike art is culturally conditioned and inspired. The individual artist who has sufficient strength of purpose to keep clear of the trivial and the merely precious and to gain a worthwhile vision, at variance with the commonly accepted, has the right to hold himself apart and to experiment. But even such art must be seen in cultural perspective. Nothing could be more strikingly individual than the work of Cézanne, Renoir, Pascin, Soutine, Rousseau, and Kisling, to be seen in the collection of the Barnes Foundation. Each has his own vision and his distinctive pictorial values. But looked at in the large their painting has its place within the traditions and revolts of nineteenth century art; is paralleled by similar experiments in poetry and music; and swings in line with spiritual impulses, tensions, and readjustments in the wider life of morality and religion.

The relations between science and art present no special difficulties or controversies. Science moves away from the picture thought of its slight beginnings to abstract terms, patient research work, relational thinking, and purely intellectual scaffolding. In its observations and experiments it comes close to the sense object—the color, form, and texture of a leaf or flower—; but its ultimate interest is in a relational scheme into which that object may be brought. In the scientist's use of hypothesis and generalization there is something of the creative imagination and intuitive vision of the artist; and his larger structures especially may show aesthetic virtues such as economy, harmony, articulated wealth of detail, and elegance.   The artist, in his turn, has much to gain from a responsiveness to science:—a responsiveness which allows him to make the scientific work of his age his own, and to find in its reshaped views of man and his world new problems and a new range of effects.   He must, however, guard against too abstract and too complete a rationalizing; nor must he move too far away from the interest in the sensuous as such, without which there can be no art.   His drama must not be merely a proposition worked to a triumphant Q. E. D.; his novel, not merely a *roman à thèse;* and he must remain within the circle of semblance which science is constantly breaking through and discrediting.   In this sense the aims and the technique of science and art are so dissimilar that if mankind were utterly and consistently scientific there would be no place for art, while there would still be a sort of general aesthetic self-expressiveness in the life and procedure of science.   But the very nature of this difference and the sharply specialized interests of both scientist and artist make actual confusion and bigoted interference, on one side or the other, a remote and infrequent chance.

The relations between morality and religion and art are more complex and controversial.   Throughout its history art has drawn for some of its material on the moral and religious experience of mankind; its task has often been the consecration of moral ideals, forms of worship, imaged deities, and aspirational needs.   From such tasks it need not suffer an aesthetic loss.   Some of the finest music is church music; much of the best architecture and sculpture is religious in origin and motive; the ideal moral content of the drama of Aeschylus and Sophocles is perfectly blended with splendor of language and artistic portrayal of character. If there is no such perfect blending in Dante and Milton, it is because there is too much theology in their religion. Art then need not suffer; and morality and religion may be the gainers. By a sympathetic response to art and a well considered use of its glorying in the sensuous, morality may become a little less narrow and unlovely, and religion a little less abstract and aloof.

There is, however, a difference, far reaching and leading to clashes. Art moves within a world of semblance; within that world it develops an artistic conscience selective of sound, colors, word images; and creatively organizing. It draws within that circle such of the materials of life as it can use. At this point there is an inherent antagonism between it and morality and religion. No moralist would be satisfied with a morality that was merely appearance and did not work its way into actual moral problems; no religionist would be content with a divinity that was not the cause of things, a real shaping influence in character, the incentive to a certain way of living, and the guarantor of a moral order.

Again, the principle of selection is different. There is no denying that Aeschylus had a deeply religious mind, and that to him Greek mythology was intensely real. In his case selection and reinterpretation are not at variance with the interests of morality and religion: his Zeus moves on a higher moral plane and is a worthier object of worship than the earlier Zeus. But he is also a Zeus of infinitely greater imaginative appeal; and it is there that the real secret and value to art of the selection lies. Raphael chose religious subjects, but the aesthetic meaning of his painting is in delicacy of line and persuasive color harmonies. When Rodin contends that every great artist is religious he is merely referring to what the Germans call *Weltgefühle*, cosmic emotions and imaginings, through which a work of art is given reach, intensity, and volume for the imagination. His own world image, in terms of cosmic stress and urgency, reflects nothing but the condition on which he can satisfy his sculptural genius; it has no other meaning for him but that; and is in no sense put forward as an only true, universal religion.

Morality and religion do not employ such a principle of selection. Interested as they are in the reality of the good and the divine, they are forced into an intolerance of evil. They are restrictive, disciplinary, and distrustful of the body and its impulses. Only if it could be shown that moral evils were less capable of being put into organized form and were of smaller imaginative value than the good, could a conflict between art and morality and religion be avoided. But that cannot be done. Rabelais in his farce; Congreve in comedy; Matisse in painting; Jeffers in his poetry; Strindberg, Wedekind, and Werfel in their trage-dies give the gross, the misshapen, the morally questionable, and redeem it by nothing but lavish genius, brilliant organi-zation, wit, and imaginative power. In Werfel's *Bocks-gesang* there is a scene which must be unendurable to the moralist and the religionist. It is damnable in its perver-sion of values—of ceremonies and ideals. Release the Beast! Worship the Beast in Man! is the cry that rolls with religious fervor across the stage. This scene, soul-shaking in its starkness, is one of the most powerful and compelling scenes in all modern drama.

How are morality and religion to defend themselves when art, going its own way, sets itself at variance with their established values? Censorship is the weapon they employ. Censorship is an attempt to become morally selective of the types of art to be encouraged and those to be suppressed. Its past attempts to control art in the interests of morality have shown much to its discredit; its record is one of almost incredible stupidity and intolerance.   But even that record does not allow us to throw aside censorship without further thought.   Each of the great human interests has a legitimate and necessary place in a complete life; each is entitled to strike blows in its own defence.   When art in its concrete effects becomes demoralizing and dangerous to the common good, a society intent on welfare has the right to seek its suppression.   But—and this is where the real difficulty and danger of censorship lie—(1) it must not allow itself the confusion of holding that all immoral and socially destructive art is therefore artistically bad; (2) it must not assume too readily that man has not the right to make himself imaginatively at home within the immoral; (3) it must be critical of its moral and religious formulas; not too ready with a moral extinguisher for every little flame that does not burn to its liking; and broadminded enough to allow a full, assertive life to all large human interests.

There is not much to choose between the carping moralist, the religious fanatic, and the petty aesthete.   Each is a special pleader, unfairly pushing his own claims and wrecking a broad and balanced life in the process.   They are alike too bigoted to see the need of having all five interests creatively active and mutually responsive in a life which cannot be without conflicts—practical life, science, morality, religion, and art being differently conditioned and aimed, but which can and ought to be lived in a large and tolerant spirit.

The Biological Function of Art

Human life maintains itself by a series of adjustments of a twofold nature:—*accommodation,* in the sense of making the most of actual conditions that confront the individual and the group; and *modification,* in the sense of an instinctive or rationalized selecting and manipulating by means of which what happens to man is swung in line with the needs of a strong, self-expressive, satisfactory life. Successful adjustment of this kind may be called life-efficiency, to mark it off from the narrower efficiency in the performance of narrow practical tasks.

It is natural to be curious about the place art has in such a general adjustment. Art is one of the oldest activities of man; it is constantly created and persistently enjoyed; it costs effort and brings returns; it appears at all cultural levels, the highest as well as the lowest; and it seems to be bound up in many ways with the existence, the welfare, and the meaning of social life.

Art in early group life—and to a lesser degree in modern life—is in close dependence on certain social tasks. War songs, rowing refrains, mimetic dances have their tribal uses; so have the ballad, commemorative and ceremonial painting, the prayer rug, the carved totem pole, the fetish, and the shrine. The uses and forms of art differ in different localities. Such ethnological variations are not our present concern; our question is a general biological one. War, love, food, collective ways of feeling and acting, magic, an instinctive search for health and vigor—one and all are the great forces and influences of early life. They set problems and offer solutions in the business of self-preservation. Art, in reflecting and serving them, serves life-efficiency as well. Thus war dances develop and give direction and efficiency to a war spirit; gymnastic dances supply physical training; songs facilitate the work of the group; tribal symbols, ceremonies, and places of worship give point and concreteness to a common life; love charms and tokens have their uses; the magic of amulets and the bid for rain or food by means of incantations, childlike and ineffective as they are, reflect ideas of economic ill-faring and well-faring, and an economically inspired art.

All this is fairly obvious and offers no difficulties. The crux of the problem appears when we inquire into the general biological usefulness of (1) certain aesthetic activities and preferences which go beyond social uses and are often not expressed in and through what is called art; and (2) art as an independent interest and structure.

(1') It has been shown that there is an interest in what might be called artistic shaping and ornamentation when there is no practical need of such things. Symmetry is sought in a paddle or a drinking cup, and form in a dance, for their own sakes. An aesthetic surplus, it seems! Much of this apparent surplus is beyond the field of art. What is called form in tennis—a compound of smoothness, grace, and elegance in the stroking—is not a necessary condition of efficiency; it often has the appearance of a luxury practised and enjoyed as such. This is true also of an elegantly solved chess problem and of a decoratively phrased gesture or carriage of the body.

(2') Again, art has achieved a mode of independence, with a domain, problems, and values of its own. It is often practised in an intensely individual way; it is neglectful of the useful, and voluntarily assumes great life efficiency hazards. Loyalty to their vision counts for more with artists than does making a living. Thus Soutine smeared his paint on thickly when he had every economic motive for using it sparingly.

With regard to (1) it may be said that an artistic interest in processes and a surplus of creative effort and enjoyment over and above the utility value of objects are not so much of a luxury as they appear to be. Not only do they make work less irksome but they assist in the cultural development of man by helping create a world which bears the stamp of his spirit, and which allows him free and pleasurable self-expression even when purposes are pointed and practical demands are insistent. Again, "form" in non-aesthetic activities at times, at least, means the easy coordination and mastery of effort which tend to make efficient performance the rule rather than the exception. But even when it has no such usefulness, it is far from being unjustified. There is no reason to believe that a life lived lavishly and decoratively is not the best life for man. Human nature craves a certain amount of leisurely and even wasteful living, of disengaged responses, of variety and fulness of satisfaction; and, from the teleological point of view at least, the process of life itself is loose, leisurely, wasteful,—giving in its formlessness opportunities both to the practical technician who seeks to harness and master it, and to him who merely looks for artistic "form" in the living.

With regard to (2) it must be said that art, in its independent and self-sufficient creations and enjoyments, has a biological part to play. Its uses are the following:—it (a) gives nobility and distinction to man's leisure; (b) affords an escape from pre-occupation with self and from the oppressiveness of what is in a sheer sense material; (c) allows man to become self-expressive in measured patterns, and thus offers an attractive combination of spontaneity and discipline; (d) permits the senses to express themselves without grossness, and reason to function both broadly and concretely; (e) offers a release from tension; (f) is an enjoyable compound of the contemplative and the motor; (g) gives concreteness and variety to man's search for the perfect; (h) supplies a highly specialized, broadly significant type of satisfaction, without which life would tend to become drab, and pleasure would incline toward the gross, trivial, and meretricious.

To attempt to reduce these uses to a single formula would be a dangerous game, which I am content to leave to any one who is so obsessed with the idea of unity that his teleology becomes a theology of the monotheistic type.

The Universe a Work of Art?

Is there a will to beauty and artistic effectiveness in nature? Many of the details of nature suggest such a formative will. There is a great beauty of form and color in flowers; grandeur in a mountain range; intricacy and a pleasing variety of design in snow-crystals; a delicate blending of texture, color, and a pattern in a snake's skin. Art turns to this artistry of nature for many of its motifs.

But there remains the larger question whether the universe, not as detail but as system, is to be viewed as a single, self-complete, artistic achievement—a work of art.

Analogies may be drawn from morality and religion. Creative attempts have been made to interpret the cosmos as a moral order and as a system of divine purposes. God looked upon His work and saw that it was good. He had given the setting for the great drama of human destiny. Back of such moral and religious readings is the desire for guidance and justification; and they reflect an aspiring faith. But did God look upon His work and see it to be beautiful? Did He completely express Himself as an artist? The question seems a little strange: the practical motive for such an aesthetic unification of the world and the faith are lacking. If the attempt is made nevertheless, it will prove unsuccessful. Nature is on too vast a scale, and too intricate and disorderly in its ensemble to allow us to confront it as we might a painting or a piece of sculpture, in a discriminating and appreciative understanding of an artistic purpose unfalteringly worked out and complete. Such attempts usually end in either a vague, unsatisfying aesthetic mysticism or a religion of cosmic beauty, in dire need of all the faith that any religion can summon and build on.

It is a significant fact that when art becomes cosmic in its motives and ideals—as it often does in tragedy—it gains less from envisaging the universe as a transparent and harmonious system than from responding to it as something huge, fragmentary, semi-articulate, and questionable—something that rouses the imagination and perplexes the mind of man.

Such then are three of the most general problems of aesthetics. They have their appeal and their worth as problems. But they must not be allowed to draw us away from the concrete facts of art and its appreciation, and from the questions that spread fanlike from these facts. For it is here that a system of aesthetics must show its life and spirit: a life flexible and responsive, and a spirit—sympathetic, careful, keen, and open-eyed—as distrustful of a formula that is too sweeping as it is eager to correlate and to weave tentative intellectual patterns.

SOME NEWER DEVELOPMENTS

The last fifteen years have yielded interesting developments in life, in art, and in an appraising thought which seeks to lift life from its turmoil and art from its experiments.

The practical recovery from the war has been marked by political and economic unrest. There is nothing idyllic about the post-war consciousness. It is tense, disturbed, dramatic in its inner adjustments and its work. It exhibits changed social and moral values, and has launched high-powered business enterprises resulting in constructive achievement and a cycle of overproduction and depression. Life is becoming more and more a thing of tremendous energy, of large and complex proportions. The mere technique of living has been profoundly affected by new inventions and discoveries. For work and pleasure alike, the machine is becoming a more and more aggressively dominant force. A new temper and spirit are to be found in the new forms and patterns of social life. The problem of an effective and happy personal adjustment to what that life demands and expresses is proving a difficult and disturbing one.

Within this life-setting the art of the last decade has moved. At this point and that it has developed a new technique. Some of these innovations have come from new industrial processes and problems. Architecture has been affected by ambitious civic planning, dearth of city space, electrified railroads, new methods of girder construction and welding. Portrait painting is setting itself off from an ever more accurate and finer photography. The dance spectacle and the drama have been reshaped by new systems of lighting. Arts and crafts, furniture, interior fittings show an experimental use of aluminum, chromium, and other processed metals. The moving picture technique has influenced the novel and the drama. Other innovations reflect interests growing directly out of the new forms and conditions of life. Such are: an interest in machinery— a keen enjoyment of force and movement—a concern with social groups and their struggles.

Experiments in technique, however, are only part of the story. Art changes in spirit as well—in point of view and liking, in the way it cuts across or drifts with the currents of the time. New movements and programs appear. Of these, one of the most striking has been called post-expressionism.

Of no less interest are thought-appraisals of art. Within the last ten years modernist art seems to have come into its own. The "crazy men" of the eighties are in the Louvre and the Luxembourg. The new music has established itself within the symphony concert. Radical experiments in architecture have been accepted. Bourdelle and Mestrovic have scored in commemorative sculpture—the one by his *Vierge d'Alsace*, the other by his Chapel at Cavtat. Elkan has been commissioned to create the great liberation monument on the Rhine. Radical departures from traditional patterns in the drama and the epic—*Strange Interlude* and *John Brown's Body*—have been popular successes. The Kronprinzen Palais in Berlin contains not only Van Goghs and Renoirs but paintings and sculptures by Marc, Nolde, Dix, Macke, Feininger, Kolbe, and Lehmbruck. The directors of small municipal museums throughout Germany show faith in even the newest art. The loan collections of the Museum of Modern Art in New York have been satisfying a genuine interest. Much money is spent by collectors on modernist painting. The money spent, not only for

Cézannes, Pascins, Modiglianis, Derains but for American artists like Marin, Benton, Rockwell Kent and others, reflects a confident, forward-looking attitude toward art. Art training in schools is becoming less conservative and dogmatic.

Such revaluation has forced into the open various thought-appraisals, friendly or hostile, of this art and its experiments, and of the nature, temper, and tone of the age that has produced and seems now to be accepting it. Of the many attempts to think the problem through, that which has called itself humanism is of special interest. It champions a view of life and art that is hostile to all but a very little of what life has been and what art has given within the last thirty years. In it are embodied certain valid preferences—preferences appearing even in modernist art. But because of an insensitiveness to anything without the credentials of tradition these preferences have been twisted into a very questionable philosophy of value.

The confines of a single chapter are such that all that can be given is a sketchy and fragmentary picture of innovations—of technique, spirit, and aim—in the several arts, and a critical estimate of humanism as a type, and a dangerous one, of thought-appraisal of art.

INNOVATIONS IN ART

ARCHITECTURE

The architecture of the day is not traditionally-minded. It has had forced upon it new problems and types of building—the skyscraper, the huge modern hotel, department stores, warehouses, signal towers, fillingstations, factories, large scale banks. For these new uses it has sought effective designs. Responsive to new conditions and aware of new resources, it borrows little from the past—classical, Gothic, renaissance, baroque—but is evolving styles of its own. It gives the impression of being an art on the move, for it has not been halted even by its own immediate past. In design and spirit the skyscraper of today has advanced far beyond the Woolworth Building, an example of modernism in 1911. The giraffe-like design of this building displeases.

The experimental reaching out and reshaping goes beyond what a new industrial life demands. It shows a desire for a new expressiveness and for original decorative effects. The spherical houses in Dresden, the new apartment house development in Amsterdam, windowless buildings, Einstein's observatory near Berlin, laborers' dwellings at the Hook of Holland all show a bold departure from the usual and the accepted. So do the designs for the next World's Fair in Chicago. At times, strange materials are used for walls—bronze, heavy plate glass, leaded pieces of glass in combination with colored stucco. Gilded or silvered metal, sheeted copper, tile and inlays, stones of different color are worked into the wall surfaces. Not all such experiments are happy. The effect, in exteriors and interiors alike, is often bizarre and garish. Mass and the large lines of design are lost. Their place cannot be taken by striking and exotic ornamentation, even if the ornament is not stuck on but is made an integral part of the building.

At one point, however, the newer architecture has found its way to solid and original achievement—in the skyscraper, whether office building, hotel or cathedral of learning.

The older type of tall building was with few exceptions horizontal in its design and patterning. No matter to what number of stories it was carried, it was layer upon layer of rows of windows with separating wall spaces. Near the top was a heavy cornice. The horizontal sky-line was awkwardly broken and reestablished by the rectangle of the elevator shaft. The walls were either uninterestingly smooth or they were loaded with heavy window facings and extraneous sculptural ornament. The many windows—gaps riddling the walls in rows—gave annoyingly the impression of the mechanical and the useful.

The newer type is vertical in its spirit and accents, and of a strong simplicity of design. Narrow rectangles of stone or concrete and sunk three-quarters or more into the very mass of the building are carried from the bottom to the top, breaking the horizontal pattern of the windows and leading the eye irresistibly and directly to heights. Cornices have either disappeared or are used as an unobtrusive horizontal motif. The horizontal sky-line is replaced by verticals of different lengths inviting the eye and the imagination to further climbing. The building at 1616 Walnut Street, the Integrity Building, the Sun Building, all in Philadelphia, the Empire State Building, and the News Building in New York and the University of Pittsburgh may serve as illustrations. When set-backs are used—building rules sometimes make them necessary—and the building rises in receding plateaus, the sense of direct climbing is even stronger. The older building we knew to be tall. This newer type gives us a direct visual and kinetic experience of height. When a triple arrangement is called for, as in the New York Telephone Building, the modern architect combines in a very effective way bilateral symmetry with verticality. The central mass rises like a towering figure with a mantle of stone falling in simple vertical folds on either side. The eye moves questingly up and restfully down. The Chrysler Building, terraced and ending in the verticals and the long spear point of the tower, is a fine example of ambitious building.

Simplicity marks detail as well as design. The eye is not to be distracted from the upsweep of walls. The walls are not to be overlaid with ornament—the half-rounding of Ionian pillars and their florid capitals, sculptures in the round, filigree stone work, and chiseled patterns. They are felt directly in their varied life of finely proportioned spacing. In the first thirty feet or so of their height there is some decorative elaboration—huge entrances of plate glass and bronze, plaques of very flat relief, flutings, rosettes, squares in color. Beyond this the height of the building is given over to its upthrust. Sculptural detail would be ineffective in any case. A clear-cut simplicity rules; and the few decorative details, minor vertical lengths touched with bronze, inserts, and the like serve the spirit and design of the building. The Guaranty Trust Building, the Drake Apartments, the University Club, the Fidelity Philadelphia Trust Building exhibit variants in the aesthetic reshaping of height and mass and in a new interest in simple design. They contrast sharply with the horizontal pattern and decorative fussiness of the Bellevue Stratford Hotel. Often beauty and distinction are being gained by fine proportions and simple, severely subordinated decorative touches. The New York Bonwit Teller Store may serve as an illustration.

Architecture has become definitely creative under new conditions and in response to the many demands made upon it by the city and its business life. It is evolving new forms and is using materials whose expressiveness, singly or in combination, it has not yet mastered. Naturally it often goes astray. Some restaurants and store fronts are little else than garish and ill-sorted advertisements. A few of the cheaper restaurants show all the confused color and obtrusiveness of a cafeteria counter. At its best, however, this new architecture is as disciplined as it is original, as true to beauty as it is to force. It is convincingly simple in its life, and of life there is in it abundance. Old labels are misleading, but it may be called a new classicism—a classicism in which is held the romance of industrial life. Similar movements toward the direct, the simple, the clear-cut may be traced in the newer sculpture and painting.

SCULPTURE

Sculpture has moved away from Rodin's subtle, impressionistic light and shade, his technique of rough surface modeling, the tension and unrest of his spirit, and the excessive dramatic and literary quality of much of his work. Something of his massiveness and power has been caught up in a new spirit of repose by Maillol, who is as far removed from the easy elegance of Praxiteles as he is from the intensity of Michelangelo or the dramatic unquietness of Bernini. The nature of the movement appears in the contrast between Bourdelle's *Hercules the Archer* in the Luxembourg and his *Vièrge d'Alsace*, or between Rodin's *Hell Gate* and Mestrovic's Chapel at Cavtat. Epstein's roughened surfaces, strongly reminiscent of Rodin, are not in the line of development. His *Conrad* may be contrasted with Mestrovic's *Wilson*.

Something of a remote past lives in this sculpture. The simple massive planes of Elkan suggest Egypt, the stylized treatment of hair and dress in Mestrovic at times recalls Assyria, at others, early Greek reliefs. There is more than a hint of archaic spirit in Kolbe's *Adagio* and his bust of a young girl. But he is essentially modern—one phase, that of directness and repose, of that complex modern spirit whose violent and tortured moments Rodin has caught.

The slow gaining of a new technique and a new sculptural form may be seen in passing from Mestrovic's equestrian statue of *Kraljevic Marko*, to his *Mother* and then to the figures of *Virgin and Child* and of *St. Rochus* in the Chapel or the *Portrait of Mme. Banaz*. In the statue of Marko there is something very like Rodin's sense of volume and *exagération des formes* in the massive horse and the treatment of the foot of the rider. But even here the feel of the modeled surfaces is different. In the fingers of the *Child* and the toes of the *Virgin* and the nose-bridge of both there is still distortion, but it is a formalized rather than an expressive distortion.   A new simple design of parallel planes has been gained.   The folds of the dress in his *Mother* have something of the severity and stiffness of early Greek sculpture.   In his later works there are a few free curves, drawing the eye sharply by contrast to long smooth surfaces. The smoothness of these surfaces is far removed from the lifeless, academic smoothness Rodin rebelled against.

The contrast between Kolbe's *Dancer* and his *Adagio* reveals much of the spirit and aim of these newer sculptors. The *Dancer* is stone turned to rhythmic flesh.   *Adagio* is a human figure, a mood, a slow movement turned into a dream of stone in repose.   There is a similar contrast between Maillol's *Etude de Nu* and *Young Runner* and his *Sitting Woman* or *La Pensée*.

A calm strength and a direct, simple design seem to speak a language of weight in this newer sculpture.   Movement and psychic interest at first glance seem to be excluded by the simplicity or crushed by the massive pattern.   But they are both there.   Kolbe's *Dancer* is rhythmically alive.   The sorrows of all war mothers speak within the monumental design of Elkan's *Heldenklage* with a passionate directness beyond the reach of Rodin's more dramatic figures.

Another, and less promising movement in sculpture is that which stems from cubism and ends in abstract sculpture. Lipschutz and Archipenko have at times broken up the human body and reassembled it as a frankly geometrical design of related plates.   Some of Archipenko's silver statuettes stop short of this—they are slightly reshaped bodies with no detail, often with legs cut off at the knee and with hollow, non-representational head-moulds.   An extreme example of abstract sculpture is Brancusi's *Flight of a Bird*. Experiments have been made in glass, aluminum and various alloys.   There is one amazing fad—of an ingenious wiring of thin strips of metal—an ear, a nose in profile, the curve of a hand.   In this way something like the allusive dependent quality of a sketch is gained, but sculptural form dissolves in thin air.

Commemorative sculpture, following the lead of Rodin, has moved away from the illustrative and the banal.   Like Rodin's it is expressive, but it often seeks something quieter, simpler, less dramatic.   In its sparing use of anything decorative and in the massive simplicity of its design it is closer to Egyptian than to Greek art.   In the spirit in which it sees its task and in the technique through which that task is mastered, the newer commemorative sculpture is less personal, more other-minded, more objective than the sculpture of Rodin.

There is renewed interest in low relief.   Mestrovic has worked in it.   Architectural sculpture has turned to it for something that will harmonize with the flat upthrust of high buildings.

PAINTING

It is not difficult to trace the main line of the modernist movement in painting back to Cézanne and Van Gogh, two original painters who rebelled against academic methods and ideals and sought something deeper and firmer than impressionistic painting.   Against the structurelessness and the shimmering surface play of light and color of the impressionists, Cézanne set design built of color and firmly put into deep space; and Van Gogh set an intensely personal type of painting—violent, forceful, searching, psychical, loose and rough in texture, and structurally firm.   It is less easy to appraise the influence these men had on others, to relate their work to such minor developments as cubism and futurism, and to discover at what points in the wide and varied front of expressionistic painting the drive of their spirit and their new discipline is to be felt.

The painting of the last fifteen years of the nineteenth

KIDD, CHRYSALIS

and the first twenty years of the twentieth century showed a dominance of Cézanne quite as strong as that of Rodin in the sculpture of the period. Other models, Renoir, Picasso, Matisse, were followed along the less used paths. It is, however, unjust to speak only of imitation. These modernist painters were inspired, and not always wisely; but they were creative as well. One who is not prejudiced must be impressed with the freshness, the vigor, and the originality of much of American painting and must watch with keen interest the burst of creativeness in painting throughout Europe.

One formula will not hold the many ways of interpreting and shaping. This painting may be called dynamic, personally-minded, and structure-minded. Its origin in its own present—a world of tensed complexities—accounts for its many divergent methods and ideals. Its double origin in the past—in the calm building power of Cézanne with life behind it and in the intense force and mysticism of Van Gogh projected into a simple design—accounts for conflicts within it.

About 1920 something strange happened. Picasso changed his style. He had often done so, it is true, being an experimenter throughout his career. But painters who had not been close to anything he ever did—the Italian futurists, Carra and Severini—changed theirs in the same direction. Chirico, Oppi, Derain, Schrimpf, Kisling, Metzinger and others were painting in a way that set new problems to interpretation. Jugo-slav and Czechoslovakian landscape painters were giving nature a new structure and a new tone.

The difference inherent in this new development can be immediately felt. There remains the problem of what it means to be within the general modernist movement.

Various phrases and labels were used by artists who attempted to interpret what they were doing in paint. Valori

plastici, verism, constructivism, neo-classicism are samples.
In 1925 Franz Roh in a book, *Nach-Expressionismus*,
sought to give in comprehensive perspective a picture of the
new movement.   He offers on opposite pages seven contrasted pairs of expressionistic and post-expressionistic renderings of similar subjects.   The lesson to the eye is direct
and convincing—it is added to in the many illustrations
that follow.   Label and text indicate that Roh regards the
movement as a departure from expressionism.   It is neither
a return to the old nor a destructive revolt.   Sharply as it
sets itself against certain qualities of expressionistic painting and strongly as it champions certain neglected values,
it carries within itself and into its experiments something
the older modernism alone could give.   Its painters may
call themselves neo-classicists or magical realists, in either
case it is the qualifying term that counts.

Roh's table of contrasts is worth studying.

Expressionism	Post-expressionism
Ecstatic objects	Sober, matter-of-fact objects
Religious	Not religious
Suppressing objects	Clearly marking objects
Inclined to be rhythmical	Representational
Wild	Severe, puritanical
Dynamic	Static
Loud	Quiet
Sketchy	Carrying through to detail
Near Image	Near Image + Distance Image
Moving toward the front	Receding
Large shapes	Large shapes with much detail
Monumental	Of the type of the miniature
Warm	Cool or cold
Heavily applied paint	Thinly applied paint
Roughening	Smoothing
Like rough stone	Like polished metal
Revealing technique	Hiding technique

Expressive distortion of objects	Harmonious purification of objects
Diagonal and acute-angled	Right-angled, paralleling the frame
Working against the edges	Firmly established within the edges
Primitive, spontaneous	Cultured

Part of this contrast concerns matters of technique—the passing from loose, rough texture to something thinly and smoothly painted—from design diagonal to the frame to design paralleling it—from schematic rendering to detail painting. Part of it concerns the objects painted. Still another marks a difference in spirit. The passionate, mobile, distorting vision and spirit of expressionism is put against the calm, static, faithful vision and spirit of post-expressionism.

An inspection of the left side of the table of contrasts and a careful reading of the text show Roh to have built his view of expressionism on an energism, a mysticism, a preference for mobile color even in the space-values of backgrounds and a distortion which are not to be found in all its types. His narrow interpretation fits the painting of Van Gogh, Marc, Nolde, Delaunay, Soutine, Benton, Macke, Kandinsky. It fits also the sculpture of Rodin, the poetry of Vachel Lindsay, Sandburg, and Jeffers, and the drama of O'Neill, Werfel, and Hasenclever. The contrast he sets up then becomes convincing. But expressionism may be broadly interpreted as including firmness and orderliness, as in Cézanne or Derain, or as loyalty to the spirit of an object to be caught through simplifying and distorting its form. From this point of view the new development is reduced to a compensatory movement within expressionism.

Post-expressionists differ greatly in technique and in their way of interpreting and shaping. Picasso, Carra, Schrimpf, Kisling, show a liking for large, static, plastically rendered bodies with little or no detail. Yet Schrimpf in his still life pictures gives an assortment of common objects—a vase of flowers, a cup, a book, the back of a chair, a pitcher—with an essential line and mass likeness, and gains a factual quality unlike any Cézanne. Chirico puts into his art an architecturally inspired, geometrical symbolism. Léger is a constructivist, he builds up a design from parts of machinery. His tubes have the smoothness and visual cleanness, if not the dull gleam, of a gun-barrel. Derain uses trees to give a skeletonized calm to his landscapes. Huber renders the minutest details of leaf and flower. Scholz's factual rendering of cactuses and Dix's carefully presented satiric types are examples of verism. In their methods of working, some of these painters go straight to nature and copy, others take from nature only the stimulus of a theme and arrangement and then build up their design in a free creative mood. Of the value of post-expressionism there can be no doubt. Much of the art from which it turned paid too high a price for onesidedness. Nolde's religious pictures are nightmares, Kandinsky sought to move painting over too far toward music. In Chagall, the futurists, and cubists the world of objects became chaotic or flew into bits. Rodin overweighted much of his sculpture with soul torture and cosmic yearning. Mobile color became disturbing and poetry was often high-pitched and harrowing in its tenseness. The mysticism became nebular, the ecstasy fantastic.

Many who admit the stimulating quality and the forcefulness of such violent art are heard to say, "this is not an art to live with." What they crave is something calm and static—something to rest in. This is a valid desire even within the modernist mood. Post-expressionism meets this desire with an art that is not an art of escape, but is courageously expressive and truly modern. Only a few of those who utter such a remark could come to rest in the deep calm of post-expressionism, for it is a calm into which has been

carried something of the depth, the strength, and the enterprise of expressionism in the narrower sense.   The still,
self-contained art of a Derain, of Kolbe's *Adagio*, of Mestrovic's *Mother* or his *Angels* in the Chapel at Cavtat, of
Bourdelle's *Vierge d'Alsace* of Chapin's *Aline McMahon*—
corrective of the tempestuous art of Rodin, Van Gogh, and
Nolde—sets problems quite as difficult to an understanding lover of cheap peace at any price.   Nor would Léger or
L'Hôte puzzle him less than Kandinsky or Soutine.

Two directions found within this new movement repay
somewhat closer study.   One is toward what has been called
a magic realism or naturalism, the other is toward neo-
classicism.

These painters are naturalists in the sense that they move
art close to the common object, which they give faithfully
in its form and often in its detail.   Their conception of
nature is one not of processes, but of a static assemblage of
objects.   This view is itself an imaginative reshaping of
what life gives.   They do not break up an object for the
sake of an abstract design, as the cubists did, nor do they
violently distort it, as the energists often did, for the sake
of something spiritual, fantastic or forceful.   Even when
they paint an exotic landscape they give it a curiously naive,
matter-of-fact touch.   They are like Rousseau *le douanier*
in this.   The closeness of their art to a world of common
objects they use as a challenge to keep to the line that
separates painting from photography.   In their use of large
color areas, their flat oil cloth-like surfaces, their sharp outlines and neglect of atmospheric perspective they are less
close to nature as a visual experience than the impressionists
were.   The ribbed trees of Derain or Alix are no more
photographically true than the feathery trees of Renoir.
The *Wild Horses* of Schrimpf are quite as much a distortion
as the *Blue Horses* or the *Deer* of Marc.   But the animal
pictures of Marc, an expressionist, reveal a mystic, rhythmic

conception of nature in sharp contrast to the post-expressionist's preference for sharp, still, finite effects.

Some are naturalists of a different type.   Grosz and Dix give to verism a Zolaesque turn.   They carry into art all that is misshapen and revolting—nudes grotesquely and terrifyingly ugly, the sensualist, houses of ill fame, capitalist and proletariat, the gross feeder and the industrial slave, the noise, suffocating nearness, and dirt of city life.   Nothing is too unsavory for an art that confesses to the belief that "man is a beast."   But this verism diverges from the naturalism of Zola at three points.   What idealism there is in it, is that of a communist Utopia.   In its matter-of-fact pictures of life and its symbolism it reaches a demonism of the ugly and the perverse that gives a new stimulus to the imagination.   Zola was unimaginative in this sense.   In its technique it is far from the structurelessness of Zola—it shows the same sharp lines and flat clear hard craftsmanship, the seizure of objects in their wholeness, and simple sense of structure that mark other variants of post-expressionism.

It is an abrupt change from the naturalism of Grosz and Dix to the neo-classicist trend of post-expressionism.   The French Revolution had its Roman motifs, and the modern Fascist warms himself at the glories of Rome and seeks the sterner Roman virtues.   The Germans, from Winckelmann to Goethe, when in search of inspiration, set their steps toward Italy.   Chirico puts into his pictures Roman buildings, columns, Pompeian fresco painting.   Mense and others give southern landscapes in a severe, restrained style.   What matters, however, is not these stage properties and memories of a classical past, but a spirit and form expressive of a classicist temper and preference within modern life.   The classicist moves his gods within his sense world, lives close to that world, and sees it in a clear light in large smooth outlines and quiet edges.   He creates and enjoys an art that is simple, disciplined, restrained, at ease within a finite world and loyal to what of sharp separateness of objects it contains. In this sense the *Hermes* of Praxiteles, the *Marat* of David, and the still life pictures of Chardin are classicist. A very large part of Greek art cannot be contained in this formula. But it is clear that classicism reflects human preferences and desires of value to art, and that it has a valid·place within the expressiveness of any age. To interpret our age solely in terms of social tensions, disruptive forces, energy, movement, noise, and psychic chaos, as some of the expressionists did, is to understand it incompletely. Again, to regard post-expressionism as an art of escape, and nothing else, is to read it falsely. It is a turning away from· mysticism, lyrical or dramatic, and from violence done to the world of natural objects. It sets itself against preoccupation with the cosmos and the self. It is to be regarded as a movement expressive of certain phases and values of our age less obvious than its turbulent energy. Science and machinery are excellent antidotes to an introvert temper and *Weltschmerz*. But they also contain new classical motifs. Just because machinery is naturally thought of in terms of function and movement it offers the interesting aesthetic problem of seeing it directly in repose and in the smooth, simple, clear-cut lines of a design.

Painting then in its chief new development joins the newer architecture and sculpture in a calm simplicity of temper and design. That aesthetic readjustment has as yet not reached the epic, the novel, and the drama.

EPIC POETRY

The situation in lyrical poetry has remained unchanged in the main. Sandburg, Frost, Vachel Lindsay, Robinson have continued true to their styles and patterns. There is one change in the bulk—less free verse is written and severe verse-forms such as the sonnet are favored. Rhyme is used more frequently.

Of the longer poems, some, like those of Masefield, show a very direct interest in narrative and vivid description; others, like those of Jeffers, are psychic and dramatic. Robinson's *Tristram* is the reshaping of an old story. Lola Ridge's *Firehead* is a medley of lyrical, dramatic, and epic moods. There are satiric and expressive poems, long and fragmentary, of the modern scene and temper.

Very little of this comes within the meaning of epic poetry. Of the epic in its truest sense there is only one example— Benét's *John Brown's Body*. This is so wide-flung in ambition and brilliant in achievement, so American and so modern, so epic in temper and so far from epic traditions that it offers many aesthetic problems of interest.

The epic is either *Volksepos* or *Kunstepos*. The former spontaneously grows out of the life and imagination of a people and slowly takes form from a mass of myths and legends. The *Iliad*, the *Nibelungenlied*, the *Chansons de Geste* are examples. The latter are single creations of an artist inspired by some great religious or national theme of the past. The *Aeneid, Jerusalem Delivered, Paradise Lost* are of this type.

In either case the traditional theme was something lofty, far-flung, and rousing—the loves and deeds of the gods, war and seafaring, the founding of cities, the deeds of Hercules or of the Argonauts, the crusades, the flinging back of the Moors. The traditional form was, like mural painting, a broad expanse of scene, narrative, and description; and set in it a single hero or heroic group. The traditional pattern was a homogeneous metre. The traditional spirit was naive, noble, and leisurely—a slow-breathing, wide-armed gathering in of the heroic and the romantic.

John Brown's Body is in many ways far from the traditional form and spirit of the epic.   This departure is not arbitrary—it is forced by the modern temper in its creative enterprise and search for new values.   The contrast must be felt in all its sharpness, and the new values sought and gained must be understood.   This can best be done by comparing *John Brown's Body* with the *Iliad*.

In the *Iliad* a single metre, the hexameter, is used.   It has amplitude and flexibility.   Narrative and description flow evenly in its slow smooth current.   Scene and time shift, but the flow is continuous.   The division into blocks of narrative, called books, is the work of an Alexandrian scholar.

John Brown's Body has many verse-patterns.   There are iambic lines, rhymed and unrhymed, mixed sequences, short trochees, long swinging dactylic lines, free verse, the prose of documents and despatches.   The arrangement is in eight books of irregular length, cut variously into short sections. The language used at times reaches the homeliest and crudest words.   The content held within the loose form has a wide range of scene, character and action—Connecticut and Georgia, the White House and the negro cabin, barrel-chested Jake Diefer and rat-eyed Shippy, dreams, visions, battles, bits of dialogue and thought, dandies and lovely ladies, the hanging of John Brown, troops on the march.

In choosing so wide a range of verse-pattern and language Benét has cut himself off from keeping his poem to one level.   There are strong contrasts in what Homer describes —Zeus hurling his thunderbolt, the misshapen Thersites, a chariot wheel or shield, a disembowelled fighter—but his verse acts like a plane which keeps the grain but gives a smooth surface.   In *John Brown's Body* [1] there is no such sliding smoothness.   Parts are left uneven.   Everything is allowed a stark separateness.   The range of this separateness can be given through three contrasted passages

[1] Copyright 1927–28, by Stephen Vincent Benét.

Hawky arrogant sons of anger
Who rode like devils and fought like cocks
And watched with an ineffable languor
Their spoilt youth tarnish a dicing-box.
The Cazenove boys and the Cotter brothers,
Pepperalls from Pepperall Ride,
Cummings and Crowls and a dozen others,
Every one with a name and a pride.
Sallow young dandies in shirts with ruffles,
Each could dance like a blowing feather,
And each had the voice that Georgia muffles
In the lazy honey of her May weather.

p. 44

It was stuffy at night in the cabins, stuffy but warm,
And smells are a matter of habit.   So, if the air
Was thick as black butter with the commingled smells
Of greens and fried fat and field-sweat and heavy sleep,
The walls were well chinked, the low roof kept out the rain.

p. 79

—and the shrill-edged bullet song
Beating down men and grain, while the sweaty fighters
Grunt as they ram their charges with blackened hands.

p. 293

The form in each case fits what it is meant to give, and
gives it with expressive directness and force.   A like expressionist motive is back of the wide content and its loose
structure.   For life, in war and peace, is a mad medley
of the important and the trivial, the sublime and ridiculous,
the picturesque and the drab, the noble and base—and each
of these moments has its right to express itself and its value
for art.

In both the *Iliad* and *John Brown's Body* the theme is
war.   In Homer the war-scene is a limited one—the walls
of Troy, the Greek ships and the plain of the Scamander
between.   The war is fought on three planes—the feuds and

partisanship of the gods, the glorious deeds and heroic words of men, and the suffering, in body and mind, that war brings in its wake. The war fought is direct and personal. It involves no great principle. Aristophanes cynically called it a brawl about a loose woman. It is more than that in Homer—a breach of hospitality is stressed, so is the decree of fate to which even the gods must bow.

John Brown's Body has as its theme the Civil War. Wide-flung in its scene, formless in its fighting, without climax and without centre, that war shows little but a loose time-pattern with shifting crises and heroisms. Benét puts this war in all its formlessness into his epic. It was a war involving a clash of types of culture and far-reaching principles. Its confused story is not one of personal gain and desire for glory. He has expressed this side of it, and has created an American epic. Two American epics are yet to be written—the story of the pioneer days and the making of a great industrial age. In *John Brown's Body* the former is hinted at in the various types of men and conditions that appear in the fighting, the latter is foreshadowed in the splendid symbolism at the close. In his epic the war is fought on four planes—the crisis of a nation—the straining muscles and deeds, heroic and unheroic, of men—the suffering of men and women—and the stray psychic reactions of thought and feeling of all caught in its toils. Such an interpretation of war means some sacrifice of the heroic, the romantic, and the picturesque, but it is a gain in true humanism. No one can deny in Homer the deep human quality of the lament of Achilles for Patrocles, of Hector's farewell to Andromache, of Priam's plea for the body of his son. But it is a humanism on broad, simple lines, and set to the heroic note. In Benét the figures of Lincoln and Grant are heroic, but he does not shrink from picturing the one in nightshirt and slippers and the other as a clerk weighing frozen hides. He breaks into the subconsciousness of his characters—the Black Horse troop waiting for battle, Judah P. Benjamin the Jew, Jack Ellyat and Curly Hatton on the march, Sally Dupré and Wingate dancing. Images, thoughts, feelings are caught in the eddies or drift along and mill about the edges of the stream of consciousness. This inner life is like the situations these characters find themselves in. The whole war is a milling about. There is confusion in its battles. It shifts men about, makes Grant and mars the old woman whom they sought to move out of range of a battle. Benét has done what does not lie within the purpose of the heroic epic—he has built war down into the inchoate mind and out into the life of all sorts and conditions of men. The sacrifice this incurs is worth making, for a new sensitiveness for what is broken, confused, inarticulate in human nature appears. Similar interests are discoverable in the modern drama and novel.

In the *Iliad* there is centralized interest. One year of the war is chosen, and the action moves in circles around Achilles and Hector. In *John Brown's Body* the interest is not centralized. No matter what character or group is in the centre of attention, there is always a strong centrifugal force moving our thought and imagination outward along this line or that.

The spirit in Homer is objective and traditional. War is accepted and described in a spirit that has nothing of the profound personal insight and sensitiveness to be found in Aeschylus. There are certain accepted group virtues—courage, loyalty, piety, self-control. There are broad human relationships and social rewards. At no point is there a searching critical appraisal of characters or events.

Such an attitude is impossible to the modern. Like O'Neill in the drama and Aldous Huxley in the novel, Benét is a thought-reagent. His pen-pictures of his characters —Lincoln, Lee, Grant, John Brown, Stuart, Ewell, Wingate, Ellyat, Cudjo are marvelously expressive. So are his descriptions of Bull Run, the Wilderness, and Gettysburg. But his mind never moves objectively and traditionally within this past. He reshapes imaginatively, comments, appraises, builds new thought-structures.

John Brown's Body is an epic on a grand scale and a fine achievement in American letters. Of the old epic it has retained little more than breadth of treatment and a lofty theme. From it it differs in its loose form, in its range, in its conception of human nature, and in its spirit. To debate whether it is better or worse is futile. All that need be said is that it is *other*, and this its otherness is of interest to the aesthetician because it reveals so clearly creative readjustments and new values in contemporary art. Like changes are to be found in the novel.

THE NOVEL

The novel is a flexible art form in which may be held one of many things—ideas, moods, images—adventure, romance or satire—interest in the social scene past or present—curiosity about the actions, motives, and feelings of men and women—dreams, observations, facts—scientific orientation and philosophical comment. It may be of many structural patterns, of many types, of many personal responses and shapings. Here lies the cause of some of the difficulties it presents to aesthetic analysis and appreciation. There is another obstacle: its content is not given on a direct visual plane and depth as in painting, but must be captured as an imagined world made accessible through the meaning of words.

The contemporary novel is in great part a standardized mass product. It rests on cheap printing and extensive advertising, and caters to a shallow popular demand. Society story, Wild West story, love romance, mystery story—it has its trite situations, cliché phrases, puppet characters, and uninspired mechanism.   It can be of little interest to the student of art forms who looks for something expressive of creative genius and for an honest, enterprising artistic conscience.

There are, however, novels of the latter kind.   Some of these achieve quality within the older traditions and patterns.   Galsworthy and Thomas Mann are leisurely and excellent in craftsmanship, urbane in spirit, wide-branched in structure, with a quiet orderliness of building.   Edith Wharton's art has amplitude and analytic subtlety; that of Willa Cather is compact, vivid, brilliant.   There are other novels, less close to tradition, which seek a new technique and form for new meanings.   Such technical innovations and changed interests are worth noting.

There is, first of all, the fact of a loosened structure. Many of these novels seem all but formless.

Dreiser and Sinclair Lewis use a free form, with some architecture to it, for their complex material.   Proust, Joyce, Don Passos, and Aldous Huxley go far beyond that. Proust and Joyce come near to destroying sentence structure.   In Don Passos' *Manhattan Transfer* and *The 42d Parallel* the body of the story breaks into brief sections and scattered episodes.   Aldous Huxley in *Point Counter Point* moves from group to group, from present to past in what seems to be a very free musical pattern.   To think of these men and their work as lawless and lacking in constructive power, is to misunderstand.   Theirs is not the naive rambling novel of a Smollett, a Dumas, a Dickens or a Thackeray.   They deviate intentionally from traditional patterns. They create new forms in response to new conditions, new problems, new interests.

It is a new world in which these novelists are set, and it is a new spirit they bring to this world.   The growth of science and of industrialism, the catastrophe of the Great War, post-war economic unrest, technical inventions, changed sex behavior, the rush for education and for diversified pleasure, psychic tensions and readjustments—such are conditions which must affect the technique of the novel in the hands of any honest and thoughtful observer and imaginative reshaper of life. The influence of moving pictures may be seen in *The 42d Parallel* with its brief shifting impressions and expressions of city life, and in Aldous Huxley's use of throw-backs and close-ups. The short sentences and vigor of Hemingway spring from an age that is tense, impatiently experimental, and far removed from slow, decorous modes of living. A form that is to hold what Proust, Joyce, and Frances Newman mean to give of the inner life must be very different from the old forms.

The loosened structure then of some of the newer novelists as a deliberate departure in technique may serve to draw attention to certain changed attitudes and interests.

The first is a changed attitude toward plot. The newer novelists are not direct story tellers and skilful manipulators of complications and unravelings. They are too close to life for that. It is only occasionally that life has the rounded expressiveness and swift inevitableness of a tragedy. Swinnerton in *Nocturne* has captured such a moment. Ordinarily life is diffuse, involved, fragmentary. It might, of course, be said that men like Dreiser, Sinclair Lewis, and Upton Sinclair, stand, as Dickens and Zola did before them, too close to life in their reporter's eagerness to observe and to record—too close to see it formed and whole. But Dickens, for all his leisurely and loose ways and irresponsible relish of human oddities, had an interest in the manipulation of complicated plots. Granted that what he gives is often only a variety show, his world is of the stage and the foot-lights. The modernist would insist that he is not at fault in the distance he chooses—that life could never take on rounded form.

Conrad is in some respects close to the novel of to-day. He

combines a story of adventure and romance with psychological studies and cosmic mirrorings. It is the pressure of the latter interests that accounts for his indirect, encysted technique of presenting characters and actions.

The newer novelists and dramatists move still farther away from plot-interest and the theatre. They at times use melodrama. Dreiser's *An American Tragedy*, Rice's *Street Scene*, O'Flaherty's *Mr. Gilhooley*, and Aldous Huxley's *Point Counter Point* are examples. But they do it either to give the crude stuff of life or to stir deeper problems. When a physical and social world is, like ours, so many-sided, so broken up, and so challenging to the imagination as it impinges on the mind of the novelist, his very desire to express and to probe will lessen his interest in a well manipulated plot.

Paralleling this refusal to give life as a pattern in logic, is a changed attitude toward character. The old interest in character lay either in marshalled feelings or in the grounding of action in motive. It was too simple and too fond of a dramatic logic. Men and women were presented as self-complete personalities who had their feelings and moods and their consciously directed purposes. Some curiosity about the inner life of feeling and some interest in what moves to action are necessary to the novel as a form of art. But the contemporary novel is equally far from the psychology of feeling of a Richardson and the psychology of action of a George Eliot, a Meredith, or a Flaubert. Several influences are back of this change. Biology has de-intellectualized character and forced it into the field of instincts and life-processes. Sociology and social psychology move it within the range of group responses and behavior patterns. Freud has dipped it into the subconscious. The I and the Other no longer seem something that can be neatly severed at a joint.

A simple directive personality with purposes sharply

pointed at a fixed world of objects does not interest the
modern novelist. To him the inner life is a stream of consciousness in which there are bits of thought and feeling
floating quietly or caught in a psychic swirl. The charting
of its depths and shallows, its currents and windings is the
subtle task of a Proust or an Evelyn Scott. Or it is a tor-
tuous cave of subconsciousness in which the sensitive, deep
search of D. H. Lawrence makes surprising discoveries.
Hergesheimer's motive-psychology seems old fashioned; and
his outer world, of country clubs, dances, drinking parties,
city scenes, and artistic bric-a-brac is uninteresting in its
fixed quality. To the modern novelist the outer world is not
separate or fixed. It is too vast to be orderly. Caught up
in fragments, it is further broken up by the refracting activity of consciousness. This changed conception of it is
directly related to the changed interpretation of the personalities into which this world sinks or against which it is
broken.

More striking than this new attitude toward plot and
character is a mental position taken by the novelist toward
all he reshapes and interprets. He is a thought-reagent to
his world. Like the modern painter he is personally-
minded, but unlike him he is working in an art form that
allows a wide and varied infiltration of thought. The new
quality of this philosophical content and spirit in the novel
offers an interesting problem in aesthetics.

The older novels had their philosophies. An evolutionary
pessimism is the subsoil in which Hardy's characters are
rooted and the cloud-ceiling into which their destinies disappear. Tolstoy in *War and Peace* and *Anna Karenina*
uses mouthpieces for his social theories and here and elsewhere sets a cosmic thought-urge into sharply observed
aristocracy and peasants and an accurately described environment. In Turgeniev's novels—*Smoke* and *A Nest of
Nobles* are examples—philosophy hangs like a heavy at-

mosphere over the scene. Dickens seldom gets beyond breezy optimism or melodrama. Thackeray, more thoughtful, still leaves his thought-values unquestioned. Anatole France, moving between a refined hedonism and social satire, is never deeply and personally engaged in the furrowing of the problems of life.

In contrast to all this, the modern novel is deeply and experimentally committed to thought-adventure. Seldom does it, as in the art of Thornton Wilder, seek a decorous escape from the welter of questions set by science, industrialism, changed modes of sex behavior, new ideals, and new needs. It is true that disillusionment and spiritual *malaise* on the part of a post-war generation have had an influence. In one sense Aldous Huxley's *Antic Hay* and *Point Counter Point* and Frank Thiess's *Devil's Disciple* are devastating books. They offer us people who have somehow become unmoored in social adjustment and war experience. It is, however, a serious mistake to overlook a deeper questioning and a search for new values. The death of the little boy in *Point Counter Point* is a challenge flung at any self-satisfied philosophy. *The Case of Sergeant Grischa*, cumulative as a Greek tragedy, strikes a new note of questioning.

The exploration of thought-ranges and the unwillingness to become settled within a single and final philosophical pattern may reveal states of mind caused by the intellectual and spiritual problems set by science and a fluctuant and disturbing social life. But whether transitional or not, they have proved a great aesthetic gain to the novel.

THE DRAMA

In the last fifteen years the theatre has offered the usual type of an evening's entertainment—revue, smart society comedy, melodrama, mystery play, local color drama, costume play, tragedy, problem play. There have been revivals of Goldoni, Grabbe, the early Schiller, Shaw, Amer-

ican melodrama, Ibsen.   Old plays—*Volpone* and *Lysistrata*
—have been adapted and treated none too reverently.   The
one has been given a new depth, the other has had modern
snickers added to its sublime ribaldry.   A few men, O'Neill,
Werfel, Toller, Hasenclever, have boldly struck out in new
directions.

A second glance at contemporary drama in its more traditional forms shows interesting readjustments and innovations.

The moving picture theatre has done the stage a double
good turn.   It offers a refuge where simple souls may indulge their sentimentality and their love for romance and
pageantry.   But there is much in us that is not sentimental,
and we are given to debunking history.   So when love appears on the stage it is seldom treated sentimentally or
handled ingenuously or glamorously.   It is either caught in
a cynical mood or is interpreted in its tensions and infinite
complexities of personal adjustment.   When history forms
the theme it is set within the critical and psychological interests of the modern temper.

The problem play of the older type, that of Ibsen, Sudermann, Brieux, Galsworthy, Shaw, was definitely pointed.
Has woman a right to a personality and a career?   Ought
sex matters to be faced boldly and discussed frankly?
What of the conflict of social classes?   Does society solve a
problem when it forces the seducer to marry his victim?
What of instinct and intelligence—of loyalty and enterprise?   In these plays conventional morality and human
stupidity are assigned the part of heavy villain.   A task is
set and a question is asked to which honesty and intelligence
can give the answer.   Even Shaw's satire, for all its brilliant
and disintegrating wit, is of this constructive sort.   O'Neill's
earlier work in part and plays like *Hindle Wakes* and *Young
Woodley* are of this type.

Our interest has shifted to a new kind of problem play—

one in which there is no answer. The clash between the old and the young was put by Sudermann into *Heimat*, a tragedy of domestic relationships. It appears cynically, with a modern note of futility, in Somerset Maugham's *The Circle;* and is handled in a shallow and mildly amusing way in Drinkwater's *Bird in Hand*. It may be a question of right and wrong, of misunderstanding that can be done away with, but not even Ibsen, constructive as he is in his social dramas, sees it wholly as that in *The Master Builder*. Profoundly considered in all its comic and tragic reaches, it is a problem to which there is no answer. Nor are answers to other problems offered in Pirandello's metaphysical puzzle plays, Werfel's *Goat Song*, O'Neill's *Strange Interlude*, Molnar's sophisticated comedies, Schnitzler's *Comedy of Seduction*, Galsworthy's *Loyalties*, and Wedekind's tragedies. The truth of the matter is we are not so much interested in arriving at a conclusion as we are in sharing sympathetically and questioningly in the uncovering of social and personal complexities. In one sense these plays get us nowhere. But to call them futile on that account is to be blind to their value as new creative interpretations of what of the sophisticated and the complex is held within the comedy, and what of deep disturbance, confusion, and imaginative reach is held within the tragedy of modern life. The wide difference between this and the older type can be felt by contrasting the problem of the right to personality as it appears in the closing scene of Ibsen's *A Doll's House* and Pirandello's *As You Desire Me* or the madness of *King Lear* with that of Pirandello's *Henry IV*.

In the melodrama and the mystery play plot is all important. Such plays have remained true to traditional patterns. An exception is Milne's *Fourth Wall*. On the whole the modern drama parallels the modern novel in the neglect of rounded, logically shaped plot construction. In moving closer to the casualness and brokenness of life it has become less theatrical and artificial. *Street Scene,* in some respects a less original play than *The Adding Machine,* expresses city life through a technique of episode. In many instances things are left, as they are in life, without beginning or end.

In moving away from plot-interest the drama has passed from a motive-psychology to a projection of mental states, of psychic imponderables, and an interest in the aimless wash of the waters of subconsciousness. Here also it swings in line with the contemporary novel.

In spirit the newer drama shows two interesting developments. One is an experimental intellectualism like that of Aldous Huxley—an infiltration of thought into characters and substance, and of adventure into thought. Molnar and O'Neill may serve as examples. The other is a turn to the fantastic, as in *Death Takes a Holiday, Green Pastures,* O'Neill's *Great God Brown* and *Dynamo,* Pirandello's *Six Characters in Search of an Author,* Werfel's *Mirror-Man,* Hasenclever's *Napoleon Takes a Hand.* The fantastic may be used as a decorative motif or in order to satisfy a desire for the exotic and the gorgeous, but the part it plays in the modern drama is a different one. It serves to express certain phases of life and certain psychic responses which can be caught only by a bold throw of the imagination. This is done for machinery in *Dynamo* and in Kaiser's *Gas,* for inner tensions in *Mirror-Man,* for a shifting and unsure sense of reality, to which the moving pictures have contributed, in plays like von Unruh's *Phaea* and Hasenclever's *Napoleon Takes a Hand.*

One of the great popular successes of the last few years, O'Neill's *Strange Interlude,* shows such a radical departure from traditional patterns and is so filled with the modern temper that it deserves a more detailed study.

Strange Interlude is in two parts and nine acts, of which four are in the first, and five in the second part. Its time span covers more than a decade and a half, and its actual length is twice that of the ordinary play. There are four essential characters—Nina and her three men. The whole play is loosely patterned. The length is the result partly of the time-reach of its purpose, partly of a technical device which projects unspoken thoughts and feelings. This device was used more sparingly in an earlier play of O'Neill's— *The Great God Brown.* One of its forms is a projected soliloquy. Thus Marsden at the beginning of the play, after a few matter-of-fact words to the maid, indulges in a rambling, inchoate musing which covers three pages of text. Or it takes the form of bits of feeling and thought washed against the spoken dialogue. The old type soliloquy was a clumsy make-shift. It meant slovenly exposition and lack of subtlety in character drawing. When Ibsen, as in *John Gabriel Borkman,* used a dialogue of double values and an exposition through reminiscence he succeeded in retaining the economy of structure which marks his mature plays. O'Neill's method, more radical and unrestrained, slows up the action, loosens the structure, and again and again gives a halting step to his exposition of character. To call him clumsy or slovenly because of this, is to overlook the fact that technical devices must be judged in relation to what content and meaning they are to carry. Whatever our ultimate appraisal of this method of projection in the drama may be, we must understand it as deliberately used by O'Neill to give something the traditional drama could not give.

Two things are aimed at in it—a more nearly complete revelation of personalities and a chance to illuminate character critically. In the usual drama personalities are revealed through such of their purposes and actions as express character. They are revealed also through what they are to themselves in moments of reflection and through the sensitive surfaces of other characters. Thus Hamlet moves

within his problem, sees himself halting or planning its solution, and is revealed through the minds of his mother,
Horatio, Ophelia, and others.   The interest is in the psychology of motive and frustrated action.   O'Neill like other
modernists, sees that the closer one approaches the line that
separates the conscious and subconscious, the broader a base
is needed for the apex of purposive action.   He also sees
that within a personality thus broadly based there are all
sorts of stray thoughts and feelings which are unrelated to
motive and action, and still of great interest in any human
portrait.   Only by means of a device such as he uses can
this deep and confused inner life be brought within the
form of the drama.

His second reason is equally interesting.   Apparently
his characters are simply expressing themselves with all their
hidden feelings and broken lengths of unavowed thought.
But what O'Neill has fashioned for himself is a flashlight
method of psychic spotting.   Shaw plays at fast and loose
with his characters, steps into and out of them with his wit
and satire and social program.   O'Neill's method is more
unobtrusive and artistic.   He turns his flashlight inter-
mittently into the recesses of the inner life.   He makes us
conscious of his own sensitively and critically shifted light
in the very revelation of the men and women of his play.
There is a new subtle presence of a dramatist on the stage.

Meanings and values then are sought which put *Strange
Interlude* closer to the more flexible, broader form of the
novel.   There is both gain and loss in the enterprise.   Subtlety and breadth have been gained, economy and dramatic
force have been lost.   It is wrong to count only the loss in
this and other bold attempts to widen the range of an art
form—useless to set against such enterprise a mechanical
doctrine of the *genre net*, of nicely blocked off, never-to-be-
redefined art forms, each quiet in a little compartment of its
own.   It is wiser to risk a misadventure in order to gain

such things as the music drama of Wagner, the mobile color of Van Gogh, the psychic drama in Rodin's sculpture, the color-motif in poetry, and the movement-motif in architecture.

The changed view of the inner life and the outer world which *Strange Interlude* shares with many modern novels, is bound up with a new type of the tragic.   The main tragic idea in O'Neill's play is contained in the words: "—our lives are merely strange dark interludes in the electrical display of God the Father."   It is the futility—loneliness, torture, weariness—of human life and purpose within an indifferent, dark world of natural forces.   There are minor tragedies within the play.   Such are: Marsden's personality, warped and frustrated by a mother complex; the chasm between Nina and her father; the love and hate neurosis developed in Nina by Gordon's death; the thwarted father's love of Darrell.   There is no conciliatory note at the end —no gathering of tragic characters and situations into an inspiring philosophy of affirmation and consecration. Madeline and Gordon, going off in an airplane are like a life-impulse hurled into the vagaries of space.   They leave behind them persons dispossessed of all but a shell of self and weary, like Nina, disillusioned and cynical, like Darrell, and fatuously contented, like Marsden, at the coming to pass of something that cannot possibly have any meaning or value.   Life is having its way with all of them.

O'Neill has been accused of giving clinical studies of abnormal types of men and women, and the question has been asked "Are such types suitable material for tragedy?" His world view has had to meet another challenge: "Can a materialistic naturalism achieve great tragedies?"

These questions are answered in the negative in two essays in *Humanism and America*.   One, "The Dilemma of Moderr. Tragedy," is by Alan Thompson; the other, "An American Tragedy," by Robert Shafer.

If these men are right in their analysis and their conclusions, then a great modernist tragedy is impossible, for the hidden forces and abnormal phases of human nature have caught our interest, and we have been affected by the tremendous, decentralized world science is offering.

Alan Thompson contends that "those who work in the modern temper are unable to discover any worthy heroism to exalt." The dilemma for the modernist is that "he cannot be both honest and sublime." Classic tragedy was elevating. It expressed and allowed us to share in impressive, lofty exhibitions of will and a spiritual order. Macbeth is "wicked, but admirable." Steadfastness, indomitable spirit, and the expression of moral law give grandeur and elevation to this type of tragedy. In contrast to it, modern tragedy is depressing. Modern democracy, science and a mechanistic psychology, and a sceptical temper have contributed to the destruction of the old heroic tragedy. The modernist does not believe in greatness, so "he cannot inspire others." Men like O'Neill and Jeffers are committed to abnormal types and situations. Madness, lust, incest, sex repression, neuroses, split personality are their tragic material; a mechanistic naturalism is their world view, and confusion of spirit, disillusionment, futility are what they close on. Of O'Neill Thompson says "Indeed he finds no man whom he can wholeheartedly admire, he can exalt no character or cause and thus does not gain the elevation of heroic tragedy. He finds life a muddle, he leaves it a muddle." The essay ends with the thought that the realm of values is that of moral laws, and that these are what is distinctively human and what ought to be expressed in art.

Shafer's essay is very similar in its main ideas. It is an attack on Dreiser's *An American Tragedy*. Dreiser does not get beyond sensationalism and the sense of futility because his materialistic naturalism forces him to deny importance to life and human purposes. His work, therefore, contains no single element of tragedy. He shuts himself off from what Aeschylus, equally sensational in his plots, but lofty in spirit, builds into his tragedies—the "faith that Moral Law uncompromisingly governs the life of man, making for an order which is divine."

It must be admitted that Dreiser does not often achieve either the tragic or the sublime. This is no fault of his materialism or determinism. Lucretius has proved that a materialistic system can be projected into sublime poetry and modern dramatists have shown that it is consistent with true tragedy. The flaw lies in Dreiser's lack of imagination. When he tries imaginative writing, as in the chapters giving the murder, he sinks very low, to the level of the reporter who is covering and elaborating a real murder story and never in his florid language gains true tragic insight. But the last fifth of his novel is genuine tragedy.

Thompson and Shafer, however, go wrong at several points. They think of the essence of tragedy as held in the centralized interest in some strong and exalted character and in a moral and divine order. They therefore regard as unsuited to tragedy the anti-heroic psychology of the modernist and his impersonal, non-moral world order. Their pattern fits even Greek tragedy only in part. Euripides, called by Aristotle the most tragic of the poets, was anti-heroic, sceptical, naturalistic. Thompson interprets noble in terms of an imaginative hold—his reference to Macbeth proves that—and slips into an identification of noble with what has moral worth. Both men fail to see that tragedy has its life not in morality, but in a ranging and probing life of the imagination. The tragedy they contemplate, with its heroic characters and its moral order, undoubtedly has an appeal to the imagination. From that appeal the modernist has cut himself off. The question then is: "Can he, nevertheless, achieve true tragedy?"

I believe he can. Ibsen's *Ghosts*, Werfel's *Goat Song*,

Toller's *Hinkemann*, and O'Neill's *Strange Interlude* have
as truly a tragic spirit and imaginative uplift as the *Oresteia*
or the *Antigone*.

First there is the question of abnormal situations, types,
and states of mind. No one could call the situation in the
Oedipus Rex normal or apply that term to the Electra and
the Ajax of Sophocles or the mad Heracles of Euripides.
In modern tragedy *Hinkemann* presents an abnormal situation, *The Captive* a perversion, *The Emperor Jones*, *The
Hairy Ape*, and *Strange Interlude* abnormal types and
states of mind.

When the modernist robs personality of its single directive purpose, cuts into it, splits it up, forces it down into the
dark confused life of feeling and thought, he sets himself
a very difficult problem. He must solve it by developing a
sensitive and deep-going imaginative insight and a ranging
imagination that carries the tragic over from single persons
to a common life that holds them in their twisted, thwarted
personalities. This O'Neill has done in *Strange Interlude*.
At no point is Nina heroic. But she is seized and projected
with the utmost sensitiveness in her neuroses and her abnormal possessiveness. She is a tragic figure, lonely at
last and defeated in her desire to possess herself of the lives
and souls of her three men. But the tragic meaning of the
play goes beyond Nina—the imagination is carried to the
lives that revolve about her. The spirit of modern tragedy
is decentralized, diffused.

Second, there is the question of the world view. Can
there be a tragedy of materialistic determination set to the
note of scepticism, revolt, and futility? That there is little
chance for moral uplift in such an interpretation of human
life and its fate may be granted. But there may be imaginative uplift even in a humanity engulfed and drowned in
the dark waters of an indifferent world. As long as the
individual is of some worth to himself he is comic or tragic

material, however little he counts in the cosmic process. Eteocles knows himself doomed, but his rough steadfastness of will defines his worth for himself and his worth for our imagination. Again, there are tremendous opportunities for imaginative shaping in the kind of world science offers us.

Modern tragedy has struck new tragic music from a changed view of human nature and a new view of the world in which men and women move. It has given moving and challenging pictures of insane mother-love and possessiveness in *The Silver Chord*, of sex perversion in *The Captive*, of twisted mentality in *The Hairy Ape*, of human confusion in Pirandello's *Naked*, of frustration in *Hinkemann*, of introversions and futilities in *Strange Interlude*. It has lost something of directness, massiveness, and finality; but it has gained in sensitiveness and human reach.

Thought-Appraisals

There are many who live within their age as an inarticulate part of its processes and values. They work and play, and enjoy or do not enjoy art. There are others who move the light of thought close to their footsteps undisturbed by darkness behind or in front. Then there are a few who seek to hold their age—or all ages—within the enveloping activity of their thought. They are the *Kulturphilosophen*. They analyze and appraise; build out the present and send their thought propellingly and prophetically into the future. There is much talk of the machine age, the new individualism, the rounded life, the life of poise and decorum, of what American civilization means, of a new morality, of the art of the future. Spengler, Dewey, Keyserling, Waldo Frank, Mumford, Lippmann, Babbitt are examples. They like to build, and feel so comfortably at home in what they have built.

Of these thought-structures, humanism is of special in-

terest to the aesthetician.   At first glance it seems very close
to the movement in contemporary art which has been called
post-expressionism.   It sets an ideal of decorum and calm
restraint against unruly power, lack of measure, noisy self-
expression.   It puts itself against its age and the main
drive of contemporary art.   But in moving away from the
aggressive art of the energists, it does not move closer to
that of the post-expressionists.   It seeks to escape "a cosmic
headache"—the phrase is Foerster's—and ends in an aesthetic coma.   It may, therefore, be used as an object lesson of
how rash constructive thinking may do an injustice to art
and to the age within which it has its being.

HUMANISM

The leaders of humanism in America are Irving Babbitt
and Paul Elmer More.   Their ideals and theories have attracted among others, Foerster, Mather, Seward Collins,
Shafer, Alan Thompson.   Within the last few years they
and their followers have sought to give humanism the
definiteness and rounded effectiveness of a creed.   Essays
appeared in *The Forum, The Bookman, The New Republic.*
A book was edited by Foerster, which was called *Humanism
and America,* and which contained in addition to a definitive
essay by Babbitt, contributions by More, Mather, and other
humanists.   Naturally there would be differences of stress
and approach in such a symposium.   Babbitt is a critic and
historian shaped by eighteenth century French thought;
More is a student of Plato and Christianity, the sober-
minded younger men who gather around these standard
bearers have their own thought-preferences.   But the main
position of all these humanists is the same.

The humanists see American life endangered by modernism.   To them there is little that is good in our age and its
art.   They fight against the turmoil and confusion in our
social life, against its headlong undisciplined force.   The

huge collective enterprises and mechanistic forms and habits appeal to them as little as do the naturalistic moral revaluings, the scientific temper, the humanitarian practices and ideals. They find a similar chaos and lack of quality in contemporary art. The novels of Dreiser and the unheroic tragedy of O'Neill are unacceptable to them. They speak of "spiritual anarchy," "temperamental overflow," egoism, emotionalism; and reject all but a little of what modernist art has created. They approve of Sophocles and Aristotle, allow that Robert Frost has the humanist temper, but insist that there must be a humanist culture before much of humanist art can put in an appearance.

This hostile criticism, expressive of a dislike of things not to be endured, and of the direction and temper of modernism, reflects partly a philosophy of escape, partly a rationalizing of fears and temperamental preferences, partly a constructive program strongly influenced by both. Opponents have made much of the academic isolation of men like Babbitt and More. A college campus, however, may be not more of an obstacle to a true appraisal of contemporary life and art than a boiler-room would be. Distance there must be, but there must also be a live interest and a sensitive response to living forms and forces in industry and art. In the humanists such a wide and sympathetic interest is lacking. They neglect formative art, past and present, and are traditionally-minded in their literary appraisals.

According to Babbitt man lives on three levels—the naturist, the distinctively human, and the religious. With the third he does not greatly concern himself; he drives the dualism of the first two deeply into his position.

The naturist level is that of appetite, impulse, feeling. It is a flux that ever tends to excess and overflow. The second level is that of reason and rational intuition. Here there is a "principle of centrality" the inner check which creates measure, poise, permanent value within the flux of the inner life.   There is something in man that "is set above the flux."   This is man's humanity.   "The virtue that results from a right cultivation of one's humanity, in other words from moderate and decorous living, is poise."— "Decorum is simply the law of measure in its more concrete aspects."   The Greek view of life is used as an example of this calm, restrained, strongly centralized spirit.

Babbitt's hostility to modern life and art is rooted in his belief that they move along the naturist level.   Our science is mechanistic, our industrialism, huge and disordered, our pleasures are aimed at comfort and animal enjoyment.   Our humanitarianism is Rousseauistic—a matter of sympathetic emotionalism.   Our art is undisciplined, expressive of "expansiveness" rather than "centrality."   It is turbulent, noisy, vulgar, anarchic.   It lacks moral elevation.

When a philosophy results in such an unfriendly, distorted image of the ideals and forms of modernist art, there must be some flaw of vision.

Babbitt tends to confuse expressionism with romanticism and to interpret romanticism as the dated formlessness, self-worship, and emotional overflow of men like Rousseau or Victor Hugo.   The modern movement in art does not stem from Rousseau.   It is not ego-centred, emotional, and formless, as this nineteenth century romanticism was.   But much of it is romantic in the sense of *The Book of Job*, the *Odyssey*, and *The Bacchae*.   The humanists who attach the label of naturalism to expressionistic art go astray in a different way.

The second flaw in Babbitt's vision is his biased view of Greek literature.   He comes close to seeing Homer through the eyes of Pope.   He overlooks the Dionysian element in Greek tragedy—and so he narrows Sophocles and passes Euripides and Aristophanes by.   To stress measure and poise and to miss ecstasy and depth, is to fall short of a grasp of the art of the Greek dramatists and of Sappho.

The third flaw is an inadequate view of wherein man's humanity consists. Expansiveness is more truly something of human value than centrality. The sympathetic width of Terence's phrase "nothing human is foreign to me" and the cultural expansiveness of Rabelais are better than Aristotle's highmindedness or the pattern of rounded righteousness the humanists offer. Of this genuine human spirit there is more in Sandburg's poems, Toller's tragedies, and Benét's *John Brown's Body* than in all humanism.

Where humanism seems most at fault, however, is in its insensitiveness to the creative temper in art. The new problems set and the new interests developed by modern life are welcomed by the enterprising artist. In them he finds new inspiration and new forms. His art must be creative if it is to be living.

CONCLUSION

Contemporary art has been shown as something free and creatively alive. It cannot be caught in some rat-trap of a mind. Nor can it be set aside for a gilt cage left open for some songster of a single melody. It is not uniformly good. It goes astray in its free life. But even the cosmic life-urge occasionally produces monstrosities. On the whole, it is evolving a discipline of its own. The desire for form is strong in every true artist. It may not be the traditional form—it may be something new to fit new ambitions and values. On it we may rely, and stand boldly within the art of our time.

PART SEVEN

PROBLEMS OLD AND NEW

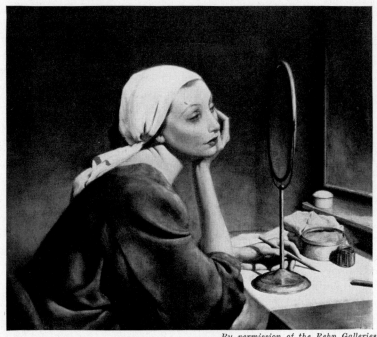

CHAPIN, ALINE MCMAHON

SEMBLANCE AND THE AESTHETIC RESPONSE

The theory that art is semblance, seeming, *Schein*, must not be confused with two others often found close to it—the play theory and the illusion theory. Plato and Schiller alike regard art as play; the one finds in this matter for rebuke, the other, for praise. Both also held to a semblance theory of art. Lange interprets art as illusion—a playful self-deception indulged in by us as we move back and forth between seeming and fact. These theories, questionable at best, are often held to discredit the idea that art moves within a world of semblance.

The theory of semblance is regarded by many with deep distrust, voiced in two objections. A work of art exists as part of a factual world. Not only does it have its uses and contexts, but into its making have gone the selection and shaping of materials by the skilled craftsman. Buildings, statues, rugs, jars, paintings are such physical objects, occupying space, observable, measurable. They must not be detached, denuded of their substance, and reduced to shadowy images. Another objection is even more forcefully urged. It concerns that inner realm of convictions, values, and ideals to which we are factually and emotionally committed and which we seek to actualize in the substance and forms of living. How can an art or a theory of art be acceptable if no place is found for an energetic pursuit of such values?

It may be said in answer that the first objection, among other faults, confuses the physical object with the aesthetic object; and that the second overlooks the fact that art, which

451

is not mere pattern, finds a place within itself for the whole inner life of man, expresses and reinterprets it within a world of its own—a world not to be judged in terms of practical achievement, and of an energizing loyalty to moral and religious ideals and a passion for social reform.

In a sense, a chair, a lamp, a building, a picture are physical objects. Wood, metal, glass, stone, pigment, and canvas are materials existing in a factual world. They have been given forms spatially definable and related to our comfort, our need, and our vanities. What we make of them depends on the nature of our response. As an experiment, instead of seating ourselves comfortably in our favorite chair by the table with the convenient reading lamp, suppose we take our position at the other end of the room and keep looking at these objects. Something curious may happen. Of a sudden we become aware of shapes, lines, textures, lights and shadows, with no thought of ourselves or of the world of fact. Objects have become images in a world of seeming. We are then on common ground with the artist. The subject matter of a painting may be flowers in a vase, but flowers and vase and table as they appear in the picture have aesthetic being and meaning only as organized images. To say that the pleasure art yields is merely one of sharpened and clarified perceptual experience is misreading the facts. What and how we perceive is quite as important as the pleasure of perceiving. Again, a strong and pleasurable stimulus to keen and clear-cut perception is often bound up with the aim of entering the practical world and of dealing with it effectively.

The world of semblance involves a double detachment— from the factual world and from self-reference. This is not something easily gained. Plato never reached a full understanding of art as semblance because he was too deeply committed to the thought that art cannot express reality and that it is an imperfect copy of the objects man creates as a

practical shaper.   It is hard for man not to pass from the
painted flowers to what he calls the real flowers, from Shakespeare's Falstaff to what such a man would mean in real
life.   Desperately anxious to understand, control, and better the world that means so much to him, he is inclined to
call art false, trifling, useless, dangerous.   He employs actuality controls throughout, and he fails to see that the world
in which art has its being is a self-sufficient world.   If one
step is taken beyond the magic circle of seeming, the spell is
broken.   The theory that art is illusion is to be condemned
because it takes that step.   Nor is self-detachment easier.
It is we who must live and be active—gain a living, escape
boredom, play, and amuse ourselves.   Many people respond
to art only as pleasurable entertainment and are neglectful
of the quality of the art they enjoy.   The motion picture
industry appeals too strongly to such popular desires.

So far our world of semblance is an impoverished world.
If art were nothing but pattern, it would indeed be something relatively unimportant.   However, a process of enriching these images or shapes is going on concurrently.
Here sympathy and empathy play their part.   The inner
life of man—feeling, mood, impulse, thought—finds expression in art.   Two points must be insisted on.   First, this
inner life exists for art only as it inheres in the form of a
picture, a poem, a sculptured figure.   Second, art must be
held to be nothing but a simulated rendering, reinterpreting,
and revaluing of the impulses, passions, and moods of real
life.   Values highly prized—deep religious feeling, love of
home and country, sense of truth and honor—cannot sustain
a shoddy design or a commonplace art.   Again, they have a
meaning for art only as the inner spirit, or soul, is manifest
in every part and accent of a form.   The second point
stresses what is essential to an understanding of what art can
and must do.   In living we are interested in passions and impulses in three ways: how they express and affect us and

others, what causes them, and how they will work themselves
out in their drive and objective. In art the interest lies
elsewhere. The dancers in a dance drama appear to be
angry, joyful, torn with grief, or sunk in melancholy, subtly
changing in mood. All this is stylized, projected into visual
image, and given the quality of patterned movement. In
real life we do not carry our anger to the mirror or turn it
into dance steps—we are too deeply concerned with and involved in its intensity and drive. The rhythmic lamentations and crooning expressions of grief found occasionally
in actual mourning cannot be cited in rebuttal; for these, far
from being the voice of sorrow at its keenest and fullest, are
rather the soothing medicine of Nature taken instinctively.

Art then calls for a new response and creates new values
as it holds our inner life over against us and gives it new
forms and meanings. Further illustration of this may be
found in poetry. Jealousy as a passion reflects the nature
of the man who is jealous. It may be mean or petty or
spiteful or tragic. Jealousy as it shatters a great personality and changes cosmos to chaos is the theme of Shakespeare's *Othello*. Incidents, characters, words, thoughts,
impulses, feeling, agonies of mind, death are alike fiction,
seeming, symbols and images created by a genius. This is
their only reality. Jealousy here is quintessentially and individually expressed, not as mere pressure, but as the quality
it has for a free, reshaping, reinterpretative imagination.

Here is the purifying function of art. The self that is so
insistently with us and so troublesome is forgotten; a world
that clamors for action, control, and betterment is changed
to the shadow play of semblance; but somehow these shadow
shapes are endowed with an imagined inner life moving
within the span of human experience. Courage is shown,
and freedom and exaltation are gained when man, forgetful
of self, of agony of spirit, and of pressure intellectual and

practical, recreates his inner life as symbol and image and changes it to an object of contemplation. But a note of warning is needed. The inner life as it appears in art is not the inner life of religion, morality, and science. These concern themselves either with an actual world or with an imagined one to be actualized. They are intent on recording, energizing, and changing. An aesthetizing religion is not religion in its depth and reality—religious painting has its own problems and values. A cultural theory like Schiller's expects of art what art cannot give. Aeschylus, in contrast to Raphael, was undoubtedly a deeply religious man, but his tragic force remains and can be imaginatively recaptured by us for whom the Greek gods have been swept away by time. Peace and war are for all of us matters of gravest import. They stir us emotionally as they affect human happiness and as they guard or destroy spiritual values. As ideas they are complexes of meanings. In art they reappear as visions newly charged and formed. A fragment of Bacchylides gives a vision of peace; in Euripides' *Trojan Women* and *Hecuba* the sack of Troy, the brutality of the victors, and the fate of the victims are reshaped to an emotionalized vision.

Bacchylides' poem, even when translated in prose, is instinct with grace and gives with splendid imagery and in an ecstatic spirit a vision of the blessings of peace. The trumpet of war is silent, spear and sword are covered with rust, the spider weaves his web. Thank offerings are given to the gods. There is rejoicing—feasting—music and dancing. The hymns of the children go upward "like a flame." The poem strikes many human chords, but spirit, image, and music are its own, not to be confused with that voice of humanity which sounds in the worker for peace and the hater of war.

Euripides has been called by Aristotle the most tragic of

poets.   In the two plays he gives incidents that would be unbearable in life, and agony and grief that would there be
merely strident or inarticulate.   These he changes to visions

> The glories of my country, even as smoke
> Which on light wings is borne aloft in air,
> By war are wasted; all her blazing domes
> Are sunk beneath the flames and hostile spear.

> Heard you that dreadful crash?   It was the fall
> Of Pergamos.   The city rocks—it rocks,
> And crushed beneath the rolling ruin sinks.
> My limbs, my trembling limbs, hence, bear me hence.

Other examples are Hecuba's speech beginning with

> Place the orbed shield of Hector on the ground

which vibrates with memories of the dead hero; and Andromache's apostrophe to her son.   In tragedy a new intensity
is born, for there we are deeply stirred by imagined happenings to persons to whom the poet has given, within his
chosen form, the semblance of an inner life.

The theory that art is semblance is no academic invention.
Goethe, Keats, Grillparzer, and Hebbel were conscious that
they were giving form to seeming.   This accounts for the
quality of Shakespeare's *The Tempest* and of Keats's *Ode
on a Grecian Urn*.   Painters are at times conscious of it.
Witness Renoir's words: "Some of our servants have admirable figures, and have posed like angels.   But I must admit that I am not hard to please.   I had just as soon paint
the first old crock that comes along, just as long as she has a
skin that takes the light."

It might be objected that this theory, while applicable to
poetry and music, is only a half-truth with regard to sculpture and painting, and fails dismally with reference to architecture and arts and crafts.

A building is a physical object occupying a portion of real space and related directly to an actual world of purpose and use.   This is also to be said of a bowl, a pitcher, a coin, a rug.   In all this craftsmanship counts for much.   The architect at his drawing-board, the painter with his brushes and tubes at work mixing colors, the rugmaker while weaving are all skilfully and meticulously employed at tasks demanding their full attention.   While they are working out plans of building or fashioning physical objects, they have little time for a full aesthetic response.   But their activity is controlled, subconsciously in part, by the vision of an aesthetic object—a vision gradually unfolding itself and gaining meaning and shape in their shaping.   Rarely does an artist know beforehand what the thing he is creating is going to turn out to be in quality, form, and excellence.   Completed, it confronts him not as physical object that shows his skill, but as something in its own world and in its own right.

A visit to a museum shows me, in cases and carefully labeled, two groups of old Peruvian pitchers and vessels for carrying water.   They are there as physical objects dug up along the coast of Peru—interesting remains of pre-Inca cultures.   I know that their narrow pipe-like openings, single or double, are explained by the semi-arid climate and the need of keeping the water they contained from evaporating quickly.   They appeal to me contextually—I speculate about the culture whose product they are.   If I should turn sentimental—which God forbid!—I might think of the lips long turned to dust which they were meant to serve.   But suppose I become first an observer and then an appreciator of what is before me.   One group shows a strong sculptural feeling.   A vessel is shaped like a human head; in another, head and shoulders are carried down into a roundness, against which in black are sketchy and distorted arms and hands; others are shaped like frogs or birds.   There is little interest in color. In the other group the shapes are simple, non-human, but color is used in stylized patterns geometrical or naturalistic. I notice, again, that in all cases there is a bold and original shaping that holds me within its spell. The stylized bird form does not call to mind this or that bird; the frog is nothing more, and nothing less, than a formed vision, existing as the quality of the artist, put by him into a physical object. Suppose I detach from either group a single pitcher and allow it to have its will with my senses and my mind. It begins to impress me as something timeless, individual, yielding an eternally renewed delight in form, design, and vision. Then, and then only, has it become for me what the unknown artist meant it to be—an aesthetic object. Craftsmanship is an essential part of art; when we regard it as a means we may respond to it aesthetically. But it is neither the beginning nor the end of art.

Granted that a pitcher or a vase may be seen and felt as an aesthetic object, is it not true that it is, comparatively speaking, a trifle? No deep emotions stir within it, no spiritual issues are involved. Is this all there is to art? Is there to be no reaching out into real life, no protest against actual conditions, no desire to change them? Does not the theory that art is semblance cut between the artist and the man, between art and life, between blossom and root and soil?

This is not an objection to be turned away from lightly. Material urged in support of it may be taken from the cartoon, from satire pictorial or literary, and from the social novel and drama. The cartoonist certainly seems to be close to life and directly involved in it. Goya was a witness of the brutalities of war and recorded them in his *Désastres*. Nast and Daumier took a vital interest in politics and the uncovering of corruption in public life. Daumier spent six months in prison because of a cartoon in which he satirized the king. Juvenal, Martial, Molière, Voltaire, Anatole

France are all satirists—standard bearers, it seems, in the fight against vice, bigotry, injustice, hypocrisy, and human folly. Nor is it otherwise with the social novel. Zola, a champion of truth in the Dreyfus affair, is filled with disgust at the social sores he so brutally lays bare; Dickens in *Hard Times* and *Nicholas Nickleby* attacks economic slavery and a stupid and deadly school system; Sinclair Lewis turns against commonplaceness and hypocrisy and warns against fascism; Upton Sinclair impugns capitalistic exploitation and the public press. Like tendencies are found in the social drama of Ibsen, Brieux, Galsworthy, and Shaw. In all these instances artists are expressing themselves as men who sincerely and boldly strike blows in defence of decent living and a desirable social order, and against vices that put at naught what they as men committed to ideals desire and cherish.

This seems a formidable array of evidence against the theory that art is semblance. Here is art leaving the shelter of a dream world, ready for a bitter fight in a workaday world, shouting for and sometimes gaining changes for the better. Is this all that can and must be said?

The artist feels the pressure of the world about him; he may be emotionally stirred by what he sees and hears and may put his art at the service of some worthy cause. Society, again, in its own practical interests, set art to work. In the novel form is held to be unimportant—ideas are to be put across, people are to be shown as they live and suffer in some part of the world; class warfare, social injustice, inbreeding, disease, frustration, are to be documented and revealed. Other types of novels are contemptuously set aside as belonging to the art of escape.

Suppose we reflect on this, the contact point between art and life. We shall be forced to conclude that (1) art quality is not inevitably the result of the championing of worthwhile causes, (2) when such art quality is present it is not because the artist is a fiery propagandist, a practical idealist and reformer, but rather because he as an artist creates new forms and meanings, in a world of outer and inner semblance, and (3) because of this, his socially pointed art tends to be practically ineffective.

There is little art value in Nast's political cartoons or in the mass of drawings attacking war, alcoholism, syphilis, profiteering. Ibsen's *An Enemy of the People*, virtually a pamphlet play, is inferior to his *The Master Builder;* Shaw's *Widowers' Houses* is a poor thing when compared with his *Saint Joan*, for in the latter play the artist for once has triumphed over the propagandist and the intellectual buffoon. The ostensible purpose of Siporin's Haymarket series of drawings, two of which, *Thanksgiving 1884* and *Haymarket Massacre*, appeared in the *Daily Worker* and are reproduced in Cheney's *Expressionism*, was to arouse class feeling. Rivera's *Division and Depression* at the New Worker's School is to instil pity for the masses and hatred for their oppressors. In Rivera's cluttered up mural there is little of art; in Siporin's drawings there is a great deal—original design is aimed at and achieved. There are groupings in threes, expressive lines, forceful shadings, distorted and simplified forms. Such artistic reshaping and reinterpreting of social problems and themes is common throughout the range of art. Lissauer's notorious *Hymn of Hate* was to give through hatred of the enemy a tempered edge to German patriotism. But Lissauer, looking back on his poem, sees in its swing and imagery merely the sensuous and imaginative projection of a mood. Aristophanes attacked demagogues and war-mongers. But how far is this from accounting for the quality of the *Knights* or *Lysistrata?* In these plays the poet disports himself in his own realm, heaping phrase on phrase, inventing expressive comic scenes, throwing against the luminous screen of his genius transformed ideas and emotions, and semblances of men and women.

A reference to Steinbeck's *Grapes of Wrath* and Picasso's *Guernica* will prove instructive. Facts are back of both— the plight of the migratory worker and the destruction of Guernica during the civil war in Spain. Pity and a sense of social injustice and of human tragedy are to be found in the novel. Its spirit is not that of propaganda, although it can be used as such. In his preface to a popular edition of his *Tortilla Flat* Steinbeck protests indignantly at the way socially minded people misread his sketches of *paesanos* as an economic brief and document. A factual record of how people were forced to leave the dust bowl and of their bitter experiences in California would be harrowing and depressing reading. The effect of the novel, however, is not depressing. Sincerity and intensity are still there. Grandeur of conception, epic sweep, reverberating compassion, the expressive sketching of imagined characters—all this shows fact transmuted to art. Nor is this art shallower than life. It has a depth and range of meaning whereby new values are added to life as it is commonly lived and contemplated. Picasso's huge mural, planned as a part of the Spanish pavilion at the Paris fair, was meant to be propaganda. The painter was filled with rage by an historical incident of destruction, slaughter, cruelty, and barbarism. But what of the completed picture? It shows one of the strangest designs ever created—there are distorted, semi-abstract human forms, light shapes set sharply against the dark. The onslaught of war and the agony of its victims supply the spirit within this design. The artist has triumphed over the propagandist. Fact and emotional reaction to it have been transmuted to something that has its meaning only in this form, and the form itelf is all but unintelligible to the factual-minded hater of war.

As art quality becomes increasingly manifest and creative in a cartoon, a poem, or a picture, art becomes less and less effective as a social weapon. Scientific reports and pamphlets on a disease, vice, and health conditions; statistics on adulteration of foods, overcrowding, occupational diseases; reasoned arguments in books and magazines are proper and effective measures of protest and reform. But many people, it is held, are indifferent and incapable of abstract reasoning. Famine and flood, the ravages of disease, the need of a civic interest must be brought home to them by a vivid image or symbol. Thus art may be made useful. Let us then have slum clearance plays, films showing the dangers of reckless driving, dramatized revelations of the microscope, educational films, pictures, cartoons, poems set to the spirit of protest and appeal. Flag waving and fist shaking, labor spies, scabs, bosses, the Five Year Plan, wealth and poverty, peace and war, race conflicts, rackets, corrupt politics—such is the mass of convictions, ideals, emotions that seek to become articulate and forceful through art. Art may be used incidentally and graphically to point a social lesson—or it may enter creatively for its own purposes the physical and spiritual drama of man. But art that is nothing but propaganda is art that is bad, and social art that is more than that is usually ineffective as propaganda. Rivera is a social rebel in many of his crowded, crudely documented murals— he is a true painter, and an impressively human one, in his simple, forceful sketches of Mexican types. It is not for the artist to thrust naked foils at living flesh, his is the thrust and parry of buttoned points. Does an art which disengages itself from the practical or reshapes it to its aims run the danger of becoming shallow and inhuman? The feeling against "arty" or merely clever art is a natural and just reaction. Sincerity, integrity, and devotion to ideals are aesthetic virtues as well as moral ones. But the two must not be confused. Verlaine wrote a few fine religious poems;

Oscar Wilde was for once artistically sincere in his *Ballad of Reading Gaol* and *De Profundis*. In neither case did art work moral miracles. We disapprove of a Falstaff in real life, but the Falstaff of *Henry IV* we welcome as a pure joy. It is wrong to expect of art the point of view and the moral selection taken and used in actual living.

However, to insist sharply on the difference between aesthetic and moral interests is not to be disloyal to the spiritual qualities and values of life. Art is a magical mirror whose surface flashes with this or that bit of the external world, sensuously and imaginatively changed by the genius of the artist. It is a magical book on whose transforming pages are inscribed the inner experiences of man, imaginatively re-created and given new meanings. Caliban, Falstaff, the Satan of Milton reveal the black ink of evil changed to letters of gold. Whoever regards the mirror as a mere reflecting surface or the book as a moral ledger, extract, or book of facts has no understanding of art. He also cuts himself off from the supreme spiritual gift of art. Man frees himself from the insistence of objects, the drive of purpose, and the clamor of desire and feeling; and as a creator and enjoyer of art makes himself a new ideal home where whatever is experienced and humanly prized may find new expressive forms, new qualities, new values. Tragedy, of all the forms of art, is most generous in this giving, for there courage, insight, compassionate understanding, depth and range of thought, a bold and interpretative imagination combine to offer a semblance which is more soul-stirring and soul-shattering than anything found in nature. There are tragic personalities and situations in real life, but they are inarticulate, chaotic, fragmentary. It is for the tragic poet to give them stature, voice, and a new wealth of meaning. Hamlet, Lear, Othello are gifts, not of nature, but of art.

Antaeus gained strength through contact with the earth. Art must seek sustenance in life if it is not to be merely clever play or trivial self-expression. Within the simpler ranges of art—an embossed silver cup, a medallion, a still life—the artist must show himself an honest and original shaper. Even here a psychic force may take form, as in the sunflowers and cypresses of Van Gogh. But the spiritual carrying power of such forms is limited. In a symphony, however, an elegy, a portrait, a sculptured *Thinker*, a tragedy, the inner life of man is vitally formed and expressed. Art must have its roots deep in life, but its blossom and fruit are its own.

PROBLEMS OF THE DANCE

THE DANCE AND MUSIC

The two arts have in common movement and rhythmic pattern. In the dance the movement is of the body in and through space; in music it is a varying succession of sounds. The dancer feels and gives rhythm directly; the musician gains and gives it through the ear. There are ballroom dancers who follow the time-beat and overlaid pattern of the music perfectly, and yet are utterly unmusical. Their sense of rhythm is kinaesthetic and not auditory. The uncovering of differences in what the two arts seem to have in common shows how dangerous it is to indulge in vague analogies and such generalities as "all art is music" or "all art is dancing." Neither art can be merged in the other. Music is a time art, and its substance is sound. The dance is a time-space art, and its substance is patterned bodily movement. The latter is in part a visual art; the other, wholly an art through the ear. The visual images music calls forth are incidental and uncertain. It cannot be denied that some compositions spring from visual images and that some listeners have vivid flashes of such imagery. Program music aims at something of this sort; but the image of the composer yields quickly to the developing tone-structure, and the directing call to the visual imagination of the hearer proves insufficient. During an experiment made some years ago in Berlin people of varied interests and capacities were asked to jot down their visual images on hearing Schumann's *In der Nacht* played. There was a bewildering variety of responses to this simple music. One person saw a moon passing through rifts of clouds; another, Leander swimming the

465

Hellespont. Different as these images are, they have one thing in common—rhythmic movement—the moon passing through clouds, the swimmer breasting the waves.

From its beginnings to its position as a fine art, the dance has stood in some sort of relation to music. This may be thought of as (1) the dance as the interpreter of music, (2) music as the servant of the dance—either as mere accompaniment or as helping to express the form and spirit of the dance, (3) both arts collaborating toward the creation of a form that preserves both and transcends either.

The simple dance forms of music present no problem. The dancer can catch the spirit and give a vivid interpretative rendering of the *Blue Danube Waltz* and of Ravel's *Bolero*. Isadora Duncan was at her best in dancing Chopin; Argentinita, in a loyal and understanding spirit, turns to visual images the peculiar quality of Spanish dance music. With other forms of music the difficulty begins.

When a musician watches a dancer attempting to interpret a symphony by Beethoven, he is apt to become critical and scornful; when he encounters the rewriting and rearrangement of such music to fit a dance scheme, he is resentful. He is right on both scores. What music of this type offers, no dance can fully and faithfully interpret.

What of music as the servant of the dance? Some simple musical sounds have from the first been used to accompany dancing. Examples are the stamping of feet, the drum beat, the rattle of sticks and clatter of castanets, the clapping of hands, shouting, the swirl of some musical instrument. Here melody and harmony count for nothing; rhythm is all-important. All the music is meant to do is to underscore and maintain the time-form in the patterned and expressive bodily movements of the dancers. Then there is the music specially written for the dance recital. In tone variation and phrasing it is to differentiate the moments, give point and substance to the moods, and express the spirit

of the dance.   Martha Graham, Trudi Schoop, the Jooss
Ballet, and Wigman, among others, make use of such music.
It may be that of a short dance or of an elaborate dance
drama.   To say that most of it is not music fine or great
enough to stand by itself is beside the point.   It is meant
merely to serve.   Even here it is only at times fully expressive.   When Trudi Schoop as Fridolin plays his agitation of
mind on an imaginary piano, and her brother's music invades the stage, nothing she can do—gesture, pose, facial
expression, movement—can reach the psychic expressiveness of that specially written music.   At times, however,
when not moods but ideas are to be expressed or when comic
effects are aimed at, music has limited resources.[1]   A facial
expression, a shrug of the shoulders, a moving arm, an unexpected slumping or tensing of the body, a psychic blot-out
on the part of Fridolin overmatch the accompanying music,
resourceful as that is.

The third possibility remains—both arts collaborating independently toward the creation of a form that preserves
both and transcends either.   Examples may be taken from
the two extremes.   In a ballroom dance—a tango or a waltz
—performed on the stage neither dancers nor observers are
conscious of two arts separately, one subordinated to the
other.   Rather are they experiencing something that is not
merely visual nor mere bodily movement nor mere rhythmic

---

[1] See the footnote on p. 317. Penkert gives many examples of the psychic
shuttling back and forth between the important and the trifling: a sudden
drop or incongruous sequence in a melody; a tone structure in a zig-zag
futile search for a goal; excessive, unexpected pauses; a tone stubbornly
held to; transpositions into other keys; two themes, one lofty and the other
frivolous, in a capricious interweaving; the transition from full-toned choric
polyphony to a single piping voice; intentional mechanization; burlesque
repetition of a form or theme.   Penkert cites as examples Strauss's *Till
Eulenspiegel* and *Sinfonia Domestica,* Beethoven's *Wut über den verlorenen
Groschen,* Schumann's *Faschingsschwank* and *Papillon* No. 2, and many songs
and comic operas.   In the main he proves his point that the comic may live
vividly and variously in musical forms.   But he makes his task easier by
including many cases where the music becomes fully expressive comically
through the mediation of words.

sound, but a new time-space art created by all three harmoniously working together. At the other end is the dance
drama, elaborately staged, costumed, orchestrated, and
danced by the Diaghileff or Monte Carlo ballet. Examples
are *Petrouchka, Bacchanale*, and *Prince Igor*. Some modern dancers speak of these contemptuously as ballets, forms
of entertainment to be replaced by simple essential dances in
which the music is strictly subordinated and the visual is
stressed only as movement. The lover of music, in turn,
finds them distracting. Neither point is well taken. The
complex dance drama, like the music drama of Wagner, has
a right to existence and approval. Wagner carefully distinguished between the old form of the opera and his own.
This was to be the joint creation of all the arts. In harmonious and expressive conjunction they were to build its
substance and carry its spirit. But Wagner saw that in a
music drama there must be variational stress—as the dramatic idea unfolds itself, one or the other of the arts must
step back or become for a time the leader and carrier. Why
not a dance drama on the same pattern? It would have the
same problem—a variational stress on the visual, the motor,
the rhythmic, the kinaesthetic, and the musical. It would
be absurd to regard this highly complex collaborative form
as the only acceptable one. It cannot discredit simpler
dances in which the music is merely incidental, where there
are no stage effects and no elaborate costumes, and in which
a direct physical and psychic expressiveness is sought and
sustained. Nor can it be banned by them.

THE EXPRESSIONISTIC DANCE

Expressionism as a modern movement affecting all the
arts goes back to impulses and interests to be found throughout the history of art. It is marked by (1) a sense of outgoing energy, (2) the creation of forms instinct with such

energy, (3) violent expressive distortion, (4) breaking down
the barrier between inner and outer, psychic and physical,
experiences, and (5) psychic weighting.

The dance uses living material—the body as it occupies
and moves within space—to create time-space patterns. Of
the two primitive types of the dance, the gymnastic and the
mimetic, the former gives directly physical energy held
within variational order; the latter by costume, pose, gesture, movement, and pantomime offers an imitative rendering of animal life or of simple human activities such as rowing, stalking game, fighting.

On further thought the distinction between the two types
seems less sharp, for even in the mimetic dance there are self-
activity and expression. Suppose a literal-minded person
sets himself the task of copying accurately on paper the
shape and appearance of a fox or a bear. Contour line, detail, and shading are perfect. We observe his moving pen-
cil, comment on his expertness, admire the lifelikeness of his
sketch. If his lines show something of the slinking of the
fox or the clumsy gait of the bear, it is only because in real
life the lines and shapes of animals are seen expressively and
as suggestive of movement. This then is our work, not his.
Nothing in this is meant to apply to the true artist in black
and white or to the painter, for, far from being a mere copyist, he creatively selects, reshapes, and expresses.

Suppose now a dancer impersonates a fox or a bear.
Costume gives the first, obvious hint. In primitive animal
dances parts of the fur, feathers, antler, or teeth are made
use of. The dancer is a skilled mimic. Using his body as
material, he projects images of animal shapes, poses, and
movements. He is never a mere copyist, passive or mechanically active. His is a free outgoing energy creative of expressive rhythmic forms. He experiences this self-activity
directly, and we who watch him dancing a bear, a puppet, a
wooden soldier feel it in the space and time images he offers.

In the gymnastic dance this kinaesthetic factor is more strikingly present.

Imagine yourself watching a ballet. There are men and women on the stage. They tense and relax their bodies, leap, whirl, bend and straighten, come to rest in a pose, pass from one part of space to another. With them you have no concern. They are aesthetically meaningful only as they appear as semblances. A mathematician might say: "With time, patience, and ingenuity I could plot the meaning of this dance, which is its surface pattern in space and time, by means of a number of graphs and musical scores." But there is something this response overlooks. These semblances are not merely visual; they are instinct with energy, alive with simulated movements, feelings, moods. The dancer projects herself into a theme, a rhythmic movement, a mood, and gives form to these through the aesthetic use of her body. We as spectators respond to this motor and psychic energy as it animates and is held within the shapes we see. This is the dynamism of the dance.

A useful analogy may be drawn from sculpture. As we stand in front of a man of stone, his arm stretched shoulder high straight toward us, we may respond in either of two ways. We may, beginning with the finger tips, send our eyes along the arm to the shoulder and move them over the modeled surfaces of the body. This is the visual response. Or we may set ourselves within the stone man and move outward with the thrust of arm or leg and the tensed muscles. This is the dynamic response. The sculptor may, like Thorvaldsen, stress the former or, like Rodin in his *Thinker*, stress the latter. Greek sculpture at its best holds sensuous design and motor and psychic qualities in perfect balance. Of this the Aegenitan *Herakles* and the *Nike* of Paeonius are instances.

One word of caution is needed. When a dancer sinks to the ground in feigned lassitude or assumes the pose of grief, when a sculptured figure holds suspended an outstretched arm, when a poet sings the ecstasy of joy, we must never refer this inner life to ourselves——how we should feel when weary or grieving or holding a tiring pose or shouting with joy. We should then be moving out of a world of seeming to a factual world of self-reference.

The modern expressionistic dance definitely subordinates the visual to the dynamic. In this it swings in line with the other arts in an enterprising revolt from older forms.

The old academic ballet breathes the spirit of the eighteenth century. It is formal, stresses ease and polish, is stylized in dress, and presupposes rigid discipline and slowly acquired skill in toe-dancing. There is an elaborate and artificial grammar of pose and movement, and the speech is that of the court and opera. It is never naturally and strongly expressive. A mannered beauty is gained from difficult poses and arm and leg movements. The dancers raise themselves on tiptoe, pirouette, flutter, and gain decorative space-patterns. When they take a few walking steps they seem awkward, for the spirit of the ballet is the denial of gravity. Pantomime plays a part and is as stereotyped and as artificial as are the costume and the movements of the dancers. The ballerina, or première danseuse, is a dancer of exceptional charm and skill, but whether she dances a solo or accents a group she is fitted into a rigid school pattern.

The Russian Ballet shows a curious combination of this type of the dance with motifs taken from the gymnastic peasant dances and with a freed dramatic and musical spirit. Fokine and Diaghileff, whose choreographer Fokine later became, rebelled against the traditional ballet. They replaced its formalism with a freer dramatic and personal form. They made use of the peasant dances of Russia and responded readily to modernism in art. In 1909 Diaghileff scored a great success in Paris. From then to the time of his death this bold organizer offered elaborate dance dramas in which Stravinski's music, Bakst's love of exotic color, and the genius of Nijinski, Bolm, and Massine, among others, produced novel and personal effects, as in *Petrouchka*, *Bacchanale*, and *The Firebird*. It must be borne in mind, however, that there was a classical strain in Diaghileff. His outstanding women dancers were the classically trained ballerinas of the Imperial Theatre; and in some of his ballets, *Swan Lake* and *Le Baiser*, he returned to the old pattern.[2]

The dancers of the modern movement have turned away from both types of dancing. They are critical of the virtuosity and artificiality of the one and of the conglomerate of many arts that marks the other. The dance recital is to take the place of the ballet and is to give the dance in its essence.

They are apt to do less than justice to Isadora Duncan and her influence. She, too, was a rebel. She and her group of pupils did much to establish the dance recital on the stage. The body was used simply and naturally as plastic and kinetic material. Her range was limited; Anna, her pupil, was a more gifted dancer. Duncan combines classicism and romanticism. Romantic by nature and the interpreter of romantic music, she found the pattern for many of her poses and gestures through a study of Greek vases, and sought everywhere, except in her last phase, something of the measure of ancient beauty and grace. In the *Marche Slave*, danced on her return from Russia, she attempted expressionism with unhappy results of excessive pantomime and grimacing. The moderns object to the place she assigned the dance in relation to music and to her stress-

[2] The repertoire of the Monte Carlo Ballet shows a disconcerting mingling of the two types. The favorites of the Russian Ballet are revived; there are short set pieces and bravuras of the academic ballet; and there are modernistic experiments, which do not quite come off because routine training and virtuosity intrude. In *Union Pacific* the expressionistic bartender's dance by Massine stood out above the rest.

ing visual grace and beauty to the neglect of other aesthetic values; and they hold that the modern dance must swing in line with the expressionistic movement that has so profoundly affected the other arts.

The credo and the technique of dancers like Wigman, Martha Graham, and Doris Humphrey offer interesting problems.

It is these groups John Martin has in mind when in his little book *The Modern Dance* he sets down four essentials: movement as substance, metakinesis, dynamism, and the spontaneous creation of new forms. He points out that movement is a basic experience, capable of direct variational patterns of outgoing energy, and contrasts the flowing movement of the modern dance with the traditional use of movement as leading to poses and points of rest. He argues that in primitive dances man expressed and conveyed directly through bodily movement, with music as a mere accompaniment, psychic experiences of himself and his world, and that the modern dance makes use of this psychic carrying power of movement. This he calls metakinesis. He comments on the confusion of the person who seeks a common technique among these dance groups and reveals how on the basis of authentic experience the dancer allows each dance to find its own form.

A few years ago Doris Humphrey gave an instructive talk during the course of which she had a few of her pupils demonstrate how her dances were built up. She made much of the energism of modern and especially of American life. This must be expressed in the dance, and can be expressed only if the body is affirmed as force, weight, and tensional accentuation. A purely visual pattern aimed at formal beauty is to be shunned.

It is clear that modernism in all the arts refuses to limit itself to beauty in the narrow sense. It aims at an effectiveness in which other types—the characteristic, the grotesque, the sublime, the comic, the tragic—have a part. Nor is it afraid of ugliness when needed. This is reflected in the modernistic ballets and dance recitals. If the dance were suddenly stopped and the dancers held immobile, ugliness would again and again be found in crouched or bent bodies, awkward contour lines and gestures, and unbalanced groups. But to stop it is to distort it, for it is essentially mobile, dynamic form. Its pattern is not that of a picture, nor is its rhythm that of music. Tension and relaxation of the body, the up and down in the intensity of movement, repetition and contrast in the emergence and merging of smaller groups in a tensional interplay, major and minor accents of expressiveness in dancer and group, supply the variational life of the dance.

Something more must be said of metakinesis. Man is not a top to be set spinning by a string, nor is he a mere thinking machine. He lives as he moves spontaneously. He has emotional experiences, personal feelings, moods which he feels and externalizes through his body. According to Martin the inception of a Wigman dance is "a vision of something in human experience which touches the sublime." This is felt through with "a sensitive body." Suitable rhythms are evolved. In direct fashion the onlooker becomes a psychic sharer. The psychic carrying power of dance movements is a well-known fact. In many tribal dances there are no crystallized concepts; in others the original conceptual idea has been lost; yet both are stirringly danced and profoundly experienced emotionally by the group.

This simple mysticism is paralleled by certain developments in expressionistic painting.

There are advantages in this position. The dance frees itself from subservience to music and from intellectualism, creates its own forms, and is not mere pattern. Few of these modern dancers stop here; they are tempted to burden the dance with an elaborate mysticism which strains its resources. They then fall into dangers similar to those that beset program music and ideational painting. The pivotal question is: how much of the inner life of man can the dance express? In one of these dance compositions a group of dancers gaze intently at something on high. The program indicates that the motif is the crucifixion. But it might be any one of many things. Other arts—music, poetry—have religious resources and ranges of sublimity which the dance lacks.

The expressionistic dance, in its narrower and broader forms, is to be welcomed as a refreshing and significant departure from traditional routine—as one proof more of the sensitive perception that art is personal, spontaneous, and ever creative of new forms.

NON-OBJECTIVE PAINTING AND
SURREALISM

A few years ago two exhibitions of radical painting were being held in Philadelphia, one at the Art Alliance and the other at the Parkway Museum. Taken together they offer an interesting contrast in non-representational painting. Abstract the one, abstruse the other, they are far apart in aim and method. The first gives a quiet excursion into the realm of pure geometric form and pattern, remote from human interests; the second explores the subconscious and moves within a world of nightmare shapes and symbols.

Both movements have their champions. Hilla Rebay in her introduction to the catalogue of the Guggenheim Collection disparages representational painting and claims for non-objective painting great spiritual and religious values. Herbert Read in his introductory essay in the volume entitled *Surrealism* shows himself an extreme, uncritical partisan. Such extravagant claims ought not to provoke an equally unreasonable attack—the denial of sincerity and skill on the part of at least some of these painters and the casting aside of what they are doing as having no place within the range of creative art. Smugness is not the proper counterbalance to excessive enthusiasm.

Non-Objective Painting

A glance at the catalogue shows Kandinsky, Rudolph Bauer, Léger, and Moholy-nagy as the chief representatives of this type of painting. As forerunners are named Gleizes, Feininger, Paul Klee, and Chagall.

The pictures are non-representational in both form and

color. They are built up of lines, circles, triangles, rectangles, arcs, set off sharply one against another or cutting into each other in many ways. These geometric forms are variously and for the most part evenly colored—there are red, yellow, purple, and blue circles; color bands; lines picked out in color. The forms are kept flat; only occasionally is there the shaded roundness of a sphere. The surrounding space is generally smoothly painted of a uniform black or blue or tan with little deep space accent. The aim is to get away from interest in subject and psychic meaning, and to create a design in pure form and color—each shape and color rightly placed and all working together to a self-contained, direct visual unity, static or instinct with the movement of music.

A complication at once arises. The Kandinsky pictures fall into two groups. The first contains his Compositions and Improvisations. There he carries out his theory of mobile color and color music. Continuity and movement are aimed at. There are no sharply delimited geometric forms. The deep space element is recognized, for to Kandinsky part of the movement of colors is toward and away from the observer. Paintings of the second group bear such titles as *Two Circles, Rigid and Bent, Long Stripe, Above and Left, Pointed and Round.* They are geometric and flat, much more in line with the designs of Bauer. The puzzle deepens with a reference to the men whose work is included in the catalogue as akin to the movement. Gleizes and Feininger stem from cubism and are strongly geometrical in their designs; Klee has been claimed by the surrealists; and Chagall, a highly imaginative and fantastic painter, somehow in technique and aim points away from Kandinsky and Bauer. The truth of the matter is that there are two tendencies in non-objective painting, corresponding roughly to the two groups of Kandinsky's pictures. They may be called the geometric and the musical.

As abstract geometric pattern this type of painting marks the end of the road the cubists traveled.   They at first took objects like houses, bridges, tables, bottles, and human bodies and radically reshaped them toward a schematized rendering in terms of line, plane, and angle.   In this they saw a double advantage—the subject interest was subordinated and new patterns of shapes and colors were created.   They did not stop here, but went to the length of abolishing objects and being content with a non-representational design.   To this influence must be added another: a movement of the nineteen twenties called post-expressionism.   Over against the turbulent energism, the restless composition, the mysticism and psychic stress of the expressionist, it set a kind of painting that was simple, calm, clear-cut, self-contained.

Plato in his *Philebus* assigns to pleasure the lowest place in his system of goods, and admits of pleasures only such as are not bound up with desire.   Of these he cites pleasures gained from simple colors and geometrical forms.   He objects to the intricate imitative music of his day and condemns tragedy for its emotionalism.   Distrustful as he was of desire, feeling and change, he cannot be said to have dehumanized art, for music, poetry and geometry are given a place in his social system.

The non-objective painter moves away from human interests, yet claims for this detached art great human values. His world seems alien and cold.   No human form is seen in it—no imagined life of desire and passion stirs in it.   No moods are projected; no inner life of memory, thought, and feeling is formed.   Shapes and colors confront us at every turn in our lives and are bound up with what we know, seek, and value.   Rarely do we experience them in the essential purity of their being and relationships.   Non-objective painting invites to such an experience.   It is an art for the trained eye, and a purely visual art.   It does not, like surrealism, carry a heavy psychic pack on its back.   It does not range far, but within its limits it moves lightly and effectively.

Are there no psychic implications to this type of painting? Extravagant claims have been made for it: it makes other painting look cheap; it is an escape to a spiritual world; it brings joy and cultural inspiration to man; it is the religion of the future. All this is nonsense. It must be granted that this type of painting, so directly visual and structural, so single-minded, pure and self-contained, offers what life rarely gives, and that it meets a psychic demand for directness, purity, and serenity. But this is, after all, only one demand of many. It cannot be held to discredit others. The human spirit, so variously alive in the meanings and forms of art, cannot so easily be cheated of its range and depth.

After such of Kandinsky's pictures as aim at color music are set to one side, the geometric group suggests a perplexing problem. Form and color in the geometric designs are not always meant to be, nor can they remain, static. Tension, balance, and movement are there—color transitions, series of diminishing circles, thrust of triangles, parallelisms of shape, variational directions and qualities of straight and curved lines, triangles cutting into rectangles. The difficulty lies here. Can clear-cut, sharply delimited colors and forms, skilfully organized, effectively express movement? The clavilux, or color organ, was meant to offer compositions in color music. At first the colors were given as those of simple geometrical shapes. The impression gained was not that of fluid music where neither sound nor structural unit is independent, but all are merged in one variational life and movement—rather was it that of a string of stones, a sequence in which each stone, for all the careful arrangement and matching, retains something of a hard separateness. There is much of a like conflict in non-objective painting.

Surrealism

No sharper contrast can be imagined than that between non-objective painting and surrealism. The meaning of the one may be had for the seeing, that of the other must be guessed at. Non-objective painting is a visual, impersonal art of design in shape and color; surrealism is a personal, psychically expressive art in which form, color, and pattern are carriers and symbols of the fantastic dreams of the sub-conscious. Among surrealist painters are classed Chirico, Miro, Klee, Ernst, Magritte, Fini, Breton, Oppenheim, Nash, and Dali. They differ in stress, style, and skill.

Here are a few titles: *Face in Growth, Two Children Menaced by a Nightingale, Head Waiter, The Water Mug Gets Lost on the Playground, Suburbs of the Paranoaic-critical Town, Daybreak, Ancestors.* They seldom allow a guess as to the nature of their pictures. Nor can an inference be drawn from these to the titles. One painting shows a slice of ham with the centre bone replaced by a wide-open eye. It is called *Portrait of a Friend*, but might equally well be named *Awareness on the Part of a Slice of Ham*.

At first surrealism seems utterly mad, marked by the clinical sincerity of disordered minds, or else a shameless hoax perpetrated on a public that is to be twitted and outraged. But there are among the surrealists honest, original, and skilful artists whose work cannot be cast aside in this way. The least that ought to be done is to give a hearing to the champions of this strange movement in art and to examine critically what it aims at and what it has achieved.

In 1937 there appeared a book bearing the title *Surrealism*. It contained ninety-six plates of surrealist painting and sculpture. The lengthy introduction was by Herbert Read, who had in 1936 prefaced the catalogue of the London exhibition. There are four essays; two by Breton and Davies, surrealist painters, and two concerned with poetry.

Read, Breton, and Davies are ardent champions, agree in their interpretative analysis, and use very much the same conjuring tricks—"in the name of Marx and Freud."

This is how a composite account of their views would read. Surrealism is rooted in romanticism. "There is a principle of life, of creation, of liberation, and that is the romantic spirit; there is a principle of order, of control and repression, and that is the classical spirit." (Read.) Classicism is rational and representative of established class interests; romanticism is anti-rational, imaginative, and rebellious. "But whereas the universal truths of classicism may be merely the temporal prejudices of an epoch, the universal truths of romanticism are coeval with the evolving consciousness of mankind. It is in this sense, then, that Surrealism is a reaffirmation of the romantic principle." (Read.) This sweeping interpretation of romanticism soon gives way to a narrower one—the romantic movement in England. There are quotations from Coleridge, Wordsworth, and Keats; Byron and Shelley are cited; and the macabre novel of horror of Radcliffe, Lewis, and Maturin is made much of. Surrealism is said to differ from romanticism in being scientific in the modern sense, free from sentimentality, anti-emotional. It rests securely on the dialectical materialism of Marx and the psychoanalytical theories of Freud. Read in an astounding passage ties surrealism to Hegel's logical pattern of change—the dialectic of thesis, antithesis, and synthesis. "In dialectical terms we claim that there is a continual state of opposition and interaction between the world of objective fact—the sensational and social world of active and economic existence—and the world of subjective fantasy. This opposition creates a state of disquietude, a lack of spiritual equilibrium, which it is the business of the artist to resolve. He resolves the contradiction by creating a synthesis, a work of art which combines elements from both these worlds, eliminates others, but which for the moment gives us a quantitatively new experience—an experience on which we can dwell with equanimity." (Read.) A special turn is given this theory of a synthesis of the outer and inner by the use of certain Freudian motifs—infantile memories, instincts freed from repression, neuroses, subterranean experiences, dreams, sublimations, and symbols. Read interprets Wordsworth's nature poetry in a Freudian manner and analyzes a poem of his own in the light of Freud's theory of dreams, pointing out the automatism of its imagery. Automatism is to Breton the limit toward which surrealism tends. This mass of disordered subconscious experience, which to most of us seems chaotic and personal, is construed by Breton as something shared and destined to bring men together. That accounts for the stress put by Breton on the practical function of the artist, on "collective myth," on the liberation of instinct, on fraternalism. Unlike the sentimental humanist and the social propagandist, the surrealist artist gives fantastic form to the latent content of the mind and the age.

What is to be made of such an exposition of the nature and aims of surrealism?

It must seem surprising that in the reading matter of a book with so many plates of surrealist art there is only one explanatory reference to a picture. René Magritte's *The Red Model*, which shows a pair of shoes changing gradually into the front part and toes of a bare foot, is cited as an example of dialectic synthesis. Of it Davies says: "he will find a visual image by Magritte of precisely this kind, an image which seems to me to possess an overwhelming profundity and power, and which in its human or 'political' aspects can compare with the best of Wordsworth." Claiming that much of medieval art might be called surrealist because of its fantastic shapes and symbols, Read remarks: "we find that a subject like Christ in Limbo is often treated

Bauer, Andante

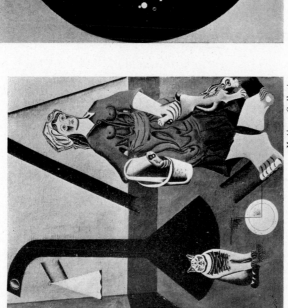

Miro, The Farmer's Wife

Non-objective Painting and Surrealism

in a manner recalled by Picasso's recent etching Minotauro-machia."

A movement in art cannot be sustained by the high-sounding phrases of its champions. It stands or falls with the quality of its work. At the risk of being called obtuse, I must confess that I cannot see in surrealist art social protest, liberated common human experiences, at once primitive and spiritually significant, or expressive symbols effectively formed and used. The symbols and shapes point back to a clinical case-book of early memories, fixations, frustrations, of interest to the artist and the psychoanalyst, but not to one who is seeking art. Of what interest is it to any one but Dali that because of childhood resentment he symbolizes his father as a grasshopper or that he sublimates curiosity by painting a woman with a chest of half-opened drawers in place of an abdomen? Not all symbols used, are, however, of this kind. When Dali symbolizes time refracted in memory as bent watches, he has created an effective and expressive symbol. But neither distrust of deeper meanings nor awareness of the frequent presence of sham, hoax, and publicity-mongering can keep me from gaining aesthetic enjoyment from certain qualities of this strange type of painting, and from admitting it to a legitimate, if subordinate, place in modernistic art.

Surrealism as an art may be set aside for the moment for a few critical comments on its explainers and apologists.

To identify classicism with the established interests of society and romanticism with the creative need and urge of the artist—to interpret the one as shallow rational pattern repressive of instinct and the other as life, freedom, imaginative force, is to go seriously wrong. There is a sharp contrast of human preferences between what Nietzsche calls Apollonian and Dionysian artists, but there is creative genius in both. When Read shifts his ground to nineteenth-century romanticism, marks it as anti-rational in contrast to the shallow rationalism of the eighteenth century, and stresses its kinship with surrealism, he lays himself open to attack. We are unresponsive to the sentiment and the fantastic horror of the early romantic novel. The paintings of the pre-Raphaelites, of the French and German romanticists, are hopelessly dated. Blake's imagination in its forays into the spirit world is inferior to Dante's—he is of interest largely because of the clear-cut direct expressiveness of line and pattern. We may learn something from Swinburne's music, but much of his poetry, like that of Byron and Baudelaire, is an outmoded rhetoric and pose of passion. Modernism does not spring from a modified romanticism. These champions of surrealism blunder in not seeing in expressionism the force that helped create twentieth-century art.

Van Gogh in his cypresses and sunflowers is not a naturalist nor a classicist in search of clarified beauty nor an emotionalist aiming at human warmth and color nor a self-analyst and symbolist—he expresses himself and the spirit of the object he paints in one bold creative forming. Here is the fusion of the inner and outer worlds the surrealists claim as their own. Their boasted synthesis is not a synthesis at all, but a mechanical combination of the subconscious and objects—a telephone, a grasshopper, an umbrella, a wormy apple, at times fantastically distorted. It is a jockeying back and forth and an arbitrary symbolism. The effect may be comic. The rotund and naïvely benevolent Mr. Pickwick dressed at a masquerade as a bandit is a source of laughter. He is not in the Hegelian sense a synthesis. Surrealists occasionally aim at what they call objective humor, but for the most part they turn to the fantastically imaginative. The secret of their image and symbol, of two worlds juxtaposed, lies not in the painting but in the psychopathology of the artist. How different from this is Hobson Pittman's picture of an empty room where there is neither

ghost nor flesh, but where there is a pervasive psychic quality in the very shape and color of table, chair, and wall.

Expressionism offers a personal and psychically weighted
art. Far from moving along the surfaces of factual observation and intellect, it expresses and projects psychic experience. The surrealists insist that they owe much to
Freud and his symbolism of dreams. In a series of essays
Freud has attempted psychoanalytical studies of Shakespeare, Goethe, and Ibsen. His analysis of dreams shows
him, the student of myth, as a myth maker of the first order.
To look for great psychic meaning in the surrealist projection of the subconscious is like expecting great spiritual
truths from the chaotic and often trite and silly communica-
tions at mediumistic seances.

Roh in his book *Post Expressionism* has shown how in the
twenties a reaction set in against the turbulence and mysticism of the expressionists; and how a magical realism came
into being—a less distorted, calm, tightly organized type of
painting. Expressionism, shorn of its excesses, remains
alive in this movement. Surrealism may be regarded as a
wild offshoot of the latter.

Leaving theories aside, what may be put down on the
credit side of surrealist painting? First, it swings in line
with a growing interest in the subconscious life of man. Of
this there are many evidences in the novel, the drama of
O'Neill, and the poetry of Robinson Jeffers. Second, it
must be given credit for originality of imagining and shaping.[1] Painting, from time to time, is in need of fresh sub-

---

[1] Even this must be qualified. The fantastic tales of Hoffmann and Poe are
highly imaginative and original. So are some of the surrealist pictures.
But while the former show a spontaneous harmony between shape and a
macabre imagination, the latter are too often marked by a cold intellectual
symbolism and a discordant visual clarity.

Again, while the imagination may seize upon the fantastic, it may show
its creative force in other, quieter ways. Thus Dante, a master of the fantastic and the horrible, gives an expressive freshness and intensity to common
incidents, sights, and sounds. Frost in *A Hillside Thaw* and other poems of

ject matter and treatment. Third, in turning to the fantastic it gives point and value to a minor but interesting aesthetic type. Again, many of its paintings show a skilled use of shape and color, a sense of original design, and an unusual and intriguing visual clarity.

In spite of its pretensions it is only occasionally successful in dealing effectively with the subconscious. It too often irritates, perplexes, or amuses. Its case must rest on the other three points set down to its credit. It is because of such qualities that some of the pictures of Dali and other gifted surrealists have an aesthetic appeal.

Non-objective painting and surrealism are one-sided and strongly contrasted experiments. The one is coldly non-human, preoccupied with design; the other is subterranean, often murky and disordered. The general public, indifferent to the former, greets the latter either with sweeping abuse or with a morbid, uncritical acclaim. The wise attitude is one of interest and caution.

---

country life achieves a very fine imaginative quality. It is easy to overrate the imagination of the surrealist—it is limited in range and of no extraordinary depth. Ask a group of people, as part of a parlor game, to sketch in a plan for surrealist paintings, and the result will prove startling. They will imagine all manner of wild things and, while they cannot paint what they conceive, their visions will be very like those of the surrealist. The very ease with which surrealism may be parodied—witness Gracie Allen's exhibition in New York—is further proof of lack of range and depth.

THE COSMIC ELEMENT IN TRAGEDY

Of all art forms tragedy has the greatest psychic intensity and strength. It gives the inner life of man directly, vividly, searchingly; and probes deeply and thoughtfully into the quality and values of life. This is beyond the power of sculpture, painting, and music. Its concentrated form holds the quintessentially tragic. The novel has certain advantages—it can give experience more completely and with subtler shadings and offer a fuller orchestration of the evil, the error, the agony that lie at the heart of living. But it is a distillation rather than an essence. Put Cassandra, Lear, or Faust in a novel, and the tragic impression is weakened.

The tragic has rightly been held to involve the universalizing of pity and fear. We do not feel sorry for this or that individual, nor are we apprehensive of his fate. Clytaemnestra being what she is, we know what will happen to Cassandra—she will be butchered with Agamemnon. But the real tragedy lies in the curse Apollo has put upon her, of seeing clearly the future, not of herself only, and being utterly powerless to change it. That is one of two curses inherent in life—the other is being bound to move about darkly along precipices. It is presented by Aeschylus not as an abstract idea, but in the impassioned, throbbing speech of Cassandra herself. Lear is much more than an old man wronged by his daughters; in him a challenge to the world order becomes a voice.

This curious power of creating individuals and suggesting cosmic issues marks tragedy at its height. Shakespeare shows it in his tragedies—in his histories the world spirit is too smugly English. Schiller fails on both scores—his characters lack individuality, and his ethical idealism is too comfortably established.

An understanding of this highest form may be led up to by turning to other types of tragedy.

Four Types of Tragedy

THE TRAGEDY OF SOME PERSONAL CRISIS AND CATASTROPHE

Love, ambition, passion, jealousy, and sense of honor are some of the commoner themes. Plot interest counts for much; and the spotlight is thrown on individuals as they feel, will, live, and die. The tragic moves within a restricted psychic circle. Examples are the *Ajax* of Sophocles, the *Phèdre* of Racine, the *Judge of Zalamea* of Calderón, *The Hairy Ape* of O'Neill, and Kaiser's *From Morn till Midnight*.

THE HISTORICAL TRAGEDY OF SOME PERSONAL CRISIS AND CATASTROPHE

This type, too, is individually centred. Some historical character is imaginatively reshaped, with the deeper and wider implications of history neglected. A good example is Schiller's *Mary Stuart*. The poet has flattened to a fresco of clashing personal forces and motives what was historically a deeper and more subtle conflict. In his *Jungfrau von Orleans* he goes beyond this type, but falls far short of the meanings packed into Shaw's *Saint Joan*.

THE TRAGEDY OF SOME SPECIFIC SOCIAL CONFLICT

Some vice or folly or fatal disability is shown emerging from social living—some condition is held responsible for the ruin of individuals and groups. It may be the slander of a perverse child, as in *The Children's Hour;* alcoholism;

economic serfdom and sodden lives, as in the earlier plays of
Hauptmann or in *Tobacco Road;* a woman selling herself
into marriage for social security as in *Hedda Gabler;* the
clash between family authority and a free life, as in Sudermann's *Heimat;* dry rot in country club life, disease, corruption in high places. Nowhere is the tragedy felt to be elemental or inevitable except within the logic of its restricted
pattern.

THE TRAGEDY OF INTRIGUE

Here some malevolent, plotting individual uses the weaknesses, passions, and mishaps of his victims to encompass
their ruin. Examples are Shakespeare's *Othello*, Webster's
plays, Schiller's *Kabale und Liebe*, and Lessing's *Emilia
Galotti*. The last offers an especially instructive instance.
There are few more effective stage plays than this. Lessing
has contracted the Roman story of Virginia, with its imaginative and emotional range, to what Hebbel calls a mere
court intrigue. He has set down the characters in clear-cut
fashion and has managed the plot with the severest economy
and the subtlest logic. But to cite Hebbel, a piece of clockwork is not a world.

THE FOUR TYPES WITH COSMIC IMPLICATIONS

Even in these first four types an enveloping thought and a
ranging imagination may carry the tragic poet, at one point
or another, beyond a limited, individual pattern. Shakespeare calls Romeo and Juliet "star-crossed lovers" and has
set the tragedy of their youthful passion within the strife of
the Montagues and Capulets. In the *Ajax* the chorus
strikes cosmic notes. Set Grillparzer's *König Ottokars
Glück und Ende* beside the studies in weakness and villainy
offered in *Richard II* and *Richard III*, and it reveals itself
as a magnificent historical tragedy with universal overtones.

It is seldom that Ibsen stops with a Hedda Gabler or a John Gabriel Borkmann. *The Master Builder* suggests and *The Wild Duck* offers cosmic tragedy. Social problems may be given a spreading meaning. Even in the tragedy of intrigue the villain may be made to express evil incarnate in the world, and in the death-cry of his victims may sound the agony of spiritual defeat.

COSMIC TRAGEDY

There are tragedies of such tremendous depth and range, of such shattering effect, that they leave us shaken and wondering. With them the formalist can do little or nothing. Aristotle responded to the perfection of *Oedipus Rex*, but there is no proof that he felt its greatness. *Othello* is formally superior to *King Lear*, but who would be willing to make the exchange?

Cosmic tragedy cuts to the roots of experience and moves to the uttermost confines of a world order, intent on its problems and meanings. *Oedipus Rex*, the *Oresteia*, *King Lear*, *Hamlet*, *Faust*, and *The Wild Duck* are of this type. In *Lear* a challenge is hurled at God for the evil, the human misery, the injustice that are part of life. In *Hamlet* and *Faust* man the thinker and seeker grows to colossal and tragic proportions. Aeschylus and Sophocles are like eagles that "have dug their talons into the ribbed rocks of the earth and thus defy its tempests" (Hebbel). *The Wild Duck* shows humanity broken on the wheel of a false idealism.

Maeterlinck's earlier plays—we have his own word for it —are tuned to a cosmic pessimism which has for its theme the intrusion on human happiness of brutal, dark world forces. But his substanceless men and women, with their flickering little life-flame, do not allow him to get full tragic intensity from his theme.

German aestheticians—Hegel, Nietzsche, Volkelt, and

others—have probed deeply into the meaning of tragedy. Butcher in his essays on Aristotle's *Poetics* and Bradley in his *Shakespearean Tragedy* exhibit a rare combination of scholarship and penetrative, appreciative insight. But the clearest light on cosmic tragedy has been thrown by Hebbel, himself a tragic poet of power and distinction. His prefaces, letters, and diaries offer a wealth of material.

Speaking of historical dramas, Hebbel insists that the poet must not merely decorate the graves of the past nor play the Angel of Resurrection to history. If he essays middle-class tragedy, he must go beyond some extraneous matter and its incidental conflicts, such as hunger, class feuds and tyrannies, petty intrigues, cruelties, and misunderstandings. He must reach something that, like spiritual agony and death, inheres in life. Tragedy is not like a game of cards in which the cards are shuffled to new combinations within a set of rules. There must be larger spiritual meanings. "There are dramas without ideas; in them people take a walk and meet with some mishap." The nature of man, the fate of man in a world not of his making—such is the theme of tragedy.

For Hebbel tragic individuals are like bits of ice floating in the world stream; they have become congealed into a separateness of being; the poet sets them colliding until through attrition they again disappear into the stream. There is a twofold pessimism in this view. Guilt is not something definite, like stealing your neighbor's wife or money, or lying or murder—these can be avoided by forethought and rightness of purpose. On the contrary, it is guilt as it appears in Hamlet and Oedipus—the need of acting in a world dark, mysterious, challenging. Rüdiger in *The Nibelungen*, enmeshed in divided loyalties, cries out: "No matter how I act, I shall do wrong." Again, tragedy, far from ending on a note of edification and reconciliation, ends on a discord. We may marvel at the great flywheel of existence as it turns and hurls individual after individual into the abyss and respond to the majesty of its inevitable moving, but the thought of broken humanity remains.

Hebbel was influenced by Hegel's theory of a world process, rational and spiritual, with tensional conflicts, triumphantly asserting itself against rebellion, one-sidedness, narrowness, unreason. He often uses the Hegelian terms *Idee* and *sittliche Mächte*. He must have approved of Hegel's analysis of the *Antigone*. But his temperament refuses to go the full length of Hegel's robust optimism. In *Macbeth* the rebel is overthrown and righteousness wins the day. Such a cosmic victory is not for Hebbel the essence of tragedy, for, while it is inevitable, it lies beyond the purpose of the poet. He keeps within an unresolved conflict. Hebbel expresses this view in a poem:

"Seize upon man, O tragedy, at that sublime moment when the earth yields him and he falls a prey to the stars; when the law that is his gives way, after a momentous battle, to the higher law that rules the worlds, but seize upon the point when both are still clashing and struggling, so that, as he escapes the cocoon, he may resemble the butterfly."

This is why, again and again, in Hebbel's tragedies the final note is not death, but an inner collapse, a doubt, a question sent into the cosmic darkness. It is the living—Judith, Herodes, Meister Anton—that are shattered and arouse in us the sense of fate. Meister Anton in *Maria Magdalene* is a man cut out of hard wood, narrow, stout-hearted, sure of himself, stern in the demands he makes on others. But when death has swept across the stage, it leaves him broken. He utters the last words of the play: "I no longer understand the world." In these words lies much of the secret of Hebbel's view of the tragic.

In 1817, when Hebbel was still a boy, an Austrian dramatist, Grillparzer, jotted down some interesting remarks on fate and its relation to tragedy. Fate as it appears in Greek tragedy may be interpreted, he holds, as natural necessity or punitive justice or as a power hostile to man. It may be one or another of all these things. It is an x which man cannot understand. Because of the origins of Greek tragedy, fate there appears within the circle of religious thought and feeling. In this sense fate ought not to be introduced into modern tragedy. There it must be a dim foreshadowing and premonition, not a thought carried to its completion. "The logic of poetry is thoughts not thought out to the end." Tragic characters feel themselves, and are felt by us, as reaching beyond their actions, purposes, and actualities to wider meanings; and the scene—a room, a tent, a marketplace—stretches to a world. To change the figure of speech, tragedy must have cosmic overtones and *Nachklänge*. This for Grillparzer accounts for the vibrational experience evoked by the tragic. The one a harsh, coarse-grained, lower-class realist, giving with a tortured subtlety the psychic life of the will, the other aristocratic, hypersensitive, self-tormenting, a marvelous poet of feeling and spiritual stress—Hebbel and Grillparzer exhibit a sharp contrast in temperament and in their art and aesthetic outlook. But they are alike in their understanding of this essential and neglected quality of cosmic tragedies.

The world admits of many different readings. Pessimism is not inevitable. If optimism is the ultimate credo, it must not be facile, but must, like Hegel's, find a place for spiritual conflicts and agonies. Time changes man's outlook on himself and his world. That of the Greeks is not Shakespeare's. In our own age, faith has lost much of its religious cast, and the sense of the cosmic reappears either as the stupendous, humanly uncentred worlds-upon-worlds vision of the astronomer or as an awareness of the subconscious forces that shape and mar human action. A new dark world of conflict, error, human misery has been uncovered. It is this that is the essence of O'Neill's *Strange Interlude* and *Mourning Becomes Electra*, as it is that of the novels of Faulkner.

It may be objected that the Germans are prone to philosophize and that their plays and novels are topheavy with thought and theory. Art is, after all, not philosophy. On this Hebbel utters wise words: "Only fools seek to banish metaphysics from the drama. But it matters a great deal whether metaphysics develops from life or whether life is to grow out of metaphysics." Art is experience sensuously and imaginatively projected and individually shaped. By itself, a cosmic problem does not suffice for tragedy. Ibsen's last play, *When We Dead Awaken,* has as its theme the conflict between art and life. This appears in broken-heart accents in Grillparzer's and Hebbel's diaries.[1] But Ibsen fails to give it creative projection. Only a poet of genius, one who thinks deeply and can create adequate images and symbols, can create cosmic tragedy. Grillparzer comments on the fact that, while an infinite distance stretches beyond the Ghost in *Hamlet* and the witches in *Macbeth*, they nevertheless are. The problem is to combine concrete individuality in the tragic characters with cosmic range. Byron and Maeterlinck fail where Shakespeare in *Hamlet* and *Lear* has shown his mastery. The others ought to restrict themselves to personal or social dramas with cosmic implications. Such are Gorky's *Below the Depths* and Lenormand's *Failures*— concrete and challenging in their theme of human wreckage —and *Tobacco Road* and *Idiot's Delight*. Even here there are dangers. Some of our playwrights—Maxwell Anderson, Thornton Wilder, and Odets are not exceptions—run a well conceived plot into a vague ending that gains a spurious

---

[1] Hebbel, *Tagebücher,* 1842: "With what I have achieved in art I may well be satisfied; it surpasses by far everything I had hoped for; it gives the full measure of my intuition—no man can give more. But I have fed my talent at the expense of myself as a human being. What in my dramas as a flaming passion brings life and form, is in my real life an evil, woe-begetting fire that consumes me and those I hold dearest and value most."

profundity.   It is not the strangeness of life, the pathos of human bewilderment, the throb of social issues that vibrates in these endings—rather is it uncertainty on their part about what they are attempting as artists.   At other times theory stalks naked in the tragic pattern.

THE ART OF THE MOTION PICTURE

The other arts appear early in the cultural life of man and show a long time-span of effort and achievement, but the art of the motion picture has a scant history of several decades and is still in its infancy. While they developed within the context of social work and play, it came into being as a new form of amusement. They antedate technology in the modern sense. True, they have been influenced by technical discoveries and inventions—steel construction, color chemistry, new musical instruments, metal casting in sculpture, improved methods in etching. Granted that they have gained some new values from this influence, the fact remains that in essence their art values are independent of technological progress. The motion picture, however, owes its very birth to technology. In one of Wycherly's plays going to "see a motion" meant going to a puppet show. Here and in that childhood toy, operated by hand, the cinematograph, and in shadow pictures may be seen hints of what came to be the cinema. But what made the cinema possible was the invention of the motion picture camera. Further growth was dependent throughout on technical refinements—in photography, in projection, in the synchronizing of form, sound, and color. Whatever art quality it may have is similarly conditioned. An early film, with its flickering lights, its breaks, its raw use of space, and its exaggerated pantomime, is not merely crude technically; it is crude artistically as well.

Motion pictures appeal either (1) to man's interest in the factual or (2) to his craving for amusement or (3) to his desire for aesthetic satisfaction.

The Cinema and the Factual

People are interested in actual happenings. They are curious about the where, the when, and the how. So they are given the Pathé News, the March of Time, bits of tennis matches and football games, travelogues, fashion news, studies of life under water. To these must be added instructive and educational films—a lesson in golf, political and social propaganda, the General Motors safety first film, flood disaster and relief, slum clearance, accounts of new inventions. The images that pass across the screen are of interest only as they record an actual world in its forms and happenings —a world we are invited to watch and be eager to change as we respond to it in feeling, thought, and desire. No one would deny that such pictures are of the greatest social value, and that they offer, within their avowed purpose, chances of artistic selecting, shaping, and stressing. But their point of view is not that of art, which moves within a world of semblance. The aesthetician must, therefore, set them to one side.

The Cinema and Amusement

The cinema offers an astounding spectacle of mass amusement. The magnetism of the movies is not an empty word. Tens of millions of people are drawn to these centres throughout the land, in city, town, and village. They come from all classes and range from the intelligent to the stupid, from the sensitive to the obtuse. Some go to escape boredom, others to enjoy a hearty laugh; still others, stunted or starved of adventure and romance or of the sentimental in real life, seek an imaginary indulgence; others, again, like to see themselves or others on an imaginary rack.

Mass amusement may grow up spontaneously within the life of a people, and may be disciplined into art. Spectacles, dramatic games, and folk dances offer examples. High spirits, craving for excitement, love of finery, a holiday mood, are to be found in all of these—but there is something else: a creative urge to achieve pattern and to project self into form. It is this that turns amusement into art.

The cinema is mass amusement, but not one sprung spontaneously from the life of the people. Rather is it provided by a small group of men to whom it is a commercial enterprise. In Hollywood studios and elsewhere pictures are manufactured. The word may seem harsh, but it serves to mark that they are the product of coöperative effort, much of which is mechanical, and that for the most part they are not art, either in aim or in spirit. The ordinary producer seeks answers to three questions: Who are the popular screen stars and how can they be used? What of outlay and financial return? What is the popular preference of the moment—romance, historical costume piece, music and dance medley, spectacle, picturized novel? They show courage, enterprise, imagination, and a shrewd appraisal of the fickle popular appetite. To this must be added a willingness to gamble for high stakes, and at times a semi-barbaric pleasure in lavish sets and spectacular effects. Colossal, glorious, glamorous are the three recurrent notes in the Te Deum of many a producer. It cannot be denied that there are others who conceive and create films as fine art, and that there are patrons who get a genuine aesthetic experience from what they see. These will be considered later. The present concern is to show why they are exceptional cases—why the pull is so strongly toward mere business and mere amusement.

The producer is too conscious of investing money and purveying amusement—too directly concerned in these two ways with his public; the movie-goer is too intent on himself and his pleasure. One fails to give, and the other fails to demand, art quality in what is shown. But there is a deeper fault still.

Consider the world as given—as fact. There are events

and persons, human experiences, localities, natural forms such as mountain, plain, desert, sea, forest. Art is never a transcript or record of these. The artist has a vision of his own; he reinterprets and reshapes. He creates another world. How different the position of the producer is in this respect may be seen by considering four types of film: one that leans heavily on actual scenery or faked actual scenery, another that exploits history, a third that is a picturized novel, and a fourth that offers directly human drama.

Nature as it appears in a film is not nature as this is part of a painting or a poem. It is mechanically recorded by an ingenious and selective camera. The appeal is factual—this is what Labrador, the Riviera, the desert, the big game regions of Africa, the Hawaiian Islands, look like. It is exploiting our interest in actual scenery and locality.

In the historical film and the picturized novel there seem to be greater creative opportunities. They both begin with fact—Henry the Eighth and Mary Stuart were personages, and certain things happened through them and to them. Their contemporaries dressed and behaved in such and such ways. *David Copperfield* and *Anthony Adverse* as novels are literary facts—they are such in plot and in the circle of their characters. History is formless—it must be reinterpreted, refelt, reshaped, if it is to reappear as art. There is then no reason why we could not have a fine or even great historical film. Our films of this type are far from that. The greater part of the fault lies with the producer. He may be naïve, crassly ignorant of historical perspective, unimaginative, or he may be a shrewd showman, giving the public what the public wants. Then the recipe reads something like this: Groom some star, Laughton, Garbo, Hepburn, Boyer, for the part, get authentic costumes, hit the high spots of some events and invent others, introduce scraps of the spectacular, the picturesque, the sentimental, the amusing—and call it an evening's entertainment.

Films offering picturized novels and plays are no better. There are dangers in transferring material from one art to another. Novels and plays are literary fact. They are written at a given time. They have their plots, their store of characters, their local color, and their span of incident and dialogue. In films of *Little Women*, *Vanity Fair*, *Captains Courageous*, *Anthony Adverse*, *Mutiny on the Bounty*, *Ben Hur*, *A Midsummer Night's Dream*, *Winterset*, and *Northwest Passage*, we are offered satisfied curiosity, spectacle, but little art. In every case there seems to be a loss in the transfer, with no counter balance of gain. Instead of dipping creatively into the stuff of life, these films borrow and cheapen in the borrowing. They lean heavily on the factual. What we saw with the eye of the mind, we are invited to see with the actual eye—quaint hoopskirts, English inns, Roman chariot races, men adrift on the sea, tricked-up scenery, and the like. Worse still, not for one moment are we allowed to forget that the reason for the picture—its box office value and its planned appeal—is in the stars it features. We respond factually, as we are supposed to do, to Garbo, Gable, Lorre, Dietrich, Gary Cooper. Here, as well as in the acted drama, there is room for interpretative genius, but it is rarely given free play. Producer, star, and public are too star-conscious and too little loyal to art to get much art from these dressed-up and changed novels and plays.

Human interest films are even worse. Most of them offer what people want: rose-water, moon-stuff, gun-play, sob-stuff. The stress is again actual. The response is that of real life. One of the deplorable features of our newspapers is the human color story, in which a fake artistry is applied to an actual happening. This panders to an indecent curiosity. The human interest film reverses this. It counts on our reacting factually to an imagined happening. We are held within our dreams, our suppressed desires, our sentimentalizing and our sympathies. But art demands a double detachment—from the world of actual incidents and responses, and from ourselves as dreaming and feeling. It is all semblance, and it asks an awareness of the quality in what is given as emotion, mood, and incident.

THE MOTION PICTURE AS ART

The foregoing criticisms are not offered in a carping or grudging spirit. Even in their present imperfection motion pictures are of educational value, have interested and amused countless thousands, and yield a pleasurable escape from the strain of modern life. To amuse oneself is one of the rights of man. Nor can it be denied that many films offered as entertainment show incidental artistic qualities. For man is not merely a pleasure giver and pleasure taker— he is consciously or unconsciously a creator of art. The aesthetician is interested in art as it appears, satisfies, and takes on many forms. The old Egypian goldsmith who was proud of his handiwork, the early designer of masks or dance costumes, the maker of puppets, the man who puts quality into lines and colors and shapes materials to new forms, the poet who uses words not merely as counters or symbols—all these offer him many problems.

Each of the major arts has had a long history of creative adventure, of new technical devices, of new materials used. Examples are the arch, girder construction, alloys, and glass in architecture; new scales and instruments in music; plastics in sculpture; new patterns in the dance. Each of these arts has its special point of view, its resources and limitations. To hold fast to this idea is to avoid such slipshod analogies as: "painting is music"—"a poem is a picture"—"architecture is frozen music." It is safer to say that each art is itself, nothing more, nothing less, and then to seek to discover what this self is.

Is the motion picture capable of being made more than a source of entertainment and a means of instruction? Is it perhaps, in promise at least, a new art? If so, what is the nature of this new art? What are its relations to painting and to fiction? In what ways does it offer new experiences? To what extent can it bend its many complex devices and effects to an organic unity? What is the nature of the form it must seek and gain? These are some of the questions that must be asked.

The Principle of Organic Unity

One of the oldest things said about a work of art is that it is marked by organic unity. Each of the arts creates sense values and psychic values and shapes both toward a variational unity. This is simplest in sculpture and is strikingly present in painting. The sculptor uses the sensuous beauty of marble, relates plane to plane and line to line, balances mass against mass and light against shadow, contrives filled and unfilled spaces—and thus forms a stone image of a man. Into this image he has infused a soul—action, impulse, mood, feeling, thought—which is not separable from the sense presence of his design. It cannot be taken out, as one might lift a jewel from a precious box, for the only being it has is in this stone body. Anything else would be literary sculpture. Painting is more complex in its sensuous design and wider in its psychic span. But it is bound by the same principle of a soul and a body that are one—a soul embodied in the unity of lines, colors, values, and textures.

The arts that employ words make the matter more difficult. There are sense qualities and design qualities in the words, the patterning, and the rhythmic sequences of a poem. They are essential, but are only a part of its aesthetic meaning. Words are arbitrary symbols. As we understand them, we create, in response to the poet, an imaginative vision, of incident, of time and space, of sense presences, of mood and passion.

In the novel the sense values play a minor role. There are still values of word quality, of style, of planned and proportioned ordering of parts, but the main interest is in the vivid and meaningful rendering, on the secondary plane alone which mind and imagination move, of the world within and without.

The matter becomes distressingly complex with the motion picture. A story is developed, and is conveyed partly by means of words. This seems closest to the novel. Further thought, however, shows that what we are given, incompletely and in snatches, is dialogue. The leisurely and evocative use of words in describing, narrating, commenting, and interpreting at the command of the novelist is quite beyond the reach of the film. All but the dialogue and incidental sounds is addressed to the eye. The analogy to painting, suggested by this, is misleading. If we look at a segment of a film we see a number of pictures. Each of these has a transformational value—it has its meaning in what precedes and what follows. As these images are projected, we are offered, within the frame of the screen, the actual transformation. People move about in a room, a train roars past, a crowd mills about. If we were at a signal to stay this movement and were confronted with a single visual impression, in color or in black and white, we should not have the equivalent of a painting. The response is radically different. A painting is immovably fixed in design and meaning. Its spirit is that of ordered space. What precedes and follows does not count. But the spirit of a motion picture, even in a single projection, is that of flowing time, made visible to the eye.

The more complex art is in its materials and technique, the looser and more varied will be its form. It is absurd to expect of a novel the simple organizational unity of sculpture; equally absurd to look in the cinema for the patterns of the other arts. But some form it must have, however complex, if it is to be a fine art.

In the new art of the motion picture there are complexities of aim and intricacies of technique which suggest new values of design. But their very nature make the gaining of organic unity difficult. Both gain and danger are bound up with peculiar, new uses of space and time. Here is the pivoting point of the aesthetic problem of the cinema. To reach it we must consider time and space, first in life and then in some of the older arts.

Time and Space in Life

Time and space may be regarded either objectively or psychically. Actual, elapsing time is mathematically measurable in years, months, weeks, days, hours, minutes, and seconds. The tempo is uniform, and the duration is marked off—so many seconds to a minute, so many minutes to an hour. Psychic time exists within the mind. It is variable in tempo and division. Interest speeds it up, and boredom makes it drag. The kaleidoscopic images of a drowning man show it telescoping. Within total space there are limited spaces, filled and unfilled. In a room there are objects variously shaped, filling with their bulk portions of space. All these can be stated in mathematical terms. They are fixed sizes and relations. We may move them about and establish new relationships, or we may change our position in the room. Objectively neither counts. But there are two other space experiences to be dealt with—visual space and psychic space. The actual distance between two light-brackets remains the same, but the visual distance changes with our angle of vision. The actual filled space of a tower, in size and bulk, is constant, but different space-values appear as we approach or recede. Psychic space may be either actual and visual space reappearing within the mind, restressed or remade, or it may have little or nothing to do with an objective world.   Hamlet marks it well in his words: "I could be bounded in a nutshell, and count myself a king of infinite space."   In its subtler forms—the sense of a contracted or expanded personality and of dreams—it all but defies analysis.

SPACE IN ARCHITECTURE AND SCULPTURE

Time plays a negligible part in the plastic arts, and may be disregarded.   A building and a piece of sculpture are tri-dimensional objects surrounded by unfilled space.   What they seem to give is actual space.   They offer dimensions, space forms and space relations which are measurable and seem constant underneath all the shifting of values that results from changed angles of vision.   But what they aim at is visual effectiveness.   Two pillars, one with a wall back of it, and the other with the sky, must be of different diameter to appear alike; the contour line of a pillar must be slightly rounded to appear straight; a roof line must be tilted from the horizontal; a pediment sculpture to be seen effectively from below must have distorted proportions.   All art is semblance—to regard a temple or a sculptured group as a purely mathematical problem of actual measurements is to go astray.   One important fact must, however, be stated. In the case of the light-brackets, seeing them one inch apart or partially super-imposed is a violent and capricious distortion of actual space relations.   As we walk around a sculptured figure and pause at different points, we are confronted with different sets of space forms, different parts of filled and unfilled space, different contour lines and angles.   It is clearly absurd to demand equal effectiveness at all angles.   At best the sculptor can offer two or three visually effective forms.   In each case, there is an organized visual image related to an actual space relationship. Even when there is a bold distortion of the body and its proportions, as in Negro wood sculpture, in Lehmbruck and Archipenko, the motive is not caprice, but the desire for a clear, intensified image for the eye.

SPACE AND TIME IN THE DANCE

In a ballet the dancers move from side to side, from front to rear, up and down, within cubical space boxed in on all sides but one. This stage setting remains constant, and is so limited in extent that the figures of the dancers remain fairly constant in size. No violent visual adjustments are needed as a dancer moves to the rear. A painted backdrop of a distant scene may be used, but this is unimportant since the dancing group never enters this space.

As the music develops its time sequences for the ear, the dance, in harmony with the music, creates patterns of bodily movement for the eye. If the music were from time to time stopped, and pose, gesture, and grouping held immobile, the impression might be thought to be a space image, as in painting, and the dance might be interpreted as a sequence of pictures. But space in the dance is always in relation to time. Every one of its space images holds within it what has preceded and what is to follow. This fusion of time and space marks the dance off from painting and hints at certain interesting problems of the cinema.

SPACE AND TIME IN PAINTING

Painting is rightly considered a space art. There are painters who seek to move their art closer to the time art of music. Kandinsky in theory and practice makes much of suggested movement in colors. He calls many of his pictures compositions—improvisations. Others aim at mobile patterns.

As regards space, there is, first of all, the constant, flat surface of the canvas. Within its bounds the painter creates a two-dimensional space pattern. Composed of lines, colors, shapes, textures, and values, this remains fixed as a visually effective ordered design.

This is only part of the story. What the painter means to give on his flat surface is the illusion of tri-dimensional space. Perspective is used to give this effect. The farther object is placed above the nearer lines; diminished size and greying color make it seem more distant. The deep space limits are the foreground and the background of the picture. These limits are not so narrow as in the dance. There may be distant vistas of mountain and cloud. Nor are the figures constant in size. The far images are mere specks when compared with those in the foreground. The painter has a right to deal creatively with space, but he must give a sharp, clear, orderly space image. This he does by holding to one angle and by a simplified grouping of a few planes, one back of another and all structurally fixed, once for all.

TIME AND SPACE IN THE NOVEL

In the loosely patterned form of the novel we are moving closer to the complicated use of time and space in the motion picture. The novel reveals a moving, shifting recorder; in the cinema there is a moving camera eye. Space and time are in the novel expressed by means of words. Their continuity is broken as the novelist constantly shifts his ground. He gives a glimpse of a landscape, then moves within a room or within the psychic time and space of a person. He gives segments of space, broken time sequences, and shuttles back and forth within a myriad of happenings.

We are continually forced to move with a differently angled, differently focused recorder.   In some cases the dislocations are violent.   Joyce's *Ulysses*, Aldous Huxley's *Point Coun-ter Point* and *Eyeless in Gaza*, and most of Faulkner's novels are examples.   The result is a technique that is confusing to one who is keyed to the clear-cut orderliness of the visual arts.

SPACE AND TIME IN THE MOTION PICTURE

Here the relations and interrelations of time and space are exceedingly complex.   There are new uses, new resources, and new dangers—all resulting in aesthetic problems of great interest.   We may begin with the actual length of a film, the span between beginning and end, and with the actual space of the screen.   A story is unfolded within this time; and visual images, either in black and white or in color, are offered in this frame.   We are tempted to interpret the film either as fiction or as painting.   Both views are false. The story addresses itself directly to the eye.   The early technique of captions gave explanatory words, which linked people who were acting but not talking.   Pantomime, jerky and exaggerated, had to supply the rest.   With the advent of talking pictures it became possible to tell part of the story naturally in terms of dialogue.   But vital differences re-main.   In the film we actually hear what is said, get directly the quality of the voices.   In the novel there is dialogue, printed and meant to be recaptured.   There are description and narration as well.   A scenario as read is incomplete and artistically ineffective.   It is a skeleton bared of the flesh and of an appeal to the senses—a skeleton, too, with many bones missing.   At best, the dialogue in a motion picture is subordinate; the story is told to the eye.   Certain producers have come to see a danger in dialogue, and insist that it must not be allowed to encroach on the pictorial.

Equally false is the other view, which interprets a film as

painting. Ralph Pearson in a short magazine article tells of a letter he received from Walt Disney, containing a plea for skilled draughtsmen to work on his staff. He answered by accusing Disney of having become less and less visually effective in his films. In this he is mistaken both in fact and in attitude. Pearson is a painter and teacher of painting. He has gained a direct and keen sensitiveness to the design quality of pictures. This may be easily carried over to other material. Leo Stein confesses that he makes his own pictures, sensing and creating design in groups of people in a car, a room, a street. This is a strange and exciting thing to do, but it has its dangers. To test a film in terms of whether it would make a good series of paintings is to overlook differences in the treatment of space in the two arts. A picture gives space; a motion picture, like the dance, represents space-time. Again, in a painting, within the limits of foreground and background, there is a simplified recession of a few planes, which holds shapes in the static effectiveness of a design seen at one visual angle. Not so with the images on a screen. There the deep space span is much greater. We are shown a facial close-up of Charlie Chaplin as a tramp walking along a road and disappearing in the distance. We are given with equal clearness what in real life would be an image blurred by its nearness, and what would be indistinct because distant. Nor is there a clarified ordering of intermediate spaces. Whether painted backdrops are used or shots taken of an actual room, the impression gained is often one of persons not living within these spaces or of a confused space perception. The single visual angle, too, is missing. The camera used in filming has been called a moving eye. The photographer takes shots at many angles, and there is a constant and often abrupt shifting of angles. As we in actual life move along a road or around a room, we see objects near or receding, at different slants and heights. Our impressions may be random, but they are rarely confused. We are aware of our position, whether we are standing in a meadow or are aloft in an airplane. Funded experience, visual and motor, makes for such an orderly space perception.

The moving eye of the camera records disjointedly and unexpectedly. It moves so close to a face that we can almost count eyelashes, shows a group of dancers from above or a train moving into the distance. It angles and tilts spaces. There is a demand for sudden and violent readjustments, and no guide as to what they are to be from moment to moment. Chaos results—and an unmoored space experience. New and enriched patterns of seeing are made possible—this must be granted. But this young art is as yet too undisciplined and insensitive to make the most of them. There is in the close-up too evident an appeal to the factual—a movie star's facial expression is the thing. Again, in the jumping about in space there is too much of a naïve delight in impressing and in a display of tricks. The cinema has not gained control of its resources. To startle and use trickery is not in the spirit of true art.

Four technical devices—the blot-out, the fade-out, the transforming fade-out, and the image-whirl—deserve some comment. The first two have been used on the stage. The spotlight might be called a pick-out. It is a violent accent —a strong highlight. .In modern stage lighting there is something less obtrusive and more effective. This is the blacking out of parts of the stage. The fade-out is the gradual disappearance of form and color in a gathering darkness. It was used skilfully at the end of the Irish play, *Shadow and Substance*. In films the blot-out is often used with the close-up or when figures are to be accented as detached from their surroundings. The fade-out is used simply, as on the stage. The transforming fade-out is a different matter. Here, as one image fades out, another emerges. There are analogues in reflections and psychic

experiences. Mirrored houses and streets appear and disappear in the burnished surface of an automobile. In certain
dream states or near dream states the inner eye sees transforming images. A group of painters, the simultaneists,
have sought to put this psychic transformation into their
pictures. They succeeded only in straining their art. The
motion picture has advantages they were without. It must
be admitted that, when this technical device is used artistically within the pattern and meaning of a film, it gives new
and exciting values.

The image-whirl seems to be an agitated camera eye, flashing here and there, picking out of the darkness a face, an
arm, a movement, a swirl of figures, a momentary accent of
light—all leading to a crescendo of ever-mobile confusion.
This is something no other art can do. Certain plays by
Kaiser and Toller when staged in their spirit of staccato
movement and expressionism come nearest. Unfortunately
it is too often used in the cinema merely as a startling trick.
The whirling visual confusion offered must be expressive.
A riot, a cavalry charge, a panic due to fire or earthquake—
here is its material. Such things in real life thunder in our
ears and strike horror through our eyes. The sense impressions made are confused, discontinuous. We get something of their essential might and turbulence, but we are not
detached as we are in art. The motion picture, moving
within a world of seeming, aims to express their essence.
Held apparently to flashes of disjointed, incomplete seeing,
we are plunged into soul drama—rage, pity, agony, despair,
hope, struggle, fear. The close-up is sometimes used effectively to increase the tension. The artistic value of the
image-spray lies in this: that it starts from but does not stop
with the eye—it makes use of the eye to project inner experiences in their essence of violence and human drama.
Unlike images that come and go, such inner experiences are
cumulative in their intensities.

Time, as well as space, is boldly shaped and technically managed. Psychic time in real life is not uniform in its movement. It may go at an even pace, or it may rush or drag. As we move our bodies through space or are aware of the distances between objects in space, we are disciplined to orderly estimates of time. A hundred yards in a walk, a run, or a sprint may be covered within so many minutes or seconds. It takes a sapling so long to grow to a tree. When a train is seen gliding from rest to accelerated speed, it is believed that an orderly computation is possible. The motion picture camera invites us to depart widely from our usual experiences of time. Time is slowed up so that a tennis stroke or a galloping horse is seen as it is never seen in actual life. This slow motion technique may be amusing or instructive, but of itself is unimportant artistically. The opposite process of speeding up—seeing a sapling grow by magic to a tree within a span of seconds or shooting objects through space—holds within it an artistic promise. It is used to best purpose in the animated cartoon.

The time pattern in a film is a very free one, and may easily become chaotic. There are gaps and violent dislocations. The throw-back is a common device. It is a flash back from the present to the past. It expresses the discontinuous timework of consciousness and the sudden recall of things gone by. When it is used in the film, the past is made visible. There are two dangers in this and similar shiftings: a mechanical shuffling and showing of cards, and confusion. In a novel like Faulkner's *The Sound and the Fury* we do not quite know where we are, and we resent a method that is tricky and messy. Films often give a like impression.

It would be absurd to hold a complex art, such as that of the cinema, to simple traditional patterns of space and time. An art is alive only as it shows the old in a new light and

offers new experiences and forms.   But a clarified forming
there must be.   We must not be set adrift on the waves of
an ingenious, wild, irresponsible technique.

Another interesting aesthetic problem of the motion picture is found in its attempt to express certin types, such as
the tragic, the epic, the grotesque, the fantastic, and the
comic.   To what extent has it succeeded?

THE TRAGIC AND THE EPIC IN THE MOTION PICTURE

To what extent can a film capture the tragic quality of a
play like *Hamlet* or the epic quality of novels such as *The
Good Earth, Of Time and the River, Anthony Adverse*, and
The Grapes of Wrath?   The epic in a novel demands a
broad canvas, either filled with many people and happenings
or marked by a wide span of space and time.   But there is
something less obvious.   A person, a place, an incident is
flooded with larger, vaster meanings.   In Freuchen's *Eskimo*
there is the pervading sense of the arctic—cold, snow, moving ice floes, walrus hunting, hunger, work, passion, and
death.   A few human notes—and a vast theme.   In *The
Good Earth* there is something similar—the unending struggle with the soil, storm, famine, migration—a vision of nature and of man.   Wolfe's *Of Time and the River* gives a
haunting impression of time moving in and around the persons and things it carries with it.   The motion picture at
times attempts the epic—examples are *Eskimo, The Good
Earth, The Birth of a Nation, The Covered Wagon*, and
Lost Horizon.   Producers like a lavish display, a vast,
crowded canvas.   The results are disappointing.   There
are effective epic touches here and there, but in inner meaning and sweep these films fall far short of the novels they
use and reshape.   As for the pervasive, inundating quality

of the epic, this they can never reach.   The film *The Grapes of Wrath* at times comes close to it, but falls short of the sweep and breadth of the novel.

The realm of the drama has also been invaded.   There are film versions of *A Midsummer Night's Dream, Romeo and Juliet, Winterset, Dead End*, and *The Children's Hour*. Some of these have been censured for their Hollywood touch; others have been widely acclaimed.   Little of the tragic intensity of *The Children's Hour* remained in *We Three*. The theme was altered, and the meaning was thinned.   *Winterset* was dressed up, reshaped, and given a happy ending. Shakespeare's comedy became a romping ground for Hollywood actors.   Max Reinhardt's genius, tested in the staging of many plays, showed to little advantage when he turned it to the film.   What is the most obvious in the dramatic and tragic—movement, farcical happenings, melodrama—the motion picture can give.   It can offer glimpses of human drama, directly by facial expression and words, indirectly by visual symbolism.   *The Informer* was an intensely dramatic and deeply moving film.   But the theme was one of violence—such material makes success easy.

At some future time there may be a picture that is truly tragic in its own way, original in point of view and technique. It will not be a film version of a tragedy.   The shadings, the subtleties, the psychic issues of a *Hamlet* cannot be held within a motion picture.

The Grotesque, the Fanciful, and the Comic in the Motion Picture

With these types the motion picture has had a greater measure of success.   They may be used separately or in combination.

The grotesque was pointed at the horrible and used effectively in two early films, *The Cabinet of Doctor Caligari* and

The Golem. The fanciful may be used decoratively—it then has a touch of the strange or weird about it; or it may be the building of a distorted, haunting dream world.   It is in this latter sense that it was used, none too artistically, in *Lost Horizon.*   With a technique of space and time distortion at its disposal, the motion picture has largely unrealized chances of exploiting the grotesque and fanciful.   But the spirit of Hollywood is against a deeper use.   It is not sufficiently creative, nor is it psychically subtle, an occasional film like *Outward Bound* notwithstanding.

Greater success has been had with the comic.   It appears in many ways and with many variants.   At times it is offered as the very madcap soul and body of a film; at others it is incidental.   There was genuinely creative artistry in the early Charlie Chaplin and Harold Lloyd pictures; the former showed an amalgam of slapstick and sentiment; the latter were farcical, fantastic, and full of exciting pranks.   There are some later films in which a comic mood is well sustained.   *My Man Godfrey; The Awful Truth; Live, Love and Learn; Topper;* and *Ninotchka* are examples.   Unfortunately they are borrowed, reshaped stories.   For incidental comic effects, the motion picture counts heavily on the personal appearance, the antics, and the genius of a few comedians, and the carrying power of ludicrous situations.   Laurel's expression is such an asset—it suggests irresistibly, set in a cock-eyed world, a Hamlet without mind.   Situations like the trout episode in *My Man Godfrey*, the involuntary ski-slide in *Paradise for Three*, and such as make up a mad sequence in *Bringing Up Baby* are vivid and unique in the sense that no other art can give what the motion picture gives here.   Falstaff is vivid to the eye of the mind; a fine actor may give him a greater vividness on the stage.   The ski-slide might be told with gusto, but it is the film, and the film alone, that can give it directly to the eye, with its moments, its accents, and the final head dive into deep snow. The motion picture may gain much by an artistic use of such novel and original effects.

THE ANIMATED CARTOON

Technically the animated cartoon is new and ingenious; artistically it shows in the work of Walt Disney exceptional quality. It has antecedents and analogues in fantastic and comic folk tales, in animal stories, in the *Münchner Bilderbogen*, in the drawings and verses of Wilhelm Busch, and in our ever popular comic strips. These strips are all more or less alike in what they give—a few stock characters, highly mechanized, a variational recurring pattern, wild, unlooked-for antics. They depend very much on explanatory tags, and are usually crude and blatant in drawing and color. Busch, on the contrary, was a true artist, expressive and bold in his drawing, creative of ever-fresh surprises, amazing in his handling of words and ideas. His Max and Moritz, the bad boys, with their pranks and mock-tragic end, and his Fipps the Monkey are a delight to child and art lover alike.

The ordinary animated cartoon has little value as art. It is either too simple and too mechanized in its pattern or it is trickery run wild. Or it is a cheap imitation of Disney, insensitive in drawing and without insight or grasp of form. This much, however, may be said of it: it is amusing and directly creative in contrast to the many films that borrow from the short story, the novel, and the drama.

Walt Disney's Mickey Mouse and Silly Symphonies and his full-length films, *Snow White and the Seven Dwarfs* and *Pinocchio*, demand and repay closer study. It is a mad world we are confronted with, distorted in its animal forms, unreal in its coloring, strange in its happenings, startling in its surprises, weird in its reshaped feelings—a world to give joy to a child and to an irresponsible god.

In form and incident, neither is this the world of animal

stories and of such fairy-tale favorites as the Three Little Pigs and Snow White, nor is it altogether original with Disney. Prototype or no prototype—the Big Bad Wolf, Mickey Mouse, Pluto the Pup, and the Flying Mouse show an unusual creative force at work. The whole animal kingdom is recreated in the image of the fantastic, the comic, the impish, and the playful.

Snow White and the Seven Dwarfs, a full-length film, is in a more ambitious way typical of his other work. A purist might say, "This is not Grimm's fairy-tale." We should have to agree with him. But if he went on to attack the film because of that, we should point out to him how easy it is for a purist to become a pedant.

Genuine folk tales have been gathered from many lands. Cultural conditions and stages account for many differences. There is, however, a strong family resemblance. They all reveal a sympathetic understanding of animal life and the sense of a bond between animals and humans. They are marked by a simple genuineness of motive, action, and feeling. Theirs is a lordly way with time and space. Summer may be changed to winter at the twist of a cap, there are the seven league boots, and a beanstalk grows to amazing heights overnight. There is to be found in them the fairy godmother motif. The good are taken care of, and the wicked are punished. They are marked, finally, by grotesquerie and by the comic and fantastic.

It is a very much reshaped *Snow White* that Disney gives. He has retained the sympathetic bond and the fairy godmother motif. But he is too much of an artist not to know that he could not possibly rival the folk tale in these respects. Rightly he has put the stress on original patterns of space and time and on the grotesque. Here he is supreme. Snow White herself has little depth, psychical and visual. She seems almost cut out of a charmingly colored bit of paper. The animals and the dwarfs steal the show.

Here and elsewhere in Disney there is a kindly feeling for animal life, its activities, impulses, and mishaps. As he draws them they are shapes of his own, equally remote from nature and from the ordinary humanized animals. Examples are the birds of prey and the turtle in *Snow White*, the Big Bad Wolf, the Flying Mouse, and Pluto. A Disney form is theirs, and it is a Disney life they lead. It is nothing short of amazing that while so many of the serious films give the impression of being mechanical and manufactured, the Disney pictures, laboriously created by animating countless drawings, are the very acme of utter and completely successful spontaneity. Occasionally a human note is struck— the Flying Mouse, over-ambitious, the animals cleaning house, the squirrel using its tail as a duster and shaking the dust out of it by knocking it against the window sill, the turtle always trying so hard and always frustrated. There is a quality here that is lacking in most folk tales. The best term for it is impishness. The seven dwarfs are equally original. They all have bulbous noses, but each is a separate grotesque and comic creation. Everywhere there is a playful, impish imagination at work, extracting the utmost out of each trait and each happening. It is a pleasure to watch Sneezy's antics and the changing lines of Grumpy's mouth.

Sound and color are used effectively, and the settings, whether castle, forest, cliff, or interiors, give a space that can be moved about in, and lived in.

Pinocchio shows Disney at his best. Technically it is superior to *Snow White* in the range and sureness of its effects. Collodi's book, a great favorite with children, lacks the simplicity of the genuine folk-tale: it is loosely patterned; the disconnected happenings are many; the amusing, the clever, and the didactic are mingled entertainingly. There is little character drawing.

Disney has reshaped the book to something greatly superior.   All the characters—Pinocchio, Jiminy Cricket, Foulfellow, Cleo, the bad boy, Monstro the Whale—come alive.   However crazy and weird the incidents are in a Disney film, there is always the sense of expressive personalities true to their fantastic patterns.   Each is at home in his or her space world—Geppetto in his workshop, Cleo in her bowl, and Monstro in his raging sea.   Novel effects ranging from the diminutive to the colossal are gained by shifting and combining these space worlds.   Thus a street seems huge as it must to the cricket, and we share his effort to make headway on it; Pinocchio is set over against a man-size world.   Never is the shifting of outlook and dimension other than orderly and original.   Nor is there the jumble of tricky close-ups and visual confusions met with too often in films.   Form, movement, and sound work together as effectively in the Monstro adventure as they did in the stampede of the animals in *Snow White*.   The lengthening of Pinocchio's nose and his being changed to a donkey show clever transforming.   The film has an imaginative lift, a vivid unity, a bold and mastering fancy lacking in its original.

It has been shown that the motion picture has at its command astonishing time and space effects, and that it too often turns into mere trickery what might be a great artistic gain.   Disney does strange and bewildering things with space and time, but there is always the sense of a pattern. Examples are Snow White in the forest, with her fears externalized; the stampede of the animals and their rush to help Snow White.   Sound, movement, a whirl of visual shapes, time accelerated and space swept through—here is a new art at its expressive best.

While the motion picture has reached for the tragic and the epic and failed, it has in the art of Disney scored an artistic success with two other types—the comic and the grotesque.

COLOR IN THE MOTION PICTURE

Color may be used representationally, decoratively, and structurally. Sound was first introduced into the motion picture in order to move people and happenings closer to what they are in real life. We have come to accept it as a matter of course. Not only do people as we know them talk, but they and all else in the external world appear in color. Why not, says the producer, make our pictures complete by using color and making it so natural that it, like sound, will be taken for granted in a life-like rendering? There is a danger here. It is like asking the sculptor to use colored wax and match its colors with nature. The sculptor could rightly reply: "That road leads not to art but to a waxworks museum."

The peculiar thing about technicolor pictures in their present stage of development is that they seem unreal. There are very strange blues and browns, which are pleasing in themselves and in combination give new decorative effects. What is needed in the motion picture is not a technically improved representational use of color, but an understanding of what can be done with color in art. Not for one moment do we in *Snow White* take color for granted as part of nature, nor are we jarred because it is unreal. It is used decoratively and structurally in a world of its own. Color is so effectively related to color that a reproduction in color of a single moment gives the impression of a good painting. The representational use of color interests the painter but little; color relationships within a design are his aim. That, too, is the right aim for the motion picture producer. In carrying out this aim he will come to see a new problem and a new opportunity: that of exploiting and ordering to a design time relationships in color. Robert Edmond Jones holds this mobile color, or color music, to be something worth moving towards.

THE FUTURE OF THE MOTION PICTURE

As an industry aimed at amusement and instruction the motion picture will beyond doubt advance with the march of a technological culture. Experiments are made with stereoscopic vision; color processes are being improved; a more effective camera and a more subtle and ingenious photography are to be looked for. But what of its future as an art form?

Technology as it creates an automobile, a crane, a winnowing machine, gains a new value—functional beauty. Aesthetic enjoyment here turns on the better, the more smoothly running, the shape in relation to the function. But something else must be taken into account—an aesthetic plus— something beyond use. A primitive people may be crude in technology, and yet be artistically sensitive and creative. A Greek coin, an Egyptian bit of ornament, an Indian basket, old Peruvian cloth or pottery, a Norse shield and a Celtic brooch reveal imaginative and creative reshaping— art conscious of values of its own. To overlook this is to hazard an aesthetic theory that says: Turn away from art in isolation, disregard the museum picture, the staged dance or concert—turn to art as living experience, to the form and meaning of an automobile and a spigot, the pattern of a factory, of a municipal project or a baseball game—understand art within a social context.

This theory when applied to the motion picture stresses the fact that here is a popular art expressive of a democratic culture, an art to be interpreted in a technological context. There is a double mistake in this. The motion picture is in no sense a democratic art springing from the life of the people. In this the contrast to the dance is striking. Nor does it aim at a technological product. Technology is used merely as a means to something else.

If the motion picture is to progress artistically, it must

allow a creative art impulse to become self-conscious. Playing with technical devices, aiming at amusement and box office receipts, borrowing from other arts—nothing of this will serve. It must develop a life and form of its own, and take its place as a new, fine art within the federation of the arts. Its opportunities are many. It offers new space-time experiences, new mobile color designs, and new visual projections of an inner life. It can gain an original unrivaled mastery of the fantastic and the comic, and may find new imagery and patterns for other types as well. The form it must seek is a complex one, and it is as yet confused in its seeking.

Such progress demands two conditions: a new kind of creative artist and a new type of motion picture theatre.

The new artist will write a scenario that is not a mechanical diagrammatic tracing of a short story, a novel, or a play. He will not allow it to express the clichés, the platitudes, the silly romance of the average commercial story. He will dip directly into the stuff of life and seek distinction and form. He cannot stop with this first forming. Hollywood can do wondrous and lamentable things with a scenario; build it out toward lavish display, absurd trickery, and stardom. He must be the directive master and formative artist throughout. This means the need of a visual imagination keener and more complex than is to be found in the other arts. It means also an understanding and skilled use of the exact value for art of any of the many technical devices at his disposal, and, finally, insight into the kind of form a film is capable of gaining.

To create or to encourage such an artist is useless unless he is given the chance to express himself under favorable conditions. These are supplied by an art film theatre. This would be an esoteric theatre within the great motion picture industry. It must be liberally endowed and be self-consciously artistic. Money, stardom, lavishness, irresponsible trickery must be ruled out. It might be objected that such a theatre would not pay, that it would be boring to all but a small group of sophisticates, and that it is a hothouse project. These objections are not well taken. It would be rash to assert that Disney's animated cartoons do not pay, are not amusing, and are not aimed at art. The belief that art should not be an unwholesome toy of arty people is back of the abuse heaped on the phrase "art for art's sake." What the phrase really means is that art creates and concerns itself with values of its own. Endless talk about the distinctive and dissimilar cultural contexts of the Parthenon, the Palace of Persepolis, and a Mayan stela is of little interest to the art lover, unless some of it has some bearing on the quality of sculptural line, sensitive modeling, fine spacing, and patterned form, as it is distinctive of each or common to all. An Assyrian Wounded Lion, an Egyptian Falcon, an Aztec Feathered Serpent, a peasant's or child's crude drawing have something of this. Instinctive or deliberate, it is there, in its natural creative strength, and ought to be fostered.

Such an art film theatre is not to be without roots in the soil of the motion picture theatre as we have it. For this has developed, incidentally and all too rarely, artistic values. Some of these may be taken over; others may be left to the hardy life that is theirs in an industry in which art counts for so little. To remove such unfavorable conditions is part of the task of the art film theatre. For some time to come it must of necessity be experimental, for, as yet, the final form and span of this, the newest of the arts, are things unknown. But they ought to be looked for, diligently and boldly, and with a single-mindedness that says: Give me a film that is not merely amusing or instructive—a film that is art aimed at, art achieved, and art to be enjoyed.

This must not be understood as a desire to belittle or to abolish the motion picture as we know it. Man has a right to flutter toward some neon sign in search of pleasure or mental profit. He has a right to slapstick and mystery and sentiment. The very hugeness of the motion picture industry guarantees something for every one. Let the big show go on. Let it explode its sensations, ply its magic, and give us the whirling wheel of its stars. But the rough and tumble life of the streets is in no sense a substitute for the school, nor is the school merely a preparation for the rough and tumble life of the streets. It fosters quality in what we do and sensitiveness to the quality of what we experience. It is in this sense that the art film theatre is to be educative. It is a mingling, smelting, and refining process by which ore is changed to the pure gold of art.

MODERNISM IN ART

The rivalry between the old and the new is a fascinating thing to watch. It appears with little rhyme or reason in the fashions of dress. There human nature shows itself as at once gregarious and restless—the old is discarded in favor of the new, that yields to the newest, and that again to the old; there is an erratic swinging toward and away from the useful and the comely. In medical science, economics, and religion, however, it appears in more serious and expressive ways. There it develops into the often bitter struggle between the conservative and the radical. The former looks upon past achievement as something to be guarded and cherished and regards departures from the accepted with distrust; the latter looks with a critical eye at the past and sees in the new the hope of something better. Here the pressure of science, the need of experimentation, the impact of problems of health and social well-being put the conservative on the defensive as ineffectually blocking progress.

In art the matter of the old and the new must be viewed from a different angle. Art, it is true, is affected by science and by the social life in which it has its roots, and from which it gains much of its substance and spirit. Technical advances have been made possible by girder construction, the invention of new alloys; chemistry has added to the range and permanence of colors; photography has helped the dance and has had a share in creating a new art. Industrialism and an age of social tensions and complexities have opened new channels of expressiveness to art. But the boon may be not an unmixed one. To say that photography has made portrait painting superfluous is absurd. Its very advance has led some painters to a poor and cheap art of portraiture; it has made others acutely conscious of the difference between a copy, however skilfully managed and retouched, and an interpretative painting. Again, art that plunges directly into social problems and commits itself to a "social statement" or economic creed is not by that fact good art. The truth of the matter is this: art is more than technique, and, moving as it does in a world of semblance, is not to be judged in terms of practical advance or cultural progress. Present-day medical science discredits that of Galen. Ibsen does not discredit the Greek dramatists. A Van Gogh or a Cézanne cannot be used to deny quality to a Rembrandt or a Titian. Nor can the latter be held to devalue the modern masters. Controlled curiosity and a persistent, controlling practical energy mark the advance of science and technology. The old is set aside for something better. In art there is no such advance.

A work of art is a spirit, a vision creative of a form within the medium and the resources of this or that art. Are there to be new visions and new forms? Here is the point of issue between the traditionalist and the modernist. The traditionalist is impressed by what has been done in the past. He has much to say about accredited masters, sound taste, the great traditions in sculpture, painting, architecture, and music, and the disciplined style of schools of art. He has no welcome for new meanings and new forms. The modernist is a rebel, a gambler, and a visionary. He sees in tradition the danger of routine. As an artist he has the utmost faith in a living, endlessly creative art. To its wealth of forms he means to add as his own something freshly seen, felt, and imagined, and effectively shaped.

Modernists there have always been—rebels and visionaries who did not conform to the art pattern of their time. They all had courage, and most of them paid the price of popular and critical disesteem. Euripides was called low-minded

MAILLOL, VENUS WITH NECKLACE

and tricky, the impressionist painters were ridiculed, El Greco until recently was slurred over in histories of painting, Wagner was labeled noisy and formless, Rodin and Van Gogh ugly and perverse, and Whitman was not writing poetry at all.

Within the last forty years modernism in art has made itself felt as never before. Some of the "crazy men" have become classics. Their radicalism has become a tradition which the conservative is forced to accept. But he has not thereby gained peace of mind. Our present-day architects, sculptors, painters, composers, and novelists are boldly in search of new forms and values. They are experimenting creatively with colors, rhythms, textures, perspective, abstract forms, and patterns. Success is not always theirs, for there are many by-paths and blind alleys to be avoided in this resolute march toward new goals.

To those who believe that the old is not to be challenged and the new is in no way to be trusted, the situation has become embarrassing. The new art is everywhere about them —in annual exhibitions, in concert halls, in modern anthologies, in city buildings and shop-windows, in arts and crafts, in stage settings. It may be attacked, but it can no longer be ignored by shutting eyes or stopping ears.

When something has so surely established itself and is marked by so rich an experimental life, abuse and shallow enthusiasm alike are out of place. Adjustment through understanding is needed.

What modernism in art means, in revolt and in visionary spirit and form, is strikingly revealed in the urge, the energy, and the attainments of this so-called new art.

While the reactionary may be left to his profitless scolding, the common man has a right to be heard. He is honestly shocked or puzzled by an art so unlike what he is used to. Modernistic painting disturbs him greatly. The modernists have made something distorted, repulsive, cryptic, of an art that is less abstract than architecture and less elusive than music—a visual art that is meant to be representational, clear-cut, and beautifying.

At the root of his trouble are two false assumptions. One is that art aims at likenesses; the other restricts art to the beautiful in the sense of the easily and persuasively pleasing.

No mimetic theory does justice even to the old art. Titian's *Man with the Glove* is acknowledged a great portrait, but who knows the sitter, and who cares? No work of art is an exact transcript from nature. Masks, wood sculptures, mimetic dances, the tragedies of Shakespeare, the paintings of Turner—all reveal simplifying, distortion, intensifying, and free imagining.

Distortion is objected to, partly because it seems a falsifying of nature, partly because it seems to the common man to lead directly toward ugliness.

It is true that the modernist distorts the lines and colors of common objects. One need only recall Van Gogh's cypresses, Cézanne's apples and oranges and napkins; Braque's cubistic designs, O'Keeffe's flowers, Marc's landscapes, Davies' animal forms, Grigorieff's heads, Benton's murals, Epstein's figures, and Modigliani's, Kisling's, and Archipenko's nudes. While decorative distortion generally moves within the beautiful, expressive distortion tends to shatter it. Superficial pleasingness is replaced by something strong, intense, complex, and of a wiser and deeper expressiveness. Not much of the greatest art, and no bold art, can be held with the thin gold circle of beauty. *Oedipus Rex* and *King Lear* are beyond it. Few would deny the quality of great and stirring poetry to that chant of the Furies in which are held within the daemonic imagination of Aeschylus materials and images that ought to make an apostle of Greek decorum retch with disgust. No modern poet could seek a bolder extreme. Neither the great art of the past nor the experimental art of the present can be understood if likeness

to nature or a narrow and superficial beauty is used as a final
test.

The right to reject modern art rests with every man.
The stark agony put by Gothic sculptors into their Christ
on the Cross is not to the liking of serene and decorous minds.
Many a modern picture is disturbing and unrestful in its
mobile color and strange design, in its direct and searching
vision.   But no one has the right to condemn such art on
false premises or because of prejudice.

Revolt and personal vision have been held to be the essential spirit and form of modernism.   This can be effectively
proved by showing these to be the qualities of modernistic
art.

The modernist is a rebel.   Three things he rebels against:
routine, a narrow and superficial beauty, and alien dominance in art.

Routine is a mechanical way of seeing and rendering, and
shows a lazy, imitative spirit.   As such it is a great danger
to art.   It may be destructively present before a man first
looks at a picture and before an artist puts brush to canvas.
There are forces within and about us that favor standardized response-patterns.   We see in terms of what we know;
and knowing is stereotyped, is not what it ought to be—
something flexible, alert, living.   This is too much like being secure in what we take for granted.   Art may be
wrongly expected to express such response-patterns—trees
and houses as they are commonly seen and known, shapes
and figures without the living, variable quality of line and
color of a visual experience.   Art in turn may fall into the
same error and substitute formula for creativeness.   It is
then marked by a mechanical way of seeing and rendering
and a lazy unoriginal spirit—witness the mechanized movements and gestures of classical toe-dancing, and the kind of
poetry that restricts itself to a few obvious rhythms or wears
so-called poetical words or images thin.   The old academic

instruction in painting had much of routine in it. Ruskin writes: "We begin, in all probability, by telling the youth of fifteen or sixteen, that Nature is full of faults and that he is to improve her, but that Raphael is perfection, and that the more he copies Raphael the better; and that after much copying of Raphael, he is to try what he can do himself in a Raphaelesque, but yet highly original manner; that is to say, he is to try to do something very clever, all out of his own head, but yet this clever something is to be properly subjected to Raphaelesque rules." And he adds: "And we wonder we have no painters."

How routine may lead astray even in the judging of the great art of the past may be read in that ludicrous chapter of art criticism—the appraisals by experts when the British Museum was considering the purchase of the Elgin marbles.

It is only fair to admit that not all modernists escape formula and dogma. There are mechanical copyists of radical patterns—and there is much parrot talk among radicals. Lachaise, Archipenko, Matisse, Joyce, Faulkner, are re-creative in terms of the stock-in-trade of theories, predilections, styles of interpreting and rendering. Even Picasso, experimenter as he is, finds it fatally easy to repeat, in his latest period, that strange shape, a flat, distorted, scissor-cut head and face in profile.

On the whole the modernist fights against routine in himself and others. He does not allow his art to be snared by a formula. The futurist Carlo Carra painted, ten years apart, *The Burial of the Anarchist Galli* and *The Talk*, the one a swirling pattern of energy and unrest, the other a counter-discovery of simple, crudely and stolidly substantial forms. Thomas Benton in an essay in *Creative Art*, 1928, tells how he came to rebel against the dogma of abstract painting, and how he felt the need of expressing an interest in factual happenings and solid space objects. So he painted his murals of American life. But these pictures of

Spaniards, Indians, Puritans, and workers are far removed from the traditional types of historical painting. Benton has recently carried personal shaping a step farther. In *Persephone* and in *Susanna and the Elders* he has projected subjects from Greek mythology and the Bible into the American scene.

The constructive force back of this, the first, revolt is the demand for a personally inspired, creatively alive and free art. If a girl is ever new to her lover, it is because, an artist, he is ever new in himself. And so, in painting, common objects—a bush, a tree, a hillside, a room—which are familiarly and mechanically responded to are to be set free within ever-fresh visual experiences and ever-new imagining and forming. An unshackled art, it is true, is not always a wise art. All creativeness is subject to error and waste. There is many a painting that is freakish and brash in failure. But there is tremendous life in this new art—new themes and rhythms in its poetry, new aims in its architecture, new moods and visions in its painting.

The second revolt of the modernist is against a narrow and shallow beauty. People are too ready to hold that nothing can have art quality unless it is beautiful and that beauty means the pleasing, persuasive rendering of agreeable objects. When they meet with something other, they call the artist wild, uncouth, perverse. An unambitious art easily slips into the inanely pleasing, and the obvious and superficial in color, imagery, and music. It then misses a deeper beauty and larger expressiveness and leaves unused great creative powers. The newer art is not one of pretty faces, facile design, and dainty, decorative touches. Of a deeper and larger beauty there is much. Many of the sculptures of Maillol and Kolbe and the poems of H. D., Frost, and Aldington are closer to the Greek spirit than the whole mass of neo-classic art. At times even such beauty is sacrificed. The *Oedipus Rex*, the *Divine Comedy*, Gothic sculpture, and the music of Beethoven are spiritually expressive beyond a worship of beauty however devout. Rodin, Meunier, and Epstein; O'Neill and Werfel; Sandburg and Jeffers; Faulkner and Steinbeck—all bold users of the ugly—move away from a shallow art of escape.

The constructive force back of this second revolt is the demand for an art sufficiently ambitious and strong to bend even the ugly to its uses—an art that is direct, searching, far-ranging, and unafraid.

The third thing the modernist rebels against is the intrusion of alien interests. He resents a non-aesthetic attitude on the part of the public, and he means his own art to be kept free. Of these interests, the practical blocks an understanding of the fine art of architecture; the sentimental and intellectual grossly misjudge painting, and the hedonic and practical distort the meaning of poetry, music, and the dance. A building is more than something useful—it is a matter of functional beauty, and of proportioned and effective design. A painting is the soul-in-body of a visual experience—it is decidedly not an item of information. Appeal to subject-interest or to the sentimental is common and dangerous. Many people in looking at pictures never reach the art of painting. They luxuriate in sentiment, become interested in what is painted, relate it to themselves, take it or leave it. They are unbelievably naïve in the kind of enjoyment they expect a picture to give. They might as well be eating bonbons, discussing flavors, or contemplating keepsakes. Much popular art serves alien interests. There is a place in art for life and its manifold interests. Religious art may be both devout and artistically good. Historical painting can be both informative and good; monumental sculpture can glorify and be of good design; poetry can be humbly human and yet have quality. But art controlled by such interests may be very bad. What Kipling, Wilcox, Service,

Edgar Guest, and certain fashionable portrait painters at their worst are doing is to exploit emotionally or glamorously, at the cost of art, patriotism, the domestic virtues, and vanity. It is a silly thing to say that modernistic painting springs from and expresses dissipated and restless spirits of Montmartre, who are without love of country or fireside. That is a cheap attack on an art that cuts itself off from appeal through subject-matter, and aims at strength and purity of design. Again, it is presumptuous to claim that art can be good only if it is socially and economically minded. An enslaved art may be made to serve many purposes, but it has none of its own. This much must be said of abstract painting—it is an extreme instance of a revolt against subject-ridden, mastered art.

The various secessionist exhibitions in Europe, the organizing of the Armory show in 1918 by eight American artists, differing widely as painters but alike in their welcome of the new art, the impact and shock of that show, the bitter and silly comments and appraisals—all this is a thing of the past. The turmoil has quieted down; the fog has lifted. What is best in the new art now stands revealed, not merely as something strange and rebellious, but as something constructively formed in response to a new vision.

The modernist is an expressionist. The term may be variously shaded. A special historical development has been inaccurately marked German expressionism. This is a turbulent and rebellious art marked by violent unrest, energism, and extreme distortion. Lately painting and poetry have moved along the quieter paths of post-expressionism. It must be borne in mind, however, that this is merely a compensatory movement within modernism.

We are here concerned with expressionism in its largest meaning. The answer to the question, "what is it the modernist seeks to express?" is a four-fold one: himself; objects in their spirit; forms expressive of himself, of the object, and of the art in which he works; and something of moment in the age in which he lives.

In one sense all art is self-expression. It is the projection of personal vision and personal skill. Raphael's smooth charm, Botticelli's decorative forms, Rembrandt's browns, Chardin's simple, strong line, the religious visions of a Giotto, a Dante, a Blake, Shelley's patterned lines and Swinburne's music, Monet's way of seeing a bridge and Turner's of seeing a landscape, the contrast of spirit and form in tragedy between Aeschylus, Euripides, Ibsen, Wedekind, and O'Neill, the direct joy of life in Breughel, and the preoccupation with magnificence in Titian—here is illustrative material in plenty. The conservative takes such personal differences for granted in poetry, and when sanctioned by time he will accept them in the other arts. But he has no welcome for the self-expressive drawings of a child, the wood sculpture of the African, and the paintings of peasants, of primitives, of modernists. The truth is that he approves of self-expression only if it can be harmonized with what he knows and with what he in common with many others sees. The world he sees—hills, streams, trees, fields, men and women, changeable as it is in color, form, and light —is to him something solidly built up of permanent impressions and items of knowledge. He knows a skyscraper as vertical masses and parallel lines. The American flag is to him so many stars and stripes and a rallying point for patriotic feeling. He turns against the painter who does not see and render this world he knows and would have all painters give. Yet in another art, poetry, he has accepted radical reshaping. Moon and stars, the pear tree and the willow, the rose and the violet may be routine impressions or scientific material. But poets have set their pattern and imagery on moon, star, tree, and flower, and seen them in many moods. To see, as Robert Frost does, the rivulets in

HOFER, GIRL WITH BATHING CAP

melting snow as "ten million silver lizards"; to describe gulls as "cloud-calligraphers of windy spirals before a storm"; to use phrases such as "peony-budded breasts" and "cloud-leaper lightning"—is to depart violently from a common and ordered experience.

The modernist plays havoc with the firmly set world of the conservative. As a painter he is personally minded and bold in his reshaping. Van Gogh alters colors, puts whorls into cypress and cloud, bends straight contour lines; Picasso and the cubists break up objects and seek new forms; Cézanne, Segonzac, Modigliani, Benton, and Dali are radical re-shapers of the human figure. In each case there is an intensely personal vision. To interpret such art, as Babbitt did, as romanticism or as mere hunger of self is utterly wrong. For it is as an artist that the modernist expresses himself. Far from being a mere swallower and destroyer, he is an honest, disciplined reshaper and creator of new forms.

The second aim of the modernist is to express the spirit of an object as related to himself. An art teacher allowed her children to choose their own subjects and left them for the most part to their own devices. A little girl chose to paint the birth of Christ. She burst out crying. When asked for the reason she said: "I can make everything else look as if Christ were being born, but I can't make the snow look as if He were being born." The desire was not to paint snow that looked like snow, but snow that somehow shared in the great mystery. Its dead whiteness did not lend itself to the emotionalized vision that she meant to project.

Accountable for much of the distortion in modern painting is this desire to capture something of the spirit and soul of an object. Simplifying and intensifying are two of the means used. An object does not live in its routine form and detail. Painting a yacht, with woodwork and brass, stanchions, spars, and salt-spotted sails set down literally does not appeal to the modernist. Sheeler in his painting has omitted detail, exaggerated speed lines, and multiplied sails beyond reason, but his distorted image gives the very wind-wave life of a yacht.   Modern art is direct, searching, forceful—it goes straight to the heart of something and catches its beat.   Examples are to be had in all the arts.   The sculpture of Rodin and Meunier, the *Heldenklage* of Elkan, the *Adagio* of Kolbe, the poetry of Frost and Robinson, the sunflowers and cypresses of Van Gogh, some of the work of Gill, Grant Wood, and Benton, are instances of such art.   Sandburg's *Chicago* and Vachel Lindsay's *The Congo*, tremendous in energy and individual in technique, respond to and express the spirit of a great city and of an alien race.   One thing is essential—the artist must respond sympathetically to something other than himself.   Such sympathy is rooted in the imagination and bears as its fruit a personal art, visually effective and emotionally intense—an art no mere self-seeker and introvert could possibly create.

A conservative in a liberal moment may grant this and still insist that the modernist is not always a respecter even of the spirit of an object, and that he is, therefore, at heart a lawless and destructive distorter.   This is true of some wilful, capricious minor artists.   It would be futile to deny that this is a problem of serious import in the case of even artists like Picasso, Epstein, and Brancusi.

The third point is this—the modernist seeks forms, in relation sometimes to the object, and always to himself and the medium he employs.   He may deal freely with an object, but at his best he is loyal to himself—as an artist and to the art he serves.   Kidd in *Chrysalis* stresses the girl's eyes, barely indicates her nose, and distorts her hair into bands of color which he carries into the background.   This is not caprice, for his aim is not a portrait but the projection into design of a mood—the dreams of an adolescent girl.   A modernist may lengthen an arm to fit into a pattern; he may for greater visual effectiveness shift lights and shadows; he may simplify or exaggerate for the sake of greater spiritual expressiveness. None of this is self-indulgence or anarchy—it is loyalty in its truest sense. Rejecting as he does alien interests, the modernist must be self-disciplined. How absurd then of the critic to speak of his painting as caricature. Bad art there is, of course, in all ages; and each movement in art has its type of badness. There are self-advertisers among the modernists, who fail to create new significant forms. For these I hold no brief. There are faddists who become slaves of a routine of their own. They may be put to one side. Painters and sculptors, etchers and architects, poets, metal-workers, and composers, are exhibiting new ways of seeing and feeling projected into original designs that give sharply and directly the feel of the medium.

The last point in the expressionism of the modernist is this—he means to give, within a personally shaped and artistically controlled vision and form, some phase or shape or meaning of the age in which he lives, and of whose spirit he is a part. There is an art of escape—the pre-Raphaelites come to mind—and there is an art rooted in and expressive of its age. The nature of this latter art, whether conservative or radical, depends on the quality of the age in which it thrives. Of late there has been a movement in American painting called regionalism, aimed at local color and special physical and social subject-matter. The discussion of its claims, promises, and dangers belongs elsewhere. The complexities of our age, its challenge to the artist, and the way that challenge is accepted and met by the modernist—this is our present concern. His now-minded art stands firmly within the noise, the ugliness, the tremendous energies of the present. That age has been marked, in praise or blame, by many labels. It has been called an age of machines, an age in which the turmoil of the factory, the noise of the riveter, and the drone of the dynamo mark the burial of art. It has been called vulgar, disillusioned, destructive of spiritual values. In defense, it has been called socially minded, experimental, honest to the point of not being fooled, courageous enough to pay the price. But it is too various and vast in form and meaning to fit into one formula. It lives incompletely and differently within many minds. This much, at least, may be said of it: it is manifold, strong, bold, and intensely alive. Our parks and seaside resorts, and the factories and wharves of our cities, reveal how varied are our pleasure and our work. We are equally eager for new chemicals and alloys and for new spiritual values. Everywhere there is a sense of life and power. To live wholly within this process, as part of its heartbeat and drive, satisfies some men; others demand an imaginative projection and reshaping. This may be tawdry or vicious. When a tabloid refers to the execution of Ruth Snyder in large headlines, "Ruth Burns Tonight," it is imaginatively reshaping a fact, but only to appeal to the love of the morbid and sensational. Far otherwise is it with the artist when he sets himself to express part of the form and spirit of his age. When Vassos in *Contempo* parallels satiric descriptions of stores, beaches, subways, tabloids, advertising, and skyscrapers with black and white sketches not at all literal, but original in design and expressive of these various forms and phases of our life, he has held within effective patterns and made vivid for the imagination something that loses much of its detail and nothing of its inner meaning. In this sense the modernist is not a recorder, but an interpreter—Sandburg, of Chicago and the grain and corn fields of the West; Frost, of farm life; Sloan, Bellows, and Marsh, of street, saloon, prize ring; Léger, of machinery; O'Neill, of the modern mind; Karfiol, of race types; and Benton, of industrialism. Nothing is so misleading as to call this art, even in its quieter and simpler examples, naturalism. It distorts and either intensifies or simplifies in order to express something other than the mere detail and surface of its age. As it seeks this kind of expressiveness, it reveals itself as manifold, enterprising, and forcefully alive—paralleling in this three-fold fashion the qualities of the age in which it works.

There is a temptation to which the modernist artist must not yield—that of finding theme and expressive value only in what is violent, crude, striking, strident, alive in the sense of flinging itself about. In an age such as ours there must be a tremendous amount of sustaining, quietly working energy. In contrast to the city, much of it is found in rural communities. Its qualities must not be neglected by art. Again, no art must be immersed in its age; it has the right and the duty to express the desire for something that the present neglects and denies. Violent in spirit and technique, intricate in design, the poems of Lola Ridge, the murals of Rivera, the novels of Faulkner are expressive of tension and social unrest. Calm in spirit, quiet in technique, simple and clear-cut in design, the poems of Robert Frost; the landscapes of Dale Nichols, Brooke, Bruce, and Sheeler; the figure painting of Grant Wood, Brackman, and Hofer are in their own way no less expressive of modernism.

When materials are absorbed by a creative artist, many imaginings, many moods, many designs result. Never has there been greater range and variety in painting. Nor has art ever been bolder in experiment and more eager. Abundance and rush of life are to be found in this art—forceful design, mobile color, creative power, a searching and mastering spirit, violence and calm, a new surface and a new spirit.

An art that seeks to make an age live in the imagination and in new sense-patterns is an art of large ambitions. It cannot be kept free of occasional failures. There are many noisy little rebels and egoists who are poor artists—every one of the arts has its freakish practitioners. Every storm centre of movement has its ungifted hangers-on and sloshers. But to collect these and mark them Exhibit in Modern Art is like marking a dime museum or a sideshow Exhibit in Human Nature. Even nature has its freakish and experimental failures. That is at best a petty and malicious sport. It amounts to denying that art and nature are variously and propellingly alive. The task of appraising rightly single works of art, special movements in modernistic art, is a thankless one. But to march with the urge and swing of the new art, and the stinging challenge of its aims, seems better than to be stolidly or indignantly dead on one's feet.

NOTES AND ADDITIONS

NOTES AND ADDITIONS

NATURE AND ART

In the following passage from Grillparzer's diaries he (1) denies that imitation of nature is the aim of art; (2) asserts that if it were art must fail, inasmuch as it cannot give the full intensity and variety of nature; (3) argues that men differ enormously in their capacity to enjoy and be stirred by nature, and that the deepest response is found where nature is psychically charged—with moods, thoughts, human fate, and human experiences; (4) holds that this is what the artist does; and (5) insists that in art nature is merely material, imitation is merely a means of bringing home to us and allowing us to share the ecstatic vision of the artist.

"Imitation has been set up as the highest law of art. But I ask—can nature be imitated? Sculpture offers forms, but lacks the ultimate charm, the movement, the color of nature. Painting presents landscapes and all it can gain is that it presents in the most lifelike manner possible the external appearance of trees, grasses, clouds. But can it give us the sound of the wind in the trees, the waving of the grasses, the movement of the clouds? These are the things that charm us in an actual landscape. What becomes of the song of the birds, the murmuring of the brook, the sound of the bells? Nor can an actual landscape be matched by one poetically described, although the latter is faintly expressive of movement. And yet the colorless immobile statue, the painted or poetically given landscape offered by art move people whom nature leaves unresponsive. How account for the fact that the faint representation has a stronger appeal than the strong original? The technical perfection of the imitation cannot move us emotionally—at best we are surprised and marvel, as we do at the feats of the strong man or when we see in our museums faces carved on cherry pits. Again—why is it that nature when she does not serve the satisfaction of our needs affects us immediately and does not so affect animals? And why does she not affect all men to the same degree? What is there in the rosy glow of clouds, in the fading of light, in the gathering of shadows at sundown to bring emotion to the point of tears? Why do I pass by the fresh green of trees and stop feelingly before a tree struck by lightning? Do I feel sorry for the tree, which cannot feel its injury, or do I subconsciously feel and regret the downfall of all that is great, the wilting of all that blossoms, 'the fate on earth of all that is beautiful'? Do I transfer my feeling to the tree, and is the tree only the image of my thought? If that is so, and it is, then it explains why nature moves only thoughtful and sensi-

543

tive men, while the others, distracted by the accidental and trivial, never reach an awareness of what is essential and effective. Suppose a man capable of comprehending and rendering what in nature appeals to mind and feeling undertakes to give permanent form to what he experiences. He omits from the observed natural object anything disturbing or unrelated to the emotional response it called forth. Through this elimination of the trivial and inessential the attention of the shallower observer may be drawn to essential matters, and he will when confronted with a work of art feel what he did not feel in nature and could never have felt but for the artist. He comes to see in art not an object offering itself to an observer but an artist living in an object. He will become aware of an artistic idea and come to regard imitation as merely a means to its sensuous presentation."—Grillparzer, *Werke,* Abteilung II, 7: *Tagebücher,* 341–343.

CULTURAL AESTHETICS

Intelligent progress in any field is marked by the apprehending of quality and the careful tracing of relationships. Grosse, like Taine, held art to be socially created and conditioned. He, however, avoided the vague generalities of the earlier writer. His are clear-cut, documented, specialized comparative studies of tribal motifs in personal ornamentation and decoration of tools and weapons, in the dance, and in painting and music. His program is restricted. But interested as he is in early art, he never confuses origin and value, nor does he exclude a direct, purely aesthetic interest in and enjoyment of color, line, and rhythmic movement.

There has been of late a rapidly growing concern with social and economic problems of all sorts. This has been carried over enthusiastically into aesthetic theory and criticism. Not long ago there was a small competitive exhibition of pictures each of which was painted "as a social statement." The very use of the phrase in that connection was disturbing, and the pictures, almost without exception, were unconvincing to the mind and a confused jumble to the eye.

There are variants of this socially minded aesthetics, and they call for a word of caution.

Contextualism

First there is the contextualism of Dewey. There is no evidence in Dewey's earlier work of a direct sensitive response to fine art or of an interest in aesthetics. A psychologist, an educator, and a practical liberal, he has bent his energies to the formulation of a general theory of integrated experience with the stress on instrumental values and on the interaction of organism and environment. With this as a tool he has dealt functionally and in a progressive spirit with practical economic and social problems. Parts of his *Art as Experience* show an aesthetic awakening, with a jostler at his side, but on the whole Dewey's philosophical interests are paramount and result in a contextual theory of art. The following sentence reflects his attitude. "Flowers can be enjoyed without knowing about the interactions of soil, air, moisture, and seeds of which they are the result. But they cannot be understood without taking just these interactions into account—and theory is a matter of understanding. Theory is concerned with discovering the nature of the production of works of art and of the nature of their enjoyment in perception." Art is not to be isolated but is to be considered within a general theory of experience. It exists in the raw in the practical work of a mechanic or a houseworker or a ball player. When it confronts us as a Parthenon, it is to be understood in terms of a civic life, to which our own life of the street and the group holds the key. While Dewey disclaims an economic theory of art, he is so intent on understanding it within the context of social meanings and a general psychological pattern that he seldom experiences it directly. A witness to that is his response to the Parthenon. It must be granted that the Parthenon reflects and subtends civic influences and ideals foreign to us and to be recaptured by the student of culture past and present. The heavy substantial tombs of the Egyptians, the little clay models found in them, and the wall paintings are completely understood within the context of religious beliefs. Greek tragedy has its roots in ritual and myth. The Parthenon, the Great Palace of Persepolis, and a Mayan stela have sprung from different cultural soils. But a glance at their reliefs will show a quality of sensitive line, of modeling, of patterned design that is timeless and individual—bearing also the mark of a common excellence. It is this art quality that a cultural method is apt to neglect. From time to time a writer appears who argues that the Greeks must have regarded the attitude of "art for art's sake" as meaningless. He cites in proof the fact that Greek temples were built with the spoils of war—that many statues were chryselephantine, displaying gold and ivory, glorifying and commemorating—and that the popular reaction to both buildings and statues was in terms of splendor, civic pride, and piety. We are all too familiar with splendor changing to showy vulgarity and with deep civic and religious feelings leading to a shoddy art. How comes it then that there is so little of either in the art of the Greeks and that, with cultural bonds broken, a Greek tragedy, a statue, a Tanagra figurine, a coin, an urn appeal to us with a freshness and directness the Greeks themselves must have felt? This theory is obtuse and confuses, as Dewey himself does, the physical art product with the aesthetic object.

Marxist Theory and Criticism

Marxism is dialectical materialism. It analyzes the social process as patterned class tension and conflict, envisages the overthrow of the capitalist and the bourgeoisie and the triumph of the worker, and interprets culture along economic lines. The editor of a radical paper drew the attention of one of his men to a news item—a collision between a Ford and a Rolls Royce—with the remark: "Write this up from the class angle." The "class angle" is only too apparent in the aesthetic theories and art criticisms of Marxist writers.

Art that is not socially minded is labeled trivial. There are two kinds of art —bourgeois and proletarian. The former is bad, the latter is good. While proletarian art is to be used as propaganda, it is also to be encouraged to become more fully self-expressive and more expressive of what Marxists consider an ideal culture of the future. Russian painting and poetry after the revolution were directed toward the glorification of the hammer and sickle and toward the new dawn. Bourgeois art was to be liquidated. In 1918 Bogdanov wrote in the magazine *Proletarian:* "Art is part of the ideology of a class, an element of its class consciousness, hence an organized form of class life, a means of uniting and welding together class forces." The theory that the artist can stand above the battle is rejected. *Voices of October,* by Freeman *et al.* (1930), furnishes materials for a study of art in Soviet Russia. Since then there have been many fluctuations and changes. Examples of Marxist criticism are to be found in Granville Hicks' *The Great Tradition,* in John Strachey's *Literature and Dialectical Materialism,* and in many reviews in magazines. In the *Nation* a young poet who had written a nature poem was taken to task for being college-bred and for not having written about factories and workers. A few lines in which he described an airplane following the course of the Connecticut River were cited as a poor description of a canoe. Such are the preoccupied and sloppy ways of many of our critics. Strachey compares two poems, one by MacLeish, *Frescoes for Mr. Rockefeller's City,* and one by Stephen Spender, *The Pylons.* In both he finds commendable an expressed love of country. Using a convenient phrase of Michael Gold's—the Fascist Unconscious—he puts MacLeish in "the camp of the capitalists" and Spender in "the camp of the workers." Parenthetically, communists welcomed MacLeish's *The Fall of the City* as a blast against dictators—this, of course, did not mean Stalin. Strachey brushes aside MacLeish's confession that his poem was art and art only. It is only fair to note that in another passage Strachey writes: "it does seem to me that Hicks falls sometimes into an error which, as I was suggesting above, is a tempting one for Marxist critics. He hardly seems to pay enough attention to the merits of writers as writers."

Any method that confuses social values and aesthetic values and judges art from the class angle is sure to be wrong. In this respect the cult of gentility or fascism is not one whit better than Marxism. One of our popular expositors and middlemen of the books of the day in commenting on novels and the characters in them comes close to the criterion "people I should like to meet socially." As for fascism, the position of art in totalitarian countries is anything but enviable. It is controlled and misused, and it has lost its creative virility with its freedom.

UTILITY

The theory that art has origin and meaning in the useful, and that as something is felt or thought to be useful it is held to be beautiful rests its case on one or another or all of the following meanings of the term *useful:*

Specialized functional utility: A pillar helps support the roof, streamlining means lessened wind resistance, a sloping roof takes care of masses of melting snow. The modern functionalists in architecture come close to regarding as architecturally bad anything that is needless or purposeless in this sense.

Group utility: A social group has special purposes to be carried out— sowing, harvesting, hunting, fighting; it also aims at maintaining an orderly homogeneous pattern of living. It is easy to prove a relation to such purposes in the design and color of body decoration, in gymnastic and mimetic dances, in the use of totem animals, in masks, and in the incised and polished tribal stones of the Australians. When economic issues and class interests are stressed, another variant of the theory emerges—the Marxist interpretation of art.

Religious utility in the sense of an attempted control through magic: The stress may be on the individual: amulet or mask is to save from disease or danger through possessive magic control over an enemy—success in hunting is sought. Or it may be on the group: spirits are to be placated, elaborate dances are staged to bring rain or to make tribal hunts successful, or devils of disease are to be exorcised. Fertility rites are common. The cloud-and-rain symbol, the squash blossom, the thunderbird, the Indian eye symbol, the spear of grain are to be found in necklaces, pottery, rugs, folk-tales, and carvings.

Utility in a general biological sense: Here, too, there are many variants. Art is to heighten life—to enhance it—to give form to subconscious dreaming and wishing—to be a force in human progress.

Of these meanings of the useful, the fourth may be put to one side as of little value to aesthetics. There is in it glib talk about life and vague talk about art.

What of the other three? In all art as craftsmanship special functional adaptations have a place. A jar, a dagger, a feathered arrow, a canoe paddle, a building call in their making for adaptive skill. Undoubtedly the awareness of such adaptedness colors our aesthetic response to such fitness. But a useful form may be an ugly one. The wavelike blade of a Malayan creese subtends more than the desire to inflict a severe wound. It offers a direct delight in a curved line, which certain medieval weapons with jagged projections and sawlike blades, even though they are more effective, cannot give. There is this fact also, overlooked by functionalists in architecture: corkscrew pillars are effective supports, but they seem to collapse under the weight of the roof. The leaning tower at Pisa stands but seems to fall. In this seeming lies the clue to all art.

As for group utility and the religious utility of fetishes and masks, anthropologists and ethnologists have proved beyond cavil the close relation between tribal interests and art. But there is a very real danger of overstressing. Even where in body coloring, decoration, and dance ritual there are traditional patterns related to specific tribal aims, a large measure of self-expression, of decorative interest as such, and of improvisation is to be found. Indian sand paintings, the masks of devil dancers, amulets and fetishes are all meant to serve curative and preventive purposes. A gymnastic dance is never merely a drill to train fighters and to arouse a warlike spirit.

Utility has a place in the theory of art. It can explain many things, but there is one quality it cannot deal with—a quality to be found in all ranges of art from the clear-cut color and delicate line of the sand paintings to the architecturally reshaped bodies of Negro wood sculpture, to grotesque masks, to the modeling of a Greek statue and the design of a modern painting.

ARTS AND CRAFTS

Suppose that at the whim of a cosmic dictator all museums of fine art were toppled over, all paintings and sculptures and poems and musical scores were destroyed, all major arts proscribed, and all men were set to useful tasks. Would that be the end of art? The answer is manifestly no. From the very first, man has been a craftsman and a shaper in response to practical need and to the strain of human vanity. He must have jars to store food and wine in, a stool for support, a rug for warmth, a good sword and shield, a property mark, a canoe paddle, coins, a fetish, a tribal emblem. He also must have something to make him look fine in the eyes of others—shells, glass beads, a feathered headdress, gems and trinkets.

A useful thing may be merely that, and a thing serving vanity may be merely ostentatious. But never in the past have they been merely that. There is, again and again, an interest in color, in line and design in the production of useful objects. This might be looked for in a people as sensitive and cultured as the Greeks, who resented a false intonation in the speech of an actor, and who in their coins, vases, cut stones, figurines, and toys showed exquisite craftsmanship and creative art quality. But it may also be seen in a Negro comb, a Peruvian jug, an Indian rug, a Malayan creese, a Swedish shield, a Celtic pin or clasp.

No cosmic dictator's command could destroy art. The galleries on Fifth Avenue would no longer be there, but there would be shop windows filled with glass and silver ware, leather work, jewelry, rugs, furniture, hammered brass, toys, lamps, lace, book ends, and books with tooled leather bindings.

Toward these minor arts two contrasted and equally one-sided attitudes are commonly taken. The first is one of distrust of the detached art of museums, of easel paintings, and of sculptures whose purpose is art and art only. It finds in arts and crafts an art spirit pervasive of and functioning in organic relation to life. This has encouraged a sympathetic study of folk-art and industrial art. But it leads easily to a dangerous contextualism and a narrow functionalism. The second attitude is one of distrust of arts and crafts as bound up too closely with utility, as superficial and alloyed. Art must be detached and pure. While this view is extreme, it contains an element of truth.

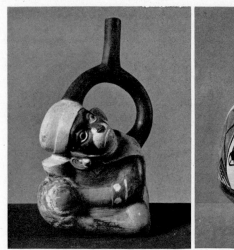

Ancient Peruvian Pottery

Pottery from Panama and Honduras

ARTS AND CRAFTS

In arts and crafts, considered artistically, craftsmanship, function, and design are all important. There is a Greek coin so small that its pattern can be seen in detail only with a magnifying glass. Only an expert with his tools could have cut these sensitive lines and filled this small space so effectively. Only an artist could have given this coin the quality of the metopes of the Parthenon. Craftsmanship and design are carried up from this underground of all art to art at its peak.

Art, however, is something more than patterning. It is inner reshaping. There is something of this even in the minor arts, but much less than there is in a picture by El Greco or Rembrandt or Van Gogh and in a tragedy by Shakespeare. In this sense arts and crafts are, relatively speaking, superficial in having less of vision and psychic depth. Many of our fine art schools make the mistake of teaching architecture, dancing, and water color painting almost wholly as crafts.

Art is more than skill or craft. But for one who inclines toward vague emotional responses to music and poetry, an understanding of technical processes and a response to the simple, functional, directly present design of a coin, a pitcher, a chair, a plaque is a much needed counterbalance.

DISTORTION

Distortion is held by many to be the cardinal sin of modernistic art, active as they insist it is in the sign of the ugly and untrue. However, distortion is inherent in all art and is widespread in nature, both in form and in image. It would be a reckless and hopeless undertaking to account for the wide departures from natural forms—exaggerated slenderness or massiveness, schematized animals and flowers—to be found in Cretan, Greek, Peruvian, and Gothic art—in terms of a lack of technical skill.

On pages 140 and 141 of Ogden's *The Psychology of Art* are two pictures of a man lying prone, at full length in the direct line of vision. One is a photograph of a model, the other a copy of Mantegna's *Pietà*. The former shows a violently foreshortened figure and grotesquely large feet. Here a natural impression, because of the angle of vision, distorts the proportions of the human body. Such distortions we are constantly receiving and constantly correcting through knowledge. In the *Pietà* the feet and the legs are unnaturally reduced in size to correct the grotesque actual foreshortening and to gain a clean-cut, satisfying visual image. Here is an interesting instance of art correctively distorting, in the presence of a natural distortion.

Art cannot imitate nature with any degree of accuracy or completeness. It follows that it must distort. Here are a few examples. A dramatist selects from a welter of historical personages and events; he omits details; pulls more tightly the knotted string of years; changes the tempo and stress of the past. The sculptor cannot give body color, the texture of the skin, the living eye. The painter is forced to simplify, to use equivalents, to redesign.

A second glance at these examples reveals art as distorting not merely because it cannot compete with nature, but because of aims and values of its own.

The following types of distortion in art may be set down:

Comic distortion: This is aimed at cheapening, playful extravagance, and an expressive simplifying and intensifying. The Paphlagonian in Aristophanes' *Knights* is a satire on Cleon, shows imagination running wild in bold conceits and the heaping of abuse, and expresses the unprincipled lowness of a demagogue. The art of the cartoonist offers many examples. It is fatal to take caricature too seriously and to think of it merely in terms of exposing and cheapening; a playful, distorted, extravagant expressiveness must not be overlooked.

Decorative distortion: This is found in early art. It appears in stylized form in architectural ornament. The rose, palm leaf, acorn, and oak leaf are reshaped to pattern. This is true also of lizard and bird in rug borders and of shells and fish, the nautilus and the squid in Cretan pottery. It is present in modern metal work and embroidery. Artists like Botticelli, Manship, Beardsley, and Marie Laurencin are fond of distorting to gain decorative effects.

Structural distortion: This is less superficial and cuts deeper than decorative distortion. It goes to the heart and life blood of design, and to the spirit it embodies. El Greco, Van Gogh, Marc, and Cézanne furnish examples in painting. In Negro wood sculpture the human body is distorted from its natural structural forms and architecturally reshaped. Munro in his *Negro Sculpture* sets aside cultural meanings and seeks to recapture this quality of design. A modernist painter at times deliberately destroys the world of space objects as commonly perceived and rebuilds it consistently in the pattern of a new, original, and clear-cut space-experience.

Expressive distortion: While not new, this type is used extensively in modernistic art. By simplifying, underscoring, exaggerating, and forcing, something intensified, compelling, imaginatively gripping, and more directly and largely expressive is sought. Shelley aims at the essence of lightness in this bold figure of speech:

> An antelope,
> In the suspended impulse of its lightness
> Was less aetherially light.

Sheeler multiplies the sails of a yacht, for here, rather than in wood and brass and detail, lives its spirit. Sandburg in *Gargoyle,* Vachel Lindsay in *Congo,* Benét in many passages of *John Brown's Body,* Hodler in his *Tell,* Benton in his murals, Rodin in his sculptures, and Barlach in his projections into sculpture in wood of vices—lust, greed, anger—all make use of distortion of this type. Seeking to express his conception of a man of destiny, a portrait sculptor of Mussolini built out his heavy jaw into a fateful, granite-like exaggeration.

Distortion may be abused by being used (1) perversely and (2) unwisely.

Certain little artists, anxious for something original and bold, succeed in creating nothing but the twisted grimace of their own vanity. To be different is to be odd, but not necessarily good. Even good artists fall into the error of perverse experimentation. New music and a stimulating freshness and creativeness are to be found in Joyce's *Finnegan's Wake,* but it exhibits a perverse desire to make of art something akin to a cryptic private world of dream and puzzle. The "fractured words" theory and practice of the Transition Group leads straight to bewilderment and boredom. Archipenko's simplified, semi-abstract renderings of the human form are very fine, but at times he offers a tangled unnaturalness that goes beyond the limits of an effective design.

Unwise distortion results from overloading. This is most clearly evident in the arts of sculpture and painting. They are, first and foremost, visual arts, and this must define and set a limit to their psychic expressiveness. In actual life there is something chaotic in thought and feeling, which is worked off through experience in focusing and clarifying. Certain actuality controls are established. These in art must be held in abeyance. When a painter or a sculptor uses distorted images and symbols in his desire to express motherhood, human misery, greed, war, he must beware of underscoring actuality controls by his very disregard of natural forms. Lachaise may have thought that he was expressing motherhood, but what he gives are women with unnaturally small heads and monstrously massive and fat bodies. Epstein makes similar mistakes. There is danger of overburdening the visual arts ideologically and of neglecting design quality. I have in mind Taft's *The Blind,* a sculptural relief called *The Significance of the League of Nations,* Rivera's overloaded murals, Benton's *Hollywood,* pictures satirizing fascism or expressing communism, Paul Engle's hodgepodges of America and Russia. The mind is not satisfied, and the eye, the ear, and the attention wander aimlessly.

RADIO DRAMA

It is strange that while people are being made eye-minded, other forces are at work to make them ear-minded. Pictorial magazines good and bad have had a mushroom growth and their range is wide. Reproductions of paintings, snapshots of celebrities, picturized scandals, bits of science, travel, sport, cultural sketches—such is their technique of making things vivid and popular. In this they are outmatched by the motion picture with its flair for instruction and amusement. The radio is the other force at work. It offers through the ear advertising, war news, health talks, concerts, political speeches, comic dialogue, telescoped novels and plays, weather and stock reports, and what not.

While the motion picture and the radio have spread happiness far and wide, neither can be called an unmixed blessing. Indiscriminately they appeal to the eye and the ear, but not always to the mind. The synthetic excitement of war correspondent and sports announcer, the glamorous radio voice of a politician, the cheap dramatizing of this or that, the posing of a movie star—these lull the mind to sleep while they excite us. The motion picture industry is apt to treat us as children; for the radio we are too often hypnotic subjects.

Art lays the senses under contribution and seeks new ventures in extending their range of expressiveness. The motion picture has within it the promise of a new art. As yet it is largely a promise; fulfilment must await the work of discriminating creative genius.

Within the last few years the art impulse has sought to make use for its own purpose of the resources of the radio. Three poets, Archibald MacLeish, Maxwell Anderson, and Alfred Kreymborg, have created the radio drama. MacLeish was the pioneer with *The Fall of the City.* This was followed by *Air Raid.* Anderson contributed *The Feast of Ortalans* and *The Bastion of Saint Gervais;* and Kreymborg, *The Planets.*

The uses of sound in radio are various. There is the spoken word, the register of facts, the conveyer of ideas, the arouser of feelings through meaning. There is voice quality with a direct force and appeal. To these must be added music and the recording or creating of all manner of noises and sounds —the banging of a door, the drone of a motor, a scream, the rattat of a machine gun, the rumbling of thunder, the tumult of a river in flood. The announcer or commentator uses sound in one or both of the first two senses. With regard to the last, the radio has many devices for controlling and organizing non-musical sounds.

In *The Fall of the City,* a half-hour radio drama in verse, MacLeish uses sound in three ways. A studio director explains the situation, after the manner of a prologue; an announcer, detached from the action, explains, comments, interprets. But for his help the listener would find it difficult to distinguish the speaking parts and follow the plot. Random noises of the crowd, muttering, shouts, chatter and clatter—and inanimate noises—of guns, bombs, airplanes, as in *Air Raid*—are either given in their mere impact or are woven into semi-musical patterns.

MacLeish claims much for radio drama. On the stage, he argues, there is a conflict between the eye and the ear whereas in radio drama there is nothing but sound. The "word-excited imagination" here functions in its purity. He makes much of the announcer, a typical radio figure, as an interpreter after the manner of the Greek chorus. In accenting, fading out, moving toward or away from the action he gives the "oblique" and "tri-dimensional" quality "without which great poetic drama cannot exist."

These claims are excessive. It may be admitted that the staging of a play can detract from its inner meaning or not measure up to it. It has been said that the tremendous stature of Lear as a poetic figure shrinks lamentably on the stage. But there is no inevitable conflict between the visual and the auditory—the direct presence in action has an expressiveness through the eye and a richness of appeal that the radio lacks. In the reading of a drama the imagination seizes and builds, goes back and forth at leisure; in a radio drama it is hurried; distraction here is the far greater one of trying to distinguish the various voices, of stepping in and out of the moment with the announcer. The studio director, like the prologue, is a clumsy device. Contrast with it the swift expository scenes in *Romeo and Juliet*.

A reference to the announcer will serve to reveal the essential weakness of the radio as a medium for a new type of drama.

The chorus in Greek tragedies at times stood outside the action; at others, as in *Agamemnon* and *The Trojan Women,* it was involved in it. But whether talking or acting, whether chanting beautiful lyrics or intoning deep moral and religious strains—in giving richness and spiritual substance to the artistic design—it always served the purpose of establishing *distance,* as masks, staging, and myth did in their turn.

The announcer's part in radio is to give and comment on facts. He summarizes the news of the day, advertises, analyzes the war situation, gives at the beginning of a concert a bit of biography. He is essentially a factual figure; he moves things close, abolishes *distance.* To use him as a figure in radio drama means a wasteful, makeshift technique; it also means ineffectually running counter to the strong factual impact of the radio. In 1938 Orson Welles as announcer in a dramatic version of Wells's *The War of the Worlds* was so convincing that people who had not tuned in at the beginning thought an actual invasion from Mars was under way. They became panicky, hysterical; scurried to escape. At this mass spectacle of scrabbling humanity malicious gods might have shaken with inextinguishable laughter. The informative function of the radio and Orson Welles's dramatic voice combined to destroy the distance from fact and self so essential to art. It is not surprising to find that radio dramas so far have had as their material matters of pressing concern such as war and peace, dictatorship, air raids. In *Air Raid* MacLeish exploits not the word-excited but the sound-excited imagination. While there is patterning of the noises that mark an air raid, the main stress is on terror-provoking sound. It is one thing to express an air raid, it is quite another thing to bring it home to us in a melodramatic, panic-arousing way.

At best the radio drama is an interesting experiment with limited opportunities for a new expressiveness in sound. It can hardly be more than that. The radio is too close to real life, too dependent on the patience of a listener hurried along, the attention flagging at the end of half an hour, too circumscribed and poor in resources to be a promising medium for the dramatic poet.

REGIONALISM

Of late there has been much talk of regionalism. The thing itself is not new. Novelists have sought and given local color to scene, characters, incidents, and dialogue either because they had their roots in a sharply set off group or made such a group imaginatively their own. Thus the types, the manners, and the speech of the Breton fisher folk, the Tyrolese or Bavarian mountaineers, the Sicilian, the Arab, the Mexican, the Wessex farmer, have found their way into literature. The Germans call such art *Heimatskunst*. But regionalism is much older than this. There is a very close relation between early small groups and the art they create. Their conditions of living, their habits and bent of mind, their religious beliefs give to their art an individual group character. A study of various types of Oriental rugs or of pottery shapes and designs will bear this out. The ethnologist is fascinated by this problem of the indigenous and the borrowed.

The recent trend has been toward regionalism in painting, in the sense of Americanism. This means a reaction against foreign influences. For many years our painters were trained in French studios and have followed French models. Glackens, to be classed with Sloan in his earlier sketches of American manners, imitates Renoir in his oils. Others are committed to the technique of Cézanne or Braque. Epstein in much of his work employs and exaggerates the rough modeling of Rodin. It is the English landscape that appears in many of our poems.

Why not express America in substance, spirit, and technique? It would be unfair to give a political turn to this demand, for it is not to be confused with nationalism, nor does it imply the stultifying pressure on art in totalitarian states.

America is a land of many racial strains, of many climates and contrasted scenes, of many groups and folkways. In substance, temper, and tone no art can comprehensively deal with it. In the past, when travel, interchange, and transportation were difficult, life was split up into groups with whom self-sufficiency was a need. Farmers did their own timbering, butchering, spinning, and weaving. Small townspeople had their local bank, their few mills, and moved within the narrow pattern of local custom. Farmhouses, barns, furniture, rugs, pottery, glassware, needlework, cooking recipes, dress—all exhibit a more or less distinctive character of some locality or region. There has been a recent revival of interest in what are called home industries and in the folkways and folk art they express.

The social pattern has become complex to a bewildering degree. The growth of industrialism, migratory shiftings, the influx of many races, specialized labor, centralized city life, and the give and take of easy communication and rapid change have had a part in putting an end to a simple, homogeneous, solidly based type of living. Regionalism as an aim in art reflects either a nostalgic regret at the loss of a simple past or an ambitious urge to discover new expressive ranges in these very complexities.

Ought art to be American in the sense of expressing with genuine insight and keen localized interest some phase or section of the American scene and of American life—the fishermen and lumberjacks of Maine, Negroes and gentlefolk of the South, the Texas cattle hand, the miner and fruit grower of the West, the types of Middletown, the hillbilly and the hobo, the Indian, the immigrant, the gangster, factory and slum life, the small town tradesman and the migratory worker? Such sectionalism is encountered in the novels of Dreiser, Sinclair Lewis, Steinbeck, Roberts, Caldwell, Faulkner; in the use of

Negro motifs in the dance and music; in the collection of Negro spirituals and shanty songs; in the poetry of Sandburg, Frost, and Jeffers.

What shall be said of painting? Part of an industrial America lives in Pennell's etchings; Demuth in his water colors has re-created the smooth functional beauty of machinery; Sheeler has recaptured that of Bucks County barns; Benton has painted American murals, and in a more sophisticated mood has in *Persephone* and in *Susanna and the Elders* put old myths in an American rural setting. There is a Gloucester school of painting; there are painters of the sun-drenched Southwest—of slums, saloons, and public parks—of the circus ring, the hot-dog stand, and the dance hall—of sailors and farmers —of racial types. Bellows, Grant Wood, Benton, Biddle, Blume, Chapin, and others are regionalists in a great part of their work.

There is much in America that is in need of recapturing, much in it also as yet unexpressed. From this angle the demand for specialized endeavor, inspiration, and a strong native technique in painting is a sign of health. Two dangers, however, must be kept in mind. Nostalgic regret may lapse to sentimentality. The desire for new special expressiveness may slip into a narrow localism or may lead to a reliance on the factual or the cheaply sensational. There are in art visions and qualities that go beyond regional boundaries.

APPENDIX

APPENDIX I

NOTES

INTERESTS IN AESTHETICS—ART ANALYSIS

Aesthetics has been haphazard in growth and is unsure in its use of method because of the many interests it expresses and seeks to satisfy. The thoughtful artist, the alert critic, the art lover, the student of social records and human motives, the analyzing scientist, and the system-building philosopher have all sought their special problems in the study of art. They have helped and harmed aesthetics in various ways. Not on the best of terms among themselves, they have built into it their conflicting interests and distrust.

Art enthusiast and artist often look with distrust on analysis. To them it seems to endanger the life and value of art. The scientist in his turn holds that enthusiasm is a cheap and superficial thing. He insists that values are facts, and that all facts come within the range of his cool work of dissecting.

Whether there is a deep-going conflict between the scientific and the artistic temper is a general problem beset with difficulties. But there is the immediate and simpler problem of bringing these interests together within the analytic study of works of art.

Unless the artist is thoughtless, he will admit that enthusiasm, while often the first, is never the last word in the enjoyment of a picture, a piece of sculpture or a poem. He will agree that if a deepened and widened appreciation is to be gained the ways of combining colors and lines, of relating planes, of creating rhythmic patterns and grouping images, of projecting moods and visions must be understood. A lover who catches love like an infection and lives it like an ecstatic dream is a poor judge of quality. Similarly, the quality of art escapes the enthusiast and emotionalist.

There are, of course, many problems in aesthetics which are not concerned with appreciation. Some of these are physio-psychological, others historical, still others social. To these the intellectual curiosity of the scientist has an absolute right. To the others he has only a qualified right. Mechanical analysis is to be avoided. There is nothing more like senseless butchery than the chopping up of a poem into metre, the counting of vowels, the search for the caesura, topical analysis, and philological jugglery when no response has been made to the poem as something living and meaningful. The initial response to a work of art ought always to be wholeminded and sympathetic—a search for its *soul-in-body*. When that has been done, thought must be sent into its structure and meaning. Only in this way will it reveal its quality, and allow itself to be critically understood and deeply enjoyed.

THE ARTIST AS CREATOR

A neglected problem in aesthetics is that of how art comes into being in the mind of the artist and how it takes shape in his creative working. What of the inception of a poem, a painting, a sonata in a thought or mood, a visual image, a musical phrase? What of subconscious elaboration, directive skill and thought, and the full and final forming? Is a work of art, like a storm, an upheaval and a flash or does it ripen, like grain, quietly and imperceptibly? What of the part played by vision, feeling, mood, thought in its forming? What of the artist— is he ecstatic or calm— happy or tormented?

There is in Volkelt's *System der Aesthetik* an elaborate and, on the whole, discriminating study of the psychology of art creation. But that is only a preliminary sketch, in view of the great mass of material still unused. There are letters by artists, diaries and journals, confessions and interviews in which this problem is forced into the open. Not all of them come to it willingly or handle it intelligently. In a collection of hundreds of letters by artists on art (Uhde-Bernays, *Künstlerbriefe über die Kunst*) only a few—by Van Gogh, Picasso, Marc, Beckmann, Cézanne—concern themselves with the creation of a work of art. But abundant material is to be found elsewhere in what has been said and written by Goethe, Delacroix, Hebbel, Wagner, Nietzsche, Rodin, Gauguin, Benton, Marin, Bruce and others. To this must be added the comment of those who were in a position to watch artists at their work.

In all this testimony there is little agreement. There are three reasons for such variations. One is the nature of the work of art created, another is the type of art in which the artist creates, and the last is the temperament of the artist.

A short lyric, a simple bit of music, a sketch may be revealed in a flash in their complete form. They may be made art quickly without thought or the effort of reshaping. Or a line, a rhythm or a visual image may act as a magnet of form. With a drama or a symphony this is not possible. There elaboration, subconscious nurture, slow and gradual structural building become necessary. This is true also of all but the simplest painting. Franz Marc insists that artists like Mantegna, Bellini, Delacroix and the architect of the Strasbourg Cathedral constantly and anxiously struggled to achieve form. Of them he says: "That they were artists and knew of art was their blessedness, and is mine also; but form was their daily study and their torment. Form is something the good God does not offer us as a gift."

The type of art in which the artist works must be considered. When an art, like painting or sculpture, requires much manual skill, the inception counts for less than it does in poetry or music, and the process of elaboration and shaping can be less easily and completely turned over to the subconscious mind. The technique becomes definitely a matter of craftsmanship in the use of the brush or the chisel.

Most striking are the temperamental differences among the artists. Van Gogh writes: "The excitement, the seriousness of the instinct by which we are guided—these excitations are at times so strong that I am not conscious I am working. Sometimes the strokes come, blow after blow, and they follow each other like the words in a conversation or a letter." Some portrait painters are tense and breathe heavily while they are painting, others are workmanlike and unemotionally creative. Shaw, watching Rodin model his bust, comments on his businesslike way and compares him to "a river-god turned plasterer." *Thus Spake Zarathustra* came to Nietzsche in drunken, ecstatic lurches, while climbing. Ibsen's workshop shows him coolly planing and nailing. Max Beckmann writes from the front, in 1915: "What a passionate love I have for my painting! I am always busy with form—while drawing, in my head, in my sleep. Sometimes, I think I shall go crazy—this lust mixed with pain fatigues and torments me so. Everything disappears—time and space— Sometimes, I think of how I can paint the head of Christ Resurrected against the red stars in the sky of the Last Judgment. Or how I can bring to decorative and living unity the mustaches of petty officer D. and his red nose.—Or how I can paint the sparkling light that is mirrored in the blinding white of flyer grenades against the bluewhite of the noon sky—and the wet, clear, angled shadows of the houses—"

On the point of what the creative mood brings of pleasure and pain, artists show less disagreement. They find the pleasures of creating intense and mingled with restlessness, pain, and torment.

The whole problem of how a work of art comes into being within the artist, how it takes shape in his art, and of how he is affected by the experience is a complex one, leading finally into the realm of individual psychology. It cannot be contained within standard thought-patterns. Here, as in so many of the more subtle problems of art, aesthetics must aim at a delicately sympathetic and discriminating study.

THE POET'S WAY

The poet reverses the process of our common speech and our common perception and experience of objects. Words in their ordinary use are markers and labels. By means of them we become articulate, record, and communicate. Some of them, at least, had a *feel* of their own—a rhythm, a forcefulness or smoothness, an architectural quality. As symbols and markers, too, they showed imaginative color and boldness. Early expressiveness and primitive picture-thought and an occasional vivid and forceful user and coiner of words combined to give language this quality. To all this we have become inattentive. In the fluent currency of common communicative speech words have been sensuously and imaginatively devalued. Thus the colorless "relatives" has replaced the vivid "kin"; and *grit, glimmer, lisp, log* are used with little or no response to their *feel;* and *interval, skyscraper,* with no thought of the imagery that is at the heart of them.

This process is reversed by the poet. In his use and grouping of words he is not concerned with intellectual conciseness and accuracy. What he seeks is color, force, music, imaginative and emotional suggestiveness. So he travels the way back to the earlier, lost qualities of language.

There is a similar reversal with the objects of experience which language marks. In the childhood of the individual and the race the response to an object is personal and individualizing—*my shield, this dog, this magnolia.* It lives for me in its details and is caught up, lovingly or rejectingly, into my life of the senses and the imagination. It is thus that it has its being within the words I use. Language, however, gradually becomes intellectualized, impersonal, generic. Dogs, houses, trees are standard labels. The original individual experience is lost.

Here, again, the poet reverses the process. He finds his way back to details lost in the practical and social use of experiences. He seeks to recapture something of the freshness and vividness of an original impression. This is done with a common barnyard object in George O'Neil's *The White Rooster.* Often he goes beyond that, and captures new sensuous, emotional, and imaginative values by a bold personal reshaping and *charging* of the common stuff and form of experience. Examples of this are Shelley's *To a Skylark* and H. D.'s *Pear Tree.*

APPRECIATION OF MUSIC IN THE LIGHT OF SYNTHESIS AND ANALYSIS BY PAUL KRUMMEICH

Since so vast and profound a subject as music cannot be adequately presented within the compass of a few pages, the writer gratefully embraces this opportunity to add some after thoughts, hoping they prove useful in further defining the nature and purpose of this art. Two methods are available for the solution of our problem, namely, the synthetic and the analytic, and we shall find that not one or the other but both will be required in their proper order and functional limits.

Some of us, by nature more or less introspective, delight in the search for the essence of things at the risk of drifting into mysticism and losing contact with the world of realities. On the other hand, there are far too many who are satisfied with the contemplation of the manifestations of life; lacking the true philosophical bent, they are doomed to remain on the surface of things and can never know the depths where the surface is anchored.

The old question: *What is Music?* can be disposed of in more ways than one, but there is no answer so comprehensive and none more true than the one which states that *Music is the product of the mind.* As such it becomes legitimate game for every hunter in the preserve of mental phenomena and the forces which condition them.

Formal analysis is as old as curiosity and enjoys both the dignity of age and the sanctity of tradition. Notwithstanding such security, older structures have been successfully attacked and proved fake or at least, unsound. There is so much *skeletal* presentation of music that the artist *pur sang* revolts; being what he is, he resents this "tearing asunder what Nature has so wondrously joined." To him, art-apart is not *art;* it is either art-in-the-making or art-disintegrated. Fully conversant with the value of science in the making of art, he respects its functions but insists that it be regarded as a means to an end and not as the end itself. Instead of dogmatically asserting the merits or demerits of analyic operations, we shall briefly consider the mind in its natural functions and abide by our findings.

There are two distinct ways by which new ideas may be perceived: they can dawn on us like the light of the rising sun, or burst forth with the startling suddenness of an apparition. In either case we are apt to misinterpret the nature of these phenomena. When we speak of the *dawning* of a new idea, we are hardly aware it is the great Unconscious which gradually reveals to the conscious mind an organized structure (Gestalt); nor do we realize that the sudden birth of such an idea presupposes unconscious labor. In both cases we are confronted with the emergence of an organized whole, generated in the depths of the Unconscious and presented to us in the nature of a gift—but with the force of a command. There can be no doubt that this initial unconscious function is synthetic. The first operation of the *conscious* mind consists in apprehending and integrating such organic units (subwholes) as it can glean through the contemplation of the synthesis presented to it by the unconscious. Thus the initial conscious function is also synthetic, but its product is not necessarily as perfectly organized as the unconsciously created original. The next, *i. e.* the second conscious performance shows all the symptoms of curiosity; it is the familiar *analysis.* Shocked somewhat by the newness of the situation and anxious to orient itself, the conscious mind carefully disintegrates the synthesis of its own constructing in order to reassure itself of the thoroughness of its earlier synthetic activity. So far, we have two synthetic, and one analytic function: unconscious-synthetic, conscious-synthetic, conscious-analytic. Having put its own creation to the crucial test of analysis, it (the conscious mind) eagerly *re*integrates the units obtained by its earlier analytic efforts. Without a doubt, the fourth and final conscious act is also synthetic. Considering the mind in its unity, we may temporarily ignore the difference between the unconscious and the conscious and count our winnings.

It is quite evident that four distinct operations are required to fix a new idea in the conscious mind; it is equally clear that three of these functions are synthetic, whereas only one is analytic. Incidentally, it is of the utmost importance to note that this single analytic performance is not creative—not constitutive, but *regulative*.

Our endeavor to observe the mind at work has not been without results. We have learned that in a psychic ensemble of four functions three are synthetic and only one analytic. We have also found that this lone analytic operation serves no other purpose than that of assuring the final reconstruction of the unconsciously created original.

Far from having destroyed the value of analysis, we have assigned to it its proper place in a complex apparatus. By so doing, we have carefully established the limits within which it must operate, and we shall no longer permit it to encroach upon other, older and more vital functions of the mind. Let the music lover be guided by the light of our discovery and draw his own conclusions. Since man can have no more than the wisdom of his own mind, let him see to it that this complex and delicate instrument functions properly. "In genius, Nature works according to her own laws"! Why should the lover of the arts mistrust his own nature? The artist will always succeed in separating the wheat from the chaff—he prefers to trust himself. The truly naive are equally blest as long as they remain untutored and unspoiled by the advice of those who listen with their heads to a message of the heart.

THE GROTESQUE

The grotesque may be seen in the masks, wood sculptures, and dances of primitive art; in folk-tales; as a decorative motif in the gargoyles of Gothic cathedrals; in Rabelais; in the work of German romanticists; in Dickens and Victor Hugo; in the dramas of O'Neill, Werfel, Kaiser, Molnar, and Hasenclever. In considering such material care must be taken to separate what was meant to be grotesque from what to us only appears grotesque. A sculpture of a dancing god with several sets of arms is grotesque to us. Its meaning is far removed from that; it is a naive attempt to render movement.

Within the aesthetic field, the grotesque may be created to serve the comic, tragic, or the sublime. Or it may be created and enjoyed for its own sake.

Aristophanes, Rabelais, Swift, Anatole France all use a *grotesquerie* of situation, character, and word in order to gain bold satiric and comic effects. Gilray, Rowlandson, and Daumier give to caricature a like spirit and technique. While such distortion is aimed at cheapening, the grotesque element in it serves the purpose of rousing the imagination.

The tragic and the sublime are sometimes found merged with the grotesque. Such a use is seen in the feast of Thyestes and other Greek legends, in *The Singing Bone* and other folk-tales from many lands and ages, in Poe and Victor Hugo. Expressionists have built it into their tragedies. O'Neill has done this in *The Hairy Ape*, Werfel in *Goat Song*, Hasenclever in *Die Menschen*, and Molnar in *Liliom* and

The White Cloud. The motives back of this use are various—to give a new range or pointedness to terror—to get a bolder projection and a deeper sympathy—to gain the tragic pity and fear from characters and situations that do not yield them easily. The effect, here also, is to rouse the imagination—to give to the imaginative life of man vigor and elevation.

The grotesque is, however, quite apart from its comic and tragic uses, something sought and created for its own sake. Primitive art shows that. Two mistakes are often met with—negro sculpture has been interpreted altogether as abstract design and masks have been analyzed with sole reference to such purposes as frightening an enemy, god control, ceremonial dances and the like. The treatment of the human figure in negro sculpture is indeed a strange one. Nose, neck, length of arm and leg, the grouped unity of the body—there is violent distortion everywhere! Some of it can be traced to design—to a feeling for lines, planes and masses inherent in the human figure, but obscured in the ordinary representational response. A reference to pages 95, 96, 100, 112, 115, 369 in Sidow, *Die Kunst der Naturvölker* proves this. But there is often a direct and keen interest in the grotesque: in a reshaping that is to leave the body a strange, wildly imagined thing. Examples of this are to be found in Sidow on pages 212, 218, 227, 407. This is not meant to imply that there is in such cases no interest in design. The desire for form marks the art of all ages.

A study of folk-tales reveals a vivid interest in the grotesque. Giants, trolls, gnomes are projections of this aesthetic type. It is also present in primitive dances and masquerades, such as the Butter Festival in central Asia, the mummeries of the Middle Ages. No explanation of Gothic gargoyles as satire is adequate. Nor can the combination of twisted spirituality and fantastic illustrations of certain medieval sermons be explained except as a creative delight in the grotesque.

Masks show the grotesque in full strength and wide range. In the oval of the actual face are certain features—the eyes, the nose, and the mouth—approximating standards. In combination these features become variationally expressive of a feeling, a mood, a thought. The Greeks, in their dramatic masks, sought to fix, in a distorted form, some expressive type for comic or tragic uses. When we pass to the masks of the negro and the Indian we find something like this. Within the oval, the features are fantastically and inevitably distorted. Eyes are set close to the nose, the mouth is extended or becomes a circle or is reshaped to a vertical crescent, the nose is bisected or becomes a long vertical from the forehead to the mouth—the natural lines of the faces are broken into by painting—the pupils of the eye seem to be caught in a strange caprice. Pages 18, 19, 32, 44, 45, 57, 74, 75, 76, 77 of Sidow *Kunst und Religion der Naturvölker* furnish examples. Quite as wide in range as this reshaping of the face are the expressions of impulses and feelings these masks give.

Every moment of calm and torment seems to be embodied in them. Tribal traditions, symbolism, primitive fear reactions all have a place in this expressiveness. But there is also, as there is in our Hallowe'en masks, something that has nothing to do with custom or fear or serious projection of an inner life of impulse and feeling. This something is the grotesque, sought and enjoyed for itself.

To recognize the presence of this aesthetic type is easier than to analyze it. A clue or two toward further analysis is all that can be given in a note.

There is, first of all, distortion. This distortion is playful, not in the sense of a lack of seriousness, but in that of a free and bold play of the imagination. This includes a wilfully capricious reforming of what experience offers and a venturing into an imagined world of the fantastic. The distortion is frank and radical. There is nothing timid or halfhearted about the grotesque. It is not disguised, nor does it stop short. Most striking is this—the distortion is created and enjoyed as something final. The breach between an orderly world and a weird and misshapen world of the imagination is to remain. No bridge is flung across it.

Imaginatively obstrusive and suggestive as a grotesque is, it has little or no emotional depth or force. We can, it is true, pass from it to the tragic or the sublime. But this is not its quintessential spirit. Masks and grotesque sculptures have a curious emotional flatness. We do not reach through them to an inner life of feeling. We are either held to the distorted surface or sent off into a fantastic world, only to be sent back to the queer distorted form, which is obstrusive but not oppressive.

The grotesque shows how far beyond the will to beauty art, primitive and modern, goes in its enterprising way with what the senses and the imagination offer.

A KEY TO EXPRESSIONISM

Van Gogh writes to his brother.

—"I am to paint the portrait of a friend, an artist who works, as the nightingale sings, because it is his nature. He is to be blond. I should like to paint in my picture all of my admiration, all of my love for him.

"I shall, to begin with, paint him as faithfully as I can.

"But that is not the end of the picture. In order to complete it, I become an arbitrary colorist.

"I exaggerate the blondness of his hair. I turn to orange shades, to chrome yellow, to light lemon color.

"Back of the head, in place of a common wall or room, I paint the infinite. I make a background of the richest, the strongest blue I can produce. And so the shining head on a background of rich blue acquires a mystical effect, as a star in the azure sky.

"When I was painting the picture of the peasant I used the same method.

In this case, however, I did not wish to give the mystical effect of a pale star in infinity. I put this dreadful man in high noon light in the full heat of the harvest.

"Hence orange lightnings like red firebrands. Hence the old gold shades, flashing in darknesses.

"Yes, my dear brother—and the good people will see nothing but caricature in this intensification."

EXPRESSIONISM IN CHESS

When there is in the fine arts a sharp turning toward new enterprises, something similar is discoverable in the applied arts, in amusements, and in the tone and temper of life as it moves beyond art. Part of this is to be explained as the effect of the movement on taste; part of it is a matter of cause rather than effect, art moving in response to life.

This is true of expressionism. It has left the mark of its technique and spirit on advertising, on illustration, on book jackets. It has made an appearance in new styles of social dancing, new behavior patterns, in new ways of looking at and doing things.

In chess it has reached something remote alike from business and from mere amusement. Chess is separate also from the world of art, although in its appeal to the imagination, the living creativeness of its play, and its constructive designs built from dissimilar units, it is close to some of the essentials of art.

Within the last fifteen years something very much like a revolution has taken place in chess. It has meant not only a new technique, but a new patterning, and a new conception of beauty. So close to expressionism is this movement that it will reward a second thought.

The early style of game lacked constructive design. It was a matter of slapdash kingside attacks and haphazard defence. The next step was due to Steinitz. Baroque in style and in many of his theories, this master, in shifting interest to pawn play and to strategy instead of tactics, laid the foundation of modern sound, scientific chess. Credit for the next advance must be given to Pillsbury, Lasker, and personally, to Tarrasch. They gave to pawn chains a greater flexibility, and put into their games a simple, clear beauty, an effective economy of effort, and a calm temper. Repose and restraint marked even the attacks of the Tarrasch School. To this Capablanca's genius brought something of its own. He saw that the balance must be a mobile one. To a degree he kept his resources *liquid* to allow for the shifting of values. But he had a like preference for the classical ideal in chess.

Not so very many years ago Capablanca, in a published statement, urged a change in the rules of the game. This, he held, was made necessary by the many draws, the lifeless, mechanical type of chess that was being played. Chess in its movement toward science, soundness, and classicism had run itself into the ground.

At the very time Capablanca made his plea for a change in the rules a new world master was in the making, and the new, the hypermoderns, were playing chess in a very original way and were sending thought deeply into their experiments. The leaders were Niemzowitch, Tartakower, Grünfeld, and Reti. Of their books Tartakower's *Die Hypermoderne Schachpartie* and *Das Neuromantische Schach* and Niemzowitch's *Mein System* are the most interesting.

The picture offered by many of these modernist games is a strange and at first glance a disordered one—wing development, a retarded centre, cramped and blocked positions, holding back and sparring, *Überdeckung,* lack of economy, no stable reposeful chains of pawns, wilful disregard of tradition in openings. The *Queen's Gambit Declined,* of all the openings, was closest to classical beauty. The new ways of playing it for white and especially for black—the *Indian* and other irregular defences—have destroyed that simple balanced beauty. A hypermodern opening, *Alekhine's Defence* involves in the shifting of the knight an utter wastefulness—it seems a blow struck directly at the sacrosanct principle of utmost economy and rapidity of development.

The picture, however, does not express and reflect chaos. A new individualism, an irruption of the imagination, a keen love of adventure, a new forcefulness and vividness—all combine with a devotion to the spirit of chess and a loyalty to art which gained, as Alekhine did against Capablanca, original creative work from very simple positions. Originality and imagination were offered by expressionism to art, in order to give it depth and range and a new complex beauty. On a smaller scale, the modernists have done a like service for chess, and given it a new life, new forms, and new values.

APPENDIX II

ORIGINAL SKETCHES

by

PAUL KRUMMEICH

The following original sketches shall serve to further illustrate the all-important creative process. These musical fragments are first consciously apprehended as sound-images, so called, but it is quite evident that they represent the product of deeper mental functions.

The degree of spontaneity manifested by their gradual or sudden appearance in the conscious mind reflects the state of development as well as the intensity of a mood, as it is unconsciously generated. Thus we can actually observe the composer in his workshop and gain considerable insight into the most recondite phases of creative labor.

I have preferred my own sketches because they furnish first-hand knowledge otherwise unobtainable.

SKETCH I.
12-27-'25

Andante Maestoso M. M. ♩=72.

"Choral-motif"

Sketch I represents a natural rebound from an overwhelming depression accumulated during a prolonged study of J. S. Bach's *Choralprelude,* "Now come the Gentiles' Saviour." Bach's composition is in the minor mode of G and expresses an austere and gloomy mood; Sketch I, also, represents a typical choral-motif, but in the major mode of G, and thus radiates an infinitely brighter atmosphere.

In my opinion, Sketch I embodies the overflow of a mood, more or less the opposite of the one expressed in Bach's composition. My sensation while playing Sketch I was one of intense relief; I felt that a temporarily disturbed psychic equilibrium had been reestablished.

The melody of Sketch II represents a tonal realization of the undulating line a, visualized as a temporal line (a graceful gesture), while the organ point on D flat (in the bass) stands for the straight line b, similarly visualized. In this case Sketch II is a kind of program music; it furnishes an example of *dynamic* correlation in music, painting and sculpture. The reader will remember that the composer's phantasy is of the audible type; whatever he expresses must first be experienced as ideal sound, and we may say that he composes "sound-images." While in painting and sculpture all lines and curves are fixed in space, in music everything is actual motion. Music is a temporal medium of expression, and we speak of melodies as temporal lines or curves.

(The second half of Sketch III is added by reflection and is, in my opinion, inferior to the first half, which is spontaneous.)

Sketch III is an old friend; it is the spontaneous expression of a mood with which I am on very familiar terms; in fact, this particular mood has haunted me for many years. I have always felt that a certain composition had deeply impressed me, but I could not recall this particular melody, although the mood which it had aroused long ago constantly returned demanding and finding spontaneous expression time and again in varied forms.

I have repeatedly caught myself employing these variations of one and the same melody for the purpose of demonstrating certain types of moods. They are represented by Sketches IV, V, VI, VII, VIII, and IX. If the reader will play Sketches III, IV, V, and VI, he will notice how the serene mood, expressed in Sketch III, gradually assumes a lighter color until it eventually grows boisterous and rather burlesque (in Sketch VI).

(Sketch VIII represents a natural development of Sketch VII.)

SKETCH IX. (Combination of Sketches VIII and IV.)

M.M. ♩=76.

In Sketches VII and VIII, we have a peculiar specimen (of spontaneous expression), which, at first, I considered a new melody in its proper harmonious garb. But I found much later that it was intimately related to Sketch IV. And I was astonished when I realized that Sketch VIII actually represented the natural (harmonious) setting to (the motif of) Sketch IV.

I have combined Sketches VIII and IV in Sketch IX without changing their original forms in any way. Since many months had elapsed between the expressions, represented by Sketches IV and VIII, we have here, in my opinion, an extraordinary example of unconscious development. About a year ago I came across Chopin's *Concerto No. I E minor* and realized, to my surprise and gratification, that it was this composition, first movement beginning of E major part (piano solo), which had originally aroused in me that mood to which I have given such frequent expression without the faintest (conscious) memory of its original excitation.

Sketch XA is an expression of a feeling of comfort—a reassurance of reestablished health after a temporary indisposition.

Sketch XB presents itself just as spontaneously several hours later; during this interval I had occupied myself with the study of one of Liszt's *Petrarca sonnets*, (consciously) quite oblivious of XA. In my opinion XB, also, expresses a feeling of comfort born, in this case, of the realization that I had conquered some difficult parts of the Liszt composition. Every musical person will at once recognize in XB a matured development of XA. I feel justified in considering XB another demonstration of unconscious growth.

Sketch XI shows how thoroughly a marginal (visional) impression may register. I had barely glanced at a program which contained Johann

Strauss' *Blue Danube,* when I caught myself improvising this variation
(Sketch XI) of the second part of the *Blue Danube* during the discussion
of an irrelevant subject.

SKETCH XII A.

Sketch XIIA represents the germ of which XIIB is the finished composition; XIIA is the vaguest form of the musical idea, which I developed
in XIIB. While sketching this musical fragment, the idea of the lullaby
presented itself, and I heard (ideally) the even, rocking accompaniment,
peculiar to the lullaby type. Simultaneously, some fragments of a typical
lullaby text appeared to me, properly rhymed and ordered.

This musical idea emerged quite spontaneously while I was reading a
German *Journal of Psychology* without having, of course, any idea of
music in my conscious mind. I do not know if this lullaby (XIIB) represents a manifestation of the parental instinct or if it is a case of cryptom-
nesia—an unconscious memory of my own childhood days. The latter
seems quite possible because the text appeared in German which I very
rarely speak.

(*Sketch XIIB follows on pages 576–578*)

NOTE: To E. A. Singer, Jr. I am indebted for an interest and a stimulation which helped me towards a crystallization of unconscious ideas and
a deeper understanding of personal reactions.

I have had the greatest encouragement from the theories of Schopenhauer, Nietzsche, Wagner, and the Vedanta Philosophy in the working out
of my ideas on the metaphysic of music.

A few titles are added for the benefit of the student who is interested
in the wider cultural and psychological problems of music.

v. Hartmann, *Aesthetik,* 1886.
  Philosophy of the Unconscious, tr.
Gelet, *From the Unconscious to the Conscious,* tr., 1920.
Volkmann, *Lehrbuch der Psychologie,* 2 vols. tr. 1894.
F. T. Vischer, *Aesthetik,* vol. 1, part 1, Metaphysik des Schönen.
Hanslik, Vom *Musikalisch-Schönen),* 1854 (formalism).
Kant, *Critique of the Power of Judgment,* tr.
H. Pfitzer, *Die Neue Aesthetik der Musikalischen Impotenz,* 1920.
Simple analysis may be found in the books on aesthetics cited in the
  Bibliography.

PAUL KRUMMEICH.

LULLABY

Andante cantabile.

M.M. ♩=84.

SKETCH XII B.

June, 1925

LULLABY—Continued

LULLABY—Concluded

TOWARDS A BIBLIOGRAPHY

The First Venture

Santayana, *The Sense of Beauty,* 1897
Brown, *The Fine Arts,* 1892
Puffer, *The Psychology of Beauty,* 1905
Vernon Lee, *The Beautiful,* 1913
Gordon, *Esthetics,* 1909
Bosanquet, *Three Lectures on Aesthetics,* 1914
Langfeld, *The Aesthetic Attitude,* 1920
Parker, *The Principles of Aesthetics,* 1920
Fechner, *Vorschule der Aesthetik,* 1876
Valentine, *Experimental Psychology of Beauty*
Clive Bell, *Art,* 1913
Flaccus, *Artists and Thinkers,* 1916

System-Builders

Lipps, *Aesthetik,* 1903–1905
Volkelt, *System der Aesthetik,* 1905–1914
Lange, *Das Wesen der Kunst,* 1901
Hegel, *Vorlesungen über die Aesthetik,* 1835
Croce, *Aesthetic,* tr. 1909
to these may be added Kant, Schopenhauer, Taine, Ruskin, and
    Tolstoy.

Origins and Social Setting

Grosse, *The Beginnings of Art,* tr. 1897
Hirn, *The Origins of Art,* tr. 1900
Groos, *The Plays of Man,* tr. 1901
Buecher, *Arbeit und Rhythmus,* 1902
Spearing, *The Childhood of Art,* 1913

Goldenweiser, *Early Civilization*
Harrison, *Ancient Art and Ritual,* 1913
Frazer, *The Golden Bough*
L. Thorndike, *A Short History of Civilization,* 1926

HISTORICAL ORIENTATION

Reinach, *Apollo*
Faure, *History of Art,* tr. 1921
Springer, *Kunstgeschichte*
Meier-Graefe, *Modern Art,* tr. 1908
Cheney, *A Primer of Modern Art,* 1924
H. Gardner, *Art Through the Ages,* 1926
Bosanquet, *History of Aesthetic,* 1904

ARTISTS ON THEIR ART

Vitruvius, *De Architectura*
Leonardo, *Treatise on Painting*
Essays, diaries, letters, prefaces by Schiller, Wordsworth, Poe, Hebbel, Shaw
Van Gogh, *Letters;* Gauguin, *Noa Noa;* Whistler, *Ten O'clock*
Marc, Contributions to *Der Blaue Reiter*
Wagner, *Prose Writings*
Gsell, *Rodin* (tr. as Rodin, *Art.*)
Hildebrand, *The Problem of Form,* tr. 1907
Busoni, *Entwurf einer Neuen Aesthetik der Tonkunst*
Kandinsky, *The Art of Spiritual Harmony,* tr. 1914

ARTISTS AND THEIR WORK

Mauclair, *Claude Monet,* 1924
Blanche, *Manet,* 1924
Vollard, *Renoir,* 1920
Burger, *Cézanne und Hodler,* 1920
Meier-Graefe, *Renoir*
———, *Cézanne*
Bell, *Since Cézanne,* 1922

C. Burkhardt, *Rodin,* 1921
Deri, *Die Neue Malerei,* 1921
Berenson, *Study and Criticism of Italian Art*
Deri, Dessoir, etc., *Einführung in die Kunst der Gegenwart,* 1919
and countless studies and appreciations of artists old and new.

The Arts and Their Special Problems

Banister Fletcher, *A History of Architecture,* 1921
American Institute of Architects, *The Significance of the Fine Arts,*
    1923
Lessing, *Laocoon,* 1766
Babbitt, *The New Laokoon,* 1910
Pfeistücker, *Das Wesen der Plastik,* 1922
Guillaume and Munro, *Primitive Negro Sculpture,* 1926
and the work of Furtwaengler, Gardner, Bulle, Hyde, etc.
Buschor, *Greek Vase Painting,* tr. 1921
Regling, *Die Antike Münze als Kunstwerk,* 1924
Hamlin, *A History of Ornament,* 1921
Ross, *On Drawing and Painting,* 1912
Poore, *Pictorial Composition,* 1903
Wright, *Modern Painting,* 1915
Barnes, *The Art in Painting,* 1925
Ruskin, *Modern Painters*
Emmanuel, *La Dance Grecque*
Thiess, *Der Tanz als Kunstwerk,* 1920
Bie, *Der Tanz*
Aristotle, *Poetics*
Lanier, *Science of English Verse,* 1880
Watts-Dunton, *Poetry and the Renaissance of Wonder*
Gummere, *Handbook of Poetics*
Lowes, *Tradition and Revolt in Poetry*
Amy Lowell, *Tendencies in Modern American Poetry,* 1917
Untermeyer, *American Poetry since 1900,* 1923
Max Eastman, *The Enjoyment of Poetry*
Prefaces to the *Imagist Anthologies*
Freytag, *Die Technik des Dramas*
Lessing, *Hamburgische Dramaturgie*

Nietzsche, *The Birth of Tragedy*, tr.
Clark, *European Theories of the Drama*, 1918
Volkelt, *Aesthetik des Tragischen*, 1906
Lipps, *Komik und Humor*, 1898
Bergson, *Laughter*, tr. 1913
Freud, *Wit and the Unconscious*, tr. 1916
Meredith, *An Essay on Comedy*
Palmer, *Comedy*
Greig, *The Psychology of Laughter and Comedy*
Longinus, *On the Sublime*
Burke, *Sublime and Beautiful*, 1756

MISCELLANEOUS

Kuelpe, *Grundlagen der Aesthetik*, 1921
Pater, *Renaissance*
———————, *Appreciations*
Shaw, *The Quintessence of Ibsenism*
Clutton-Brock, *Shakespeare's Hamlet*, 1921
Fry, *Vision and Design*, 1920
Hind, *Art and I*, 1921
Havelock Ellis, *The Dance of Life*
Bradley, *Oxford Lectures on Poetry*, 1909
Zola, *The Experimental Novel*, tr. 1893
Essays by Goethe, Coleridge, Carlyle, Corneille, Brunetière, Maeter-
    linck, Matthew Arnold, Huneker, Anatole France, and many
    others.

ADDITIONAL TITLES

Butler, *Painter and Space*
Casson, *XXth Century Sculpture*
———————, *Some Modern Sculptors*
Cheney, *Expressionism*
———————, *The New World Architecture*
Deri, *Die Malerei im XIX. Jahrhundert*
Dewey, *Art and Experience*
Einstein, *Die Kunst des 20. Jahrhunderts*
Epstein, *Let There Be Sculpture*, 1940
——————— and Haskell, *The Sculptor Speaks*, 1932

Fry, *Transformations*
Gatz, *Musik-Aesthetik,* 1929
Gilbert and Kuhn, *A History of Esthetics,* 1939
Gordon, *Modern French Painters,* 1929
Greene, *The Arts and the Art of Criticism,* 1940
Hambidge, *The Elements of Dynamic Symmetry,* 1926
Listowell, *A Critical History of Modern Aesthetics,* 1933
Lowell, *Poetry and Poets,* 1930
Martin, *The Dance,* 1936
Munro, *Great Pictures of Europe*
Ogden, *The Psychology of Art,* 1938
Parker, *Analysis of Art*
Parkhurst, *Beauty*
Pearson, *Experiencing Pictures,* 1932
——————, *How to See Modern Pictures,* 1934
Prall, *Aesthetic Judgment*
Read, *Surrealism,* 1939
Reynal, *Modern French Painters*
Stein, *ABC of Aesthetics*
Sidow, *Die Kunst der Naturvölker*
——————, *Kunst und Religion der Naturvölker*
Uhde-Bernays, *Künstlerbriefe über die Kunst*
Wright, *Modern Architecture,* 1931
——————, *Autobiography,* 1936

INDEX

Aeschylus, 226, 235, 236, 400, 455, 460, 490, 528, 550

Aesthetic indirection, 37, 73, 75, 80, 177

Aesthetic response

disinterestedness, 58, 61, 63, 290

flattening and enriching, 60-66, 134, 177, 397

genesis, 56-57

and semblance, 59, 451, 453-454

relation to practical life, 13, 64, 396-397, 451

Aesthetic types, 225

Aesthetics

affiliations of, 4-9

"botanizing," 22

field of, 3, 13-14

haphazard growth of, 3

methods of, 15-30

cultural, 544

Aldington, R., 161, 382

Anderson, Maxwell, 494, 552

Anderson, Sherwood, 371

Andreyeff, 373

Animated cartoon, 516

Animation, 232

Animism, 65

Apollo, 228

Apollonian, 46, 208

Arabesque, 207

Archipenko, 123, 530

Architecture

aesthetic meaning of, 92

balance in, 99-100

color in, 96-97

light and dark, 96

light and shade, 95-96

elements in, 109

functionalism in, 547

harmony in, 105

material in, 96-97

new developments in, 410-413

patterning in, 100

rhythm in, 106

texture in, 97-98

Aristophanes, 178, 261, 460

Aristotle, 284, 350

Art

analysis of, 451-452, 454-455

and ceremonial, 16, 49

and group life, 6, 37, 49, 390, 403

and morality, 399-401

and nature, 11-14, 63, 140, 543

and personality, 42-44, 364, 394, 531

and play, 25, 45

and propaganda, 460, 462

and reality, 19-20, 452-453, 534

and religion, 399-401

and semblance, 59, 451, 470

and sex, 49-50, 298-299

and social control, 401-402

and taste, 23

and work, 36

biological function of, 402, 403, 548

circle of, 400

human interest in, 5, 35

imaginative venture of, vii

oldest, 34

purifying function of, 454, 463

uses of, 405

Artistic idea, 193

Artistic painting, 141, 143

Artistic sculpture, 117

Arts and crafts, 548-549

Babbitt, I., 445-447

Bacchanale, 468

Bacchylides, 455

Bahr, 44

Bakst, 472

Balance

and symmetry, 100

in architecture, 99-100

585